GHOST STORIES
FROM THE AMERICAN SOUTHWEST

Compiled and Edited
by Richard Alan Young and
Judy Dockrey Young

GHOST STORIES
FROM THE AMERICAN SOUTH

Compiled and Edited
by W.K. McNeil

WINGS BOOKS

NEW YORK • AVENEL, NEW JERSEY

This omnibus was originally published in separate volumes under the titles:

Ghost Stories of the American Southwest, copyright © 1991 by Richard and Judy Dockrey Young.
Ghost Stories from the American South, copyright © 1985 by W. K. McNeil.

This 1993 edition is published by Wings Books,
distributed by Outlet Book Company, Inc., a Random House Company,
40 Engelhard Avenue, Avenel, New Jersey 07001,
by arrangement with August House, Inc.

Random House
New York • Toronto • London • Sydney • Auckland

Printed and bound in the United States of America

Library of Congress Cataloging-in-Publication Data

Ghastly ghost stories.
    p.   cm.
    Contents : Ghost stories from the American Southwest / compiled
and edited by Richard Alan Young and Judy Dockrey Young — Ghost
Stories from the American South / compiled and edited by W.K.
McNeil.
    ISBN 0-517-08927-0
    1. Ghosts—Southern States. 2. Ghosts—Southwest, New.
3. Ghost stories, American—Southern States. 4. Ghost stories,
American—Southwest, New. I. Ghost stories from the American
Southwest. 1993. II. Ghost stories from the American South. 1993.
BF1472.U6G474 1993
813'.0873308979—dc20   93-19514
                                         CIP

8 7 6 5 4 3 2 1

ONTENTS

GHOST STORIES FROM THE AMERICAN SOUTHWEST

In memoriam
Lewin Hayden Dockrey
January 22, 1920–May 11, 1989
For his love of life and the stories he told

PREFACE AND ACKNOWLEDGMENTS

"The preservation and presentation of American heritage through crafts" is one of the objectives of Silver Dollar City, a theme park and crafts village in Branson, Missouri. One aspect of American heritage and one art form (or craft, depending upon your judgment) preserved there is storytelling. The Ozark Mountains, near whose geographic center Silver Dollar City is located, are rich in oral tradition, and the local residents share their stories with visitors from all of the United States and many foreign countries.

We two—Richard Alan Young, a native Texan, and Judy Dockrey Young, an Oklahoma native—have worked at Silver Dollar City as storytellers since 1979 and are the collectors and editors of this anthology of narratives. Many of the stories come from our states of origin; others come from our current homes in Harrison, Arkansas, and Stoneridge, Missouri (a suburb, if you like, of Kimberling City). Still others have been collected during travels to Louisiana, Kansas, Colorado, New Mexico, Arizona, and California, as long ago as 1952 and as recently as 1990. Another source of stories has been the continuous stream of visitors to Silver Dollar City—more than five million of them —since we began storytelling there.

From the "oldest" stories of our childhoods to the most recent acquisitions collected from others in their home states, this anthology represents a broad sample of ghost stories and other supernatural narratives native to, or told in, the American Southwest. Such scary stories are the most popular and most requested stories we know and tell, and it is our pleasure to present them to you.

5

We wish to express our thanks to all the storytellers and informants who contributed tales for this anthology, whether they did so with recognition, without recognition, or even (at their own request) anonymously. We especially thank those guests of Silver Dollar City who shared stories with us before we ever thought about putting them into an anthology.

Our special thanks go to Teresa Pijoan de Van Etten, New Mexico storyteller and petroglyph expert, who gave us many stories and many story leads; Kathy Costa and the Library Storytellers Guild at Oliver LaFarge Branch of the Santa Fe Public Library; Jim Moeskau, entertainment manager at Silver Dollar City, Missouri; Dr. Gloria A. Young of the University of Arkansas Museum in Fayetteville; Margaret A.E. Miller, resident storyteller at King's Mountain State Park (as of this writing); Shelley Harshbarger, storyteller, of Tallahassee, Florida; and Texas folklorists George D. and Peggy Hendricks of Denton, Texas.

We are grateful for research assistance to Mary Roberts Bishop, Janet Watkins, Lucille Pratt, Bill and Kathy Drake of Sherman Texas, Tilman and Kathryn Cavert of San Antonio, Texas, and Fern Peterson Dockrey of Wagoner, Oklahoma.

We also wish to express our gratitude to Bob Coody and the staff of the Special Collections Library at Northern Arizona University, Dottie House and the library of the Museum of Northern Arizona, Louise Merkel and the staff of the Flagstaff–Coconino County Public Library, and Keith and Kathy Cunningham and the staff of *Southwest Folklore*, all of whom are in Flagstaff, Arizona.

CONTENTS

Supernatural and Preternatural 118

Possessed By Spirits 155

NTRODUCTION

THIS COLLECTION OF GHOST STORIES AND SUPERNATURAL NARRATIVES IS A representative sampling of the broad spectrum of such oral folk literature from the American Southwest. It is not definitive or all-inclusive; it is only a taste of a rich oral tradition that spans centuries of human habitation in the Southwest, from the preliterate societies of native Americans through the illiterate and literate explorers, colonists, and settlers, to the current oral tradition that persists alongside literature both printed and electronically transmitted. The modern Southwesterner will read the latest novel, watch the newest episode of his favorite television program, and then sit around a crackling campfire with fellow hunters or campers or co-workers, listening to and spinning yarns for entertainment and the enrichment of the human experience.

Folklorists document details about the teller as carefully as they document details of the story; the question of whether the teller believes the story to be true is important to a folklorist's scientific interpretation of the meaning and purpose of the story. To storyholders and storytellers, such a question is unimportant to the quality and enduring nature of the story and potentially insulting to the informant or source. For example, many Southwesterners are deeply religious, and the narratives they tell are often part of their belief system. For a storylistener or collector to ask about the personal beliefs of a storyteller with respect to a given story would not be a natural part of the storyholder's task. For this reason, the sources of the stories in this collection are noted in order to give credit to sources and informants, and not solely to illuminate the reader's understanding of the story.

Psychologists and academic folklorists try to explain why human beings tell stories and why they tell stories about the supernatural. As to the question of why people are drawn to and tell stories, storyholders only accept that *it is so,* and thus that it is our task to listen attentively and hold the stories for telling to future generations and broader audiences. This is the task we have undertaken in editing this collection. As to the question of why people listen to, retell, and seem to benefit from the telling of supernatural narratives, storyholders only acknowledge that such stories are the most popular and most often requested narrative type among storylisteners. Having accepted without trying to explain these psychosocial phenomena, we have assembled this collection for a new generation and a broader audience of listeners and readers.

The issue of the religious beliefs of the Southwesterner as they relate to ghost stories is worth further consideration. The editors offer the following observations:

❖ Traditional Christians often tell supernatural stories that are clearly outside the dogma of the Christian church (e.g., narratives about ghosts existing in post-Biblical times, about Satan manifesting himself as a physical being who seems easy to outwit, about God manifesting Himself to humble people, offering them worldly wealth instead of spiritual benefit, and so forth). They are often sensitive about the relationship of such stories to their stated religious beliefs, and many have presented their stories anonymously to us.

❖ Evangelical or charismatic Christians often refuse to listen to or retell supernatural narratives because they seem so outside the stated dogma of their churches. (One may tell the stories of Balaam's talking ass or of the Witch of Endor raising the ghost of Solomon or of other Old Testament events, but not the story of a ghostly figure seen in a supposedly haunted house nearby.) In those rare instances when such a believer does relate a non-Biblical supernatural narrative to us, he or she may also do it anonymously. One such person, asked casually about ghost stories, replied, "Stay away from the occult! Stories like that are the work of the Devil!"

❖ Some traditional Christians simply do not tell supernatural narratives. One commented, "We talked about ghosts every day, but it was always the Father, the Son, and the Holy Ghost." Others clearly distinguish between Scriptural truth and fiction for amusement, permitting the latter as long as the narrative is not accepted as fact.

These Christians most often tell "ghost jokes" and non-personal, third-person narratives.

❖ Traditional Christians who accept the possibility of modern-day miracles and manifestations often tell supernatural narratives about the works of the Holy Spirit, fully believing the events of the narratives, in the same way "superstitious" people tell ghost stories and accept them as the truth. We have collected some of these.

❖ Traditional practitioners of native American religions tell sacred stories that are part of their belief systems and will often only relate such stories if they are accepted anonymously. Sometimes they will pass them on only when certain small changes have been made during the telling to remove the spiritual power from the stories without altering their message content.

Understanding the deep religious feelings many Southwesterners have is just one aspect of what makes the supernatural narratives of the American Southwest so fascinating and often difficult to collect. Another source of fascination and difficulty is the great variety in interpretation of what constitutes a "ghost story" or supernatural narrative.

Southwesterners may regard as ghost stories or supernatural narratives . . .

. . . stories about the works of the Holy Ghost

. . . stories about spirits or beings in the Ancient Times of native American belief systems

. . . stories about witches and witchcraft, especially among Hispanic people and among the Navajo

. . . stories about preternatural beings

. . . stories about unexplained natural events

. . . more traditional stories about ghosts as the spirits of deceased persons who have either never left this earth or have returned to it for some reason.

This wide variety of supernatural themes makes the Southwestern narratives much more varied than their Southeastern counterparts, where English, Scottish, Irish, and German ethnic groups share a common interpretation of what constitutes a ghost story.

Another issue that arises in a collection such as this is the definition of the American Southwest. For us, the Southwest is the area west of the Mississippi River and south of the Santa Fe Trail. This vast area encompasses Missouri from the trailhead at St. Louis across to Independence and southward; all of Arkansas, Louisiana, Texas, and Oklahoma; those parts of Kansas south of the Arkansas River; Colorado along and south of the Arkansas River; and all of New Mexico and Arizona. The southern portions of Utah, Nevada, and California are partly Southwestern in culture and partly Great Northwestern. Our collection touches them only briefly. (There is ample material from these states for other anthologies of narratives from the Great Northwest—the Pacific Northwest, the Rocky Mountain States, and the western Great Plains—or even just from California itself.)

No attempt has been made to collect from traditional narratives state-by-state or by ethnic groups; rather, these stories came to us from interested people living in the areas listed. The stories are arranged by general theme rather than by region or ethnicity, but there is an index of stories by state of origin.

The method of collection was simple: storytellers generally share stories, each teller present offering his or her narratives around a fireplace or some other appropriate storytelling setting.

The stories come in many forms:

. . . complete stories with well-developed plot lines and character delineation, rising action that culminates in a climax, and all the aspects of a well-told story

. . . short, almost summarized, versions of what was previously heard by the teller as a complete story

. . . fragments of a story, with many lacunae ("holes" where elements have obviously been lost or forgotten) and often no ending

. . . sometimes just a single item or element, such as the name of a story, of a character, or of a place associated with the supernatural.

When stories come to us incomplete, we do not try to fill in the missing portions ourselves; we wait patiently until another teller gives us another version with some of the missing portions included. Eventually the story is filled in and becomes complete, ready for telling. When one version has an "extra element" that is missing from all the other versions we have heard, and does not seem to supply a lacuna, we often choose to omit that extra element from the finished story.

Our purpose in this collection is not the preservation of numerous variants verbatim, but the preservation and presentation of the story in its complete, if generalized, form. This "retelling form" of the narrative represents the way it is told in its most complete version by the majority of those who tell it. This is not the folklorist's method of preserving a single variant ("frozen in time and space"), but it represents the story-teller's method of preservation with minimal alteration by the collec-tors/tellers. The storyteller himself or herself is one link in the human chain that transmits the story over time, and is one of the "folks" in the unbroken chain of folklore; the same is true for the story collector or storyholder. The folklorist, on the other hand, is likely to be more emotionally detached from the story and is a scientist and scholar out-side the actual folklore chain, looking in as an observer.

Ghost stories range from the disdainfully-told fragment or summary of a legend to gripping personal narratives that bring a tear to the eye of the teller. As storytellers and storyholders, we listen without judging, without trying to decide if the story is true or not. It is not the truth that matters, it is the story—and there is a general truth even in stories that are not specifically true. Here are examples of the extremes of personal emotional involvement with a narrative:

> They say that years ago at Fort Sill [an Army outpost now in the state of Oklahoma], you could see two ghosts quarrel in one of the barracks buildings. Two cavalry soldiers were in love with the same girl. They died in the Indian Wars, and their ghosts keep coming back to see their girlfriend. This is an old story.[1]

> I saw her! *La LLorona!* I was nine years old, and it was late in the day on a Saturday, late in the fall, around Hallowe'en. Me and my friend—another nine-year-old—and two eleven-year-olds and a thir-teen-year-old, we decided we were going to go over to the school-ground and play on the merry-go-round, in my hometown of Las Vegas [New Mexico]. *La LLorona,* you know, she was the one who killed her children after World War I. I saw her.

> You see, to get to the school from my house over near the railroad tracks and Gallinas [River], we went down the tracks where it's real dark. We were at some abandoned sheds, along the tracks, and I picked up some rocks and was throwing them to see if I could get one to go in the holes in the wall of the shed.

> I was just getting to the last shed, and I saw this mattress folded over lying beside the last shed, and on it this white, white shape. I took a rock and I threw it. It hit the white form, and it . . . started to come up off the mattress. I crouched down and put my hands up over my head, and this form, it just came up off of the mattress and it started floating at me and wailing that terrible wail . . . *"Ni-i-i-ño-o-o . . . ni-i-i-ño-o-o . . .* [My son, my son]."

The other kids ran away. Me, I was so scared I couldn't run.

I crouched down with my arms over my head, and when I looked up, she went over my head, and she went over the railroad tracks, and she went over to the river, and she disappeared.

I got up and I ran. I ran so fast that I caught up to those older boys, and we all looked at each other and we knew, we knew. We had seen *la LLorona!*[2]

In the first narrative, the teller merely summarizes the events of a story he has heard, or heard of. He does not tell the story himself (nor, as the folklorist would point out, does he seem to believe the story). In the second example, collected by Betsy McWilliams, a Hispanic folklorist, the young Hispano teller is deeply involved in this very personal narrative which, according to the collector, was related with strong emotional context.

One type of story that shows the extremes of personal involvement is the "ghost-light story." There is no scary story type more beloved. Almost everyone in the Southwest has heard at least one ghost-light story, and there are several very famous lights or sets of lights in the region: The Marfa Lights in Texas, the Hornet Light in Missouri, and others. Visiting these lights is a favorite pastime, especially for young adults. Serious studies and frivolous legends have yet to explain the phenomena, even though such diverse groups as the U. S. Army Corps of Engineers, the film crew of television's "Unsolved Mysteries," and scientists from local colleges and universities have tried. When we asked for "spooklight" stories, we got many answers, such as:

The spooklight at Hornet [Missouri, near Joplin] has been explained by a scientist as a phenomenon of lights on the Will Rogers Turnpike across the [state] line in Oklahoma. But the light was seen long before that road was ever put in, or even before there were automobiles with electric lights.[3]

Most spooklight stories are explanations of why the light exists or are chilling personal accounts of going (often on a dare) to the site of the ghostly glow. We have included both kinds of narratives in this collection. Here are further examples:

This story is called "Bailey's Lantern." Out on Bailey's Prairie [in Texas] there is a ghost-light that can be seen on the darkest nights. It has been seen for over a hundred years. A settler named Bailey, who arrived before Stephen F. Austin's band, quarrelled with Austin over his squatter's rights [which Austin would have claimed violated the terms of Austin's land grant from Mexico]. Bailey, a hard drinker, swore "never to leave his land, dead or alive."

As he lay dying, years later, he asked to be buried standing up, holding a bottle of good whiskey, facing west, since he'd been going west all his life anyway. Some relatives saw his ghost as early as the 1830s; now there's only his light, a lantern, seen near the [presumed] site of his unmarked grave.[4]

Next, an example of the somewhat rare "second person narrative," in which the teller uses the American English tendency to replace the pronoun *one* with the pronoun *you,* and in which a feeling of immediacy is created for the listener:

You know the Rio Grande [River] along at Laredo [Texas]? You can see a ghost-light there! The Mexican town of Dolores is there, too. They used to mine silver there, and if you go there along by the river at night, you can see a lantern moving along the trail in the darkness. You can't see who's holding it, just the lantern. You might see just a hand with no body attached, holding the lantern. It's a miner who was killed in a cave-in and he lost his hand. You can see him still looking for his silver.[5]

One final example of a very personal ghost-light narrative:

My father is a riverboat man, and he calls two very different things by the name *feu follé* [also spelled *feu follet* in some books]. As you go down the river you can see images in the swamp gas that escapes out of holes or bubbles; sometimes it would shoot up like a jet, and sometimes it would look like fire. Most often it looks like fire: *feu follé.*

Also, when it is stormy and lightning is dancing on the wire fence, like what some people call St. Elmo's Fire, he also calls that *feu follé.* [The informant pronounces the phenomenon as if it were written *fifollé* in French.][6]

From the folklorist's point of view, the stories we have collected are one small part of folklore. "Folklore" is often defined as material that is transmitted orally, is usually traditional and formulaic (unless it is a very personal experience being passed on), changes with time and retelling thereby creating variants (changing with the style of the teller and the signs of the times; e.g. a traveller on horseback becomes a driver of a car, etc.), is often anonymous (except for personal experiences), and often has no title (unless the teller thinks of the story as being traditional and easily identifiable by the title).

Storytellers are often described as "active bearers of folklore" who actively retell and keep alive their stories. Carl W. von Sydow, who conceived of this classification, called "passive bearers of folklore" those who only know summaries or have dim recollections that they can repeat if asked to, but who are not likely to tell the stories or remember them without being asked. Here are examples:

> In Valencia County [New Mexico] three dead men who were hanged as outlaws come back and haunt the place of their death. Some people call it *El árbol de la horca.*[7]

Sometimes the narratives are disconnected thoughts that reflect a more complex folk belief or that refer in fragmentary form to a longer story, heard in childhood and now forgotten:

> You know, if a place is haunted you can put a thin layer of ash on something—a table or something—and leave a feather. Then the spirits will write in the ash what it is they want. And you can give them what they want, and they will go away. They have to use a feather because it is light, and they are not very strong, you know. [Collected in southern New Mexico.][8]

Sometimes the narratives are told in story form, but only as a summary, not as an "adventure tale":

> A story about a hairy man is told by folks east of here [Waco, Texas]. He lives along Richland Creek and the Trinity River. He hasn't been seen recently, maybe in the 40s, but he has a huge head and—this is the interesting part—his hands and feet are alike, as if he were really a four-footed creature. He's usually seen near the creek or near a well.[9]

Finally, the narratives are sometimes told as real stories, often complete with appropriate gestures and sound effects, as the events are presumed to have happened to a third party or as the teller asserts the events actually happened to him or her. These stories are generally the work of active bearers of folklore who will offer their tales "at the drop of a hat."

The most active bearers of folklore and the most ardent tellers of ghost stories often offer narratives that are actually death beliefs or events associated with death beliefs. In spite of the fact that these are not "stories" in the strict sense, they are folklore, and have sometimes been included in this collection. Here is a lengthy example from a good teller:

> My mother is an L.P.N. and was hired a few years back to sit with [an elderly man] who was dying at home. The old man had lost his mind and was very threatening and abusive to his family, but he was too weak to do anything, and my mother wasn't in any danger. She was sitting with him one day, reading a book while he was asleep, when he rattled and died.
>
> When she was sure that he was really dead, she informed the family and started the long walk to a telephone at a house a mile away to call the ambulance and the coroner.
>
> As she was leaving the house, one of the menfolk was slowly peeling the wallpaper in the room with the dead man and another was outside with a clawhammer pulling off siding. When she got back an hour later, and the ambulance came, the family had taken off the siding, opened a hole in the lath, and peeled back the wallcovering to make an opening two feet tall and as wide as the studs. They made the E.M.T.s pass the body out the hole in the wall rather than letting it be taken out a door or window. When Mother asked why, they said simply, "to keep his ghost away."
>
> As everyone left, they were nailing the siding back in place.[10]

All the sources and informants who told us stories used vivid language imagery to describe the ghosts or supernatural and preternatural beings and events being narrated. The most striking words were those chosen by the tellers to denominate the ghosts or beings themselves. Tellers who were dubious about the objects of their narratives used works like *shape, form, figure,* or just *thing* to name ghostlike phenomena. A few believers in ghosts or psychic phenomena used words like vision, aura, emanation, or materialization. Others used the terms shadow, specter, soul, or the skeptical terms illusion or hallucination.

The most common terms were ghost, phantom, spook, phantasm, apparition, spirit, wraith, spectre (specter) and even will-o'-the-wisp (will-o-wisp). The poetic word shade and the rather technical term revenant have never come up in stories told to us. In the Ozarks, the terms haint [haunt] for ghost and booger (as a prefix, e.g. booger dog) for preternatural being are very common; these terms are also found (less frequently) anywhere the "mountain folks" or "hillbillies" settled in the late 1800s.

A few ethnic groups have unique words in their native languages that come into English stories (e.g., the Irish banshee), or names for specific beings that are universally accepted (e.g., la LLorona), but for the most part the stories we have heard, retold, or collected used common but expressive English vocabulary. (One exception is the very few Native American Indian stories in which the informants used indigenous language names that we have phonetically rendered without tonal or diacritical markings.) Although some Southwestern states have passed legislation in recent years making English the "official language" of that state (e.g. Arkansas, California), it is common usage that makes English the preferred language (even as a lingua franca) of the Southwest. The Vietnamese grocer tells the Navajo customer what his Hispanic neighbor told him about a haunted place; the story is in English.

Each ethnic and linguistic group has its own rich heritage of oral traditions in its native tongue, and each such heritage richly deserves study and preservation in that tongue. We think this collection of narratives, a general sampling of the American Southwest with all its cultural diversity, is equally rich in the unique dialect we call American English.

NOTES

[1]Collected from an unidentified Oklahoma man, a white male in his thirties, in 1988.

[2]"I Saw Her!" collected by Hispanic folklorist Betsy McWilliams in September, 1990, at Cochiti Lake, New Mexico, from "Miguel," a young hispano in his twenties.

[3]Collected from Bill Frenchman in October, 1989. An Oklahoma resident, Mr. Frenchman has travelled and observed the ghost-light phenomenon in several Southwestern states.

[4]"Bailey's Lantern," provided by a patron of the library in San Antonio, Texas, in November, 1989. A white male in his fifties, he told the story enthusiastically but did not seem to believe the events of the story.

[5]Collected from a stall-keeper at the Mercado in Nuevo Laredo, Mexico, across from Laredo, Texas, in the 1970s. The Hispanic male in his forties told the story in English and appeared to accept the events as the truth. He used the English "you" to mean "one" as native English-speakers do.

[6]Collected from Louis Darby of Opelousas, Louisiana, former Louisiana state fiddle champion, in August, 1989.

[7]"El árbol de la horca," collected from a young Hispanic male in his twenties, from southern New Mexico, in late summer, 1988.

[8]Collected from a young Hispanic male waiter in a restaurant in Mesilla, New Mexico, in January, 1987. The young man, in his twenties, seemed to believe the data to be true.

[9]"The East Texas Hairy Man," provided by a librarian in Waco, Texas, who declined to be identified, in November, 1989. *Compare this summary with the events in story number 104.*

[10]Collected from a teen-aged white male living in Boone County, Arkansas, in 1972. The events took place in Newton County, Arkansas, in about 1969. To avoid any unethical implications of patient confidentiality, names and some details have been deleted.

There always exists the possibility that stories told orally to the editors of this collection may have passed through the print medium (i.e., the stories are told orally, written down by a collector, and read by someone who then tells them orally to another collector). It should be noted that "Bailey's Lantern" (note 4) is also recorded in Catherine Munson Foster's *Ghosts Along the Brazos* (Texian Press, Waco, Texas, 1977), and the Dolores-Light story (note 5) resembles a series of statements in Henry Yelvington's *Ghost Lore* (The Naylor Company, San Antonio, Texas, 1936). Both stories, however, are well known in their respective areas and may have reached our informants purely through the oral tradition.

Notes on the Text

The spelling of certain American Indian names and words is often phonetic rather than the official spelling used in each language, especially if the official spelling involves tonal or diacritical markings. The editors apologize for any inconsistencies or errors with respect to the American Indian languages, in which we are not conversant.

The spelling of words in Spanish follows the forms given to us by native speakers or the correct forms for the dialect of Spanish most familiar to the editors. The capitalization of the Spanish letter *ll*, as in *la LLorona,* follows the historic, though antique, pattern for the American Southwest and conforms to the spelling the editors learned from parents and collateral relatives who spoke the language. We use it everywhere except in story 132, where we preserve the spelling of the title in the original printed version.

The spelling of the name Jean Laffite (instead of *Lafitte*) is based on the fact that Laffite himself is known to have signed his name with that spelling.

Parentheses in the introduction and the text of the narratives indicate normally parenthetical material; brackets represent insertions, deletions, or explanations by the editors. In all cases of deletion, personal names or personal information was left out at the specific request of the source or informant.

Titles have been given to the narratives to make the book easier to browse. In most instances, they are simply descriptive phrases chosen by the editors to help keep track of separate stories. Where the title is one used by informants or customarily attached to a story, it will be indicated in the notes, all of which are gathered in the back of the book.

# Ghost Jokes

1 The Pawpaw Lie

IT WAS AUTUMN, AND TWO BOYS HAD BEEN OUT STEALING PAWPAWS FROM under a neighbor's tree. Their families didn't have good pawpaw trees, and the fruit was just ripe, so they waited until the fellow with the good tree was out milking, and they crept into his yard and stole a whole bagful. With two boys and only one sack, they had to divide up the goods. They figured that since it was sundown, the least likely place for them to be disturbed was the graveyard.

So they went to the graveyard, and hid behind a big, tall head marker just inside the rock wall, and started dividing up the pawpaws, saying, "You take this one, I'll take that one."

While they were counting, this big old cornfed country boy came swinging along the road whistling to himself. He stopped just as he got alongside the boys on the back of the wall. He heard them real clearly saying, "You take this one, I'll take that one."

It scared that country boy to death. He took off running all the way to the house.

When he got to the porch, he hollered, "Pop! Pop! I heard them! It was the Lord and the Devil out in the graveyard dividing up the souls!"

By the time he got inside the house, his father said, "Son, you've been in the liquor again, haven't you?"

"No, Pop, really!" said the boy, jumping up and down with excitement. "I heard them dividing up the souls, going 'You take this one, I'll take that one!' Really I did!"

"Son," said the old man, "if you heard that, I want to hear it, too."

"Well, come on, let's go!" said the boy, starting out the door.

"Son," said the old man, "you know I ain't stirred a step with the rheumatism these ten solid years. You'll have to carry me. That's what I raised you big old boys for. Pick me up and carry me down there."

So the great big boy grabbed the skinny old man and set him on his shoulders, and off they went to the graveyard. As they got closer and closer the boy went slower and slower, until he was creeping up on the graveyard wall, old man and all. Those two boys were still there, but they were through dividing up the good pawpaws, and were down to the last two.

Just as the country boy and the old man got to the wall and leaned over to listen, one of the thieves said, "There's not but these two left. You take that big fat one and I'll take the old shriveled-up one."

That was it! The country boy reared back and threw his old grey-haired father off and lit out running toward the house. And his pop, who hadn't stirred a step with the rheumatism for ten solid years, beat the boy home by a full minute!

2　You Can't Get Out

A YOUNG MAN WAS WALKING THROUGH THE GRAVEYARD ONE NIGHT, AND he fell into a fresh-dug hole left open for a funeral the next day. He wasn't hurt, and he tried and tried to get out. No matter how he scrambled and jumped, the hole was just too deep. He finally settled down to spend a cold night in the ground until the mortician would come in the morning.

A few hours later, a drunk came walking through the graveyard, whistling loudly. Sure enough, he fell in, too.

The young man sat in the corner watching the drunk jumping and scrambling, trying to get out.

Finally, to be helpful, the young man said to the drunk, "You know, you can't get out."

But, you know, he did!

3 I Can't Get In

MY GRANDDADDY GREW UP IN NEWTON COUNTY [ARKANSAS]. HE'S DEAD now, but when I was a boy he told me that this happened to him. He and a friend had been to a dance and had got drunk on moonshine. It was real strong stuff, and both boys were sick and staggering. They lived side-by-side and were walking each other home, trying to stay standing-up on the road.

They came to the graveyard and knew they could shortcut through it. They got about halfway through, and the other boy got sick and sat down on a grave to let his head stop spinning. Granddaddy went on. About five minutes later, the other boy ran past Granddaddy like he was standing still.

Granddaddy ran crazily, trying to keep up, and when he got to the other boy's front porch, there he was, shaking like a leaf and stone-cold sober.

"What happened?" asked Granddaddy.

"I was sitting on that grave," said the other boy, "and somebody starting poking me on the shoulder. I looked up. It was a skeleton standing beside me, poking me on the shoulder and saying, 'I can't get in. You're in my way! I can't get in!' "

Granddaddy swore it was the truth.

4 The Haunted Car

ONCE THERE WAS A CIRCUIT PREACHER IN NORTH TEXAS WHO WAS PREACH-ing in a small town on a Sunday that fell on Hallowe'en. After the service was over in the old wooden church house, the preacherman stayed to let the fire die out before he locked up for the month and walked to the farmhouse where he was staying with members of the congregation. He scattered the coals and covered them with ash, turned the damper down, and shuttered the windows. The wind was blowing cold when he locked the door and started down the dirt road toward the farmplace.

He had to walk over three hills and down through two gullies to get where he was going, and on the middle hill sat the old graveyard. As he walked, he pulled his scarf up and his hat down to turn the wind. Soon he heard something on the road behind him. He stepped aside and looked back in the darkness, but a grove of live-oak trees on the eastern horizon kept him from seeing the outline of whatever was behind him.

He turned back around and kept on walking. A minute or two later, he heard something behind him again, getting closer. There weren't any hoofbeats, so it wasn't a horse; there weren't any tracechains jingling, so it wasn't a wagon; there wasn't any motor noise, so it wasn't a tractor or an automobile. He stopped again to listen, but the sound had stopped. He kept on walking, up the slope toward the graveyard.

The preacherman heard the sound again, and it was so close behind him that it made the hair on the back of his neck stand up. He turned around, and saw a huge, black shape coming silently at him. He stepped aside, and the shape pulled alongside of him. It was an automobile, but without its lights lit.

"Well," thought the preacherman, "this is some deacon of the church who's taken some sister home and is stopping to offer me a ride." He stepped over, opened the side door, and got into the back seat. He leaned forward to thank whoever was driving, but he found he was alone in the vehicle.

And the automobile began to move . . . silently . . . toward the graveyard!

The preacher sat very still and waited until the vehicle rolled to a stop—right in front of the iron gate to the burying ground.

"Well," thought the preacher, "I guess this is where I'm supposed to get out." He stepped out of the automobile, shut the door quietly, and walked quickly away from the ghostly vehicle. Suddenly, he heard something breathing heavily, like a huge animal, just on the other side of a tall marble monument.

Very slowly, the preacherman walked around the marble stone and saw . . . one of the deacons of the church, leaning on the marble and breathing loud and hard.

"Don't go near that automobile!" said the preacher. "There's something wrong with it!"

"I know that, Brother John," said the deacon. "I've been pushing the damn thing for a mile!"

 ## A Ghost Story for Folklorists

ONCE, ON A DARE, A YOUNG MAN H1416. HE FELL ASLEEP, AND AT midnight the E273 and suddenly E279.2. The young man jumped up and saw E530.1 all around him and heard E401! Up from behind a huge tombstone D1641.13 and it F1083.0.1 toward him.

He began to run, and it chased him as F990!

He ran all around the graveyard and finally took a cough drop and stopped the D1641.13.

Translation

Once, on a dare to prove his bravery, a young man spent the night in a graveyard. He fell asleep, and at midnight the ghosts of the dead woke up and started talking to each other. That woke the young man. He jumped up and saw the ghosts glowing and talking to each other, and just then a coffin floated up out of an open grave and came toward the young man.

He ran and ran, and the coffin chased him.

He ran all around the graveyard and finally took a cough drop and stopped the coughin'.

6 Scary Song

There was an old woman,
She was just skin and bones,
Oh, oh, oh-oo!
There was an old woman,
She was just skin and bones,
Oh, oh, oh-oo!
Well, she looked up and she looked down,
She spied a corpse upon the ground,
Oh, oh, oh-oo!
She went to the parson and she said,
Will I look so when I am dead?
Oh, oh, oh-oo?
And the parson said
[shouted] *Yes!*

❖ Editors' note: The editors have heard many other "ghost jokes" through the years, but these six are the most typical and the best examples of this popular Southwestern genre. We have heard dozens of variants on each, from countless tellers. Many other such narratives base their humor on racial or ethnic insults, or are scatological, or lack good narrative form, and have been omitted. While such narratives have value to a folklorist, a storyholder or storyteller might choose not to pass them along.

_U_rban Legends

7 Last Kiss

LATE ONE NIGHT, YEARS AGO, A TEEN-AGE BOY WAS DRIVING HOME ON A Saturday night, on a rainy road in the country. Just as he rounded a long curve, the headlights lit up a teen-age girl standing by the highway. She was wearing a white party dress, but she was all wet from the rain. He knew at once what must have happened: her date had dumped her after a quarrel. He felt so sorry for her that he skidded to a stop before she even had a chance to hail him.

He leaned over and opened the door for her, and she got in.

"Would you take me home?" she asked. "I just live a mile down the road."

He noticed for the first time how really pretty she was. He almost couldn't speak, she was so pretty. He mumbled something and she smiled. He quickly took off his letter jacket, and she leaned forward in the seat so he could drape it over her shoulders to keep her warm. It was too crowded in the car for her to get her arms into the sleeves.

The boy put the car in gear, and they were at the two-story house by the graveyard before he could even think of anything to say.

"This is my house," she said.

He stopped the car and got out and went around to open the door for her. He walked her up onto the porch of the dark house, and before he could think how to ask if he could see her again, she kissed him. He was so surprised that she opened the screen door, opened the front door, and was gone into the darkness before he could speak. Then he realized that she still had on his jacket.

It was a perfect excuse to see her again. He could come back the next day after church and ask for his jacket.

Sunday afternoon, he was back at the house and knocked on the door. A haggard woman came to the door.

He asked if he could see her daughter.

"My daughter died one year ago last night," said the woman sadly. "She was killed in a car wreck at the big curve down the road, there."

He told her that wasn't possible, that he had given her a ride home the night before.

"If you don't believe me," she replied, "go look in the cemetery, there. Her tombstone is in the third row."

The boy walked slowly into the graveyard. In the third row of headstones, he found the one he was looking for.

There was his letter jacket, draped over the rounded grave marker, just like it had hung around her shoulders on Saturday night.

 ## 8 Laffite's Hook-Arm

THERE'S THIS CEMETERY IN THE OUTSKIRTS OF NEW ORLEANS WHERE THE ghost of Jean Laffite is seen walking on moonless nights. He wears a pirate hat and has a hook instead of his left hand.

One night, two kids were going parking on the old road by the cemetery, where no one would bother them. While they were parked, the girl thought she heard something outside in the graveyard. To get her to snuggle close to him, the boy told her the story of Laffite's ghost.

The trick backfired, though, and the girl got so scared that she demanded he take her home. He had just about decided she must not like him. To be polite, he started up the car, and just as they pulled onto the road, there was a loud thud on her side of the car. The girl screamed, and the boy stomped on the gas and spun out down the road.

Back at the girl's house, the boy got out and went around to open her door. He just stood there, staring down at the door. At first the girl couldn't figure out what was wrong. Then she realized the door was locked, and he must be waiting for her to unlock it. But even when she unlocked the door, he just stood there staring.

The girl rolled her window down, and looked out at the door handle. Hanging from the handle was an old brass hook, with a stream of dried blood trailing off the door!

 9 The Baby's Milk Bottles

THEY TELL A STORY ABOUT A STORE OWNER IN THE SANTA CLARA VALLEY during the Great Depression. One rainy day, a woman in a print cotton dress, drenched by a sudden rainstorm, came into the store with two empty returnable milk bottles. She set them on the counter without a word, folded her arms, and looked down. The store owner assumed she wanted two more bottles. He got them from the cooler and set them in front of her, putting the empties underneath the counter. He told her the price was ten cents.

She took the fresh milk without speaking, and left without paying. The store owner just sighed; she probably didn't have any money anyway.

The next day she came back, and put the empties on the counter. She stepped back, folded her arms, and stared straight ahead. After a moment, the owner put the empties away and gave her two more fresh bottles out of the cooler. She left without paying, almost running out the door.

The third day, she came back with the empties. The store owner felt so sorry for the skinny, bedraggled woman that he took her empties and gave her fresh milk. But this time he followed a few yards behind her when she went quickly out the door. Maybe he could find the migrant camp where she was staying and give someone in her family a job around the store.

Instead of going to the migrant camps by the road, the woman went to the graveyard by the river. She disappeared behind a stone marker just as it began to rain again. The owner stood there for a few minutes, getting wet, and then he decided to leave. Just as he turned to go, he heard a baby crying in the distance. He looked all around the graveyard for a tent or migrant camp. Then he realized the muffled cries were coming from under his feet.

From inside a shallow grave!

The man ran back to the store and called everyone he knew that had a phone. In a few minutes trucks began to descend on the graveyard. Men with shovels had the grave open in a matter of moments. Inside was the woman in the cotton dress. She was dead, and had been for days. In her arms was the baby who'd been buried with her—but the baby was alive.

Beside the baby were two bottles of fresh milk.

10 Pair of Pants

AN OLD WOMAN AND AN OLD MAN LIVED TOGETHER IN A SLAT HOUSE BY the river. When the old man died, the woman sold most of his clothing to pay for the funeral. When the funeral director told her the casket's half-lid is opened only from the waist up at funerals, the old woman sold the old man's pants.

After the funeral, the ghost came to her at night. He stood in the door to the bedroom night after night, staring at the old woman. She'd just scream and cover her head with the bedclothes until dawn. Finally she went to the preacher and asked what to do.

"Ask him 'what in the name of the Lord' he wants," said the preacher.

That night the ghost came again.

"What in the name of the Lord do you want?" she asked.

"I'm cold," he said. "I want my pants."

"All right," she said. "I'll go get them."

The ghost went away and never came back. And the old woman didn't go get the pants back, either.

Freshman Initiation

YEARS AGO, WHEN I WAS IN JUNIOR HIGH SCHOOL, I WAS ON THE TRACK team. The senior high boys made us freshmen spend the night in a haunted house outside of town as a kind of initiation. They'd been doing it for years, and no one thought much about it, except that the kids that had come from the house always said it really was a scary place. We always expected that the seniors would be doing something to try to scare us, anyway, so we were ready for it.

The night started out pretty normal, with the five of us—I come from a small town—in the living room. We didn't have any lights, the seniors didn't allow that, and we'd been told to split up, one to a room, to get some sleep. I took the old living room, Dave got the back room, and so on; John took the lonely upstairs room. Well, we heard pebbles hit the windowpanes from time to time, and ghostly moans came from the barn out back, but by midnight the upperclassmen hadn't done anything really scary, or that we could conclusively blame on them, and it got real quiet and still. I guess we all fell asleep.

I awoke past midnight and could hear John in the room upstairs pacing slowly back and forth in his big heavy work boots that he always wore. I guess it woke everyone up, because the other four of us all got to the foot of the stairs at the same time, looking at each other kind of scared. We called to John and he didn't answer, but the pacing stopped.

The wind was blowing outside, and the old curtains were blowing in at the windows. Slowly, we climbed the stairs to the loft, in the inky darkness. Then, at the top of the stairs, we saw it: it was John, at least it had John's big shoes and John's clothes. We couldn't tell if it had John's face, because it had no head. Then the thing slowly lifted its head from the darkness beside itself, and threw the head right at us!

We ran as fast as we could back down the stairs and scattered out of the way. The head hit the floor. It was a burlap bag full of barn dirt. We ran back up the stairs, realizing we'd been tricked. John must have been in on it with the upperclassmen. They were probably laughing themselves silly somewhere out on the roof. In the loft, we found muddy tracks. The window was open. We ran back downstairs and scattered out to surround the house.

Around back, we found John all right, and we were sure it was John, but he had tried to climb out the back window and slide down to the low part of the roof for a drop to the ground. He must have slipped and slid faster than he planned. The old roof was sheets of tin, and a gable cut across over the kitchen. He must have hit the rusty edge of the gable sliding pretty fast. He was on the ground. His head was lying on the edge of the kitchen gable, staring down at us.

We let out a scream, and Dave turned and ran. While we tried to think of something to do, Bob noticed Dave was nowhere in sight. As we started the long run to town to get the sheriff, we saw Bob standing over the well. There in the light of the rising moon, was Dave, lying in the shallow well where he must have fallen when he ran, with his neck broken.

The upperclassmen denied having John "in" on the trick; it must have been his own idea. At least Dave's funeral could have an open casket. Bob went catatonic and has been lying in a bed in the state hospital ever since. Butch committed suicide the next year.

That just leaves me. But I'm all right, aren't I?

Aren't I?

12 Call from the Grave

ONE TIME THERE WAS A LITTLE GIRL WHOSE GRANDFATHER HAD JUST DIED. She had loved her grandfather very much, and she missed him a great deal. He was buried in the cemetery just a hundred yards from the home. She could see his grave from the living room window.

One night her parents were going out, and the babysitter hadn't come yet. They knew she was very reliable and would probably arrive in just a few minutes, so they kissed the girl goodbye and left for the drive into the city. Hours passed, and the babysitter still had not come; the girl began to be afraid. A storm was brewing outside, and thunder and lightning began to move closer to the house. Suddenly the lights went out just as a flash of lightning struck close to the home. The wind blew and branches fell all around the yard. Alone in the dark, the girl began to cry.

Then the phone rang. Just once. She went to it and answered, hoping it was her parents. She said hello, but no one said anything for a long time. Then a voice said, very softly and very far away, "Don't be afraid, honey. There's nothing to fear. You'll be safe in the house, and the storm will pass over . . ."

It was her grandfather. She waited a long time, but there was no other sound on the line. Slowly she hung up and sat down on the sofa, smiling.

Her parents drove hurriedly into the driveway, dodging the fallen branches, and rushed up to the door. The girl met them at the door, smiling, in the dark.

They told her that they had tried to call, but the phones were all dead. She told them she had gotten just one call. From her grandfather. The parents just shook their heads and put the girl to bed.

The next day, the family went to the cemetery to clean up around the grave after the storm. Branches were down everywhere; the power lines were down, and the phone lines were hanging off the poles. The phone line from the house was intact up to the first pole, then it fell into the cemetery—where they found it lying with its broken end across the grandfather's grave.

13 Eleven-Eleven

THERE'S A MYSTERIOUS TIME OF DAY; YOU ONLY NOTICE IT IF YOU HAVE A digital clock. Once you've heard this story, you'll know that it's true. That ghostly time is 11:11. Here's what happened:

It was the big party at the high school. All the kids were having a great time. Nobody noticed that the captain of the football team and his girlfriend, the head cheerleader, had left early to go out and get drunk.

Nobody alive knows how it happened, but their car skidded off the road and hit a tree, killing them both instantly. Back at the dance, it was like everyone had this same feeling all at the same time. They all turned and looked at the digital clock on the desk. It was 11:11, the exact moment the kids had died.

And after that, the teenagers began to know that their dead friends were trying to communicate with them, trying to warn them with the ghostly message. They began to notice the clock when it said 11:11.

And now that you've heard the story, it will happen to you, too. You'll get the ghostly message. You'll start noticing the time, over and over again, for the rest of your life, just as the digital clock reads 11:11.

14 La LLorona at Waldo

NOW THIS HAPPENED TO A FRIEND OF MINE, AND SO I KNOW IT'S TRUE. HE was in his pick-up, driving from Cerrillos to I-25, and he was drinking beer and throwing the cans out the window. He was at Waldo [a ghost town], and he saw this girl hitchhiking. It was real late at night, and so he picked her up because she looked like she was lost or had run away from home.

And he was driving on this gravel road, and there's no houses or anything near. And she says to him that he shouldn't drink so much. And he just laughed and threw another empty can out. And when he looked over at her, she was all ugly, and her face was starting to rot like she'd been dead for a long time. And he looked away because she was so ugly, and when he looked back, she was gone.

And it was *la LLorona,* and that's true.

 **hostly Lights**

15 Michael and the Ghost Light

ON A DARK NIGHT, IN THE HEAT OF SUMMER, WE LEFT THE SAWMILL WHERE we worked and drove eighty miles to see it: the ghost light at Crossett. Four of us in a convertible with the top down; one of the guys had been there before and knew the way. It was about ten o'clock when we stopped on the gravel road and turned out the lights. The railbed is elevated in that part of the state. The road rose about three feet above the level of the fields to cross the single set of rails.

We sat in the car drinking and talking, waiting for something to happen, daring and double-dog-daring each other to approach the light if it appeared. Somebody retold the legend in the steamy darkness:

A train had rolled to a stop just at this crossing sometime after the turn of the century on a dark, hot night like this one. A brakeman was walking the railbed with a lantern, checking the cars or the couplings. Something, no one knew what, caught his attention between two cars; leaning in at the coupling, he found something wrong.

Trying to fix something, a loose coupling or a dragging chain, he bent closer and closer to the metal mechanism. The locomotive lurched a few inches along the track as steam engines sometimes did, and a heavy ripple of movement surged down the long line of flatcars and boxcars. The brakeman's lantern fell to the railbed.

Looking back past the coal car, the engineer saw the lantern fall. He took his own lantern and ran back, car after car, to where the brakeman's lantern lay. The body was lying across the track. The head was lying under a bloody coupling. Some folks say the body went that night in a boxcar, but the head was left behind, no one having the courage to pick it up. Or maybe the head just wasn't in the boxcar with the body.

Anyway, by night, people still see the light of the lantern moving slowly along the tracks about three feet off the ground. "It's the decapitated brakeman," people say, "still looking for his head!"

The convertible got very quiet after the last retelling of the legend.

An instant later we saw it. A faint, yellowish ball of light about a foot in diameter was floating slowly along the tracks, three feet above the rails, going south to north. It just crept along, not bobbing or weaving, just slow and steady.

Finally, I left the car and walked toward the tracks, not ever taking my eyes off the light, trying to meet it at the intersection on a double-dog-dare. I was sweating, but I wasn't sure why. There wasn't any fear, or any feeling at all, just that light. I got onto the tracks and turned and faced it as it came slowly toward me. When it got within ten feet of me, it just vanished.

I was almost disappointed. After a minute, I turned to walk back to the car. There was the light, north of me on the tracks, moving away. The guys were all wide-eyed as I came up to the car.

"What did it feel like?" they asked.

"What did what feel like?" I said.

"We saw the ghost light pass right through your chest!"

Then, and only then, was I afraid. Really afraid.

16 Dawson Cemetery

THE DAWSON CEMETERY SITS ALONE ON A HILL, THE TOWN IT ONCE served long gone. In the silver mining country near Cimarron, New Mexico, Dawson was a boom town, and it went bust just as quickly when a cave-in killed most of the men in town. A second cave-in twenty-five years later ended the town's life. Most of the headstones in the cemetery have one of the two cave-in dates. The town itself was dismantled board by board and carried off by the mining company when the second cave-in made the mine unprofitable.

Some of the rangers from Philmont Ranch would drive out to the cemetery with a guitar and something to drink, and sit around watching the moon and enjoying an evening off. Myself and three other rangers from the [Air Force] Academy, and two civilian rangers, went out one summer night in 1980 and sat around enjoying the high desert view and the old songs.

[One of the rangers present] got uneasy, and wandered back to the car, parked a hundred yards away. Later, another ranger went down to the car to check on the . . . not exactly scared, just uneasy . . . friend. Only minutes later, the second fellow came walking quickly back to the grave sites. He grabbed me by the arm and whispered, "We all need to leave here, right now!"

He was dead serious, as serious as a stone, and we all packed up and left calmly but surprisingly quickly.

When we got to the cars, fifty yards down the hill at the road, we all asked, "What's wrong? What's the problem?"

The ranger who had been sitting back at the car said, "While you were sitting up there singing, we saw these green lights floating down the hillside toward the graveyard. They floated down to where you guys were sitting and standing, and they mingled in among you like they were part of the party. They weren't flashlights or anything; maybe a dozen of them were milling around you."

We were kind of skeptical, but the deadpan looks on these guy's faces convinced us. We drove back toward Philmont and talked about it. "There were two levels of light," they explained, "some about as high as your chest, and some up around your heads."

That was when we began to realize it. Miners would have two kinds of lights: lanterns held at chest height and carbide lamps on their hard hats. Those of us actually in the graveyard never saw them, only the guys at the cars down the hill, but we knew that it must have been the miners coming home from the mine to sing and have a drink with the living, just as they had done three-quarters of a century before.

17 Senath Light

IN THE BOOTHEEL OF MISSOURI, AT THE SMALL TOWN OF SENATH, THERE is a ghost light. We got some directions on how to get there: you turn off the pavement at a certain point, drive a certain distance down a gravel road, cross a couple of bridges, then you're out in a soybean field and you come to a corner where there's an old, gnarled tree with a lot of character.

We knew the tree the minute we saw it in the dusk-light; it was a tree you might see in a horror film. You take another left, go down to another bridge, and park on the bridge. The hollow sounds echoing up from the old wooden bridge made the place pretty scary just to begin with. Real or imagined, the creaks and groans of the wooden bridge heightened our awareness as we waited for the light.

Then we saw the lights far ahead of us. There are all the usual explanations: swamp gas, lights at some distant airport, but these lights didn't look anything like that. They drifted slowly toward us, fairly high up, yellow-white in color, moving about above the road and the fields. Five of us sat and watched them come closer and closer. Then the bridge noises and the slow approach of the lights combined to give us all the excitement we had been looking for that night.

We left.

In reverse.

Quickly.

18 Ghost Light in Red

ON THE OUTSKIRTS OF JONESBORO, ARKANSAS, THERE IS A MYSTERIOUS grave haunted by a ghostly light of a very rare nature and color. College boys at A.S.U. [Arkansas State University] often take their dates to "park" beside the cemetery, where they can scare their dates with the obviously true story that explains the ghostly light.

The area is lonely and secluded, and many old stones and monuments rise high into the night among dark, twisted trees and sinister shrubbery. The ghostly light is easy to spot: unique in all the ghostlore, this light is red! You see, it's the grave of a prostitute buried almost a century ago.

The white monument is an obelisk, standing tall in the midst of other smaller stones that are more modern. The brazen hussy won't be still even in death, because if you park just in the right place, near a moss-covered monument carved from marble in the shape of a tree-trunk felled by the Grim Reaper, you can catch a glimpse of a pale red light, glowing from the orb at the top of the obelisk.

[The teller adds: and you must be careful to keep your date's attention on the graveyard, because if she looks directly opposite the graveyard on the other side of the road, she will notice the tall radio transmitter tower with the huge red light on it. The ghostly light is a romantic hoax.]

19 Ball Lightning

YOU KNOW, I'VE NEVER TOLD ANYONE THIS UNTIL TONIGHT, BECAUSE I never heard of ball lightning before. I live right by the Illinois [River in northwest Arkansas], and my bedroom window looks out on the river. One night in the summer, when I was real young [about 1953], I was looking out the window and I saw a ball of white light come down out of the sky, fast, but not very fast, and it came down like this [she described a concave arc] over the water.

It flew right down the middle of the water, following the river, about three feet above the water, right down the middle of the river. It was about two feet in diameter, and it was white. I thought it was a ghost.

20 Ball of Fire

ONE NIGHT GRANDMA AND GRANDPA HAD GOTTEN IN THE BUGGY TO GO somewhere, and as they drove along, there was a mild storm going on, but not real close. There was some rain falling, and when they got to the bridge that had to be crossed in order to get to town, a ball of fire came rolling down the river toward them.

They were scared bad. They had never seen a fireball, but Grandpa told me what it looked like: it was big, it was yellow and orange, and it rolled like a bowling ball down the river toward them. They turned around and went back to the house, they were so scared.

The next morning when they went to make the crossing again, the bridge had washed out.

21 The Lights in the Nursing Home

WE WERE TALKING ABOUT STRANGE LIGHTS: I SAW SOME UNUSUAL ONES when I worked at the nursing home here in town. At [this] nursing home, there are three small lights at night before someone dies. Small, little, round lights, a group of three. I had never really thought very much about the story. Apparently it goes all the way back to [the previous owners of the home]. This went on then, and when [the current owners] took it over, they didn't like rumors about their nursing home, and they told all the employees that rumors and gossip like that would not be tolerated and anyone caught spreading rumors or gossip like that would be fired.

Once or twice I had caught a glimpse of something out of the corner of my eye, but not anything I could pin down. Usually someone else would see it, too. It could be anywhere in the nursing home. It could be down the hall [from a patient who later died], in the room, or even over the bed. And usually after the lights had been seen, within the next twenty-four hours, someone would pass away. And the deaths always seemed to come in groups of three. Usually the lights were in close contact to the person who would die. A lot of times they would just be seen down the hall, but several times they were in the room or actually over the bed when they were seen.

22 Ball of Fire II

AT NACOGDOCHES [TEXAS] OUT BY THE OLD NORTH CHURCH GRAVE-
yard, the local people have seen a ball of fire run along above the
ground near the graves shortly after a new burial. The ball of fire always
runs along barbed-wire fences or hog-wire fences, never along the road
itself. They say it's the spirits of the newly dead, complaining about
their lot.

23 The Texarkana Light

DURING THE WAR BETWEEN THE STATES, A CONFEDERATE SOLDIER CAME
home looking for his family. He had deserted having heard that his
home had been raided. He went upstairs in the dark and discovered his
family all murdered by jayhawkers. He found them when he lit a candle
and raised it high to look around. He killed himself with his saber.

There is a ghostly light in the window still.

A casual acquaintance took me and a friend out on the dark road to
see this light. We parked at the modern home of the land owner, within
fifty feet of the empty old house, and as the driver went up, politely, to
tell the occupants that we had come to see the ghost light, I looked over
at the dark, empty dwelling from the past. There it was: a ghostly
fluorescence in an upstairs window! It rose into view, then lowered back
out of sight, almost like a candle raised as a signal to someone outside. I
had never seen anything like it before.

It didn't look like a candle—but then, what else was it?

24 The Big Thicket Light

THE TEXANS CALL THE AREA "THE BIG THICKET." BETWEEN THE TRINITY River and the Neches River, around the town of Saratoga in Jefferson County, near the Old Bragg Road, the Texans see "The Big Thicket Light."

As you can tell from its name, the area is dense with undergrowth and was an ideal hideout during the early period of Texas history, and during and after the Civil War. The only clearings through the Thicket are the roads, the railroad right-of-ways, and occasional clearings where hunters gather around pine knot fires to tell the ghostly tales of the region after a long day's hunt.

The story has it that a jayhawker [used here to mean "union sympathizer"] was killed in a burn-out at the town of Kaiser by Confederates seeking out "slackers" who were avoiding military service to the Confederacy. The man ran burning from the house and ran into the Thicket, setting some of the underbrush on fire. His ghost still walks the Thicket as a small ball of flame.

When the Santa Fe Railroad came through, the ghost light often followed the tracks. When the tracks were pulled up in 1934, the light followed the empty railbed. After the road through the area was paved in 1952, the light was seen more often as more passers-by looked into the Thicket on dark nights and watched the ghostly light moving slowly in the undergrowth.

25 The Miami Spooklight

ON A DARK, FOGGY NIGHT ONE AUTUMN JUST OUTSIDE OF MIAMI [OKLA-homa], a woman sent her daughter out to look for the cows and drive them back to the lot. This was at the turn of the century, so the daughter took a lighted lantern with her to cut the fog. The girl never came back. The mother became frightened and began to search for the girl about midnight. She also carried a lantern.

She searched all night and never found the daughter, but the cattle were scattered across the rolling hills. The mother continued to search, night after night, insane with grief. When she died of remorse, her spirit continued to walk on foggy nights in the fall. She can still be seen, or her lantern can, on cold, foggy nights. I have seen the light; it's yellow like a lantern, and it swings just a little bit as if the ghost were carrying it while walking.

26 Spooklight at Hornet

IN 1886, SETTLERS ABOUT ELEVEN MILES SOUTHWEST OF JOPLIN, MISSOURI, began to see a ghostly light. It was blamed on the ghost of a Quapaw Indian (the Quapaw Agency was at Seneca a few miles away) looking for his lost lover, who had committed suicide rather than give in to her father's wish that she marry a man of his choosing instead of the young Quapaw. The light scared some settlers so badly they abandoned their farms and moved away. Today, the light is called the Hornet Spook Light for the settlement a few miles away.

27 Hornet Burial Ground

I USED TO KNOW AN OLD CHEROKEE MAN WHO RAN A LIQUOR STORE JUST outside of Seneca [Missouri], south of Joplin, about where [U. S. Highways] 71 and 66 cross. This Indian man told me that when the road was cut through the area, they disturbed an Indian burial ground near Hornet. Those [spook] lights you see started being seen about the time the graves were disturbed.

The lights are the spirits of those disturbed burials, wandering in search of their scattered parts.

28 The Split Hornet Light

YEARS AGO, WHEN I WAS QUITE YOUNG, I HAD JUST GOTTEN OUT ON MY own, and was working at a job in Joplin [Missouri]. A young man that I had been seeing came to me one evening and said, "You've got to come see this."

He said he wanted me to see the spooklight south of Joplin. I assumed that it must be . . . an excuse, you know. We were sitting parked at the side of the road with the lights off, and as we were talking and cuddling, a very bright, white light came up behind the car. It was beautiful! It was glowing white with blue fringes. It came directly toward the trunk, and when it got to the car it split in two and slowly passed by us on either side of the car, up about as high as the windows. It made no sound at all!

When it reached the hood, it rejoined and went on down the road.

29 The Still Hornet Light

WHEN I WAS IN HIGH SCHOOL, A WHOLE BUNCH OF MY BUDDIES AND I decided one night, girls and guys, to go up to Hornet [Missouri] to see the spooklight. One of us knew the way from up in our corner of Oklahoma, closest to Missouri, and they wanted all of us to go up and look, and check on it.

We saw the spooklight do something it hardly ever does, just sit absolutely still. It was yellow, shaded toward orange. It was about the size of a basketball and it was sitting in an open field about three feet off the ground.

Very quietly, from about two hundred feet out, we encircled the light, all the way around it. Some fools will tell you that what causes the spooklight is headlights from the Will Rogers Turnpike (in Oklahoma), but when I was in high school, the Turnpike hadn't been built yet. And the light is seen in the hollows between the hills; there's not any way that the intelligence this light displays in its movement could be headlights.

Very quietly, speaking to each other, we all took one step forward, then another, then another. The light was just hanging there, three feet off the ground. We all took one more step and when we got about fifty feet from it, it winked out.

The light immediately appeared a hundred yards away, off to one side, just hanging in mid-air. At that point, a lot of us had reached our tolerance and we left.

30 Ghost Light Along the Chisos

ALONG THE RIO BRAVO DEL NORTE, WHICH WE CALL THE RIO GRANDE, near the Big Bend in the river, there is a ghostlight that moves among the Chisos Mountains. The Mexicans call it *la luz espantosa*.

If a cowboy is lost in the twisting, turning valleys and watersheds of the Chisos Mountains and singing to himself as he searches for the way back to camp, he may hear the echo of his song go on longer than the verse he was singing. The ghostly singing will echo off the cliffs and around the chasms.

Then he will see a ghost light moving along at the level of a rider on horseback, as if the rider were carrying a lantern. He may imagine he hears a woman singing, but then a lonely cowboy often imagines that, even when a coyote howls. He follows her, whatever she may be, with her light.

Some cowboys say the light will lead the cowpoke to safety. Others say it will lead him off a cliff in the blackness of night. Even if the cowboy dies, he dies happy and hopeful, better than dying in the desert sun the next day. But I like to think the ghost light leads the cowboy out safely.

Singing as it goes.

31 Bayou Bourleau

AT THE BAYOU BOURLEAU, JUST BESIDE THE PLANTATION HOUSE POINTE Chrétienne, there is the ghost of a girl who was killed on the bridge over the bayou. She appears in a white shroud. Sometimes she is called a *feu follé*, because she glows like fire.

She stands still on the bridge as you approach her and you can get very close to her, but if you try to touch her, she will disappear.

32 The Marfa Lights

MARFA, TEXAS, WAS ESTABLISHED IN 1881 AS A WATER STOP ON THE OLD Texas and New Orleans Railroad. In 1883, someone driving cattle between Alpine and Marfa saw the most famous ghost light of them all. For over a century, the Marfa lights have been seen moving slowly along the ground.

One story says that back in the 1850s, West Texas was just beginning to be settled and people were very scattered. One winter, a bad blizzard blew in and a rancher who had not been prepared, went out to get firewood. His family became worried when he did not return, and they went out with lanterns to search for him. None of them ever returned to the house, and the Marfa lights are the family out looking for the rancher.

33 Lights at Silverton

I HAVE SEEN THE PHENOMENON OF LIGHTS IN THE OLD GRAVEYARD AT Silverton, Colorado. It's an ancient cemetery [the teller later explained that he meant "very old" by that] from the heyday of mining in Silverton. The mines were abandoned long ago, but the cemetery remains.

I was standing up on a kind of a nob of a hill above the cemetery, and I saw between twenty and seventy softball-sized lights. They're white and they rise from just above the grave and they rise up to about fifteen or twenty feet in the air, and then they go back down, and then they rise again.

How many there were fluctuated, and how fast they were moving fluctuated, too.

34 Ball of Fire III

AT LUCERO, THEY SAY A WOMAN WAS KILLED BY DOGS. THE DOGS WERE demons working for the Devil, and they got hungry, so they killed her. Her spirit is still there, and she is angry. She comes up from Hell and rolls around as a ball of flame. She only comes out when the moon is full. They only come out then, you know.

35 Ball of Fire IV

AT THIS OLD HOUSE THAT WAS ABANDONED, SOME PEOPLE WERE GOING BY in a wagon and they saw light in the house. They went to look, but nobody was in there. Then a big ball of fire, a *brasero,* came out of the chimney and rolled at them. They really ran. And as they left, they saw sparks coming out of the chimney.

Ghosts of the Roadways

36   Raw Head and Bloody Bones

DEEP IN THE WOODED HILLS AND HOLLOWS OF THE OZARK MOUNTAINS of Missouri there lived an old conjuring woman who knew all the herbs and roots and cures and magical spells. Everybody in the hollow came to her for remedies, but she only had one friend: a lean, mean wild razorback hog. The old boar came by her house and ate her kitchen garbage; he ate so many of her leftover roots and discarded magical potions that he got to where he could walk and talk like a man.

The old woman and the old boar got along fine for many years, but one year in October, at hog-slaughtering time, a lazy hillbilly who didn't have any hogs rounded up his neighbors'. He must have rounded up the conjuring woman's pet, too, and taken him to the Hog-Scald Hollow where all the neighbors had gathered to shoot the hogs, cut their throats to bleed them out, and hang them up for gutting. After gutting a carcass, they would scald it with boiling water and scrape the hair off. After the meat was ready for the smokehouse, nothing was left but the bloody bones in a pile at the bluff wall. Even the hogs' heads were skinned and taken back to the house to boil and make souse.

When all the meat to be smoked was loaded into burlap bags, and loaded into the wagon, and the heads laid alongside, and the sun was going down, everyone would leave the hollow. The last one to leave was the lazy thief, looking about for one last morsel to scavenge. As he rode off in his wagon, the skinned head of the old conjuring woman's pet bounced out into the dirt road.

The skinned head spoke: "Bloody bones, get up and dance!"

Back at Hog-Scald Hollow, the bloody bones of the conjuring woman's hog got up and danced around. The bones got back together and ran down the road and collected up the head. The ghastly creature followed the wagon to the lazy thief's house.

Raw Head and Bloody Bones went to all the critters in the deep woods and borrowed things to wear. He borrowed the panther's fangs; he borrowed the bear's claws; he borrowed the raccoon's tail.

At the cabin, the old man and the old woman were in bed asleep. Suddenly there was a noise like something falling into the fireplace. The fire flared up and the old man awoke.

The old man got up to see what was the matter. He looked and looked but couldn't find anything amiss. Then he looked up the chimney.

"Land o' Goshen," said the old man, "what have you got those big old eyes for?"

"To see your grave . . ." said the deep hollow voice up the chimney. The old man ran and hid under the bed. After a few minutes he got curious and came back and looked up the chimney again.

"Land o' Goshen," he said, "what have you got those great big claws for?"

"To dig your grave . . ." said the deep, dark voice. The old man ran and hid under the bed again. After a few minutes he got curiouser and curiouser. He came out and went back to the chimney.

"Land o' Goshen," he said, "what have you got that big bushy tail for?"

"TO SWEEP YOUR GRAVE . . ." said the rumbling rolling voice. The old man ran and hid under the washtub. After a long time he got so curious he couldn't stand it any more. He came back out and looked up the chimney one last time at the raw head and the bloody bones.

"Land o'Goshen," he said, "what have you got those long sharp teeth for?"

"TO EAT YOU UP!" said the Raw Head and Bloody Bones, and it came down the chimney and carried off the lazy hillbilly and stole his horse, too.

They never saw the old man again, but they saw Raw Head and

Bloody Bones wearing the old man's shirt and overalls riding on the stolen horse. It carried its old raw head in its hand, up high against the full moon. Old Raw Head and Bloody Bones!

37 The Guard at San Marcos Bridge

THE BRIDGE OVER THE SAN MARCOS RIVER ON OLD U.S. HIGHWAY 80 IS guarded by a ghost. He wears high boots and grey pants held up by suspenders, an underwear shirt, and a Confederate cap. He stands at the parade-rest guard stance so many Confederates used, leaning on his rifle, guarding the bridge.

Local legend says that brothers who volunteered for the South during the War Between the States swore to return home, dead or alive. The one who came home alive is buried and gone. The one who died in battle is still on duty, one-and-one-quarter centuries later.

38 White Wolf

BETWEEN THE CLEAR FORK AND THE DOUBLE MOUNTAIN FORK OF THE Brazos River, U.S. 180 follows one branch of the Old Southern Trail to California. Fort Phantom Hill was built to guard that trail across the empty grasslands and low mesas of Central Texas. Hundreds of wagons passed Westward along the trails, and many wagons and inhabitants vanished, the prey of marauders, wild animals, or disease and starvation. Thousands of unmarked graves must lie along those trails. And one that is marked by legend.

Among the many wagon trains that passed, one wagon slowed and stopped to wait for death. A young boy was ill with a high fever, and the family camped to spend the boy's last days. One night, the boy asked to sleep outside on the ground instead of in the wagon. His fever was so high and he was so hot, the mother finally consented.

Sometime after midnight, the boy awoke, feverish, and looked toward the dark mesa that overhung the camp. High, high up on the mesa's rim sat a ghostly white form with red, red eyes. A long, low howl echoed down the stone incline. The boy fell asleep.

The moon set and the night grew deeply dark. Only the pale light of the stars lit the camp when the boy awoke again. Across the dead campfire sat a great white shape with red, red eyes. At first the boy was afraid, but the figure never moved and gradually the youth decided it was just some laundry laid out on the water barrel. He fell asleep again.

One last time, some before dawn, the boy awoke.

The thing sat beside the boy's bedroll, looking down at him with red, red eyes.

"It's just a dog," thought the boy with a smile, "a big, white dog."

The great creature lowered its muzzle to the boy's face and gently licked his fevered brow. The boy laughed and closed his eyes for the last time. A long, low growl began outside the wagon and rose to an unearthly howl that climbed the mesa walls and rang out over the prairie.

The father leapt up and grabbed his rifle, but by the time he was down from the wagon, the camp was empty and the boy was dead. They buried him after dawn under the prairie mound beside the camp.

As the wagon rolled away, a huge white wolf watched it go—a wolf with red, red eyes.

Through the years the grave was seen by many passing travellers; one wagon even stopped and saw small white bones sticking out of the sand. When the men went over to investigate, an enormous albino wolf leapt over the prairie mound and sent them scattering with a snarl.

The legend grew. Some settlers said the wolf guarded the grave. Others said it was the wolf that killed the boy. But finally, the legend came to say that the ghost of the boy was the wolf himself. The white wolf.

With the red, red eyes.

39   The Ghostly Battle

MOST FOLKS DON'T KNOW IT, BUT DURING THE WAR BETWEEN THE States, volunteers from California went East and fought, some for the Confederacy, some for the Union. A lot of volunteers went from Northern California. After the war, many of the dead were transported back and buried here. On the winding road between Redman and Elkhorn, there is a little cemetery in the valley where the war is still fought, day and night, by the ghosts of those brave volunteers.

High up in the mountains, the graveyard holds both Confederate and Union dead. A precarious, crooked road works its way down off one mountain, through the valley, past the graveyard, and up the other valley wall. From the overlook on the road, high above the grass-covered graves, many drivers swear to have seen a battle going on in the valley below.

I was just a young man, twenty-five or thirty years old, just out of the armed services and I had a truck-driving job delivering machine parts between Redman and Elkhorn and other places. One day I came up the side of the mountain with the loaded truck laboring, and as I came around the horseshoe bend at the overlook, I chanced to look down at the graveyard far below me. I had heard the legend that if you saw the battle in progress, you wouldn't live to climb the other side of the valley; you'd be killed on the twisting road going down. I didn't believe that part of the legend. But even though I'd heard about the battle all my life, I wasn't prepared for how real it all looked.

Because, there was the battle, going on—and these didn't look like ghosts, these looked like flesh-and-blood men, easily a hundred soldiers, fighting on one side or the other. I could see the puffs of smoke coming out of their rifle-barrels; I could see the sunlight glinting off their guns, their uniform buttons; I could see them, but I couldn't hear a thing. It was completely silent.

But a fierce battle was taking place between men in blue uniforms and men in grey. I pulled over to the side of the road at the overlook, stopped the truck, and sat there and shook for several minutes, not daring to look again. And then I reminded myself of the rest of the legend, that "you wouldn't make it to the other side," and that I was now probably going to be killed if I didn't go back the way I'd come, and back around another way.

After a long wait, I started the truck and pulled out down the hill toward the valley, against the warning in the legend, driving at five miles an hour, around the sweeping curve to the other side of the valley. As I got even with the graveyard, I dared to look.

At that moment the sun was setting. There were no ghosts in the graveyard, just old, weather-worn stones. I drove to the next town, parked the truck, and I never drove that road again.

40 The Head on the High Road

THERE WAS A YOUNG SPANISH *CABALLERO* IN THE REGIMENT AT SANTA FE who was proud but lonely. All the other *caballeros* had ladies, but not he. It was the custom to hold a dance on the last night of each month for all the regiment, and for each dance, one of the *caballeros* would be the host and his lady the hostess. It was the lonely *caballero's* turn to host the dance for October. He had no one to serve as his hostess, and the dance was only weeks away.

He had noticed a lovely young *señorita* who ate every day at Sena Plaza; she was the daughter of one of the Sena family. She ate alone at a table every day, and she was beautiful. He dressed in his best uniform to meet her one day. She had a cup of coffee, and it was half-empty. He came to her table and asked if he might serve her more coffee; in this way he hoped to gain permission to join her. She agreed. He poured her cup full and joined her. She smiled but did not speak throughout the meal. When she had finished, he pulled out her chair for her, and she left without a farewell. Every day for a week he offered to pour her coffee, each day she left without a word.

On Sunday, after Mass, he approached her family to ask if he could escort her to the regimental dance. They ignored him and rode away in their carriage. At lunch the next day, he returned, offered to pour her coffee, she agreed, and as he seated himself, he saw her handkerchief laid on the table. He decided to take it so she would think she had lost it and returning it, he could gain her favor. He took her handkerchief when she wasn't looking, and she departed without it. He went to her house that night, but the servant who answered the door refused to admit him.

He joined her the next day and tried to bring up the "missing" handkerchief. She said she was not missing anything, and after that she said nothing else. Another week went by without any success. Every attempt failed. At last, he resorted to the last remedy. While he was drinking in the cantina, a friend advised him to go to the two *brujas* who lived in the Oldest House. He gathered all his money and polished his boots and went to see the witches.

Up the narrow, dark street was an adobe house with a low, crooked door. He knocked, and finally an old woman answered, an old woman with white porcelain skin, fragile, and very old.

"What do you want that you cannot leave us in peace?" she demanded.

He explained that he needed to see the witches and why.

"We have been called many things," said the old woman, *"viejas* [old], *feas* [ugly], but never *brujas!* How dare you call us witches?"

He told them he was in desperate need, and the woman admitted him in an apparent change of heart. Behind the door, as she closed it, he saw another old woman cooking at a great *calderón* [cooking pot] over a smokeless fire. Behind her was a wooden case filed with different vials and bottles. He explained his problem again, and called her *bruja,* again.

"Don't call me *bruja,"* she said. "If you have to call me anything, call me *abuelita* [little grandmother]. Love brings nothing but trouble. But for all those coins, I will give you this." She walked to the case and picked out a tall, thin purple vial, and she blew the dust off of it and cackled.

"You can take this vial and give me all your coins, or you can leave with your wealth and leave this vial here. Either way, I promise you, you will still have a problem. There are no guarantees in life."

The soldier took the vial and gave her the coins. He left at once. The next afternoon he met the *señorita* at Sena Plaza and when he poured her coffee, he held the vial beneath her handkerchief and poured its contents into the cup as he flaunted the kerchief to her. She drank the coffee and snatched the *pañuelo* from him; she stood up and left with a look of contempt that told him she never wanted to see him again. The contents of the vial seemed not to have worked.

It was All Saints Eve, and the *caballero* was humiliated to have no hostess for the dance. He marched back to the house of the Sena family and forced his way past the servant to see if the potion had worked. The *señorita* slammed the door in his face. Her feelings for him were unchanged, but more intense. He marched back to the Oldest House and pounded on the door.

He had been drunk the night before, bragging to his friends in the cantina; now he had nothing. He wanted revenge. His sword rattled in its scabbard as he knocked. It reminded him that he should defend his honor with his sword. The old woman opened the door and looked at him with such a glare. He drew his sword and demanded his money back.

"Give me back the vial and I will give you back your coins."

He pulled the vial from his waistcoat pocket and presented it to her.

"This is empty. Give me what was in it and I'll give you the coins."

The *caballero* screamed that the witches were powerless.

"I never claimed to be a witch," said the old woman. "You called me a witch. I told you there are no guarantees in life!"

The *caballero* held his sword to the old woman's throat and demanded his coins. Out of nowhere a long knife flew through the air. Did the other woman throw it? Or was it witchcraft?

The knife took off the *caballero*'s head. The head fell to the street, and rolled slowly down the sloping street, down toward the plaza, making a ghastly thumping noise as it rolled. Its eyes were open and its mouth was ready to scream.

And now today in Santa Fe, on Hallowe'en Night, if you stand by the Oldest House, you can hear the head rolling down to the plaza.

41 The Headless Caballero

AROUND THE HERB SHOP of DELFINIO LUJÁN, ON GALISTEO STREET, THEY tell the tale of the headless *caballero* of Alto Street. He lost his head to two witches when they sold him a love potion that didn't work. Now he rides his fine horse up and down Alto Street, along the river, looking for his head.

He brandishes his sword at you if he sees you, and acts as if he'll cut off your head, too, for spite, for staring at him.

He never has found his head.

42 La Malogra

THEN THERE'S *LA MALOGRA [LA MALHORA,* OR *MALA HORA,* THE BAD hour]. You see her when you are walking at a crossroads and someone is going to die. She foretells death. She takes on human form and sometimes to see her drives you insane. Sometimes she wears a sheepskin, like the *borregueros* wear. She is like *la LLorona.* She is a bad thing.

43 Ghost Girl of the Mimbres

THE OLD-TIMERS SAY THERE'S A LONELY GAL WHO RIDES THE MIMBRES AND lures cowboys astray. They say she was a pretty lady in life, but one who lived so far out that she seldom saw anyone but her brothers and the ranch hands. And that, as the old-timers say, would be like kissing your sister.

One day she caught a glimpse of a handsome rider, and she followed him, hoping to find out whereabouts he lived. He took a sharp turn in the deep canyons, and she lost him, and she lost her way. The ranch hands found her months later, dead beneath a mesquite tree.

When the cowpokes see a well-dressed lady on the Mimbres now, a pretty Anglo lady in turn-of-the-century duds, they know not to follow her. She'll lead you into the twisting canyons and you'll never come out. Unless you come out riding with her, forever, on the Mimbres.

44 La LLorona

PEOPLE OF SANTA FE HAVE ALWAYS CELEBRATED THE END OF *ZOZOBRA* [Old Man Gloom] with a fiesta where we burn him [in effigy], but now the people of Santa Fe are interested in a true tale or belief of the people. She is *la LLorona* [The Weeping Woman].

Once this woman was a widow, and she had two children. She fell in love with a rich nobleman, but he wasn't interested in her because he didn't want to have to raise her two children by her first man. So she took the children to the *acequia* [irrigation ditch] and drowned them, and let their bodies float downstream. When she told the nobleman that she was free of the children, he was horrified. Now he really didn't want anything to do with her.

She went back to the *acequia,* looking for her children. They were gone. This was a long time ago. Now she continues to wander the valleys and weep and wail over the loss of her children. She warns drunkards to mend their ways and tells people to go back to church if they've quit going for some reason.

She's like the bogeyman, and she's the conscience of those who don't have a conscience anymore. She is *la LLorona.*

45 La LLorona II

THAT'S *LA LLORONA,* YOU KNOW [THE TELLER GESTURES AT A PAINTING IN the Museum of Fine Arts]. She comes at night to the people who are out too late or who are doing bad things and makes them stop. She wears this *rebozo* [shawl], and when she has warned you to stop what you're doing wrong, if you don't listen to her, she takes off her *rebozo* and she is a skull. Sometimes someone will shoot at her and try to kill her, but she turns into a snake to get away in the grass. You can't kill her anyway, because she's already dead. She murdered her own children, and now you see her by waterways because she drowned them. The *abuelos* and *abuelas* [grandfathers and grandmothers] use her to scare the little children and make them obey, but grown men see her, too. I've never seen her, but I know people who have. That's what people say. But it all sounds like *pozole* [hominy stew] to me.

46 Hitchhiker at Tierra Amarilla

THERE IS A GHOSTLY HITCHHIKER ON THE ROAD UP NEAR TIERRA Amarilla. An anglo boy who drank too much and drove too fast got drunk one night at a party. He tried to drive home and crashed his truck into the solid granite wall where the road had been dynamited through the mountain. His father had a grotto built into the granite, with a scene of the Holy Family in small statues, there at the spot where the wreck took place. Every year on the anniversary of the boy's death, the father goes there and lights vigil candles.

When I was a little girl, young women who might be driving alone, to a dance or something, on the anniversary of the boy's death, might drive by the grotto late at night. They would see the ghostly image of the boy, standing out on the road, trying to flag them down.

Everyone always said that if the girls had been drinking or doing things they should not have been doing, the sight of the ghost would make them slam on their brakes [to keep from hitting him] and they would crash into the granite wall right where he had been killed years before.

That kept a lot of the young girls from going out at night.

47 Booger Dog

THERE IS A GHOST DOG THAT WALKS BY NIGHT IN THE OLD SECTION OF Waco [Texas]. He is bigger than a dog, almost as big as a mule, and black as the night that he comes out in. Some folks see the ghost dog when they've been haughty to their elders or when they've been lying or cheating, but some folks see him just because they're out alone on a dark night.

He'll jump out and scare a lone walker and send him scurrying. He'll step out of the woods in front of a mule or wagon-team and they'll stop dead in their tracks. He's even been known to jump on the hood of a car, and the weight puts the frame down on the tires and ruins them.

Folks that know better get home before two [a.m.] if they know what's good for them. But if you can cross the Brazos [River] when you see him, you'll be safe: ghosts can't cross running water.

48 The Headless Outlaw

TWO TEXAS RANGERS, W. A. A. "BIGFOOT" WALLACE AND CREED TAYlor, used to tell the tale of the headless rider, now known across Texas from San Antonio to Waco. Wallace had come to Texas in 1836, and became a Ranger after his brother was killed at the Goliad Massacre and the new State of Texas needed to track down outlaws with a newly created law enforcement agency.

One of the outlaws in those early days had a price on his head. The reward was for bringing in the outlaw, dead or alive, for identification. One Ranger caught up to this outlaw, killed him in a fair gunfight, and cut off the head to transport back for the reward, because he was too lazy to take the whole corpse. This practice was frowned on by the Rangers and especially by the ghost of the outlaw.

Sometimes the headless outlaw is seen riding the trails between the Brazos and the Trinity [Rivers], searching for his head. Sometimes the headless outlaw is seen riding with his severed head, which he has dug up from its ignominious grave, tied to the saddle horn, and the eyes of the head glow with the fires of Hell, where the soul has presumably spent some time in the Devil's calaboose.

Sometimes, when the headless rider is seen, cattlemen are heard to remark, "Why doesn't he go on back down to Hell? It's cooler there than it is here in Texas."

49 Ghostly Express

AT HANOVER, IN NORTHERN KANSAS, WAS THE OLD HOLLENBERG STOP ON the Pony Express trail to Sacramento. The Pony Express only ran for eighteen months, but in that time many riders died or disappeared. They say you can still hear the faint sound of hooves, like distant thunder, and the warning cry of "Hello-o-o-o" that meant a rider was coming in and the station master should have a fresh horse ready. Some of them [the riders] are still riding, refusing to believe that they were cut down by a bullet or an arrow over a hundred years ago.

50 The Lady of White Rock Lake

THERE'S THE STORY OF A YOUNG GIRL WHO APPEARS REGULARLY AT WHITE Rock Lake in Dallas. She is wet and alone and is given a ride by an unsuspecting motorist. She is taken to an apartment, at her request, and says good night; then she disappears, either while still seated in the car or just after stepping out. A wet spot on the upholstery proves that she was not a hallucination.

The motorist asks around among the apartment residents, and they do not know anything about her. Sometimes—for this has happened very often, we are told—the girl tells a tale of terror about having been left at the lake by a boy who tried to drown her.

(It may be that the girl, who is often described as wearing a white dress, died so long ago that no one at the apartment building lived there when she did, or that the apartment building is built on the site of her former home and she disappears when she, as a ghost, recognizes that her home is no longer there.)

Haunted Houses

51a The Ghost Smokes A Pipe

HAVE YOU HEARD THE STORY ABOUT THE GHOST WHO SMOKES A PIPE? IN A big, old brick house down by the San Antonio River, there lived a young Army Air Corps pilot named Sidney Brooks. He was learning to be a pilot before World War I. He died in a crash. Brooks Air Force Base is named after him.

Some people say the young pilot used to smoke a pipe.

Every family to live in the house since 1917 has sometimes . . . when the person is sure he or she is alone . . . smelled the smoke from a pipe. Even when no one who smokes a pipe lives in the house . . . they smell that sweet pipe smoke.

Sometimes, on Hallowe'en, small pieces of furniture seem to move on their own. Sometimes people who live there think they see someone out of the corner of their eye . . . someone dressed in old-fashioned clothes. Perhaps a young man with a moustache.

Maybe it's the young pilot.

The one who smokes a pipe.

51b Ghost Who Smoke Pipe

(The story "The Ghost Smokes A Pipe" was told in San Antonio by deaf clients of the Southwest Center for the Hearing Impaired. One way it might be told from one hearing-impaired person to another is by following this written American Sign Language version.)

UP-UNTIL-NOW YOU HEAR FINISH STORY NAME GHOST WHO SMOKE PIPE?

Long ago [use two hands and make the sign slowly] young man airplane pilot live house [point with index finger as if to indicate where] near San Antonio River.

Man name (fingerspell) S-i-d-n-e-y B-r-o-o-k-s [repeat SB to designate his name in the rest of the story.]

Before World War One start SB learn fly airplane [gaze upwards as if you see the plane overhead]. Later (long time) SB fly-plane crash SB die. B-r-o-o-k-s (fingerspell) Air Force Base here [point to indicate here] San Antonio.

Name why? Young man name S-i-d-n-e-y B-r-o-o-k-s.

Up until SB die he [point as if he were present] smoke pipe [classifier]. SB die finish. Now (present time) family live there [point as you did before to where the house might stand] same house SB live before die.

Sometime family live there [indicate] and no person smoke and sometime person alone [indicate] sometime pipe smoke [slow the signs down and look around as if you smell something] smell.

[Sign very close to your body and dart your eyes about as if you were now frightened by the story you are telling.] Sometime Hallowe'en night chair move itself table move itself. Sometime people live house [indicate] think see person [dart your eyes to the right and back, as if you thought you saw someone] person clothes past [sign past with both hands to indicate long ago].

Maybe [pause] young man who live past [sign with two hands to indicate long ago] fly airplane who [slow gestures down] smoke pipe [let the sign for pipe seem to float in the air as if it were floating away].

52 The Ghost Door

MY GRANDPA AND GRANDMA BOUGHT A HOUSE OVER IN NEWTON COUNTY not too many years back. An old man had died in one of the bedrooms, and Grandpa left that room more or less empty, just for storage. It had a solid wooden door that wouldn't stay closed. He would shut the door every night, and the plunger would click, but about midnight the plunger would click again and the door would swing slowly open.

The hinges needed oiling, and the door would creak.

Some nights it scared Grandma and Grandpa pretty bad.

Grandpa decided to oil the hinges and put one of those screen-door latches with an eye-hook on the door. He put the eye-hook into the frame and shut the door. It clicked the same as always, and he latched the latch.

About midnight the plunger clicked and woke Grandpa up.

Then he heard the latch drop against the door, loose from its eye-hook.

Then he heard the door creak open, the same as always.

He got up the next morning and unscrewed the latch and eye-hook and threw them away. He left the door standing ajar that night and every night after that, and they were never awakened again.

53 The Ghost at Hughes

AT HUGHES, ARKANSAS, TWO BROTHERS, JAMES AND JOHN, LIVED IN A house that they had been told was haunted. The previous owner, an old man, claimed that his dead wife haunted the house. When he died, the house went up for sale. After the brothers bought the house, the ghost of the wife was seen for the first time by anyone other than the old man. She always wore a long, white gown; she had died young and was very pretty for a ghost.

One afternoon the brothers came home from working in the soybean fields, and they were walking toward the refrigerator for a soda. A friend of theirs who had come home with them looked down a hallway from the kitchen, and he saw a woman pass by, and he dropped his drink. It scared him, because he knew the house should have been empty, and he asked James and John who was home besides them. They said, "Nobody's here," but he swore up and down that he'd seen a woman in a long white gown. That old boy left for home shortly after that.

Jim and John both just laugh about this story, because even though the house is haunted, they've lived there long enough to know this haunt wasn't going to hurt them. They'd become comfortable with the idea of a ghost in their house. Several times the ghost had appeared; they had seen her, other guests at the place had seen her. But finally even the brothers were scared by the lady in the white gown.

One day their father had come home. He thought his wife was around the house, and doing some work upstairs. He could hear her footsteps upstairs, and he called up, "I'm just going to get a sandwich and go back to the fields." His wife didn't answer, but he heard her moving around upstairs. In a few minutes he called up, "I'm going back out, now, honey." He could hear her rocking chair upstairs rocking. Then his wife walked in the front door. She'd gone to town and come back.

They ran upstairs and opened the door to the sewing room. The rocking chair was still rocking, but it was empty. That scared their father, and after that, the whole family was not so comfortable as they'd been before to share their home with a lady in a long, white gown.

54 The Baker's Ghost

MANY YEARS AGO, MY GREAT-GRANDMOTHER KLUSSMAN HAD A MOST EX-traordinary experience. Her family lived in a two-story house whose foundations rested directly on the ground, without a cellar or any underground rooms beneath it. In the front hall stood a great curving stairway that led to the bedrooms upstairs. One evening as she was leaving the parlor, having bidden Great-great-grandfather good night, she approached the stairway to ascend.

She stopped at the foot of the steps and looked down, catching hold of the front of her floor-length dress to lift it so she could climb the stairs. When she looked up to begin her ascent, she saw at the head of the stairs a ghostly white figure on the second floor landing, looking down at her!

The figure was entirely white, unnaturally tall, and spectral. It seemed to stand with its arms hanging at its sides; then, it raised its right arm, bending it at the elbow, and seemed to gesture downward toward her, as if telling her to go away.

She dropped the gatherings of her dress and ran back into the parlor; she brought her father into the hall, but the figure was gone. Great-great-grandfather seemed concerned but not at all afraid. Great-grandmother thought that perhaps he had not believed her story.

For many nights she climbed the stairs without incident.

Suddenly one night, for no apparent reason she could see, the figure returned. As before, she had stopped at the foot of the stairs to lift her dress front, and as she looked up to begin the ascent, the figure reappeared. This time he was very distinctly visible.

It was a man, dressed in a white baker's costume. He was not incredibly tall: his height was augmented by a high, white baker's or chef's hat. His face was calm, not at all threatening. He again gestured, but this time she could see more clearly what he meant. Starting with his arms at his sides, he raised his right arm, bending it at the elbow, and with a downward sweep of his arm, he pointed his index finger toward the earth.

Down . . . he seemed to say. Down . . . or perhaps, below.

He continued to slowly gesture as the young girl studied him. She turned and called to her father, but when she looked back up the ghost was gone.

Great-great-grandfather believed what Great-grandmother had told him, and he summoned the parish priest. After some discussion, when the priest had determined that the family had only lived there a few decades, and that the house rested directly on the earth, he suggested that they open the area beneath the stairs.

With the gardener's help, the three men opened the wall below the steps and found an empty cobwebbed space with a dirt floor. Digging there they found, three feet down, a very old skeleton. In the dark earth they removed, there were tiny white flakes of rotten fine linen. Above the head, figuring horizontally, they found the rusted and crushed wire frame of a baker's hat.

The priest took the bones to the ossuary and blessed them. The wall was closed up and the baker's ghost was never seen again.

 ## 55 The Haunted House at Howe

I WAS PREACHING ONE SUNDAY AT HOWE, AND AFTER THE EVENING SER-vice some of the elders of that congregation were waiting for me in the back of the church, shuffling their feet and talking amongst themselves.

When everyone else was gone home, one of them approached me and said, "Brother John, I have a favor to ask of you."

I listened intently as he explained.

"One of our congregation owns a house in Howe, and he wants to sell it, but he can't. No one will buy it because everyone says it's haunted. In the middle of the darkest nights, folks riding by say they see ghostly lights in the dormer windows. We were wondering if you would spend the night in that house tonight and quell these rumors for me."

Well, I agreed; I got my pipe and my copy of *Railway Through the Word*, from which I was preaching that week, and blew out the lanterns. We loaded into two automobiles and drove to the house, which sat in a grove of live oaks. The house was two-and-a-half stories, long empty, and some of the windows were out. The lights of the automobiles gave me a brief view of the house before we parked. We sat about discussing the matter for several minutes, and the deacons announced that they would "stay out here and keep watch."

I put some Prince Albert in my pipe and puffed it up enough to see by, took my book, and went inside. The owner had told me about the stairs, where the ladder to the loft was, and so on. Pretty soon I was in the upper floor, which was a child's bedroom.

It was empty but for an old bedframe and a rocker gathering dust. Four windows looked out of the hipped roof, one to each point of the compass. The panes were mostly out, and some ragged gauze curtains hung there and about, but the room was dark except for the glow of my pipe.

I sat in the rocker and began to read, with my pipe upside down to read by. I guess I fell asleep, because the next thing I knew, the pipe dropped out of my mouth and hit the book in my lap. I jumped up and brushed the ashes off the book to keep from starting a fire, but the pipe was long since cold and the ashes dead. Then I began to realize something else.

With the pipe out, it should be dark. Instead it was lighter than before I'd sat down. I put down the book and put the cold pipe in my pocket and looked around the room. It was filled with a faint, flickering blue-white light—not the yellow light of a candle or the pure white of an electric bulb—a blue-white light that came from nowhere and flickered on the walls.

First I looked out the north window. It was dark all the way to Sherman. Out the east window, there were only live oaks. Out the south window, there was light toward McKinney, but nothing like the ghostly light in the room. Then I looked out the west window.

There in the distance, over the horizon, invisible from the ground, the Katy [Missouri, Kansas and Texas Railroad or M.K.T.—"Katy" for short] was rolling south from Oklahoma City to Fort Worth, making a big sweeping turn north of Denton. The big battery-electric headlamp of the train, sweeping both sides of the tracks, was shining in the windows and lighting up just the top floor.

The former occupants must have known, but on the street below the owner and passersby thought the light came from the loft.

I gathered up the book and made my way down to the street. I kicked the fender to wake the menfolks in the automobile and said, "Let's go home, boys. It's a train."

The house was sold the next day.

56 The Healing Lady of Los Luceros

THE SPANISH SOLDIERS WHO CAMPED AT CABEZÓN PRESSED NORTHWARD for Taos in their search for the Cities of Gold. They did not stop at Española along the way. They were off the regular trail, and they came to a mysterious three-story adobe building. No one knew how old it was, or who had built it, or why. The kitchen took up one-half of the ground floor and was tiled with Mexican tile. Some said it was built by Mexican Indians trying to reach Chaco Canyon, seeking refuge from the Spanish conquest of Mexico; others said a group of Spanish foot soldiers who had separated from their cavalry to become mercenaries and collect slaves had built it. When the young soldiers traveling to Taos found it, the building was deserted.

It was at the place called Los Luceros, and they came upon the adobe structure after nightfall. The third floor glowed in the darkness with light from windows and balconies. When the boys pushed open the heavy door and went inside the first floor, there was food cooking on the stove, even though there was no wood burning in the stove. The food was hot. They ate in the dark, for they could not find any candles or lamps, and they did not build a fire, for there was no wood in the kitchen.

The *capitán* wanted to find out what was upstairs. He and the scout went upstairs while the others remained below, watching them. The bottom stair was a single piece of wood with box stairs going up, and the stairs turned partway up; the *capitán* and the scout went out of sight, and they stopped talking. They stopped calling out. The soldiers couldn't hear them anymore.

When the *capitán* and the scout didn't come down, they sent up the cook and his helper. The cook took two wooden spoons and a piece of string and made a cross, and held it to his forehead as he walked up the stairs. When they were up the stairs, the helper stopped talking, and the cook became afraid, but he didn't look back. He walked all the way around the second floor, calling down to the soldiers below, and then he came back down alone. When he removed the wooden cross, it had left a brand on his forehead, and he was blind.

The cook started to tell them that when he went upstairs he saw a large room, and all the walls were lit. Because the *capitán,* the scout, and now the cook's helper had all vanished, they decided to send up the youngest boy holding a large cross, and with him others of the youngest soldiers with crosses. And instead of walking, they would go on their knees and recite the "Hail, Mary" as they went. Four young boys were picked, and they took crosses, and they left their swords below and went up, very scared, without their boots, in stockings only. At the top of the stairs, they said the "Hail, Mary" of the Cesarean Order, holding their crosses up to their foreheads in front of their faces. One brash boy looked out from behind his cross: the cross flew to the wall and embedded there, and the boy disappeared from the earth. The other boys saw it from behind their crosses. They walked on their knees back down the stairs in fear.

They had to leave without their missing commander, and they went on to Taos. There, at Taos, there were wounded men, and sick people, and some of the soldiers were eventually wounded, too. It was decided that the sick and wounded of Taos would return with this contingent of soldiers to the Sisters of the Holy Faith at Santa Fe for treatment, and only the well and strong would remain at the outpost at Taos. A storm drove the group to seek shelter, and it happened that they were at Los Luceros when the storm struck. The building glowed its beckoning light again, and the ill and wounded with their canes and crutches went inside.

They had knocked, and rung the heavy Mexican bell that hung there, called, and no one answered, and they had gone in. Once again, hot food was waiting. They ate and rested and rewrapped bandages, and whatever they needed to do. The soldiers, who knew about the house, went out to find shelter for the horses from the storm. Only the sick remained inside, and when the horses were hobbled, they found the heavy door locked: they could not get back in.

Looking through the windows, the soldiers saw a woman all in white, with white hair and a necklace of red roses, floating down the stairwell, glowing with light. She lifted each ill person and carried him effortlessly upstairs where they were out of sight. At morning, the door opened by itself, and the soldiers went in. The stove was cold, the kitchen dirty; in the other room, there was the travois and bandages and their baggage, but the people were gone.

On the second floor, all the canes and crutches had flown to the walls and embedded there, and they could not be removed. They heard a rattling on the third floor, above the *vigas* and *latias,* but there was no stairwell. Perhaps it was only birds, nesting from the storm the night before.

A week later, many leagues away, a pack train came upon a great group of people, whole and healthy but wandering and suffering from amnesia. They were led to Taos, where they were recognized, fed, cared for, and gradually came back to their memories. But they could not explain their incredible healing or their mysterious transport to far away.

Later, the territory became more settled and populated, and a chapel was built at Los Luceros, and eventually a coach house. Those who were afflicted would go to service in the chapel, go to the great kitchen and prepare a feast, and then take candles and go upstairs. They would sing hymns and pray and admire the canes and crutches in the walls, and they could hear rustling on the inaccessible floor above.

Then, in this century, one owner cut an opening and put stairs up to the third floor. There the owners found huge wooden trunks of woman's clothing—dresses, rebozos, all of it white—the garments of the glowing Lady of Los Luceros, who healed the sick.

57 Winchester Mansion

FISHER WINCHESTER, THE "RIFLE KING," HAD A SON NAMED WILLIAM; HE married a fine lady named Sarah, and they planned to have a long life together. He died not too long afterwards, and their only child died at birth. Sarah Winchester believed that their deaths were the curse on her for marrying into the family that had made its fortune manufacturing the rifle that had killed so many thousands of people in the West.

Sarah became afraid that the ghosts of all the dead people killed by Winchesters were coming to haunt her at her home, having been somehow denied their mansions in Heaven. And all these ghosts would move in when her mansion was finished. It was as if she were to "go to prepare a place" for them here on Earth, like Jesus said he had to "go to prepare a place" for his disciples in Heaven.

She found an uncompleted mansion in San José, California, and spent the rest of her life "completing" it so the ghosts could move in. The mansion had a hundred and sixty rooms, and she had carpenters constantly building blind stairways and whole rooms sealed off with furniture in them. Fireplaces were constructed without chimneys and windows were put in that opened onto blank walls. She had inherited millions, and she spent it all endlessly preparing a mansion for the ghosts.

She never finished, she could not have finished since there was no plan, just whatever ideas she had at the time. And she died in 1922, with the mansion not yet "prepared." No ghosts of the rifle dead were ever reported in her lifetime, but now employees of the trust that operates the mansion for tours say that they often see or hear a ghost—the ghost of Sarah Winchester, dressed as she did in life, wandering the mansion still, never finding peace after all.

58 Helen

WHEN I MOVED TO CALIFORNIA IN THE EARLY 1970s, I LIVED WITH MY aunt and uncle just outside Los Angeles in the San Gabriel Valley, right up against the foothills, in a house they had bought recently. After about six months, I was walking back to the house one day and saw a lady kneeling, working in the flower beds—a middle-aged lady with kind of grey hair, wearing a green dress, kneeling at one of my aunt's elaborate flower beds. I didn't think anything about it. I just thought it was someone who worked for my aunt. I didn't mention it.

A couple of weeks later, beside the living room with its open-beamed ceiling and fieldstone fireplace, as I was sitting on the couch in the small den watching television with my uncle, I saw the lady again. She walked by the door to the den and went to the kitchen. She was wearing a black suit-skirt and tailored white blouse with long sleeves. In a few minutes, I got up and went to the kitchen and no one was there. I went to my aunt and asked where the lady that worked for her had gone.

She said, "Tell me what the lady looked like!"

I told her, and she dragged me by the arm back to the den and planted herself in front of the TV. "Ira, listen to me," she said, and then to me, "Tell him who you saw!"

He was very quiet as I told him. He said, "That sounds like Helen."

They told me a strange story.

The former owners were a couple who had quarreled. He shot her in the living room—they showed me the bullet holes in the wall beside the fireplace. Then he burned her body in the huge fireplace and hanged himself from the huge beams in the living room with its cathedral ceiling. No one but my uncle would buy the house because they all feared it. Since my uncle didn't believe the house was haunted, they had never seen her.

I didn't know any better, so I saw her, just as plain as day. Still living in her house, still working in her garden. No one else ever saw her, but from my description they knew who she was. They knew her when she was alive. I didn't meet her until after she was dead.

59 The Ghost Plays Pool

WE BOUGHT AND MOVED INTO A HOUSE THAT HAD BEEN OWNED BY A MAN who never married, and had died of cancer while lying in the living room under the bay window in about 1982. From the day we moved into the house, we had trouble keeping it warm. It was a perfectly nice house, but it had cold spots in it. And it would creak; I always put it to the house settling after the heat of the day. We had put our pool table in the basement, the same room the old owner had loved and used as his rec room, and one he spent a lot of time in, being single. We had the table all leveled, and the kids had been down playing pool one night, and I didn't ever know if they would rack the balls for the next night before they came up, or what. But one night I woke up and heard a ball hit the bottom of a pocket and roll down the return trough to the storage rack.

The table was a weighted one, and it was leveled properly, so the balls weren't rolling into the pockets from gravity or anything. I checked on the kids, and everyone was in bed but me and whoever was playing pool downstairs. It happened once in a while, and I would never go down to see what was happening in the middle of the night. One night I decided to rack the balls and leave them for a game myself, and I watched to see that, in fact, no one went downstairs after I'd done it.

About 2:00 or 3:00 in the morning, I awoke when I heard the balls break. I came up out of my bed . . . I levitated! And I came down on my feet. My daughter and I, and a nephew staying with us, hit the hall at the same time. We all went to the head of the stairs to the basement, and listened to the balls dropping, one by one, like someone was playing, into the pockets, into the return trough and rolling down into the storage tray.

My daughter said, "Mom, go down there and see what it is."

Well, I didn't go.

I got up early the next morning and went down in the daylight. All the balls I had racked the night before were in the tray. One cue, which I had put in the rack on the wall, was lying catty-cornered across the end of the table.

The answer was simple. When we were through playing, we just left the balls in the tray. The old man had to find some other ghostly entertainment after that.

60 Yellow with Brown Trim

OUR FAMILY BOUGHT AN OLD HOUSE FROM A HISPANIC FAMILY; WE MOVED in the spring, and by fall of that year we noticed that when we got up in the morning, the lights would be on in the kitchen. Then after a while, we noticed one morning that the lights would be on, and the door would be open and the fire would be lit. At first we thought it was something in the electrical wiring that turned the lights on, and we were worried about the house catching fire with an unattended cooking fire, but it was always only in the morning.

We began to be aware of a presence on those mornings, and sometimes the little rocking chair in the corner of the kitchen would be rocking when someone came in, all by itself. We lived there for years and just accepted the fact that someone was getting up early, like a Hispanic mother might, and was getting the kitchen ready for the morning.

We were getting ready to sell the house after a few years, and we decided to repaint before we showed the house. We were deciding what colors to paint the rooms of the house, and someone suggested that we paint the kitchen yellow, with brown trim. All of us thought about it and agreed that that was a good color for the kitchen. We had never lived anywhere with that color combination, and no one knew why we all thought it was such a good idea, but we painted the kitchen yellow with brown trim, and the very next day, the early-morning events came to a stop.

We sold the house a few months later, and the next year we saw the eldest son of the family that we had bought the house from; they had owned the house for generations before us. We told him about the early morning visits to the kitchen, and his eyes got bigger and bigger and bigger. He said that his mother had been a saint; she had been a lovely woman who had raised eight children. She had always been up before everyone else, getting breakfast ready. He said they were always sad that, before she died, they had never given her the one thing she had always wanted.

She had always wished that someday they would paint the kitchen yellow with brown trim.

61 The Staab House

THE STAAB HOUSE AT LA POSADA, AT 330 EAST PALACE AVENUE [IN Santa Fe], was the home of the socialite wife of a wealthy German merchant. She furnished her home with the costliest goldware and crystal instead of "laying up her treasures in Heaven" a century ago [in the 1880s]. When she died, she was disconsolate over the loss of her worldly goods. Her spirit still walks the house.

When she comes into the room, a faint cold wind is felt. The candles blow out, and her sobbing is heard as she mourns the loss of her finery and, perhaps, of her immortal soul.

62 The Fremont House

IN FREMONT, CALIFORNIA, ACROSS FROM SAN FRANCISCO, DOWN THE coast and out a ways, lived our friends the Browns. He is a computer analyst and she is an executive secretary. They bought a new house, and got a ghost at no extra charge. It's a poltergeist.

He worked nights a lot, and she would lock all the doors while he was away. He would come home to find them unlocked. Hairdryers fell from the cabinets in the bathroom. Canned food moved around in the kitchen and ended up in strange places. The ghost would steal shiny things: keys, tools. Then he'd return them in odd places. They would disappear, things like jewelry, then reappear in plain sight nights later.

They decided his name was Charlie—I don't how they knew that—and that he was a child, or childlike. They'd say out loud, "Now, Charlie . . ."

I don't really know if I believe that kind of thing or not. But who am I to doubt my friends?

63 The House on Chalet Road

OVER ON CHALET ROAD, AT LAKE TANEYCOMO [MISSOURI], THERE IS A haunted house. A man murdered his wife back in the '30s and buried her body in the cellar. She was from out of state, and when her family called, he just said she was out of the house. No one was suspicious for months. When the family finally came down to find her, they couldn't even find him. Eventually they suspected the awful truth and dug in the cellar: there were the remains. The story has been told around at parties for decades.

Then a close friend named Mike told me his version. He was at a party in this house—a very nice house, by the way—and so were, he said, other friends of mine, whom he named off. Others present that very night agreed they, too, had been in "that" house on "that" night.

One young lady had gone in to use the toilet, and looked up to see someone looking in the window. She fled out the door partially dressed. The guys present ran outside to catch the "peeper," being very protective of their lady friends, and found to their shock that the house is built right on the edge of the cliff above the lake, with a very small passage space between the house and the steep drop-off. It was pitch dark; only a fool would walk that narrow way at night. Furthermore, the window to the bathroom was over eight feet up the outside wall!

There had been people—partygoers—in the front yard, so no one could have pulled the prank, even if it had been possible, and gotten away. They asked the girl to describe the "peeper."

She said it was "an old guy with grey hair." The murderer had been an old man with grey hair.

Years later, I met a man who started telling me about a house he had once lived in with some other entertainers I knew. He said water would come on suddenly. Milk would be spilled when no one had been in the house. Silverware and glassware had slid across the counter and fallen to the floor. He had finally moved out, he said, because one night when all four 'mates were home with the front door latched, he had been sitting on his bed taking off his socks. He heard the screen open and close, and the door open and close, and footfalls come across the floor toward his bedroom. One of his 'mates came into the room, and said, "My God!" He looked up to see a cloud of smoke evaporate from the air beside him, just outside his peripheral vision. "What was it?" he had asked.

"Didn't you see the man standing next to you?" his friend had said. "He had his hand reached out toward you. It was an older guy with grey hair."

I didn't believe the first story until I heard the second one.

All four guys moved out.

64 El Monte Ghost

My mother lived in El Monte, California, and had a ghost at her house. It wasn't quite a poltergeist; it didn't throw things. What it did was shuffle things around. It was a woman ghost, because it was always in the kitchen, and it took things like beans and macaroni and mixed them together. It would leave the cabinet doors open, too. No matter how often Mother would close the cabinet doors, especially one particular door with the condiments behind it, it would always open.

Sometimes she could even smell the presence of the ghost, because the ghost favored heavy floral, sweet perfume. Up to a point my Father didn't believe there was anyone—or anything—to it. Then one day, he turned to Mother and said, "Did you get enough perfume on?"

She said, "I'm not wearing any perfume. That's the ghost!"

Then he believed her.

Not long after that, my parents moved out and moved away. When they went back to visit old neighbors not too long after that, the neighbor said, "Well, we got your spook. The smell of that perfume is about to drive my wife crazy." The ghost had moved next door when my parents left!

65 Tiny Baby Footprints

GRANDMÈRE LIVED IN KAPLAN AND CROWLEY [LOUISIANA] AT THE TIME she was growing up. They lived far out of town in an old wooden house with a wood floor. It had a fireplace of fine stonework. In front of the hearth a little distance, so it wouldn't catch a spark, was a country-style braided rag rug.

One night, my cousins told me, there were noises—two particular noises. Something bumped about near the chimneyplace. They also heard a clicking sound they didn't recognize. The dogs began to bark outside. The cousins were so scared that they hid under the covers and didn't get out of bed to see what it was.

In the morning, between the fireplace and the rug, were tiny baby-sized footprints only two or three inches long. The footprints were in the fine ash that had drifted out of the fireplace. It looked as if someone had come down the chimney, scattering ashes as he came, and then left footprints as he walked around the room.

Those footprints are still on that floor today. You can wipe up the ashes, and wipe away the footprints, but they always come back when a new layer of ash settles out on the floor. They're a little fainter now, but you can still see the tiny baby-sized footprints made when there weren't any babies in the family anymore.

 66 Quarai

SOUTHEAST OF ALBUQUERQUE, IN THE MANZANOS MOUNTAINS, STAND the ruins of Quarai Mission, which housed missionaries and early Indian Christians. There would have been soldiers there, also, and at least one soldier seems to remain on guard three centuries later.

In the autumn of 1913, visitors to the ruins saw, very late at night, a blue-white light glowing through one of the openings in the ruined adobe walls. In the center of the light stood a Spanish soldier [wearing a tabard emblazoned with a large, red cross whose points ended in *fleurs-de-lys,* the symbol of the military-religious order of Calatrava, and not an uncommon symbol in Spain].

The figure pointed his finger three times and said [most probably], *"Asiste, viador."*

[*Asiste* might mean "attend" or "frequent this place," and *viador* would mean "traveler on a mystic journey." These meanings used in the seventeenth century fit the time period of the mission and of the soldier's uniform, but the message is still unclear.]

67 Horseshoe Ranch

NIGHT VOICES ECHO IN A BARN THAT WAS ONCE THE HEADQUARTERS house for the Horseshoe Ranch, outside Tucumcari. Soldiers from old Fort Bascom nearby were escorting a payroll shipment to Fort Sumner in the late 1870s. While they slept in the house, riders, perhaps even hands at the Horseshoe, attacked and killed the soldiers, with only one trooper escaping out the back to bring help.

Reinforcements came, led by the escapee, and the ensuing gunfight killed all the riders. The money was never found; it was not on the bodies of the riders, nor was there any evidence of it having been buried.

Now [as of 1952] the sounds of heavy chain and strongboxes being moved about are heard in the cabin at night, along with the faint voices of the riders.

One Quay County resident who didn't believe in the phantoms in the empty cabin spent the night there while trail riding. In the middle of the night, something shoved him out of his bedroll and said, "Move over!"

The man jerked on his boots, jumped on his horse, and moved all the way over to Fort Sumner!

68 Riordan House

I USED TO WORK FOR THE RIORDAN FAMILY [IN THEIR MANSION IN FLAG-staff, Arizona]. I used to like to sit in the corner seats of the big dining room when my work was done. When I was sixteen, I went to work for the Riordans, and worked . . . for about five years. This other girl . . . Henrietta . . . and I would work here, and we'd stay in the house, or we'd go down to the reservation . . . on Fridays, I would serve the dinner.

My dad worked for the lumber mill [owned by the Riordans] and I worked here at the house.

They say there's a ghost here in the house . . . but I don't know . . . the other gal that used to work with me, she was two years older than me, she was always scared to go by herself to the upstairs, but I told her there's nothing to be scared of. She used to say,

"It seems like I hear the wife . . . Caroline . . . she's still here."

After she [Caroline] had died, my youngest brother and my nephew used to come and stay at the house every night . . . so there would be somebody in the house besides [Mr. Riordan]. My friend, she heard the lady [Caroline] around the house, like when we were doing laundry, and she'd hear her moving around upstairs.

*O*ther Haunted Places

69 El Camino Real

RIDERS ON THE OLD *CAMINO REAL* [ROYAL ROAD] THROUGH JIM HOGG County once met a phantom known as *el blanco* [the white one]. As the rider slowed to pass under branches that overhung the trail, the frightening white spectre would step out of the trees and grab the horse's bridle or reins. The terrified animal might rare up and struggle, but *el blanco* would hold it fast.

One *caballero* [horseman] dared to ask the figure, *"¿Eres de este mundo o del otro?"* [Are you from this world or the next?]

After a moment, the figure answered, *"Del otro."* [From the next world.]

Some horses managed to break away from the grip of *el blanco*. One *caballero* drew his saber and cut the offending hand from the phantom and rode away with the hand still clinging, bloodlessly, to the reins; at sunrise, the hand vanished in a mist.

No one knows what would happen to a rider who did not escape *el blanco*.

No one alive, at least.

70 Palace Hotel

WHEN CRIPPLE CREEK, COLORADO, WAS IN ITS GLORY DAYS AS A MINING emporium, the palace hotel was lighted by candles. One of the former owners still prefers it that way. Except that she's dead.

The current owners have come into the dining rooms in the dead of winter when the hotel is closed and found candles from the tables lit and often moved to other places than the table on which they belong. The owners say they believe it's the ghost of Mrs. Chambers, who, with her husband, owned the hotel at the turn of the century.

71 White Woman Creek

IN GREELEY, WICHITA, AND SCOTT COUNTIES IN WESTERN KANSAS RUNS the White Woman Creek. There, a peaceful Cheyenne hunting party was attacked by white men, and many Cheyenne were killed. Riding after their attackers, some of the survivors raided the white men's camp and recovered what had been stolen from them. They also took some captives as insurance against further attack.

The prisoners lived with the Cheyenne a year, and when offered their freedom as the Cheyenne moved further west, they decided to stay with the tribe. Several chose husbands or wives among the tribe, and one woman married Tonkawa, a great war chief.

The cavalry attacked the tribe one day in retribution for the taking of prisoners a year before whom the Army assumed to have been killed. Tonkawa was killed, and his bride buried him at the bank of the creek.

She never went back to her own people, and the rest of the Cheyenne moved on west. She wandered the creek until her death, and still wanders the creek at night as a wraith. She sings Indian songs and is heard crying in the wind, wandering along the creek that holds her husband's corpse and bears her name.

72 Old Chief Tawakoni

WE [THE AUSTIN COLLEGE FOOTBALL TEAM] USED TO PLAY TRINITY UNIversity when the school was located in Waxahachie. We [the Young family] had relatives there, and knew some of the members of the opposing team personally. They told a school spirit story that involved a real spirit.

Old Chief Tawokanny [or Tawakoni] was the ghost of an Indian that walked the hill Trinity had been built on in Tehuacana. He was seen many times in the single old college building or on the campus. Students saw him at night only, and co-eds at the Waxahachie campus were told that he had followed the school to its new location. This absolutely guaranteed the boys a walk home with the girls.

Old Chief Tawokanny was a handy ghost to have around.

73 The Ghost of Rancho de Corrales

DIEGO MONTOYA BUILT THE HACIENDA NOW KNOWN AS RANCHO DE Corrales in 1801, but the murderous revenge came after the Emberto family bought the property in 1883. Luis and Luisa Emberto threw elegant parties and dances, but one night the son killed a woman at one of the parties—a woman rumored to be his father's mistress. Luis then moved out and threatened to kill Luisa and her lover, believing that their son had been prompted by his mother in the killing of Lola Griego.

The night of April 30, 1898, Luis returned and shot Luisa as she ran for her own gun. A running gun battle followed, with Luis being killed by José de la Cruz, a one-eyed Indian sharpshooter who was among the posse chasing him.

The manner and circumstances of the Embertos' deaths caused them to be buried on the property, instead of in the *camposanto* [churchyard]. Their graves are somewhere on the opposite side of the irrigation ditch, away from the hacienda, which is now an elegant restaurant. Their ghosts are believed to wander the property even today.

"Have I ever seen the ghosts? Yes and no. I have not seen them, but have felt a pressing sensation here, on the back of my neck, in the old part of the restaurant, which used to be the hacienda itself. Almost everyone who works here feels or sees them sooner or later."

74 Hell and Its Horrors

THE NECHES RIVER CROSSES SOUTHEAST TEXAS AND EMPTIES INTO THE Sabine Lake and, by way of the Sabine Pass, into the Gulf of Mexico. The pirate Jean Laffite sailed his ship to the Neches seeking a place to bury some of his vast treasure. Near the river's mouth, his men secured a chain around a sturdy tree and tied off to it. After the treasure was buried, they left the chain in place and sailed back into the gulf.

Over a century later, a Port Arthur man came into possession of a chart left behind when the American Navy ordered Laffite off Galveston Island in 1820. The man followed the chart, found the tree trunk with the chain, and dug at the prescribed place. As he dug, an unseen ghost, perhaps that of Laffite himself, grabbed the man by the throat and began to strangle him. The man fled, leaving his tools behind. He never regained his wits or the power of speech; only by wild gestures could he explain what had happened to him. A week later, he died in his sleep, with his vocal cords and perhaps even his breathing paralyzed, or crushed by the ghost's unseen hand.

A neighbor named Meredith bought the chart and with a partner sought out the chain, the half-dug hole, and the rotting tools. The two began to dig the hole deeper. The pair came to a skeleton, perhaps the hapless pirate who first dug the hole, and was murdered and buried to keep the secret—or to guard the treasure. The bones were gently laid out beside the hole, and the digging continued.

Meredith's partner was in the hole, taking his shift with the spade, when he let out an unearthly scream and jumped from the hole.

Grabbing Meredith, he cried out, "For God's sake, we've got to get out of here!" When Meredith asked what was wrong, the man cried out, "I have seen Hell and its horrors!"

For the second time, the tools were abandoned.

When Meredith dared return much later, and alone, the skeleton was mysteriously back in the hole, but the tools were undisturbed and the hole had not been touched. Solemnly, Meredith covered the skeleton, and never returned to the treasure grave near the mouth of the Neches.

75 Hell's Half-Acre

THERE'S A PLACE IN ARKANSAS CALLED HELL'S HALF-ACRE. HUGE ROCKS are piled in a sinkhole there, as if something had exploded or torn up the Earth itself. The local folks know: it's the exact place where the Devil is chained, under all those rocks, since he got thrown out of Heaven. When hunters go by, or foolish children play nearby, or tourists come by with their cameras, they hear and smell the most bloodcurdling things at sundown or just at dark.

The old Devil under that rock pile cusses something awful, and you can smell his sulphurous hot bad breath floating up out of Hell itself. After all, you're at Hell's Half-Acre on Earth!

76 Dance of Death

IN THE TURKEY MOUNTAINS OF NEW MEXICO, NORTH OF VALMORA, WAS Old Fort Union. During the Apache Wars, it was a lonely island of safety in an empty land. A young cavalry lieutenant had fallen in love with the younger sister of his captain's wife. When the troop was ordered out to fight the Apaches, the lieutenant made a grim promise to his beloved.

"No one else will have you, my love. I will return and dance with you again at the wedding, no matter what!"

Weeks later, with no news from the cavalry troop on patrol, the regularly scheduled military ball was taking place at the fort. The young woman attended and received the usual kind attention from all the young officers. During the dance, some of the absent troop returned and reported that many men had been killed and others were missing in action. Among the missing was the lieutenant. The young bride-to-be was much too quickly consoled by another officer, and soon the two were engaged. On the day of the wedding, months later, everyone had gathered for the wedding dance. Before the groom and bride could lead the first dance, in the door strode the missing lieutenant.

His uniform was dirty and bloodstained, but this was not unusual for a man who had been on patrol for months. He was dirty and unarmed, but he did not remove his hat or even greet the crowd. He walked straight to the bride, and bowed as if to dance. Both pleased and saddened to see her former lover, the bride bowed back, and the regimental band struck up a waltz.

The lieutenant danced faster and faster, striking his boots against the floor faster and faster. The band leader followed, and soon the waltz was a thunderous mazurka. The bride seemed to grow faint and pale, but the lieutenant danced on. The woman fainted dead away in his arms, and the dance stopped.

When the lieutenant coldly dropped the bride to the floor, her husband stepped forward and struck the lieutenant, knocking off his hat.

The lieutenant's scalp was gone, and a steel hatchet blade protruded from his open, crushed skull. The grisly figure stood its ground, and slowly faded from human sight, leaving behind only the bride, who was found to be dead.

The following spring, the lieutenant's body was found in a canyon, with a steel hatchet blade embedded in its skull.

77 "Dame, pues, mi asadura"

IT WAS THAT THERE WAS AN OLD WIDOW-WOMAN WHO LIVED ALONE IN A small house beside a great pastureland. When her husband had died, she had become very wealthy, and much of the pastureland was hers. Then the cruel *hacendado* [landlord of the hacienda] whose land adjoined hers courted her and persuaded her to sign her land over to him preparatory to their intended nuptials. Like a giddy schoolgirl she signed the parchment. Then his affections grew cool, and her only recompense was a small sum of silver pesos.

Now she sat alone, abandoned, in her little house on her little piece of land, growing older and more bitter with each passing day. One night, having nothing to eat in the house, she decided on a sordid vengeance against the *hacendado*. She would kill one of his prize cattle, slashing its belly to make it look as if the wolves had killed it, leaving the meat to spoil and taking only the innards to make *menudo* [tripe stew].

She wrapped her *rebozo* around her and drew her sharpest knife from the cupboard. Blowing out the candles in her house, she waited at the front door for darkness to fall. As she waited, a funeral procession walked slowly by.

Six men carrying a coffin walked slowly and in step down the road in the gathering darkness. Six old grandmothers dressed in black walked along behind wailing and singing, *"Ay! Qué luto!* [Oh, what sorrow!]"* But the widow-woman knew all six of these women, and they were not related to one another. This could only mean one thing: the deceased in the coffin had left money to pay for mourners! Whoever he was, he was alone and unloved.

Then it struck her! She squinted into the gloom and examined the coat of arms on the coffin. It was the *hacendado*! At first she laughed. Then she grew angry. How dare he to die without giving her the chance for revenge?

Then, in her heart, she devised the most horrible revenge.

Wrapping her *rebozo* about her head to conceal all but her eyes, burying the knife deep in the folds of the garment, she joined the procession at the rear. No one took any heed of one more paid mourner. "Oh, what sorrow!" she cried out aloud, but her heart was saying, *"Ay! Desquite!* [Oh, retribution!]"

When the procession reached the holy ground, she stepped aside and stood behind a monument, out of sight. The men laid the coffin into a stone sarcophagus. One of the men passed coins out to the women; he looked for the seventh mourner he had seen, but she was nowhere in sight. He shrugged and pocketed the remaining coins. The old women took their coins, but then spat on the ground, and walked away crossing themselves. The men tried to lift the lid of the sarcophagus, but it was too heavy. They walked away, planning aloud to return the next day with more men.

When all was still and quiet, the widow-woman came out. She walked slowly to the sarcophagus. She bent down and drew out her knife. She pried up the top of the coffin. She reached deep into the dark interior with the knife. She cut out the dead man's entrails to make *menudo. Ay! Desquite!* Back at her house, she put the great black pot on the fire and began to make *menudo.* Soon the pot was boiling. Outside the wind began to blow as if a storm was coming down from the mountains. In the distance, out on the pastureland, the cattle of the dead *hacendado* began to low and call. "Auu," they called, "Auu."

The fire burned bright. The pot boiled high. The wind blew. The cattle called, "A-uura, a-uura." Gradually the call of the cattle seemed to come closer. Gradually it began to seem that the cattle were saying a word: *"Asa'uura, asa'uura* . . . [Entrails, entrails . . .]"

The old woman began to become afraid.

Suddenly, she heard the gate of her yard bang open. Was it the wind? Suddenly, she heard footfalls on the pathway to the house, heavy footfalls. Was it the mesquite tree blowing against the wall? Or was it . . .

The fire blazed. The pot boiled. The wind blew. The cattle called, *"Asadura* . . . *Asadura* . . . Give me back my *asadura* . . ."

The old woman ran to the door and pulled down the bar. She ran around the house, slamming the shutters and latching them. She ran to the table and cowered beneath it.

Something huge and unimaginably heavy struck the door, knocking once . . . twice . . . thrice! Slowly the heavy footfalls began to circle the house, and the wind rattled the shutters one by one, as if someone was trying to get in. The old woman crawled out from under the table and lifted the heavy pot from the hearth. The chimney shook; bits of brick fell into the fire. The old woman struggled to the door, lifted the bar, and set the boiling pot out on the stoop. She slammed the door, pulled down the bar and ran back under the table.

The fire grew low. The wind ceased. The cattle were silent.

After a moment she began to think, "What a silly I am! It was only the wind . . ."

She crawled out from under the table.

She walked to the door.

She lifted the bar.

She opened . . . slowly . . . the door . . .

Outside, the big black pot was empty.

78   The Ghost on the Third Floor

AT THE MUSIC BUILDING AT HARDING COLLEGE IN SEARCY, ARKANSAS, there is a tradition that a ghostly piano player practices by night. From the second floor of the music building, you can hear a piano being played on the floor above you.

According to the story, there were a young man and a young woman who were deeply in love, who came from the same town and were both attending Harding at the same time, and both majoring in music. Soon after the school year began, the young man died in an automobile accident. The young woman began to pine and grieve; the only way that she could comfort herself was to go up to one of the private practice rooms on the third floor and play the piano and sometimes sing.

Soon afterwards, she, too, died, apparently from loneliness and grief, before the first semester was even over. Years passed, and people say they still hear her playing on the third floor.

But what makes it mysterious is that since the year she died, the old music building has been torn down, and a new one built in its place.

When you stand on the second floor of the new building some nights, you can hear her playing above you . . . even though the new music building is only two stories tall!

79 The Weeping Lady of Colfax

A FRIEND AND I WERE DRIVING FROM THE AIR FORCE ACADEMY IN COLO-rado Springs, Colorado, to our summer jobs at Philmont in New Mexico, when we left I-25 in Colfax County for a rest stop to get out and stretch. We found ourselves in the town of Colfax, which was a ghost town of burned-out adobe buildings and a large one-room schoolhouse-church with a steeple on top. We climbed around the adobe ruins, and walked up to the schoolhouse.

The frame was fairly solid, and the roof looked dilapidated but intact, but inside the flooring was either rotted away or carried off. Old slate chalkboards and other school and church items were still hanging loosely from the walls. We wondered what might have happened there, how come the people had moved away, and where they had gone. As we left, I could hear a low noise behind us in the schoolhouse, but I didn't think anything of it.

It wasn't until weeks later, at a campfire, that an older ranger who had been away from Philmont for twenty years told a story that gave the visit to Colfax new meaning. He told local tales, and one of them was this:

"A long, long time ago, there was a man and his family living in Colfax. His favorite son grew ill and died at the tender age of ten, at the turn of the century. The boy had attended the one-room school, but that building was also the church, so the funeral was held there too. The mother sat in the back during the service and wept and wailed with uncontrollable grief.

"For weeks after, day in and day out, the grieving mother would go to the school and sit in the back on a bench and mourn and cry.

"She was so sad and morose that she just pined away, and within a month, she also passed away. The dozen or so families of the community held services for her in the schoolhouse-church, and she, too, was buried, beside her son, in the graveyard.

"In the months ahead, every Sunday, in the evening or at night, the ghost of the grieving mother would reappear in the back row of benches at the church, wailing and weeping. She became know as the Weeping Lady of Colfax.

"The sight and above all the sound of the Weeping Lady was so unnerving that one by one the families moved away and abandoned the schoolhouse, and the sight of the Weeping Lady so alarmed drifters and other passers-by who sought refuge in the structure that someone tore out the flooring to discourage visitors from staying at dusk.

"Since Colfax was halfway between Cimarron and Raton, wagons often stopped at Colfax for water or rest, and many travellers who reached Raton told of seeing the Weeping Lady. Many of those who saw her never knew she was a ghost, she looked and sounded so real."

Then I knew why the floorboards were gone . . . and what I had heard in the old schoolhouse-church at Colfax.

80 The Devil's Neck

FROM THE ROAD HERE IN PLACITAS, LOOKING TO THE WEST, OVER BY Mount Taylor, you can see the *Cabezón*. The story goes that this mesa is the Devil's Neck. When young Spanish soldiers came from over the sea to the New World, many of them were only teenagers. One young man was only fourteen when he left Cadiz; he took his sword which his grandfather had given him and had it blessed by the bishop at Madrid and had its double edge sharpened anew. He brought the sword across the sea to Mexico and north to El Paso, and he was among the few chosen to come northward seeking the Lost Cities of Gold.

The young hero's troop came up to Zuni Pueblo, and then to Zia Pueblo, and then attempted to travel northward to Taos. They wandered off course somewhat and encamped on the farthest northern reaches of Mount Taylor at a spring where they could spend two or three days and rest the horses. The last night at the spring, it was the young hero's stand at watch. The fire burned low and all the men were snoring, and the young man fell asleep, a mortal sin for a sentinel.

He awoke with a hot wind blowing against the side of his face, even though it was spring and shortly before dawn, when it should have been the coolest time of the day. It was not a desert breeze, it was a harsh, hot wind. He stood and turned to face this hot wind, and he saw the Devil's head, as large as a mountain, staring at him and breathing down on him. The Devil's mouth opened and his red-hot tongue unrolled toward all the sleeping soldiers.

Since he was the sentinel, and it was his duty to protect them, he responded with all the courage and fortitude that he had, knowing that his grandfather and everyone at home had believed in him. He drew his great, double-edged sword from its scabbard and swung it with all his strength. With the first blow, he cut open the front part of the Devil's neck. As he swung the sword back, he finished severing the huge head from the spinal cord of the Devil. The grotesque head rolled back, behind the Devil's neck and shoulders, back down into the Underworld, with a horrible, horrible scream that woke everyone up. The Devil's neck and shoulders slowly lowered back into the Underworld, and everyone stood and praised the little hero with the great sword.

And now, every morning, if you go up in the high mountains, and you look to the west, here, you see the Devil's shoulders and the Devil's neck, rising up in the west, and he waits all day for the boy to come back and put the head on its rightful place. That is the story of *el Cabezón* [the Great Head].

81 The Devil's Breath

SETTLERS CAME WESTWARD AND WENT UP ON *CABEZÓN*, KNOWING that the Indians would not disturb them there, because the Indians did not like that place. These pioneers thought that the high vantage of

Cabezón would be a good place to sit and look out on the valley. They built a village there, with farms and schools, on the flat top of *Cabezón*, the Devil's Neck.

The only contact these settlers had with the world in the valley below them was a circuit priest who came up every six months to hold marriages, baptisms, and hear confession. And to bury the dead. On his first visit, the priest took a census. A flood in the valley prevented him from returning his next appointed time, but at the end of one year, when he returned to the mesa top, he found all the people dead.

The people had fallen over wherever they stood. One man lay dead in the field, still holding his plow tied to a dead ox. One woman fell over churning butter, and overturned her churn. The children in the schoolyard lay dead at their games. The priest thought that the people had turned to sin and lost their Holy Spirit, and evil had come and taken them away.

The priest brought a company of men from the valley below to bury the dead and bring the possessions down to sell them off in Bernalillo and Santa Fe and Cuba. Everyone who knew the story of how *el Cabezón* came to be knew that the people had died from the hot sulphurous breath coming out of the Devil's Neck.

Later in the 1950s, some squatters went back up there to try to live, but the people were getting ill from the spring water. The EPA [Environmental Protection Agency] went up there and found that the spring waters were full of strychnine [or poisonous alkaloids]. Nobody lives up there now.

82 The Ghost of Ella Barham

IT SEEMS THAT GHOSTS MOST OFTEN WALK IN THE PLACE WHERE THEY WERE murdered. They most often haunt a place where they died by violence, or mutilation, or without warning. Fox hunters and 'coon hunters along Crooked Creek near the Killebrew Ford, about eighteen miles below Harrison [Arkansas], say they still see the ghost of Ella Barham, dressed all in white, walking near the mine shaft where her body was found.

On November 21, 1912, Ella was out riding; her horse came back without her. That night, hunters spotted a herd of hogs loudly rooting around some suspicious looking objects under a loose pile of rocks near an abandoned mine shaft. It was a corpse, cut into pieces by a saw. There were signs the body had been carried over the Crooked by the murderer, who must have surprised her on the road, to be disposed of.

Even though he joined in the search for the girl before her body was found, a young man named Odus Davidson was suspected of the crime. A local justice of the peace was of the opinion that Odus had been jilted by Ella not long before. The day afterward, the local judge swore out a warrant for Odus's arrest. At his family's house, when the posse came to get him, Odus jumped out a back window and fled to the woods. He had peppered his socks to keep bloodhounds from trailing him, but he was taken without resistance and admitted to having been cutting wood near the place Ella had last been seen. He had come through my yard not long after that time of day.

The flight, the peppered socks, the presumed jilting, the admission of being near the death scene, and the blood on his socks when he was caught were enough to sway the jury for conviction. We deliberated a short time and returned a guilty verdict. Odus Davidson was hanged just before the Arkansas death penalty was changed to electrocution at the state penitentiary's death house. Odus Davidson was the last man hanged legally in Arkansas.

The body of the victim had been cut up horribly, into seven pieces, but the ghost the hunters claim they see down on Crooked Creek is all in one piece. The prosecutor at the trial had quoted Bible verses, turned to Odus shouting, "And where is Ella Barham?"

I guess the answer could be, "Still down at Crooked Creek, near Pleasant Ridge."

83 White River Boy

IN THE 1920s, WHITE RIVER [ARIZONA] APACHE RESERVATION HAD A Lutheran Mission, with an assistant rector whose wife had had a child. The boy seemed fine until he reached the age of walking and talking, but he didn't do any of the latter; he was probably autistic, but they didn't have a word for it then. He was a beautiful child, and he walked and ran and played, but he never spoke. He was dark, with the most beautiful eyes, almost yellow, and had the most intelligent look, as if he were trying to get through to you but couldn't.

He constantly tried to get away, as if he didn't belong in the house. He had a sandbox to play in, and they had built a high fence to keep him from climbing out and running away. They had to watch him constantly. One day the mother left him alone in the sandbox for just a moment while she stepped inside; when she came back, he was gone. He had climbed the fence and headed for the river.

They found him later, drowned.

None of the Anglo people ever saw it, but the Apaches said they saw the boy for years thereafter, walking along the river. It was as if he were a visitor from another world who wanted to go back where he came from.

84 Cousin Jack and the Buccas

"COUSIN JACK" CAME FROM CORNWALL [ENGLAND] TO MINE THE COM-stock Lode in Nevada in the 1880s. Hiding in his knapsack was a *bucca,* a Cornish hobgoblin, who had come from the deep mines in South-western England. The *buccas* prospered more than the miners did, and soon every deep mine had one or two living in its walls. When Cousin Jack ate his pasties at lunch, he always left a bite behind in the shaft for the *buccas.* Bad luck came for sure if he neglected his imp-friends: his tools got misplaced, his lamp went out suddenly, or gravel fell in his lunchpail. But if he fed the little beasties, they would tap inside the walls and warn him in time of an impending cave-in. Englishmen claimed the ghosts of dead miners haunted the mines and tapped: Cornishmen knew it was the *buccas.*

85 Wailing Women of Katzimo

THE ACOMA PEOPLE USED TO LIVE ON KATZIMO, THE ENCHANTED MESA, over there [near Acoma Mesa]. The crops were good and life was so easy the people forgot to do the dances to pray to the gods, and they did not teach their children properly. One day three old women who were ill stayed in the pueblo while all the others were in the fields on the valley floor below. Only a young boy was left with them to see to their needs.

The Great Thunderbird came over the mesa and showed the gods' displeasure by shaking his wings and bringing great rain. The rain was so great that the pueblo was falling apart; the mud and rocks were giving away. The women sent the boy to go down to the fields and bring the men back, even in this storm, to the pueblo. As the boy was climbing down the rock-face ladder, one part of the cliff fell away, the part with the handholds cut in it.

No one could get back up to the pueblo. The old women looked down and saw the people, but they couldn't get down. They starved up there, punished for the pueblo's not teaching the children properly. In the winter, at night when the wind blows, you can still hear those old women wailing on Katzimo, the Enchanted Mesa.

86 Dead Man's Curve

IT WAS A LONG TIME AGO, AT DEAD MAN'S CURVE, BETWEEN PARADIS AND Des Allemands [in St. Charles parish, Louisiana] on an old road that runs along the railroad track. There was a little cemetery where the relatives set out voudou regalia on the graves. My friends and I used to run through and pick up black candles to use in séances when we were in high school. The road goes on past the cemetery to a real sharp curve that they call Dead Man's Curve. In the forties or fifties, before—I think—the road was paved, a young couple in a roadster took the curve too fast and were killed. I heard it said that they had sped away when they saw something in the cemetery.

If you slow down or stop after midnight at the curve, you can hear them scream, and you see these pillars of blue light moving among the trees. There's a "swamp phosphorous" that glows, that is used as the explanation for this, but that's ridiculous. We drove through slow one night and stopped because we heard the screams; we watched. These lights were moving. Now, swamp phosphorous doesn't move. These lights move, big pillars of blue light, taller than a person, coming toward the road, then turning and "walking" back off into the woods. Needless to say, we left—very quickly.

I've heard this story over and over, but I saw this! We heard, like, tires screeching, then a boy's voice screaming, then we saw the lights. Then we left!

87 The Presence at the Lodge

IN THE EARLY '70S, MY HUSBAND AND I WERE "INTO" YOGA, AND WE WENT to an old, converted hot-springs resort in northern California where a yoga group ran a yoga retreat guided by a swami. The resort was built in the '20s, with individual cabins as well as the main lodge. There were also the hot baths, with hot mineral water, in another building. About twenty people were staying there.

The unmarried men were in one dormitory, and the unmarried women in another, and the married couples lived in the cabins. We weren't encouraged to talk with others; we did our chores and studied, meditated, or whatever you were doing. So, there wasn't a lot of conversation, and I did not hear any "warning" of what was to come.

My husband was away for the weekend, and at night—I had no clock or watch so I don't know what time of night it was—all of a sudden, an energy mass appeared before me and was pulsating toward me. I was terrified. It was not a shape of a human being, it was just a pulsing mass. I don't know if I visually saw it or sensed it; it was dark and I was not aware of a color. The energy was definitely feminine, I felt, and hostile.

It is customary for a student of yoga to progress along her spiritual path, and at some point to confront interference. At this point, she would go for a meeting with the swami, or the head of the retreat, for planning the future path to follow. I thought that I was sensing interference, but it was not a happy presence, and it frightened me. I was not prepared, however, for what he told me.

Yes, he said, this is an old place, and there are spirits still lingering here. Every married woman who had been left alone for a time since the first retreat several years before had experienced and reported this same thing. They had—every single one of them—felt something was in the room with them, and felt threatened. The presence had not been discussed individually among the retreat participants; its existence had come out in a group meeting after married women had reported it. The single women were not a virgin community, but then again, they were seldom alone in their dormitory.

The head teacher explained the presence by saying that there are beings that are not ready to leave and, lacking bodies, try to relive their existence through whatever live beings are present. I left a light on all the time until my husband returned, and never felt her presence again.

88 The Lady of the Ledge

IN OLD ORAIBI, ON THE HOPI LAND, WHERE NO NON-INDIAN IS ALLOWED to go, there sits a black ravine known as Coal Canyon. On nights when the moon is full, from the canyon floor looking up, you can see her dancing on the rim: The Lady of the Ledge.

She was once an old woman, insane, wandering the endless canyons and mesas. She walked off the edge one day, ending her life of her own will. That is not the Hopi way: she was not accepted into the Other World. She returns to This World on nights the moon is full, dancing on the ledge, slow and white in the full moonlight, dancing on the ledge.

Some people who have seen her suspect that she is an optical illusion caused by the shimmer of heat rising off the rock wall as the cool of evening comes to the desert. But I have seen her, and she is dancing. She is The Lady of the Ledge.

89 Rancho de las Chimeneas

IN MAVERICK COUNTY [TEXAS], YOU'LL FIND *RANCHO DE LAS Chimeneas:* Chimney Ranch. On the property, far off the beaten path, stands the ruin of the old stone hacienda from Spanish Colonial days. Sometimes a lone rider or a fence-repair gang would sleep in the old house, with a fire in one of its many chimneys, one in almost every room.

One night a group of cowpokes slept in the house. In the darkest part of the night, they awoke to hear heavy footfalls on the dirt floor and the jingling of old-fashioned, large-roweled spurs, like the Spanish used to wear. The spurs got closer and closer until one cowboy, a Mexican, let out a scream of fear and managed to light a match. No one was there but the bootless men in their sleeping bags.

The *vaquero* was so scared, he got the *susto* [dread], and the *curandero* had to clear his mind of evil spirits by sweeping him with a broom.

90 The Exchange House Well

IN LA FONDA, THE INN AT THE PLAZA IN SANTA FE, THERE IS A DIS-traught gambler who dies over and over again. When the hotel was called The Exchange House and gambling was legal, a travelling sales-man lost in a card game all his own money and all the money entrusted to him by his company's home office. In despair, he expiated his shame by jumping into the hotel's water supply, a well, and drowning.

The dining room called La Plazuela is located over the site of the old well, long since covered. Diners there sometimes see the ghostly form walk to the middle of the room and jump into the floor and vanish down the no-longer-visible well. His expiation was incomplete and goes on over and over again.

91 The Lookout Rider

ACCORDING TO LOCAL LEGEND, THERE WAS A CONFEDERATE LOOKOUT post on Inspiration Point [the highest point along the ridge road west of Branson, Missouri]. A lone rider could spot any kind of large troop movement and take the word to nearby encampments. On that site today is a theme park honoring "The Shepherd of the Hills," the novel by Harold Bell Wright. In a nighttime pageant—which involves a ghost as a character, by the way—actors on horseback move in and out of the woods as part of their roles.

Every once in a while, there's one horseman too many.

In about 1964, a panther was bothering the horses kept on the park for trail rides and the nighttime play. Some of the local folks claimed it was a booger cat, not a real cat at all. All the employees were especially watchful around that time, keeping an eye out for a panther. This increased state of watchfulness led to them seeing something else, or someone else: a horseman who did not resemble any of the employees, on a horse that no one recognized, riding the trails at night.

Some of the actors, the best horsemen, chased the rider at night and could never catch him, almost as if he weren't human-and-horse-flesh. It may all be a scary story told around campfires, and not true at all, but at least one actor swears it's true, and that he knows who it is: a Confederate sentinel, fleeing the actors dressed as Baldknobbers, a post-Civil War vigilante group that was pro-Union!

92 Unseen Hands

. . . [T]WO MEN WERE PROWLING AROUND IN THE BALTIMORE MINE] . . . for the purpose of seeing whether there was ore enough in sight to extract profitably on tribute. Climbing into a stope, they heard the click of hammers and were very much surprised . . . to see two striking hammers hard at work on the head of a rusty drill which was being deftly turned by unseen hands, and though not a soul was in sight except themselves, they heard a lively conversation; they could make out no words. They looked and listened for some minutes, until fear took hold and drove them out of the mine quickly.

At the Toll House, they related their experience and were laughed at, but to prove that their heads were clear, they conducted a couple of skeptics to the spot and found the hammer still at work.

[Extract from the Virginia City, Nevada, *Chronicle,* October 8, 1884.]

93 The Statue That Moves

IN SOUTHWEST CITY, MISSOURI, THERE IS A GRAVEYARD WITH A STATUE that moves, a very frightening statue that moves. There is a woman carved in stone on top of a headstone. I myself have seen this happen: sometimes you will look at the statue and it's kneeling with its hands clasped in front of it, with its head bowed. Other times, the head is up and the arms are lowered. The statue changes position from time to time.

94 Great-Uncle Pius's Gold

GREAT-UNCLE PIUS BURIED HIS GOLD DURING THE CIVIL WAR BECAUSE HE had heard that the Union Army was coming toward his home. He buried it at the foot of a tree in one of his pastures, where his big white bull kept everyone out. Pius died in the war, and ever since, the family has looked for this gold.

Two separate fortune-tellers have said that the treasure is guarded by something white. These were *traiteures* [people who heal by prayer and the laying-on of hands] whom the family had consulted. They didn't know about the white bull. He died a long time ago, too, but he must still be guarding the treasure as a ghost.

The family would drive iron rods into the ground trying to strike the chest. They never found it, so the ghost must be doing a good job.

95 Superstition Mountain

ALONG THE SOUTHERN BELT OF THE COUNTRY, FROM THE CAROLINAS TO California, from the Cherokees in the east to the Apaches in the west, the Indian People tell about the Little People. Little People are about three or four feet tall, and they are associated with sun-worship.

One tribe of Little People lived in the Superstition Mountains. With them lived a woman with golden hair who was a special friend of the Sun. The neighboring Zunis coveted the golden-haired woman and attacked the Little People to take her captive. The Zunis said that they had brought the golden-haired woman from the place of the rising sun, and she belonged to them.

When the Zunis approached the village of the Little People, the golden-haired woman came out and confronted them. She carried a clay pot and poured its contents out into the Salt River. The pot was full of fire and sparks of the sun. Sparks jumped from the river and bounced off the rocks. Balls of fire rolled down the river and drove the Zunis away.

The Little People went and hid in a cave near the Salt River, and the Apaches came and tried to take the golden sun-woman. Again, she rolled balls of fire and sparks at the Apaches, and they were driven away.

The Apaches say that the Little People are still hiding in a cave in the Superstition Mountains, and it is they who have made so many miners and prospectors disappear. The sparks and balls of fire are still sometimes seen in the Superstitions today.

Supernatural and Preternatural
(Including the Miraculous, the Devil, Death, Monsters, Witches, and Such)

96 The Specter of Death

AS MOST OF YOU KNOW [THE TELLER NODS TOWARD A NEWCOMER IN A circle of friends gathered for ghost-story telling], I run the one-hour photo in the mall. About four years ago [1985], a man with a whole roll of negatives already developed came in and wanted some prints made while he waited. I ran the film through, but the pictures were so dark, I wasn't getting a decent print. We did finally get one negative to print out where you could barely see the image. I told him I might get a better print if I knew what I was looking for. Here's the print [he produces a dim color print and passes it around], and here's what the guy told me:

Quite a while ago, four men went on a hunting trip in Colorado. They had been told that the spot they'd picked to camp in was a valley that strange things had happened in before, but they camped there anyway, because they didn't believe it. The first two nights, they heard strange sounds on the wind, but the third day they went out to hunt, and as they came back to camp at sundown, they saw this! [He refers to the photo, and describes it.]

That's a four-man tent, there, and it's seven feet tall. You can see standing beside it is a figure dressed in black, about ten or eleven feet tall. He looks just like the figure of death. [Those present examine the photo. It does, indeed, seem to be what he is describing.] They had one camera with them, an old one-twenty-six, that's why the picture's square; they shot about two-thirds of the roll of this thing. That's the only picture that came out on the whole roll, the rest of them were just about black. They abandoned their equipment and walked or ran out right then, and never went back.

Within two years, I was told, one died accidentally, one died under mysterious circumstances, one guy committed suicide, and the last one, who shot this picture, had been in an asylum for many, many years. The man who brought me the photos is a researcher from California who had heard about this and finally came all the way here to talk to the only person still alive who witnessed this.

From there, he got a-hold of a relative and had to dig through all his negatives to find this one roll, and, as I said, that's the only picture on the roll that came out. He wanted that one picture badly enough that we worked with him for about two hours getting it. We ran several prints, and he took the best ones, and I put this one in a drawer at the shop, and it's been there until tonight.

You can have that one, by the way.

97 The Fouke Monster

MY GRANDFATHER TOOK A SHOT AT THE FOUKE MONSTER. NOT MANY folks have ever done that. The thing was seen many times, usually at dusk, always near the riverbed or the creeks, usually along Boggy Creek where it crosses U.S. Highway 71.

The Fouke Monster is best remembered by those who heard its roar.

Some people said it was like a panther screaming, but most said it was unlike anything they'd ever heard before. Those who said they'd seen it said it was as tall as a man, hairy like an ape, and walked upright. It had a foul smell that hunting dogs wouldn't track, and some people claimed it left three-toed tracks in the field mud.

The monster was reported on the national news after it terrorized two families sharing a house near Boggy Creek. The sheriff came from Texarkana and reported finding panther tracks, but the believers around Fouke were sure it had been the monster.

Later, they made a movie about it, and my grandfather played himself in it. The thing was messing around his chicken pens.

The monster was blamed for killing hogs or stealing chickens, and most of all, for the unexplained deaths of hunting dogs; torn and broken carcasses were found in yards or fields or woods. Dogs were scared of the thing; they howled when it came near.

The dogs were howling at my grandfather's place around dusk one day, and he loaded his shotgun. The squawking from the henhouse told him what was happening. From the back porch, he fired into the dark shadows in the chickenyard. The thing fled noisily through the underbrush. He never saw it clearly.

I think he preferred it that way.

98 Death and the Curandero

THERE WAS AN OLD MAN WHO KILLED A CHICKEN AND WAS COOKING IT over a fire. St. Peter came along and asked for a bite. The poor man said, "No, blessed Saint Peter, for you neglect the poor. The rich have so much, and the poor have so little. You do not treat us all equally."

Saint Peter went away without saying anything.

Then along came Saint Anthony and asked for a bite. The poor man said, "No, blessed Saint Anthony, for your bishops neglect the poor. The poor box [in the cathedral] is very small and the offering basket is very large. You do not treat us equally."

Saint Anthony went away with a sigh.

Then along came Death herself and asked for a bite. "Yes, Sister Death," said the poor man, "I'll give you a bite, for you take the souls of the rich and the poor. You don't play favorites. You treat us all equally." And he gave her a chicken leg, which she ate.

"I will give you a *merced* [boon]," said Death. "What do you wish?"

"Give me what you will," said the poor man, "and I'll be glad to get it."

"I will give you the *merced* of being a *curandero* [folk healer; herbal healer]," she said. "And when you come to cure someone, you must look and see where I am standing. If I stand at the head of the sick man's bed, he is doomed and you will not be able to cure him. If I stand at the foot, you may heal him. But never, never try to heal the ill person if I stand at the head of the bed."

And she went away.

The man became a *curandero* and grew wealthy giving out herbal remedies and teas, chanting over the sick, and blowing away the bad airs from the sick. Each time, if he saw Death at the head of the sick person's bed, he said, "This one is beyond help, only call a priest and pay me nothing."

Then one night he was called to the bedside of a very rich old man. There stood Death at the head of the bed. "This one is beyond help," said the *curandero,* but the old woman said, "I will pay you a thousand silver pesos to cure him." The *curandero* found he could not finish his sentence.

He took out his medicines and began to chant and gyrate in a loud silly way, and he circled the bed, and he shoved Death around to the foot of the bed in the process. Then he healed the man by his normal means and took the thousand silver pesos home. He put the money in a bag for safekeeping and placed it under his pillow and went to sleep.

During the night he awoke and turned to look at his money under the pillow. In the moonlight, there was Death, at the head of the bed. He was found the next morning, with his cold dead fingers around the money bag.

99 Pedro de Urdemalas

THEN THERE'S THE STORY OF PEDRO DE URDEMALAS (TRICKY PETE) THE *pícaro* [young vagabond who lives by his wits] who tricked Old Mister Death and his wife and children. Pedro earned his living as a beggar, and one day as he whistled and walked along the road, a beggar asked him for alms!

"You must be very poor indeed," said Pedro, "to beg from a beggar!"

Pedro gave the beggar all the coins in his pocket, and the beggar said. "Now, you may ask me for something in return."

"Very well," said Pedro, thinking it was a playful chatter just to pass the time, as beggars often did. "Give me a magical deck of playing cards wherewith I always win, and no one can quit playing unless I say so."

"Done," said the beggar.

"Give me a flute-and-drum," said Pedro, "that, once begun, no one can quit playing until I am tired of dancing and say so."

"Done," said the beggar.

"Give me a dense greasewood thicket [creosote bush; *Larrea mexicana*] wherein I can throw those to whom I owe money, and they can't get out until I say so."

"Done," said the beggar, "but shouldn't you forsake these vain and worldly things and concern yourself with your soul?"

"Very well," Pedro sighed. "Let it be that when I knock on the Doors to Heaven, St. Peter will let me in, no matter what."

"That's more like it," said the beggar, and he stood up. His dirty robe became white, and the keys to the Kingdom hung at his belt. St. Peter went away and left behind the things Pedro had requested.

Pedro gambled a lot and always won. He danced a lot and never paid the piper. And he threw a lot of creditors into the greasewood until they forgave his debts to them. Finally, it came time for Pedro to die.

Little Death [one of the children of Old Man Death, an Aztec concept] came along and claimed Pedro's soul to take it to Hell. "Very well," said Pedro, "but let's play some cards first." Little Death agreed, and couldn't stop playing. Soon, those predestined to have died were walking all about and Little Death begged to be set free to go about his business. Pedro let him go on condition that he allow Pedro to live twice as long. He agreed.

Finally, the day came for Pedro to die, and Old Lady Death came for him. "Before I go," said Pedro, "let me give all my worldly goods to the poor." Old Lady Death agreed. "Here," said Pedro as he gathered up belongings, "you carry the drum." Old Lady Death took up the flute-and-drum and was soon playing them and couldn't quit. Pedro went away for seven days. When he got back, Old Lady Death begged to be set free to go about her business. Pedro let her go, on condition that she let him live twice as long. She agreed.

Finally, the day came for Pedro to die. Old Man Death himself came for Pedro. "I'll go peacefully," said Pedro, "wait here by this greasewood bush." Pedro tried to throw Old Man Death into the greasewood bush, but the Old Man was too smart for him. He broke off a thorny switch and chased Pedro down the road to Hell.

Pedro ran around and around in circles until Old Man Death was dizzy, and then he ran up the road toward Heaven. When got to the doors of Heaven, with Death right behind him, he knocked, and St. Peter came to answer the door.

"Where have you been?" said St. Peter angrily.

"I've been busy," said Pedro. "Let me in as you promised me!"

St. Peter let him in, and Old Man Death crushed the greasewood switch until it bled grease and burst into flames. And that's the story of Pedro de Urdemalas.

100 The Flying Head

ONCE THERE WAS A GREAT FLYING HEAD. IT WAS SO HUGE THAT IT WAS AS big as a lodgehouse. It had great big eyes, as big as wagon wheels; it had great big wings growing out of its sides where its ears might have been;

it had a big wide mouth with hundreds of teeth like the points of double-edged knives. But its nose was a little-bitty nose no bigger than a child's.

When the Flying Head was hungry, it flew through the skies grinding its teeth together—*gnash, gnash, gnash!* It flew through the skies beating its wings—*whoosh, whoosh, whoosh!* The Head would fly over a pueblo and swoop down, eating whole herds of pigs or goats or carrying off a cow or a burro or even a person! When the People heard the Flying Head coming, they would hide under the floorboards of their houses. The Head only came out at sunrise or sunset, so the People were safe if they went out in the heat of the day.

There was a young mother in one pueblo who could only let her baby outside in the hottest part of the day, and she was sad that her child only saw the sun high in the sky. She wanted to be able to go out in the cool of the morning and the beauty of the evening. She decided to do something about it!

One day near dusk, when the People expected the Head might come, the young mother took her baby to a neighbor and asked her to watch the child for a while. Then she went to another neighbor and asked for some firewood, which he gave her. She took the wood to her house and built a fire. Then she went down by the river and picked up a basketful of round, smooth stones. She put the stones on the hearth, and slowly pushed them into the fire with a stick.

Soon the Flying Head was coming! *Whoosh, whoosh, whoosh,* went the wings in the sky; *gnash, gnash, gnash* went the teeth in its mouth.

The young mother heard the sound coming. She took a wooden spoon and lifted the red-hot stones out of the coals. One by one she put them in a bread bowl. She put the bread bowl on the table. Outside she heard the People calling out from house to house, telling everyone to hide under the floorboards. But she sat at the table, and did not look to either side.

The Head flew into the pueblo and swooped about, looking into the houses. The young mother said loudly, "Good bread . . . good hot bread," and she lifted a hot stone towards her mouth. Then, at the last moment, she dropped the stone into the sand beside the hearth. The Flying Head flew over and looked in the window of the house; he flew back and forth, looking in first with one big eye and then the other.

"Good bread," said the young mother, "good hot bread." And she lifted another hot stone towards her open mouth, dropping it into the sand when the Head was between eyes at the window. She rubbed her stomach and smacked her lips. The Head put its little nose in the window, but it couldn't smell any bread. *Sniff, sniff, sniff,* went the Head. The young mother didn't look to either side.

"Good bread," she said, lifting another hot stone, "good hot bread." The Head was at the doorway, looking in. She passed the stone by her open mouth and dropped it over her shoulder into the sand. She rubbed her stomach again.

The Flying Head reached its wings into the doorway and took the bread bowl off the table. The Head tipped up the bowl and swallowed all the hot rocks. The frightened young mother didn't look to either side; she sat still and looked straight ahead.

The Head dropped the bowl and began to beat its wings. It flew up in the sky and flew around and around, blowing smoke out its mouth. The Head flew way, way up into the sky and burst into a thousand, thousand pieces, and never bothered the People again. The young mother went and told the neighbors what had happened, and thanked them, and brought her baby home. And after that, she and her baby sat in the plaza in the morning and in the evening, any day they wanted.

The Lady in Blue I

THE GREAT FATHER ALONSO DE BENAVIDES CAME TO THE UPPER RIO Grande valley in New Mexico in 1629. When he arrived, he found that the Jumano Indians were already asking for missionaries instead of rejecting them as other tribes did. When asked why they were so blessedly eager and how they had known of the Christian missionaries, they told a strange and miraculous story.

A European woman with light skin, dressed in a blue robe from neck to feet, came among the Jumanos for many years, for many generations teaching them in their own tongue and promising missionaries would come to them in the future. As far away as Texas, the Blue Lady was seen for years before the arrival of the missionaries.

The Blue Lady was very beautiful and kind, and spoke all the Indian languages.

One woman from Spain said that she had been the Blue Lady, and that she had been transported miraculously to the New World for the visits, but this explanation seems inadequate, for the Blue Lady was seen before this woman was even born back in Spain. The Franciscans of the seventeenth century believed that the Blue Lady was even more supernatural than miraculous transport: they believed she was a visitor from the Other World.

 ## The Lady in Blue II

IN THE PUEBLO, THEY USED TO TELL THE STORY OF HOW IN AGREDA, Spain, there lived a beautiful girl named María Coronal de Agreda. She was born in 1602 and she died in 1665. As the story goes, this young woman, who had heard tales of the New World and the Indians, spent a lot of her time praying for the conversion of the Indians, who at that time knew little of God. It so happened that around this time, she was offered a trip to go to New Spain.

After her very long journey, illness, and prayer, she found herself among the Indians that were unheard of in Europe. She could not stay long because of her health, and she had to return. But she promised that she would send teachers to help the Indians who also suffered from illnesses.

In the 1680s, a missionary named Damián de Manzanet discovered in New Mexico the Indians written about in the writings of María Coronal de Agreda. They joyfully received Manzanet, and one day the chief asked Manzanet for some blue baize to bury his grandmother in, for she had recently died. Manzanet asked why he wanted such a strange color of cloth. No Europeans wearing blue were there.

The Indian replied that it was because he had once seen a beautiful woman who had come to help them and whom they honored in their stories, and who wore blue. The chief said he wished to be like the Blue Lady and pass into Heaven, where his spirit could be at peace.

But María de Agreda had never gotten as far north as New Mexico, and yet the Tanoan [language group of] Indians remember her in legend and tell that where she walked, her footsteps had caused wild blue flowers to bloom.

102 The Disobedient Granddaughter

IT HAPPENED THAT THERE WAS A LOVELY YOUNG GIRL FROM EL PASO DEL Norte who had come to her fifteenth spring and wanted to go out into the world and dance with young men. Her old grandmother with whom she lived disapproved, however, and forbade her to go to the parties that season. One night she slipped out a window with a loose grill and went to the dance anyway.

At the dance, she met a handsome young man with dark flashing eyes and a gracious manner. They danced and danced almost until dawn. He asked her to run away with him and be his bride. The foolish young girl was infatuated with the handsome man, and she agreed to elope. As she climbed back in through the loose grill, she told him to wait.

As he waited, he paced back and forth, and then he sat down for a moment to remove his boots, which were hurting his feet. As he paced back and forth under the window, he left footprints.

Rooster footprints.

When the young woman came back with her portmanteau, the young man had his boots on, but she saw the huge rooster tracks in the dirt. Realizing the young man was the Devil in disguise, she opened her bag and pulled out her crucifix, which she had packed.

When the Devil saw the crucifix, he ran away and never came back. And the young woman never again disobeyed her old grandmother.

103 The Wolf Girl of Devil's River

HUNTERS FROM ALL OVER TEXAS GO TO SAN ANGELO TO HUNT SOUTH OF there in Crockett and Val Verde counties. On the Devil's River, which flows out of Buckhorn Draw to the *Río Bravo del Norte,* called in Texas the Rio Grande, hunters watch for many kinds of game. And one kind of ghost.

Texas' most famous ghost is the Wolf Girl of Devil's River, seen as a feral child in the 1800s and as a white phantom until recently. No one really wants to see the Wolf Girl, who is variously described as a white shape, a naked woman, or an albino wolf.

Settlers in the territory west of San Antonio in the early 1800s were prey to many dangers, including unfriendly Indians and Mexican *bandidos.* A couple with a baby was murdered and the baby left to die. Passersby found the bodies of the couple, but the baby was gone. Wolf tracks seemed to indicate the baby's fate. For years afterward, a wild child was sighted roaming with the wolves. Some ranchers claimed to have captured the girl, only to have her escape with the help of a pack of howling wolves. She was seen again in 1852, and 1875. A wolf might live fifteen years, a woman might live seventy, but the Wolf Girl was seen for over a century and a half.

Very few people see the Wolf Girl, and fewer admit to it. But she is still seen, as recent books testify in reports by hunters who ask to remain anonymous. She's Pecos Bill's spiritual cousin, and may even be the origin of that coyote-raised boy's legend.

If you hear the call of a canine at night along the Devil's River, it may not be a dog. It may not be a coyote. It may not even be a wolf.

If the cry sounds neither human nor animal, that may be exactly what it is!

104 The Hairy Man

IN CENTRAL TEXAS, WHERE I USED TO LIVE, PEOPLE TALK ABOUT A HAIRY man who lives in the woods. I didn't ever believe in him until two years ago. My mother and I were living alone together in a rundown house near a creek bed. We . . . didn't have any money, and so the place only had a well and an outhouse. It was my job to go out and get a bucketful of water when Mother needed it.

One morning real early, I got up and there was a fog on the creek bottom. I couldn't see but a few feet in front of me. It was cold and wet, but I had to have water, and Mother wasn't up yet because she slept late on Saturdays. And usually, I did too, except this morning, I didn't.

It was real foggy and I walked out to the well on tiptoe because I was barefoot and the ground was cold. So I was looking down at my feet all the time. And I got to the well, and I was looking down as I lowered the bucket. And when the bucket came up, I looked up.

Across the well from me, in the fog about five or six feet away, was this hairy thing. It was taller than me—well, almost everyone is taller than me—and it had big brown eyes. And it wasn't a man; it had long brown hair all over its body. And it just looked at me, almost sadly, like a dog might look at you. And I just stood there too scared to move.

It turned and went away into the fog. I stared after it for a long time and went in and locked the door. But it didn't really scare me, because it had those sad eyes.

105 Lord of the LLano

OUT OF THE NIGHT, OVER THE PLAINS, SNORTING FIRE AND BRIMSTONE comes the White Steed. His eyes glow like coals, the coals of a cowboy's campfire just before dawn. His hooves are steel, striking sparks off the stones. He throws back his head and calls his *manada* [harem] of mares. He is the lord of the *LLano* [the plain]. He is the *mestengo blanco*. He is the White Steed.

No cowboy can corral him. No lariat can lasso him. No rustler can ride him. He is the White Steed.

106a Sally Baker

I GREW UP IN A SMALL TOWN IN SOUTHWESTERN ARKANSAS, AND ABOUT twenty miles south of my home, in Louisiana, is the little town of Cotton Valley. When I was growing up, I would often hear stories about a woman who had once lived in Cotton Valley, named Sally Baker; the story went around that she had been a witch. All the people who lived around her held her in awe and terror.

Children gathering blackberries along the road where she lived would disappear mysteriously. Weird sights could be seen around her tumble-down house when the moon was full. She had married seven times, each time by casting a spell on the man, and murdered them all by poison, burying each one in the woods around her house.

When she died, her evil was too strong to be bound by the walls of the grave. She was buried near the narrow dirt road that ran past her old home place, and the story went that if anyone was brave—or foolish—enough to go out there at night, and furthermore was so stouthearted—or stupid—as to run up and push over her gravestone, a spirit—the ghost of one of her husbands, still under her thrall—would emerge from the thick woods, white and glowing, to drive away the intruder and set the stone back up again. I spoke with at least one person who swore he had seen just that happen.

 ## Sally Baker Debunked

THE LEGEND OF SALLY BAKER IS WELL KNOWN THROUGHOUT THE AREA I grew up in, and as I became old enough to drive and curious enough to wish to see such things for myself, I began to ask exactly where Sally Baker's grave was.

One day I happened to mention it in front of my father, and he said, sort of grumpily, "There's nothing to that story. Sally Baker was just an old widow woman."

I asked him how he knew that, and to my astonishment, he said that he had met Sally Baker himself. He and my mother had actually visited her in her house! I was taken aback: it was as if a maiden aunt had offhandedly mentioned that she used to date the Fouke Monster! I asked my father why he had never said anything about this before, and he replied, maddeningly, that he hadn't thought it was particularly important.

It seems that one day in the late 1940s, my mother and father and my two older brothers, who were just toddlers then, were out for an afternoon drive. My mother wasn't sure, but thought that they might have gone down Sally Baker's road looking for an oil rig that a friend of my father was working on. In any case, they came upon Sally Baker's house.

It was a small farm house with a little fenced dooryard and a shed off to one side. The grounds around were weedy and grown up, and the place had an unkept look about it. Even then, there were stories about Sally Baker and her weird ways. It was said that she was crazy and dangerous. But my father was very matter-of-fact and not one to believe all the gossip he heard, so, apparently on a whim, they decided to pay a call on Sally Baker, right then and there.

Looking back, my mother thought maybe it was the fact they had two little boys with them that got Sally Baker to come out. She normally did not talk to anybody except a niece who would bring groceries to her and look in on her. But come out she did. Everyone introduced themselves, Sally took on about the children, and they had a nice little talk.

Sally Baker was neither witch nor maniac, but merely an eccentric little old woman who was deathly afraid of people. She had indeed threatened children picking blackberries, but the threats were inspired by a fear that the children were going to do something to her. She invited my parents in, and they noticed that there was a hole cut into the ceiling in the front room. She explained that she was so frightened there all by herself that at night she would climb up into the loft and pull the ladder up after her.

Before my family left, she showed them around the place, letting my brothers play with the goats. She showed my father a 1936 Ford in the shed which had not been driven since her one husband had died years earlier—of natural causes. Finally, they all said goodbye and went on their way.

Not too many years after that, Sally Baker died and was buried there by her house. In the years that followed, the stories of her infamy grew and grew. I remember that when my parents told me all of this, I was disappointed. The truth, I felt then, made a much less interesting story than the legend about a witch.

Years later, when I was visiting home, I decided that I would finally go and find Sally Baker's grave. After asking around Cotton Valley, I got directions to it. The man who gave them to me chuckled about the whole thing. It seems that when his kids were teenagers, one of the big fun things to do was to drive ten or fifteen miles north to Springhill and find some poor sucker who didn't know any better and tell him the eerie story about Sally Baker's grave.

They would then drive the unsuspecting victim out to the gravesite, having first planted one of their friends out there with a sheet and a flashlight. After goading the out-of-towner to push over the gravestone, the "ghost" would emerge from the trees, moaning horribly, and the victim would usually react by screaming off down the road, telling all his friends the tale of horror and creating more suckers for subsequent evenings of entertainment.

I realized that if I had kept asking around when I was younger, chances are I would have ended up out there as the main feature one dark night.

My wife and I found the grave with no trouble, though it was far out in the lonely woods. It was near the road. There was no sign of where the house had been. There was a concrete slab covering the grave, but I don't know what the locals have the Springhill folks do now, as there was no gravestone there to knock over; it had apparently been stolen. All around the grave, the ground was packed down from foot traffic, and littered with broken beer bottles and other trash. There were the remains of a bonfire, apparently from a scare-party held on Hallowe'en night, which had been three or four days earlier.

After all these years, I had finally found Sally Baker's grave, and all I could think about was the real woman buried there amid the trash and beer bottles—that poor little old woman, so afraid of everyone that she hid in her loft at night.

And I wished that I had brought some flowers.

 ## Medicine-Meal Mush Boy

THERE WAS ONCE A GREAT GHOST SPIRIT WHO CAME DOWN INTO THE *pueblo* and stole children. The People were afraid that someday all the children would be gone. The elders met in the *kiva* and decided that the only way to rid themselves of this gigantic spirit would be to use spirit magic against it. The medicine men looked for some magic and a prayer to get rid of the ghost giant.

One of the medicine men went to the north, and he left a pouch of sacred corn meal that had been blessed. Another went to the east and left a pouch. Another went to the west and another to the south. When they returned and met, they did a song asking that all the pouches would be like a gate, closed, and that the giant ghost would not be able to get in to the *pueblo*. The magic did not work at this time [certain small changes were made at this point, by a pause] because people going out to pick piñon nuts saw a great pot on a fire up on the mesa rim. The people crept up along the mesa and hid behind pine trees and saw the ghost giant boiling water getting ready to eat another child.

The people ran back to the village, but the medicine men were all in the *kiva* at that time and there was no one to tell what they had seen, the medicine men not permitting anyone to disturb them in the *kiva*. The people ran about gathering cornmeal to put around their doorways in hopes that it would help keep the ghost giant away.

At sundown, the medicine men came out of the *kiva* and saw all the white cornmeal sprinkled around the houses; the people told about having seen the fire and the great pot, a basket coated with pitch.

One of the medicine men decided to take a pot of water into the *kiva* and put it on the shelf by the *sipapu* [the doorway from the Spirit World] and let it heat. He put white cornmeal in the pot and stirred it and made a poultice, and shaped it into the shape of a tiny boy. When he removed the cornmeal boy, by the *sipapu*, and blew it to cool it, the cornmeal-mush boy became alive and ran around him on the floor of the *kiva*. He picked up the cornmeal-mush boy and they went out of the *kiva* and out of the village.

The medicine man said to Mush Boy, "Go. Go and find the ghost giant."

Mush Boy ran up the side of the mesa to the place of the giant, but he was so small it took four days for him to go there. For four days, Father Sun shone on Mush Boy as he climbed, and the giant saw Mush Boy and caught him and put him in storage in a basket in his giant house and went to sleep. Mush Boy didn't seem like much of a threat.

But Mush Boy climbed out of the basket and went to the giant's arrow pouch. He took four arrows and the bow, and with all his magic strength, he shot the ghost giant four times. He went outside and kicked over the pot, and boiling water spilled over and ran in on the giant. Then Mush Boy ran in and melted in the boiling water, sending white corn meal through the four arrow holes into the ghost giant's heart, and killing him.

Medicine-meal Mush Boy had saved the People, and now they do a masked dance in his honor in the spring.

108 The Ya-hah-nas at Mat-Sak-Ya

AT MAT-SAK-YA VILLAGE, THERE WERE TWO GHOST-SPIRITS WHO SAW, every night, children playing and wrestling near the *kivas* [meeting places of worship]. Children should be quiet and show respect near the *kivas*.

Because life was so good and the crops were so plentiful, the parents were always busy with the crops and seeing who could harvest the most, and they ignored the teaching of the children, and the children were becoming impolite and disrespectful.

These ya-hah-nas, these spirits, were watching the children with great sadness and disapproval. They knew that when disrespect comes, other bad things come. So the ya-hah-nas went down and went to Koh-thlou-wah-la-wah and told them that the children of Mat-sak-ya were being disrespectful to the ancestors. The ya-hah-nas wanted to punish the children and show them the error of their ways. They had a dream-sleep, and they decided that the next evening they would wash up, and after they had combed their hair, they would put on human clothes and would paint their faces the way the People do to portray *katsinas* [or *kachinas*].

The ya-hah-nas looked very handsome dressed and painted like the People. The two were ready to leave and come up from the Spirit World into the *kiva*, when the leaders of the ya-hah-nas came up with some instructions, and the sacred smoke was made (which you have to make to come up from the Spirit World—you come up in the smoke). They were to leave a home-rolled cigarette and make marks on the floor with corn meal, and in that number of days [as shown by the number of corn-meal stripes], some punishment would come to any children who had been disrespectful.

The ya-hah-nas came into the *kiva* [here some details were omitted with a pause], and they climbed the ladder out into the village. When some of the rude children came by loudly arguing and wrestling when they should have been at home in bed, one of the ya-hah-nas who had a liking for children came out and called to them in a scolding but loving way, "Stop this. Show the proper respect for your ancestors." But the children thought it was just one of the men of the village and they threw dirt at the spirit, and he went back into the *kiva* sadly.

Then the children looked down into the *kiva* and saw sacred corn meal at the foot of the ladder and saw the *katsinas* in the good light inside, and they knew that these were ya-hah-nas. They ran away, and one older boy went to his father and told him what he had seen. The father frowned thoughtfully and followed the boy back to the *kiva*.

The father went down into the *kiva*. He found the home-rolled cigarette and he blessed it. By blessing it, he also blessed the ya-hah-nas, to counter any magic that the spirit had planned against the children.

After the number of days given, the ancestor-spirits were going to put their costumes on and have a dance in the *kiva*. One of the ancestors did not paint himself but rather put on a mask of black powder. They started singing the song in the *kiva*. As they sang, the elder lead-singer changed the song to a song about women, for the mother and mother's family were the ones responsible for teaching the children the traditional ways. The song sang about catching a woman. On the way out of the *kiva,* the ancestor with the black mask caught a young woman. When he touched her and let go of her, she became empowered by him.

The woman knew what was wrong in the village and how the People had failed to teach the children and how punishment would come on the children. She knelt and begged the ancestor in the black mask to put the punishment on her and not on the children. She was allowed to go into the *kiva* with the ancestors, and she went with them into the Spirit World, leaving her dead body behind in the *kiva.* The brave young woman gave herself for the People's good.

When the men of the village went down into the *kiva,* the body was there, and they knew all that had happened. The people mended their ways and taught the children respect. But if they ever forget again, the ya-hah-nas will come.

109 Ghost Train

THE LITTLE MINING TOWN OF MAYER, ARIZONA, DIDN'T THINK MUCH about a mining train thundering through town in 1893 on its way to one of the nearby smelters, but folks noticed something about this train: it passed through without an engine. The story telegraphed to mining towns as far away as Crown King and Cleator that a runaway train had rolled through Mayer. The story grew when, a few hours later, the train came back through from the opposite direction . . . Mayer sat in a basin, and the train looked as if it would just roll back and forth through town "forever"!

On its third pass through town a couple of retired railroad men jumped on the train and set the brakes. The mystery train skidded to a stop at the edge of town. All the mines and railyards were telegraphed: no one claimed the runaway train. It sat there for days; then, one morning, it was gone.

No one heard an engine, no one saw the train leave. It vanished in the night without a sound and without a trace. The story circulated around Yavapai County, until one old miner offered an explanation. Old copies of the Mayer *Daily Progress* confirmed the miner's story: in 1871 twenty-two miners had escaped the Iron King mine flood disaster by crowding onto the engine of mine train No. 22; they uncoupled the engine and steamed out just as the remaining cars sank below the black water. Twenty years before, twenty-two men rode to safety on an engine without a train—twenty-two years later old No. 22 came back to earth —a train without an engine!

110 Bloodsucker

DOWN BY THE RIO GRANDE, WE HAVE MOSQUITOS IN GREAT QUANTITY. IT all began at twilight when this horrible ghost would go up and down the Rio Grande many years ago. This ghost would come upon people who were walking up or down the river, and suck all the blood out of their bodies. It was terrible, and no one could stop it.

There was then a young Indian man who had married a beautiful woman. In the cool of the afternoon she gave birth to a beautiful baby girl. Now, the father had come from the old pueblo of Oke-Oyunke, but that place had flooded several times; the young man had built his house by the river on the east side, near the pueblo of Yunque-Yunque. The house was high above the riverbed but all alone. In this house, the girl was born, and the young man wanted to take his daughter down and show her to his family.

He started to go, but his wife said, "No. You can't go down there in the evening because of the spirit that goes up and down the river!" On the next day, the man went to get wood and did things to care for his wife. This was the time when the sisters should come. He wanted to go down to the pueblo and tell her sisters about the baby, because they were the ones who would name the baby.

But his wife didn't want him to leave her, because if he left early in the morning, he wouldn't be coming back for a long time. They waited until four days had passed, until she was healthier and the baby was strong and it was the time for the mother to go through the first cleansing ceremony. The three went down to the pueblo to do the ceremony there; they went down that day and had the ceremony.

But the young man's mother was very superstitious, and she said that until the child had been given its own name, it should sleep in the house in which it had been born. So the three left, and were walking along the river just as the sun was going down. The man and wife were quarreling about the traditions and why he had built the house so far out, and they were just about to cross the little footbridge, not seeing that it was getting to be twilight.

The man was on the bridge, and the spirit came down the riverbank like the wind and took the blood from the woman and the baby. There was nothing he could do, and the young man ran to his house filled with anger and grief. He sat there all night and asked the spirits to give him strength.

He took the sacred corn meal and rubbed it on his face, and finally he knew what to do. He spent all the next day making spears. Many very sharp spears. Then he followed the trail of blood droplets on the grass along the river until he came to a cave. This was where the spirit stayed in daylight.

He took the spears and drove their shafts in the dirt with their points inward, ringing the cave mouth. Then, at twilight, he stood across the river and called out with a wailing sound and called out the spirit-that-sucks-blood. The spirit came out like the wind.

As the spirit hit the spear points, it was cut into thousands of pieces —and each of those pieces became a mosquito. So now, when you go down to the Rio Grande, between Oke-Oyunke and Yunque-Yunque, where the Indian paintbrush grows, there are mosquitos there, and they will suck the blood right out of you!

 Joe and the Devil

YEARS AGO, ONE OF OUR HANDS, NAMED JOE, HAD A DRINKING PROBLEM. His wife always begged him not to drink hard liquor so much; she took him to church a lot, and the priest warned him that if he didn't stop drinking hard liquor, someday the Devil would come for his soul.

He had been drinking a little beer, and sometimes he would drink a little wine, but one day he got a-hold of some hard liquor and had been drinking it, and he was driving home. He rolled down the window and threw the liquor bottle out, but the wind blew the empty bottle back in and it hit him in the head. Just then he saw a black top hat in his rear-view mirror.

He was still facing front, but he was craning his neck all around looking in the rear-view mirror from every angle to see what he could see; but he couldn't see anything. He finally turned around for a quick look over his shoulder. There in the back seat was a man wearing a top hat and a tuxedo. He was driving pretty fast down the road, and he had to look back ahead, but he was craning all around trying to see who was in his back seat, in the rear-view mirror. But he couldn't see him in the mirror.

He slowed down to a crawl, and turned around in his seat. There behind him sat a man in a tuxedo, pulling long, black gloves out of the pocket of his coat, as though he was getting ready to put on his gloves and get out of the car when it stopped. The man was just about to put on the glove, and Joe saw that instead of a human hand, the man had a cloven hoof that came into view slowly as he was about to draw the second glove on.

Joe slowed the car even more, now almost to a stop, and turned back around with horror and fascination to see what the man was doing. Now he saw a woman all dressed in white seated beside the man in black; she was staring at Joe sternly and disapprovingly. The man in black now had both gloves on, and looked normal, but he, too, was staring sternly at Joe with eyes that glowed red like a fire. Joe pulled over to the side of the road, stopped the car, slid across the front seat, and threw open the passenger door.

Joe knelt at the running board with his knees in the sand and his elbows on the car and began to pray in a loud voice as fast as he could. He recited the "Hail, Mary" over and over and over. After several minutes of prayer, the rear passenger door opened, and the man stepped out into the sand. Joe saw his feet under the door. Instead of fancy dress shoes, the man had large cloven hooves. The hooves left deep imprints in the sand as he—the thing—walked away from the car and into the *bosque* [woods].

Joe stayed there and prayed for a long time after that, with his eyes closed. When he was sure he was alone and safe, he got up and drove home. He told the story to men who didn't believe him, and he offered to take them to the place and he would show them the hoofprints, which he said were still in the sand by the arroyo.

Joe never took another drink of hard liquor again.

112 The Wild White Mare

THERE'S A WEIRD GHOST STORY TOLD AT ESPAÑOLA, ABOUT THE RODEO: IT tells of Don Paulo, who would arrive the day before the rodeo in Española in July. He would have one white stallion and one white mare in his trailer. He brought them for the [wild horse] roping contest, and no one was ever able to rope them.

One roper came up from Texas, the best lasso man around, to compete in the contest, and I know the story to be true because my uncle was there! Everyone lined up [in the Spanish-style arena] to rope Don Paulo's white stallion and Don Paulo's wild white mare. The Texan joined the line-up. None of the first ropers could even come close—it was as if the rope moved away at the last moment. Then it was the Texan's turn.

The Texan rode a shiny, polished bay; his saddle was elegantly tooled, and he had a rope the likes of which no one had ever seen before. It didn't look coiled; it was a square-braided rope. He went after the mare first. He threw his lasso high into the air and it landed right around the mare's neck. As he jerked on the lasso to tighten it, the rope cut right through the mare's neck and the mare's head came right off!

But that didn't stop the ghostly mare. She jumped over the fence and galloped into the trees which are by Ranchitos, between Española and the rodeo grounds at San Juan Pueblo. And my uncle said that you can hear this ghostly wild white mare whinny at night. Right after this happened, she didn't make a sound, but through the years her whinny is getting stronger and stronger . . . because her head is growing back!

113 Stampede Mesa

IN THE STORMY AUTUMN OF 1889 A TRAIL HERD OF OVER A THOUSAND steers moved up the Blanco River [in Crosby County, Texas] and the drovers chose to let the herd overnight on level ground at the top of a mesa after watering at the Blanco. The outfit was bedded down under a threatening sky when the night guards came upon a lone cowpoke cutting out some cattle in the dark. The man claimed he was cutting out some unbranded mavericks of his own that had drifted into the outfit's passing herd.

The night guards didn't believe him, and didn't bother to check. The lone cowboy was tied up in the saddle and his horse led under a low tree on the mesa rim. A lynching rope was over the branch and the night guards ready to hang the rider when a flash of lightning and loud roll of thunder spooked the horse. In a bolt the horse and its hapless rider went over the edge and disappeared into the dark canyon below. The night guards were shaken; it wasn't supposed to have happened like this.

Deep in the darkest night, the thunder and lightning came again, and spooked the herd. The outriders tried to mill the herd to a halt, the death of the supposed rustler still on their minds. Then, in a bright flash of lightning they saw him: the ghost of the dead cowboy, white as lightning, riding bigger than life through the herd. The herd spooked again, and in a thundering stampede, a thousand cattle and the lynch-happy outriders went over the cliff in the raging storm.

No herd ever held on that mesa again survived. They were always stampeded by some unseen force. Sometimes trail riders saw the ghost of the lone, misjudged cowboy in lightning that startled their herd. Sometimes, in late evening, when the sun cut across the mesa onto low storm clouds, trail riders saw the ghost and the ghostly herd standing high as a mountain moving across the storm clouds. And sometimes they saw the murderous night guards, huge and hellish, riding with the stampeding herd across the storm clouds, damned to ride drag forever across Stampede Mesa.

114 Corpse Walkers

WHEN A PERSON DIES, HIS BODY IS AN EMPTY SHELL. IF THE BODY IS LEFT unburied, it is like an empty house that an evil spirit can enter and live among the Living People. This is why one must bury a body, and the [Buddhist] monks will bury any body that they find very quickly. But the monks do another thing with a dead body, also.

In the mountainous regions, if someone dies high on a narrow trail where the way is too steep and narrow for two men to carry the body out, and the family does not want the body buried in the high mountains, then they call the monks who are Corpse Walkers. The Corpse Walkers go up the trail to the body, and they put their spirit into it, and they come back down the trail with the corpse walking, more like hopping, stiffly along behind them. This is in Old China, but it is spoken of in America among the Chinese of California.

115 The Spirit in the Milk Shed

AN HISPANO MAN TOLD THIS STORY TO MY FRIEND, WHO TOLD IT TO ME: When I was a boy, I wanted to go to the dance. My father said that I should not go, then he ordered me not to go, but I went anyway. When I came back from the dance, my father was waiting for me on the porch of the house, with his rifle across his lap. It was late, but I had not done my chores before the dance, so he said to me, "Go milk the cow."

I said, "Well, can't I have a lantern to go out to milk the cow?" and he said, "You disobeyed me. You don't deserve a lantern. Just milk the cow in the dark." So I went out and got the cow and led her to the shed where the milking was done. When I got partway into the dark, dark shed, the cow planted her hooves, stood firm and lowered her head, and refused to go into the shed. She began to blow [to snort] as though she was angry or afraid.

I began to be afraid; I went into the shed, and saw a light above me in this small shed. I looked up, and there was a beautiful woman dressed in white hovering in the air above me.

She said, *"No tengas miedo; soy tu madre. No permito que nada te haga daño.* [Do not be afraid; I am your mother. I will not permit anything to harm you.]" When she said that, the cow relaxed, walked on into the shed, put its head into the yoke and began to eat the feed that was there. I took the pan and milked the cow. I remember distinctly the sound that each squirt of milk made against the metal of the pan.

I went back to the house, and there was my father, still angry with me for going to the dance against his orders. I brought the milk into the house, and explained to my father that the cow had not wanted to go into the shed, frightened by something. But then I had seen the spirit of my mother. She had told me not to be afraid, that she was my mother, and that she would not allow anything to happen to me.

My father embraced me, and held me very close, and wept.

He said we should return to the shed together, to see if she was still there, so that he could tell her how much he loved her, for she had died about two years before and he missed her terribly, as did I. We went out to the shed, and when we walked into the shed this time, instead of the spirit, there was hovering in midair a black catafalque, resembling the carriage body of a horse-drawn hearse, with the decorations and the black curtains but with no wheels and no team of horses.

One of the black curtains was pulled back, and my father looked in. Lying inside was the body of my mother. He told her that he missed her and that he would always love her. Then he and I walked out, and just as we were in the doorway, we looked back for one last glimpse at the catafalque, but the shed was empty.

The Holy Spirit and the Blind Man

THERE WAS ONCE A THREE-TIERED SPIRE ON THE CHURCH OF SAN MIGUEL [in Santa Fe], but a great and mysterious storm blew it down, with its great bell along with it. The spire, which had been a fairly recent addition, was not built back. The bell was left much where it had fallen and now hangs by a buffalo hide *reata* [braided rope] woven by one of the custodians of the Church about a hundred years ago. It is the oldest bell in America, cast in Andalusia [in Spain] in the year of Our Lord 1356. It bears the legend "Saint Joseph Pray For Us." It bears another legend that is told aloud.

A century ago [the bell fell in 1872], a blind man came to pray every day at noontime. While he was praying, sometimes, even though no one was present at the bellrope yet to ring it, the old bell would begin to toll. As it rang, impelled by the Spirit, the blind man could see and describe and point to the icons in the chapel. When the tolling ceased, he was blind again. Ringing the bell by its rope had no effect on his sight. Only the miraculous ringing restored his sight. And that is the story of the Holy Ghost and the blind man.

 ## Wham-Slam-Jenny-Mo-Jam

ONCE UPON A TIME, THERE WERE A LITTLE BOY AND A LITTLE GIRL WHOSE maternal grandmother was said to be a witch. People said the old witch had a magic ball that she used to hunt down children. The boy and his sister were so curious to know if what they had heard was true that they begged their mother to let them go visit the old woman. When their mother heard that the children wanted to go and spend the night with the old woman who had raised her, she became worried.

"No, my dear children," she warned, "you cannot go, for no child has ever returned from that place but me."

When the boy and his sister began to cry, the mother finally consented to let them go if they would be very careful and remember the few good magic spells she had already taught them.

They kissed their mother good-bye, and before they left the boy said, "I will put my twelve dogs in their pen, but if we are in danger, I will whistle the magic call that only they can hear. If my dogs begin to bark for no apparent reason, let them out and they will come to our rescue."

It was about noon when the children started out for their grandmother's house in the thicket, and before long, they found her working in her twisted garden. When she saw the children, she clapped her hands with glee. She asked them their names.

"I'm Jenny," said the girl.

"I'm Mo," said the boy.

She invited them to come into her yard and play with her own children, who were about the same size and age as Jenny and Mo, but whose ears were just a little too pointed and furry, and whose teeth were just a little too long and sharp.

The children played in the yard, but the old woman's children didn't know any of the right games. Meanwhile, the old woman was sharpening on her grindstone a sharp knife she had taken from her belt. Mo helped her by turning the grindstone while she sharpened the knife.

"What are you going to do with this knife?" asked Mo.

She answered, "I'm going to kill a wild hog."

She built a large fire beneath an old iron kettle and filled it with water. Soon the water was boiling and boiling. By this time the sun had set, and the old woman told all four children to eat the cornpone on the table in the house and go on upstairs and get ready for bed. She followed them and showed them which pallet to sleep on. To her own children, she gave a dark bedsheet, and to Jenny and Mo she gave a white sheet. Pretty soon her children were asleep and snoring in a grunting sort of way, and Jenny dozed off, too, but Mo was afraid to go to sleep.

The old witch told him to go to sleep, but he replied, "When I'm at home and can't sleep, my mother gives me my fiddle to play."

The old woman brought him a fiddle from off the mantlepiece. Then she sat down at the bottom of the stairs and waited with her long knife hidden beneath her apron. As Mo played the sweetest songs he knew, the old woman fell asleep. He could hear her snoring. Quietly he awoke Jenny. Together they spread the white sheet over the other children, and put things from around the room under the dark sheet to make it look like someone was asleep under it, too.

Tiptoeing past the sleeping witch, the children headed for home in the moonlight. Pretty soon the witch woke up and went to the white sheet and killed the wild children. When she lighted a candle and found she'd killed her own children, she was very angry.

Immediately she went to the cupboard and took down her glass ball. She flew to the door and down to the path. She rolled the ball down one path, but soon it came back, and she knew the children had not gone that way. Next she rolled it down the other way. When the ball did not come back, she knew that was the way the children had gone.

The children heard the magic ball rumbling along the ground and figured the witch was coming, so they climbed a catalpa tree. At the top of the tree, Mo gave the whistle for his dogs. Back at his house the dogs began to bark, and the mother came and turned them out.

Soon the witch came with an axe and began chopping down the tree.

As she chopped, she chanted, "Wham-Slam-Jenny-Mo-Jam! Wham-Slam-Jenny-Mo-Jam!"

The chips flew in all directions as the axe fell again and again. As the chips flew, Mo chanted, "Catalpa Tree, when the axe goes 'Chop!' grow big at the bottom, grow little at the top! Catalpa Tree, when the axe goes 'Chop!' grow big at the bottom, grow little at the top!"

Every time a chip fell out, another one grew back. But the witch kept chopping and chanting. It wasn't long before the twelve dogs came running toward the witch. They yelped and jumped and tried to bite her, but her long knife killed all except one last dog. He jumped at her throat and sank his teeth in and killed her. After the old witch was dead, the children came down and cut the witch's heart out and rubbed it on the noses of the dead dogs, and they all came back to life.

The children and the dogs walked home and got there just as the sun came up.

118 Booger Deer

NEAR CANTIL, CALIFORNIA, IN THE KELSO VALLEY, HUNTERS HAVE SHOT at a huge deer that bullets do not touch. He's a magnificent stag, of the like not seen in this country since the Indian days of the 1500s, and you can't kill him no matter how hard you try. You see, he's already dead.

The Booger Deer of Shepp Springs was first seen in the 1930s, larger than life. Every deer hunter covets that rack for a trophy, but bullets can't touch him. He leaves no trail of blood even when the finest marksman shoots at him. He doesn't even leave spoor.

How could he? He's a ghost.

119 Creature-in-the-Hole

BEFORE THE EUROPEANS CAME TO THIS COUNTRY, THE INDIANS SAW A great water panther in the Red River above Heber Springs. This ancient spirit-monster lives forever and has killed any number of people as sustenance. Frontiersmen, then loggers, then later hunters, were killed and eaten by the thing. Down through the years the legend persisted.

When Greer's Ferry was impounded by a dam, the last time I heard the story [about 1961], was when some friends of mine and I were in a car trying to scientifically "observe" the "dragon of the Little Red River." A drowning victim's body had not ever been found in spite of searches that year, and the monster was blamed for "pulling" the victim under and consuming the evidence. The older boys said the creature had been spotted—always using the latest technological update in legends—at or near its den, a hole or cave on an island in the river, before the dam created the lake. The supposition was that now, with the creature's lair two hundred feet below the surface of the lake, the creature would no longer be a threat.

But no! A scuba diver reported having his mask ripped off by a creature coming out of a hole—the "Creature in the Hole." Senator John McClelland had a house built on the shores, incorporating a natural cave as his boat house, with an elevator being installed in a sinkhole that connected the cave with the hillside above. The workers installing the elevator were said to have heard the creature's unearthly cries late at night, echoing up the sinkhole as if the thing were just below them in the cave.

And hungry.

If you're ever out on Greer's Ferry Lake at night at this time of year [around Hallowe'en] fishing in your boat, and you hear the distant cries of the water birds, and you see the forms moving in the shimmering water, remember this story.

 ## 120 Changing Man

My mother used to run a boarding house in Arkansas. One of our boarders was a man named Wesley Paddy. I called him Pa Paddy. He swore this story happened to him in central Arkansas around the turn of the century. There was a bandit who robbed travelers. He was tracked back to a house deep in the woods, and the sheriff and a posse surrounded the house and called for him to come out. Shots were exchanged, and in a practice common in those times, a lantern was lit and thrown in through a window.

The house caught fire as intended, and a huge black dog came running out the front door. The posse ignored it and waited for the house to burn to the ground. In the ashes, there was absolutely no sign of a corpse. Pa Paddy was in the posse and explained very calmly that the robber must have been a changing man, who could change into animal form. He told me that as the plain and simple truth.

121 Three Nephites

JESUS CHRIST CAME TO SOUTH AMERICA DURING HIS MINISTRY HERE ON earth and gathered followers just as He had in the Holy Land; three of these Nephites asked Him for the same blessing John the Beloved had, that is, that they would not pass away until He had come into his Kingdom. The Nephites broke away from their sinful brothers, the lazy and quarrelsome Lamanites, and the Three Nephites are still seen in North America around Utah.

One lady picked up a hitchhiker near here [Ogden, Utah], and while he was riding—in the back seat—he warned her to set aside enough food and supplies to last for two years, because there was to be—is to be —a time of trouble, and she should be prepared. When she tried to ask him questions, he didn't answer. When she looked in the rear-view mirror, she couldn't see him. When she turned around, he was gone!

122 Killer-of-the-Alien-Gods

THE DINEH HERO KILLER-OF-THE-ALIEN-GODS [WHO ALONG WITH HIS brother had killed Yeitso and other Evil Giants and cut off their heads and left them as landmarks at Tshotshihl, to become *el Cabezón* and the smaller hummocks near Mount San Mateo] went out to find another evil demon he had heard of. A ghoul named He-Who-Kicks-People-Down-Cliffs lived on a trail on Gray Mesa, and Killer-of-the-Alien-Gods heard of him and set out to find him and kill him.

The Hero walked along a trail, and where the trail grew narrow, he saw an ugly old man reclining on a rock just above the trail, seeming to be asleep. The old man seemed harmless, and as the Hero started to walk past below him on the narrow part of the trail, the old man suddenly kicked one leg out at him. The Hero stepped back, dodging the kick.

"Old One," said the Hero, "why did you kick at me?"

"My son," said the ugly man, "I did not kick at you. I only stretched my leg out as I turned to sun myself."

The Hero Killer-of-the-Alien-Gods started again to pass the old man on the narrow part of the trail. Again the old man kicked at him, but he dodged the kick and stepped back. A third and fourth time the Hero tried to pass and the old one kicked at him. The Hero knew that this was the demon he had sought.

The Hero took out his stone knife and killed the demon with a blow to the forehead, but the body did not fall from its resting place on the rock even though the demon was dead and the rock face was steep. The Hero looked under the body; the demon's long hair grew into the rock face like roots.

The Hero cut the demon's hair and the corpse slid off the rock face, off the trail, and down the cliff face out of sight below. At once the Hero heard snarling and growling and quarreling below. When he went ahead on the trail, he found that it led to nowhere.

Killer-of-the-Alien-Gods went back the way he came, past the rock face with the hair-roots, hearing the sounds of animals feeding below him, to another trail that led down the cliff face to the valley floor. There he saw twelve ugly children of the demon, devouring their father's corpse. "This would have been my body they ate of," thought the Killer-of-the-Alien-Gods, "if he had kicked me down the cliff."

The Hero took his knife and killed eleven of the ugly children, whose mouths were dripping with the gore and blood of their father, but one child ran swiftly away up into the rocks. Killer-of-the-Alien-Gods chased the ghoul-child to the top of the rocks, but when he looked upon the ghoul-child, he said, "You ran from me so swiftly that I chased you, thinking you might be a creature worthy of killing. Now I see that you are just an ugly eater of dead flesh like your brothers. I will let you live." And he went away.

The People were never again troubled by alien gods, and the one ghoul-child lived on the rocks and became the father of the carrion birds that live on the mesa rim today.

123 White Riders

ALONG THE GILA RIVER IN ARIZONA, THEY TELL THE STORY OF TWO ranchhands traveling along the Diablo Trail who got caught in a two-day sandstorm. They holed up in an outcropping of rock beside a dry water hole. By the second day, their horses had dropped over dead and were covered with sand, their food was gone, and they'd been out of water for a solid day.

Gradually, the storm grew quiet, though the two cowpokes couldn't see any letup in the wind and sand. Then, out of the distant wall of sand came a lone rider, dressed in white, on a white horse. Behind him came a long line of riders, single file, twelve of them, dressed in pure white.

Their spurs and belt buckles were silver, the bits and snaffles and curb chains were silver. Their boots were white cowhide; their shirts and trousers were white linen; their hats were white fur felt. They rode in slow, leading a thirteenth white horse.

Two of the white riders got down and lifted one of the stranded ranchhands up from the sand and helped him onto the riderless horse. The other fellow called to them through his dry throat and begged them to take him, too.

As the line of riders disappeared back into the storm, the last rider turned and smiled at the cowpoke left behind. "Sorry," he said, "it's just not your time yet."

The other hand passed out from thirst; when he woke up, he was back at the ranch. His bunkmates had found him still alive after the storm died, but his partner was dead in the sand.

124 Hopi Bones

I ONCE WORKED FOR THE MUSEUM OF NORTHERN ARIZONA, FOUNDED BY Dr. Colton and his wife. One of Dr. Colton's informants was a Hopi who was a member of the Masau Clan. Bloody-faced Masau is the god who has given the Hopi permission to live in this world; his visage is a partially-decomposed face, and members of his clan have as their special privilege the ability to talk with the dead.

There is an area of the old part of the museum where the physical anthropology collection is housed. [The Hopi informant] told me not to go there at night. The spirits of the dead who were evil return to those bones at night—especially, I believe, in October. At night, he says, you can feel the presence of many spirits and hear them converse. It is best not to go in there at all, but if you do go in, you should offer apologies and an offering of cornmeal or pollen.

125 Monster of the Mogollón Rim

BEFORE THE TURN OF THE CENTURY, SOME MINERS WENT OUT ON THE Mogollón Rim searching for gold. Knowing that miners going into the Superstition Mountains to the south often did not return, these men were watchful of any Indians, fearing an attack. The miners came upon women and children at a waterhole and killed them all to keep them from reporting the miners' whereabouts and number. One miner was a lazy thief who bummed off his friends, and he stole from the dead bodies.

The brothers and fathers of the dead women and children scouted along the Mogollón Rim until they caught up to the miners. They killed the miners, and the miner who was carrying things stolen from the women he had killed was hung up by his hands and skinned. The Indian men left him for dead, but he did not die. As he hung there from a ledge, he stretched and stretched until the rope broke and he fell to the ground.

Now he walks the Rim at night. He is eight feet tall and has no skin. He's still looking for gold, and he "gets" any Boy Scouts that wander away from their camp and kills them for the gold and silver fillings in their teeth.

ossessed By Spirits
(Including Stories of People Driven by the Sight of Ghosts)

126   Mary Calhoun

ONCE THERE CAME FROM IRELAND A FAMILY BY THE NAME OF CALHOUN. The eldest child was the daughter Mary, the apple of her father's eye. And one day, passing through the graveyard on the top of hills near their house, the father of the family stopped to rest on a sarcophagus and watch the sun go down. When he got up and walked on, the old man was so refreshed that he forgot his walking stick.

At the house, where the supper table was all but laid, he mentioned his walking stick, and Mary said she'd go back and get it and be to the house again in a shake. Out the door she went, before anyone could stop her.

Entering the graveyard, she walked toward the sarcophagus her father had mentioned, and there she found the walking stick leaning up against a stone. She bent down to pick it up, and noticed in the moonlight an old, broken-down grave at her feet.

It was an old grave, and it been dug shallow, as if those who dug it were in haste or as if there was no family to re-mound the grave when the coffin inevitably collapsed and the grave caved in. As she stood there, staring fixedly at the cracks in the ground, a bony white hand reached up out of the grave and grasped the hem of her dress.

She started to let out a scream, but she found she could not. Out came another hand, and grabbed her dress higher up. And slowly, something very, very old and dead climbed up her garment until it sat on her shoulders.

"Walk," said the Thing in a voice like wind in dry autumn leaves.

And Mary Calhoun walked, against her will, held in thrall by the power of the Thing. Down the lane they went, towards the houses along the path beyond the fallow field. The Thing on her shoulders was light, like husks at shocking time, but it was also heavy, with the weight of unspeakable evil buried in the cold earth for a century or more.

"I'm hungry," said the Thing, "for I've not et in many a year."

"Turn in here," said the Thing at the first house. Then, "No, turn away! There's holy water in this house!"

At the next house, "Turn in here." Then, "No, turn away! There's holy water here, on garments blessed at Mass!"

At the third house, "Turn in here . . . Go in, for there's no holy water in this house."

Inside, Mary found that all the family, neighbors whom she knew well, were fast in bed. Somehow time had flown for them but crawled for her as she had stared at that broken-down grave.

"Go to kitchen." She went, all unwilling.

"Get a knife and a bowl." She got as she was bidden.

"Upstairs." She went up, with the Thing a-riding her shoulders. In the loft slept the three fine sons of the family, Mary's childhood playmates. "Cut their throats!" And with trembling hands and tears in her eyes, Mary cut the boys' throats.

When the first drop of blood fell into the bowl, each boy stirred. With the second drop, each boy grew cold and still. With the third drop, each boy was ashen and dead. Mary took the blood in the bowl and returned to the kitchen.

"Make gruel," said the Thing, and she did. When the water was boiled, and oatmeal and the blood poured in, the Thing commanded, "Serve us."

Mary took two bowls and spoons from the cupboard, and napkins from the dry sink, and the bowl of bloodied oatmeal from the stove, and set the table.

"Now, take a morsel," the Thing bade her. Mary's hand shook as she lifted a spoonful of the horrid gruel toward her mouth; her hand shook so violently that she dropped the bite into her kerchief at her neck, where it could not be seen. The spoon went on up to her lips. Her jaws worked and her throat swallowed, all against her will.

"Now that you've et in the house of the Dead, you're one of us." The Thing climbed slowly down and sat at table, unaware that Mary had not eaten the morsel. When it let go of her garment, its power over her faded away, but Mary was a clever lass, and sat down stiffly and pretended to eat as if the spell still held her.

As the Thing slavered and drooled and ate away at the bowl of gruel, Mary lifted spoonful after spoonful towards her mouth, and when the Thing was not looking, she dropped each bite into the folds of the kerchief at her breast. When both their bowls were empty, the Thing stood up and said, "We'll leave now."

"I'll take up first," said Mary, and she took the bowls, the serving bowl, the spoons and the napkins to the dry sink in the kitchen. She took off her kerchief, folded it over the gruel, and set it in the sink. When she returned to the parlor, the Thing climbed her dress again, and sat on her shoulders. The powerful spell returned and Mary did as it bade her.

"Back to the graveyard!" And they went out onto the path and past the houses towards the fallow land.

"Now you're one of us, you can know what the Dead know," the Thing said. "That gruel made you one of us, but if any had been left and fed to those dead boys, why, they'd rise up alive again."

A little further along the Thing said, all chatty-like, "That cairn of stones there: under it I hid all my gold—ill-gotten in life, but little good it did me."

Back in the graveyard, Mary saw the sun was about to rise. Time had flown again as they ate their gruesome meal. The Thing climbed down, and Mary felt the spell fading away.

"Come down, Mary Calhoun, into your new home."

"I'll not come down," Mary cried, "for I've et none of your hideous gruel!"

The Thing let out a terrible oath and started to climb back out of its grave and clutch at her dress. The sun rose over the hill and sunlight struck the Thing. Mary grabbed her father's walking stick and struck the Thing. It flew into a thousand sparkling shards like husk or vellum, and the sun rose over the graveyard. Mary took her father's walking stick and started home.

She turned in at the third house, where the family was awake and wailing their sons' fate. Mary went in and spoke with the father. "There's fever hereabouts, perhaps they've only swooned."

"Ah, you're daft, Mary Calhoun," said the father of the boys, "I know dead when I see it!" Still and all, he let Mary go to the kitchen, where she got a bowl of water and her kerchief, as if to mop the boys' fevered brows. Upstairs, she fed them the oatmeal. With the first morsel, each boy stirred. With the second bite, each boy blinked and awoke, and with the third bite each boy sat up and yawned or stretched and said, "What terrible nightmares I've had."

Mary Calhoun lived a long and comfortable life, and she came into some money later on, after she'd saved for years and bought the fallow land beside the graveyard. But throughout her life, no matter who died, rich or poor, great or small, her friend or not, she never went to the burial. In fact, she never, ever, went into that graveyard again.

127 The Possessed Girl at McKinney

WHEN I WAS A BOY, THE YOUNGEST OF THREE SONS, WE LIVED NEAR Celina, Texas, not far from the larger and better-known town of McKinney. There, when I was a teenager, the McKinney newspapers said that a young woman had become possessed by an evil spirit. The whole county was soon talking about it. In the dark of night, dried beans flew around the room where the girl was. Things flew through the air and clattered off the walls. The girl lay in bed and moaned and thrashed at times. In daylight hours, or when the lamps were lit, the spirit manifested itself in other ways.

The gossip said that three old women called sisters, all dressed in black, had come from the local spiritualist group to "assist" the family in its time of need. The sisters began to hold séances, and in the daytime, or if the room was lit, the sisters would call upon the spirit to knock on the table, on a wall, or on some other piece of wood. We knew two young men who had been to see the possessed girl, as half the population of the county must have done, and they told us all about trying to debunk the spirit knocking.

These two boys claimed to have tried two different ways to get at the truth or falsehood of the event. On their visit, while a séance was being held in the sitting room of the house, one of the boys went down under the house, where the floor joists sat up two feet off the ground on rock pillars, and crawled around looking for signs of fraud. He found nothing but cobwebs. Later, up inside the house itself, during the same séance, one cousin tried to trick the "sisters." He asked them to call upon the "spirit" to knock inside a solid wood door, thinking that would be impossible to fake. He stood at the half-open door, and touched it lightly from both sides with the tips of all ten fingers. Sure enough, when the "sisters" called for it, he jumped away from the door and claimed to have felt the knocking—which everyone in the room had heard—inside the door!

My brothers and I and all the boys in our town sat endless hours in the shade of a tree or porch, telling and retelling all we had heard about the possessed girl and speculating about the "spirit" and what-all it could and could not do. Finally, we determined that we would all go to McKinney ourselves and prove or disprove this supernatural event once and for all.

Unfortunately, none of us had a car.

For almost a week we worked on Fred, an older boy with a Model-T Ford, trying to convince him to take us to McKinney to see this possessed girl. Unfortunately, Fred was somewhat easily alarmed, to put it mildly, and he wanted no part of the whole adventure. After long hours of cajoling and pleading, collecting nickels to buy his gasoline for the trip, and promising like a bunch of Tom Sawyers to do all manner of favors for him, Fred's sissiness was overcome by his basic greed. The trip was on!

The appointed time and day came, after dark. This was dictated by the fact that the possessed girl got "wound up" more after dark, and the dried bean crop took to the air with the lamps blown out, and by the even more crucial fact that Fred worked by day. My brothers and I and more local teenaged boys than wisdom would allow piled into the Model T and began the trek across dirt roads to McKinney. Being the youngest of the crowd, I was squashed over against the side wall with no door, with about half my anatomy hanging outside the car. It was awkward, but the night breeze was pleasant.

With the darkness deepening around us, we began to talk about the possessed girl and the "sisters" and the knocking and the séances and the beans. We were equally divided into two camps: one camp averred that anyone could throw dried beans in the dark, and in fact, some of them had done it before; the other camp retaliated with the inexplicable knocking.

"I'll bet that old spirit could knock anywhere it wanted," said one of the town boys. "I'll bet he could even knock right here in this motor-car!"

Well, at that point the temptation was too great.

With the half of my anatomy that was hanging out of the car, I knocked on the side wall three . . . loud . . . knocks.

The reaction ranged from yelps to laughter, but the worst possible thing happened. Fred went white as a bedsheet, grabbed the brake and threw it on, skidded the car to a stop, and headed back toward Celina. No amount of explanation, pleading, or apologizing would make him go to McKinney, that or any other night.

Well, I was a worse outcast than a leper for days after that, and my brothers and I secretly plotted revenge on the sissy.

There was a blacksmith in town, a great greasy man with a bad reputation. Dad had told us not to hang around the blacksmith shop, so we spent as much time there as possible. We were dawdling around the shop and the shed he lived in, generally getting in his way, when we discovered something remarkable. He was resting on a dirty old mattress while we were boring him with talk; suddenly he yawned and dug his huge hands into the mattress in a finger-flexing grip.

To our amazement, the foot of the mattress curled upward from the sheer strength of his grip. As he gathered a handful of mattress where his hands rested near his waist, the whole mattress buckled and the end turned up.

Well, in no time at all, we had talked the smith into helping us. We covered him with a ragged blanket and someone ran to get Fred and tell him the blacksmith was possessed by the same spirit as the girl at McKinney. Sure enough, Fred came to the shed, along with several other boys. Curiosity had gotten the best of him.

As we gathered around the bed, the smith played along wonderfully.

"Oh, boys," he moaned, "That old spirit's got me!"

At that, under the blanket, he dug his enormous hands into the ticking and gripped for all he was worth. The whole foot end of the bed

—blacksmith, blanket, and mattress—began to quiver and rise as if lifted by some invisible force.

Fred screamed and ran; we didn't see him for two weeks.

128 Ghost of Vengeance

THE OLD PEOPLE TELL THIS TO FRIGHTEN AND WARN THE YOUNG PEOPLE:
From Yotsuya, in Tokyo, came a samurai warrior who married a beautiful lady named Oiwa. She was very faithful and attentive to him and only called him "Husband," in the old style, instead of by his name. So I do not know his name, but her name everyone from Japan knows. Her name was Oiwa.

Oiwa and Otto-san were very happy together at first, but with time the warrior's eyes began to fall on other women. He was especially pleased to meet Matsue, a younger woman from a great family. He began to resent Oiwa and plotted to free himself to marry Matsue. As he and Oiwa were walking home from a great banquet on the darkest night of the month, he pushed Oiwa over the cliffs into the bay.

At dawn, he and his friends combed the beach below and found the broken body of Oiwa with her face crushed and her hair full of seaweed. He claimed her fall was an accident. After the funeral, the warrior slept alone on the mat in his empty house, glad to be free of Oiwa, dreaming of Matsue.

Outside the wind blew, and the sliding paper walls of the room shook. Slowly, in the moonlight, one wall-door slid open. There stood Oiwa. Her long hair, so neatly arranged in life, hung loose about her shoulders; her beautiful kimono was gone; she wore a long white robe. Her face was ugly and dirty. Some of her teeth were missing. One eye hung out of its socket. Her arms were bony, like an old woman's. Her hands were like claws.

She said one word to Otto-san: "Vengeance."

The warrior screamed and ran from the house. The next night he slept in an abandoned house nearby, hoping the ghost could not find him. He awoke with a start at midnight. The single paper lantern he had left burning hung above his mat. Vines of ivy grew through a break in the wall. Slowly the vines began to writhe like snakes, and moved into the shape of Oiwa's body. The wind blew through a crack and the paper lantern swung. The candle inside guttered and the paper caught fire. The burned places on the lantern looked like eyes. The bottom of the burning lantern dropped away partially and flapped like a jaw talking, and two holes burned like eyes looked at the warrior.

"Vengeance," said the lantern.

The vines reached up at the warrior. The warrior cut his way through the vines with his sword and ran down the road screaming.

The next day at an inn, the warrior sat with two friends drinking tea. The steam was rising from the teapot. The steam became the shape of Oiwa. The two friends rose and drew their swords and tried to kill the warrior. When he shouted at them, "Why are you doing this?" it was Oiwa's voice that answered from their mouths.

"Vengeance."

The warrior ran out of the inn and looked back. The ghost of Oiwa was there. Her body stood at the doorway to the inn, and her neck grew longer and longer, so that her head followed him down the road. He drew his sword and cut off the head. It fell to the ground like a melon, then lay there and laughed at him.

The warrior prepared to marry Matsue. He persuaded her family to come and see his house and see how finely Matsue would live after they were married. When he and Matsue were alone in one room with Matsue behind a screen, Oiwa came and spoke to him. Matsue heard the woman's voice and thought that the warrior was seeing another woman. Matsue did not look out from behind the screen. Oiwa became more and more beautiful. Her eye went back into her socket. Her broken teeth were restored, her hair was combed and neatly pinned up. She looked younger and younger. She came to Otto-san and she whispered in his ear.

"Vengeance," she whispered.

Matsue began not to trust the warrior and became jealous. He begged her to forgive him and marry him. He held a great feast for their intended engagement. All his friends and relatives came. Oiwa came, too.

The ghost came into the feast room and stood in the corner. The warrior tried to distract everyone with loud boasting and laughter; he did not know that only he could see her. Slowly, Oiwa's face began to grow larger and larger, filling the room. The warrior stumbled back out of its way, knocking over a table and tea service. His friends thought he was drunk. They could not see the hideous head with its loose eyeball and broken teeth, its seaweed-tangled hair and rotten skin, filling up the room.

The warrior began to rant and rave. He drew his sword and swung it at the head. His friends thought he was trying to kill them. They overpowered him and left in disgust. Matsue ran from the place, ashamed and frightened. All the guests laughed in scorn and disgust. Oiwa laughed, too.

The night was dark, as before. The moon was dark, as before. The warrior and Oiwa walked the path above the bay, as before. It was too late for regret or repentance; it was time for insanity and death.

"Vengeance," said the skull-face of the corpse.

The samurai warrior stepped off the cliff and was gone.

Oiwa was gone, too.

129 The Legend of Vivia

THERE IS A STRANGE GRAVE MARKER IN THE CEMETERY WHERE MY FATHER IS buried, in Fort Gibson, Oklahoma. In the Circle of Honor, there is the grave of the only woman ever to serve as a man in the cavalry.

Vivia Thomas had fallen in love with a young man back East, where they both lived. When he joined the Army and was sent west to Indian Territory, she followed him secretly, suspecting that he would not be faithful to her.

She dressed as a fair young man and enlisted in the same fort as her lover. No one recognized her as a woman, and he didn't recognize her since he would never have expected to see her there. She secretly followed him, and sure enough, she found that he was spending time at night in the home of a local girl even though he had been engaged to Vivia when he went West. She became enraged with a desire for revenge.

On a December night in 1869, she waited by the road near the local girl's home, and as her former lover rode by, she shot him with a rifle. Because the local girl was an Indian, the Army assumed that the Indians had killed the lieutenant to keep him away from the local girl.

No one would have ever suspected, except for the fact that Vivia began to see the dead lieutenant's ghost, visiting her each night, filling her with grief and remorse. She confessed the killing to a chaplain, and began to go nightly to sit at her dead lover's grave and cry. She froze to death on January 7, 1870, a victim of the bitter cold, of bitter remorse, and of the visitations of the ghost of her former lover, murdered by her own hand.

130 Hand of Time

YEARS AGO, MY FAMILY AND I LIVED IN PRESCOTT [ARIZONA] AND I worked at the Yavapai County fairground. I drove a blade grader between the horse barns whenever it got muddy or churned up. When the ground firmed up some, I bladed it smooth again. The fairground sits on an ancient Indian burial ground; pottery shards and arrowheads have been found there for over a century.

One February, after a three-inch snow had melted, I began to blade when something caught my eye: a piece of pottery with black-and-white designs, upright and intact in the mud.

I climbed off the grader and dug up with my bare hands three pots, a perfect spearhead, and a piece of basalt rock. When I touched a human jawbone with teeth, a chill went through me, and I filled the hole back in.

At home, I soaked the muddy artifacts in a basin. The next morning, I was stunned to see the water in the basin blood red in color. As the water drained out, I found red pigment in one bowl and ash-white in another. The artifacts were put on display on a shelf in the den, to show to friends when they came over.

Within a week, I was laid off from my job and my wife began to have nightmares. In a month, the car was repossessed. Our family life took a turn for the worse. My wife blamed the artifacts, but I didn't believe her. Finally, she said either the artifacts had to go or she would have to go to get away from them.

Late on a Tuesday night, I climbed the fence to the fairground, crept back between the barns with a hand-spade, and dug a hole near where I had been before. I buried the artifacts deep in the earth.

As I drove away from the fairground and stopped for a red light, my old boss pulled up beside me and said that the board of directors had come up with some money and would I like my old job back.

We got caught up on our bills, and everything went back to normal in our lives, untouched by the hand of time.

One night that May, we put our daughter to bed, but she came walking into the den a few hours later, crying.

"What's the matter," I asked, "are you sick?"

"My friend went away," she said, shaking her head.

"All your friends are still here," I said. "Nobody's moved away."

"No," she said, "the old man is gone."

"What old man?" I asked.

"The old Indian man. His face was painted red and white. He used to sit at the end of the bed and sing to me."

I hadn't an answer for that. Only goosebumps.

 ## The Legend of Polly

In 1867, Ephraim Polly came to Fort Hays, Kansas, with his wife Elizabeth. There was a great cholera epidemic, and Elizabeth worked to help the sick and dying. She finally took the fever and died. She was buried in a lonely grave on the prairie.

Years later, a woman in old-fashioned clothing was seen walking among the outbuildings and empty barns near the gravesite. She was dressed in a plain light blue dress. No one knew who she was, and no one ever got near her. She would go around a corner and just vanish.

Some people called the woman "Polly," but that was her last name. It's Elizabeth, Elizabeth Polly, still tending the sick and dying, who alone can see her spirit.

132 La Llorona at Yuma

THERE WERE MEN COMING IN FROM SPAIN WHO MARRIED INDIAN WOMEN in Mexico. And at that time there was a Spanish soldier who married an Indian girl by common-law. They were very much in love and had two children. And at that time if you were married by common-law you couldn't have any inheritance or rights to good jobs. You had to be married to a Spanish woman. So, he legally married a Spanish woman who came by ship from Spain. The Indian woman became angry, bitter, and jealous over the man having left her. She became temporarily insane, and she drowned her two children to get revenge. Later she came to her senses and regretted that she had drowned them. She then actually became insane after realizing what she did. She was cursed to forever roam Mexico where there was a body of water to look for her children. And because of the sadness she wails a long sad cry. And to this day people say you can hear her wail, looking for her children. She is cursed to do this forever for what she did.

[The motif of passing into, out of, and back into insanity makes this variant unusual, and resembles the plotline of stories about insanity caused by the vision of the ghosts of the victims.]

*L*ifestyles of the Dead and Famous

133 Lafffite's Treasure at LaPorte

ONCE THERE STOOD IN THE TOWN OF LAPORTE AN OLD HOUSE HAUNTED by the ghost of Jean Laffite. The house sat facing Trinity Bay, which opens into the Gulf of Mexico at Galveston Island in Texas. More than once, someone tried to seek shelter in the old abandoned structure. Each one was awakened in the middle of the night, usually during a wind storm, by a ghostly figure that hovered near his sleeping place.

It is Laffite, the pirate of the Gulf, the lord of Galveston, dressed in a red coat and breeches. It points to the place beneath the floor where, in life, it buried treasure long before the house was built.

"Take the treasure. It is mine to give you. I earned it with the forfeiture of my immortal soul."

The ghost fixes the traveller with its sad gaze.

"But the money must all be spent in charity. Not one penny may you spend in evil or in selfishness. What was taken in selfishness and evil must be spent for good."

The ghost vanishes in the sudden light of a lightning flash in the storm outside. The traveller seldom sleeps again that night. And no one has ever touched the treasure, Laffite's treasure at LaPorte.

134 Petit Jean

HIGH ABOVE THE ARKANSAS RIVER STANDS PETIT JEAN MOUNTAIN. ON its southeast overlook is a tiny grave surrounded by a rusting iron fence. People who live in the valley below often see lights hovering around the grave late, late at night. Some say it's just kids or tourists; the rest know it's what the Indians saw for years before the valley was settled. It's the ghost of Petit Jean.

When the French explorer Cheves set sail from France to come to the New World, he left behind his fiancée, Adrienne, in the town of Calais. Just before he sailed, a new cabin boy signed on, a youth with a lovely face. The boy followed the troupe up the Mississippi and up the Arkansas. When the explorers reached the escarpment above the present town of Morrilton, they stopped.

A little settlement was built with log houses, and the friendly Indians of the area were fascinated with the mysterious boy. They saw in him features of both man and woman, and considered this to be a sign of spiritual gifts. His name was Jean, called "Little."

When Cheves announced that he would return to France and bring his fiancée back to this pleasant land, the cabin boy asked to go, too. When Cheves refused, the lad fell very ill. The Indians cared for the lad and learned the strange truth. They told Cheves that the cabin boy was Adrienne, who had followed him in disguise.

Cheves rushed to her side, but she died in his arms, telling him that she loved him and this place and these Indian people. She was buried atop the escarpment, and her ghost walks the cliff edge still as the beautiful Little John—our Petit Jean.

135 Marie Laveau

THEY WHO BELIEVE IN VOUDOU COME TO THE ST. LOUIS CEMETERY ON moonless nights, and by candlelight, they see the ghost of Marie Laveau passing forth and back between the Two Worlds, carrying blessing or curse to those who believe or do not believe.

In life, she danced in Congo Square and sold potions and charms from the house at 1020 Ste. Anne Street. They see her ghost there, too. She comes all dressed in white, sometimes with a snake for a necklace.

She was killed in the hurricane of 1890, but she was reborn from her open grave before it could be closed. Then she lived long years and died again. She is a good ghost to those who believe.

136 Kit Carson's Ghost

KIT CARSON'S WIFE AND GOVERNOR BENT'S WIFE WERE SISTERS. THE Carson home sits about two hundred yards from the Bents' home. Both are now museums. Both families named a daughter Maria. Both houses are said to be haunted.

Kit Carson's wife was a very pretty lady. Most of the Hispanic women here in Taos were very short of stature. All of my family [the receptionist's] are of short stature, and we were some of the first settlers to come to Taos directly from Spain, following the Old Santa Fe Trail. My family settled in a district that is now designated a historic district; my great-grandfather donated the land that the Chapel of St. Anthony now stands on and got permission from the king of Spain to dedicate the chapel to St. Anthony.

Much of Taos is the same today as it was in Kit Carson's time, and his house here is very well-preserved. It started out with just the three rooms facing the road; then they built these rooms back here for their children. The descendants come around to visit the museum, but the ancestors are here, too. Kit Carson is still here, his spirit. He's in the house. If you are sentimental, or nostalgic, or whatever you want to call it, you can feel his presence. I do.

It's a good feeling, because I've never been afraid of his ghost; I've never been afraid.

 ## The Ghostly Mob

GOVERNOR BENT OF TAOS WAS KILLED JANUARY 18, 1847. AN ANGRY mob had gathered around his residence just off the Plaza to protest American rule, enforced in the Mexican War. Governor Bent went out bravely and tried to reason with them. They shot him with bullets, shot him with arrows. Indian men came forward and scalped him.

Inside, his family escaped by burrowing through the two-foot-thick adobe walls into the house next door, and the neighbors let them go out a back door.

The men who killed Bent were eventually caught, tried, and hanged. It's not Bent that haunts the house, it's the ghostly mob, the ghosts of the hanged men, that come back and can be faintly seen or heard at night some still nights.

138 Father Juan Padilla's Coffin

FATHER JUAN PADILLA SERVED THE MISSION AT LAGUNA PUEBLO IN 1733. He was murdered, some say by a Spaniard, others say by Indians who had renounced Christianity. He was buried beneath the floor of the church at Isleta Pueblo where his horse had carried the murdered priest. His spirit, indeed his very body, did not rest in the grave. The coffin in which he was buried, hollowed from a cottonwood log, rose back out of the earth in front of the altar and was reburied.

It rose again, almost twenty years later, in response to the prayers of the Indian believers in time of famine or epidemic, or in response to Indian dances, which are also prayers, held inside the church. An investigation was held in 1819, and another one after the coffin rose in 1889, after a *Noche Buena* [Christmas Eve] dance. Ordered by the bishops at Santa Fe, the investigations never found an explanation for the periodic reappearance of the coffin and its ghostly contents.

The coffin rose for the last known time Christmas Eve in 1914, as the world went to war.

Geologists suggest that shifting sand in the soil accounts for the coffin rising. The inhabitants know better. It is the ghost of Father Padilla, who does not rest well, returning to the world of those awake.

139 Howling Ghosts of Goliad

GENERAL SANTA ANA [THE MEXICAN DICTATOR] WAS CAPTURED AFTER THE battle of San Jacinto [Texas] and taken to Velasco at the mouth of the Brazos River. He was needed alive to enforce the treaty he had signed. [If he were executed in Texas, a subsequent Mexican ruler might renounce the treaty.] To protect Santa Ana from Texans seeking vengeance for [the massacre at] Goliad, he was imprisoned at the Patton Plantation (later the Hogg Plantation) near old Columbia, the first capital of the Republic of Texas.

Later, to prevent discovery by loyalists or escape attempts by Santa Ana himself, he was moved to Orozimbo Plantation until December of 1836. Despite the move and attempts at total secrecy, Mexican loyalists living in Texas found out and crept toward Orozimbo by night to attempt a rescue of their President. They were driven away in fear by the unearthly baying of hounds in the trees near the plantation. The loyalists fled and never returned.

This alone would not prove strange, but Orozimbo had no dogs. Nor were there any strays known to be in the trees at the time of the rescue attempt.

Guards at Orozimbo who heard the howling had an explanation: The baying was not hounds, but the hellish cry of ghosts—the ghosts of the victims of the Goliad massacre.

Only very rarely, and not at all in the last few decades, visitors to Orozimbo claim to have heard the howls.

The howling of the ghosts from Goliad.

140 The Ghost at Chrétienne Point

CHRÉTIENNE POINT MANSION IN LOUISIANA WAS THE INSPIRATION FOR THE interior sets of Tara in *Gone With The Wind*. In fact, the grand staircase at Chrétienne Point is copied exactly in the scene where Rhett carries Scarlet up the steps, but the scene is reversed, with the windows on the opposite side from where they really are. The story goes that the set designer took a picture at Chrétienne Point and the negative was printed backwards.

Madame Chrétienne was a wild woman, long ago. She had lived with her husband's gambling all their married life, and after he was killed over a gambling disagreement, she turned into the wildest woman of her day. She gambled, smoked, drank, and carried on in a way unknown among ladies at the time. She turned her mansion into a gaming house and would join the men with a drink and a box of cigars, and sit and gamble all night. Her Negro servant would pass among the guests serving drinks, and he gave her winks and nods that told her what her opponents held during the card games.

Jean Laffite and his crew were good friends of Madame Chrétienne and would often come to drink and gamble at the Point. After Laffite's death, his men became renegades and turned from organized privateering to plain burglary. They came one night and tried to break in to the Point, but the house was well locked after closing time. They knew she was quite rich, and where the wealth was kept, so they broke down the door.

Hearing them outside the mansion, Madame Chrétienne had gathered all her belongings—her money, her jewelry, her gold, everything she had that was of value. She had thrown it into her long dress and held it up from the hem making her dress a long bag. She was in the act of escaping, with her dress up and her hoops showing, when the doorframe gave way and a pirate entered the front hall and stopped her at the head of the grand staircase.

"Stop, Madame," he called out, aiming his single-shot pistol at her, "and throw down the money you have in your dress!"

She stood up proudly and dropped the front of her dress. Money, jewels, and gold cascaded down the grand staircase, tumbling and rolling toward the astounded pirate.

As he dropped to his knees to grab the first coins to reach the hardwood floor, she drew her small hidden pistol and said, "Excuse me . . ."

When he looked up, she shot him square between the eyes. His blood stained the stairs and cannot be scrubbed away. If there were others with the pirate, they fled at the sound of gunfire. Madame Chrétienne stuffed the body into a closet and left it three days until the sheriff could be reached.

Today, the ghost of Madame Chrétienne walks the mansion, and one can hear the pistol shot, the fatal blow to the skull as the ball strikes the pirate, and the sound of the pirate's body striking the floor or rolling loudly down the bottommost steps.

Those who manage the mansion today do not relate the final point of the legend: not only will the pirate's bloodstains not scrub away, but when the ghost of the Madame walks by night, the bloodstains again reliquify. The steps are now carpeted, but those who know the whole legend say that the blood boils up even underneath the carpet.

141 The Ghost of Lunt Mansion

I WORK AT A RESTAURANT IN ST. LOUIS THAT WAS ONCE LISTED BY *LIFE* Magazine as being one of the three most haunted houses in the United States. It's the famous Lunt Mansion.

There were four suicides in the mansion in its heyday, and that's the source of the ghostly happenings there. My mother works in the kitchen and she has many times heard someone calling her name when she was all alone in the kitchen, and no one outside the kitchen said they had called her.

The most spectacular suicide, as I recall, was in 1949, when Charles Lunt led the family dog to the upstairs attic landing and shot it and then himself. When television crews came in one time, I'm told, the only sound they could get on tape was the barking of the ghost dog.

Mother also says that sometimes pans will rattle by themselves. She can be looking directly at them, and they shake on their hooks and rattle and almost fall from the rack.

The mansion originally belonged to the Falstaff Brewery owners and is just up the street from the Budweiser Beer family mansion. The recent owner of the restaurant stayed at the home one night after some vandalism had been done. He heard a large commotion, and he began to work his way through the mansion looking for a source of noise. All the doors were locked from the inside, but the doors inside the mansion were all standing open, as they do during business hours. As the owner came to one entryway, the two heavy wooden doors slammed shut in front of him with no visible cause.

The main source of the haunting is the ghost of Charles Lunt. He is not buried in the family mausoleum and his ghost still walks his old home, to the delight of restaurant-goers who enjoy the atmosphere.

142 They're Still Home

TONY LUJÁN WAS A TAOS PUEBLO INDIAN; HE MARRIED MABEL DODGE after a divorce. They built a beautiful home and a small adobe house on Tony's land—Indian land. Years after both these prominent members of Taos society had died, actor Dennis Hopper bought the house.

He saw these phantasms—it was in all the newspapers in the mid-70s—just the upper half of the Lujáns, from the waist up, floating in one room of the house, laughing.

His wife saw Mabel once, just a vaporous emanation, moving through the hallway near a bathroom, going right through the walls.

Collection Notes

These collection notes are provided to give proper credit to informants and sources and to answer some of the reader's questions about the background or origin of a given story. These notes do not provide all the data a folklorist would wish or would have obtained at the time of collection. Many of the stories have come from the repertories of the editors themselves, and many were collected before this anthology was planned. Often notes are very brief or tellers described as "unidentified"; these and other stories labelled "collected before January 1, 1989," are from that pre-anthology period. In other cases, notes are very brief or tellers listed as "anonymous" at the request of the teller.

Notes may begin with any of the following phrases:

Collected by . . . indicates that another storyteller or a folklorist obtained this narrative and passed it along to the editors.

Collected from . . . means that we obtained this narrative ourselves, directly and orally, from the listed informant or source, or from the listed informant and others not listed specifically.

Learned from . . . refers to stories in the repertories of the editors that we have told for years.

Provided by . . . indicates that the listed source or informant was the primary source of fragmentary material or wrote the story down for us (usually transmitting it to us by mail) when oral collection was not feasible.

Retold from . . . refers to a story we heard from another storyteller and are passing along to the reader. Some unconscious addition or deletion may exist in our variant of the story in as much as all storytellers are likely to alter a story slightly with their own telling style, even when it is not their intention to do so.

Numbers refer to the number of the story, not the page number.

1. This ghost joke exists in many variants in the South and Southwest. This version was learned from Lewin Hayden Dockrey in Wagoner, Oklahoma, in the 1950s. The father of Judy Dockrey Young, and the man to whose memory this collection is dedicated, Mr. Dockrey told this as his favorite ghost story, even though no ghosts or spirits appear therein.

2. Learned from Homer Harry Young, Ph.D., in the 1950s. Sometimes known as "You Can't Get Out," this ghost joke is also very well-known throughout the South and Southwest. Dr. Young was the uncle of Richard Alan Young, and the source of much of this editor's love of ghost stories.

3. Collected anonymously from a teen-aged boy in Harrison, Arkansas, prior to January 1, 1989. The young man swears the grandfather told the story as the truth. The "victim" who saw the skeleton had long since died or the boy would have sought him out for more information. The young man called this story "I Can't Get In."

4. Learned from the Rev. John Morgan Young, a Baptist preacher in Dallas, Texas, in the early 1950s. After the Rev. Young's death in 1957, his son Morgan Martin Young, Ed.D., also told the story. Richard Alan Young heard it from both grandfather and father, although the former called the car a "darn thing."

5. This tongue-in-cheek story was submitted anonymously for this collection as "A Ghost Story for Folklorists." It is constructed of folktale motif numbers used to classify traditional narratives. It is a well-known "ghost joke," and reads, approximately, thus:

"Once, on a dare to prove his bravery, a young man spent the night in a graveyard. He fell asleep, and at midnight the ghosts of the dead [were] in the graveyard and suddenly [the] ghosts awaken [the] sleeper. The young man jumped up and saw ghostly lights all around him and heard the voices of the dead conversing in the graveyard!

Up from behind a huge tombstone [a] coffin moves by itself and it [object] floats in [the] air toward him.

"He began to run, and it chased him as [object behaves as] if [it were] alive!

"He ran all around the graveyard and finally took a cough drop and stopped the coffin [that] moves by itself."

The pun of *coffin* on *coughin'* works best, of course, when said aloud. Since the motif numbers are phrases instead of clauses, the grammar of this waggish tale has been both added to and subtracted from with the words in brackets. Our apologies to the folklorists among our readers, but this unique tale was too good (or too bad) to pass up.

6. "The Skin and Bones Woman" as sung by Lillian Deaver Sears, 1887–1973, learned in childhood at Elm Springs (Washington County), Arkansas, by her daughter JoAnne Sears Rife. Passed along to the editors March 13, 1990. This song and others of its type, wherein young listeners are frightened at the end, are a common Hallowe'en practice in the Ozarks.

7. The most famous of the American urban legends, this story is often called "The Vanishing Hitchhiker," and is told in hundreds of variants in every state in the Union. This version is sometimes called "Last Kiss," the name by which the editors of this collection first heard it in Texas in the 1950s. Other elements sometimes included are: the boy sees a photograph in the dead girl's home for positive identification, the girl has been brought home by a different boy each year for many years, or the mother accuses the boy of making a cruel joke in claiming to have seen the daughter. Jan Harold Brunvand's *The Vanishing Hitchhiker* gives this legend well-deserved attention and presents innumerable variants on it. Learned in adolescence by the editors, this version comes from many informants and sources in Texas and Oklahoma.

8. Jean Laffite (his own spelling) never wore a hook, and although he privateered off Barataria Island south of New Orleans, there is no reason to associate him with this story, which is usually named "Hook-Arm" or "The Hook Man" and is one of the most popular urban legends of this century. This version was contributed by teenagers from Louisiana prior to 1989.

9. This is a well-known urban legend, told in California and in Oklahoma, where it is purported to have come back home with returning workers who had fled to California during the Dust Bowl. The legend entered the editor's collection long ago, and has been heard by them in many variants, including a recent telling by California storytellers at the National Storytelling Festival in October, 1990, in Jonesborough, Tennessee.

10. Homer Harry Young, Ph.D., was a professor of education at Rice Institute and later Rice University in the 1950s and 1960s. Since Rice had no summer school for education, he taught summers at Texas Southern University, Bishop College, or Paul Quinn College. From teachers and students in summer school he collected folk tales or urban legends. While there were no collection notes among his papers at the time of his death in 1967, he passed many stories along to his brother Morgan Martin Young, Ed.D., and his nephew Richard Alan Young, one of the editors of this collection. This story is from the Waco, Texas, area, and is a variant on the classic English folktale "Golden Arm." This variant is sometimes called "Pair of Pants."

11. This complex scary story is told in many variants throughout the Southwest, especially at Girl Scout and Boy Scout camps. Heard from numerous tellers since 1963, our version is based on the tellings of Scott Doss of Dallas, Texas, and Carl Christofferson, formerly of Hillsboro, Missouri. Although this version has no ghost, some variants tell of the headless ghost tormenting one or more members of the team until they commit suicide. The story often ends with the teller screaming or jumping at the audience; experienced campers move slowly to the rear during the telling, putting the "greenhorns" who've never heard it up front for the ending. Other camps use it as the last story of the evening to try to insure nightmares or at least very nervous latrine trips afterward. The story has numerous names but seems to be most often known as "The Freshman Initiation."

12. Learned from Bobby Dahms of Whittier, California, in 1967. Mr. Dahms had heard it in California and tells it purely for entertainment. This urban legend is well-known throughout the South and Southwest and is usually known by the name "Call from the Grave."

13. Collected numerous times in variants from adults and teenagers over the ten-year period 1980–1990. This variant is largely that of Tom Phillips of Edmond, Oklahoma. Mr. Phillips and many others we have talked to point out that for some reason, one does begin to notice 11:11 more often after hearing the story. The phenomenon persists for a very long time, perhaps indefinitely. Mr. Phillips suggests that you see different times on a digital clock readout and don't "remember" or "notice" the odd times like 1:27 or 3:52; but since there's a story about it, you "notice" and remember noticing it when the time reads 11:11. In some versions of the story, the time is given as 1:11. The editors suggest that this reflects a later curfew for kids in the 90s than in the 70s and 80s. The older versions also have the clock in the car stopping at the time of the wreck at 11:11, but battery-operated digital clocks don't "stop"; they just flash 12:00 over and over and over. This variant was collected August 6, 1990, in Edmond.

14. Collected from a young Hispanic man in his 20s in Santa Fe, New Mexico, in December of 1987. He firmly believed the story to be true, and "sightings" of The Weeping Woman (or "The Wailing Woman") are common among the Hispanos of New Mexico and Arizona. *La LLorona* is the "Bogey Woman" of the Southwest, either warning miscreants to change their lives or visiting retribution on wrongdoers who persist in their sins (or who have ignored her previous warnings). She appears most often to children and drunkards (who are, after all, childlike when intoxicated), but is also seen by others. She usually appears as a woman dressed in black, although she also dresses in white. She often appears first as a young woman and then changes to a hag (although she has also been seen to appear young and simply vanish, appear old and simply vanish, appear young and turn to a skeleton, or appear old and turn to a skeleton). *La LLorona* seems to be a purely Mexican and Mexican-American phenomenon, based on an Aztec mythological character. Various authorities suggest she is Civacoatl (Cihuacoatl), Tonantzín or Coatlicue. As Coatlicue, she would be a bogey woman; as Civacoatl (also called Tlillan, or Blackness), she would call for sacrifices by carrying a basket-cradle containing a stone knife instead of a baby and leaving it with some unsuspecting woman in the marketplace. Another possibility is that *la LLorona* is one of the Cihuapipiltin (Mothers-of-children-who-died-in-first-childbirth). They came to earth one night a year to cry for the loss of their dead children. They often haunted crossroads and were often associated with the *ignis fatuus*, or fool's fire. *See stories numbers 44 and 45, and the Introduction for more about* la LLorona.

15. Collected in the winter of 1967 from the late Michael Olin Poe, who saw the light as a teen-ager from Sheridan, Arkansas. The light appears near the town of Crossett, Arkansas, in Ashley County. Residents from there and nearby Hamburg claim the light has been seen for at least half a century and is still seen as of this writing. Poe died in the line of duty as a policeman in Texas, and this story is a fond memento for the collectors of this anthology. The same narrative explanation is given for other ghost-lights or "spooklights," including one seen along the tracks at nearby Gurdon, Arkansas, and in other states as well.

16. Collected from Sean Bishop of Altus, Oklahoma, on June 25, 1990. *See the note to story number 79.*

17. Collected from Tom Phillips of Edmond, Oklahoma, on August 5, 1990. Mr. Phillips, in his 30s, relates an experience from his college days and suggests that the New Madrid Fault near the site may somehow be the cause of the lights.

18. Collected by Tom Phillips (*see note above*) from college pal Bobby Box, in Jonesboro, Arkansas, in the 1970s, this story/event was passed along with a laugh to the editors on August 6, 1990. This narrative is an excellent example of how a hoax may enter folklore to the frustration of serious storyholders or folklorists. Mr. Phillips swears he knew other college students who "fell" for the story and the hoax event, never bothering to look at the radio tower or make the mental connection.

19. Retold from a teen-aged girl's account in Siloam Springs, Arkansas, in 1962. She requested anonymity at that time. This is the only instance the editors know of this phenomenon being reported as ball lightning.

20. Learned from Jimmy Carter on October 18, 1990. Mr. Carter resides in Kansas, but the events of this story took place in Nebraska. Mr. Carter tells this family narrative as the truth. Mr. Carter assumes that the explanation is ball lightning. The association of the ball of fire with a bridge over a river follows the general belief that ball lightning follows "conductive material" (e.g., water, railroad tracks, etc.) as it moves along above the earth. Mr. Carter's grandfather was Joseph Augustine Wright.

21. Collected from an anonymous informant whose employers indicate that this story is not to be spread. The editors regret presenting such a fascinating story with the deletions and lack of annotation, but this is what the informant requested. The informant is a white male Emergency Medical Technician in his 20s, and he believes the story to be the truth.

22. Retold from Dr. H. H. Young, who collected it in the 1960s in central Texas from black educators studying in summer school. *See also the note for story number 10.*

23. Collected from Terry Bloodworth of Kimberling City, Missouri, in October, 1990. Mr. Bloodworth saw the light near Texarkana, Arkansas, personally, as described in the narrative. Mr. Bloodworth is a fine storyteller and has contributed many stories to this collection.

24. Provided by two informants from East Texas prior to January 1, 1989.

25. Collected from Katie Wamser of the Miami area during July of 1989. Ms. Wamser has seen the light and accepts its ghostly nature as the truth. Some other informants suggest the light is caused somehow by the nearby mining operations. The Hornet spooklight is only about thirty miles away in southwestern Missouri, and both lights might have the same explanation.

26. Retold from a dozen Missouri informants during 1989 and 1990. This is the "standard" folkloric explanation for the Hornet light.

27. Collected from Johnny Brewer from Grove, Oklahoma, (just across the state line from the Hornet spooklight) in August of 1989. Mr. Brewer did not accept the explanation, but found the story fascinating.

28. Collected in October, 1990, at Silver Dollar City from Betty Gresham, a resident of Stone County, Missouri.

29. Collected in August, 1989, at Silver Dollar City from Bill Frenchman, a resident of Disney, Oklahoma.

30. Provided by more than one informant from West Texas between 1957 and 1985. This well-known story has several conflicting versions, depending on the ending (which seems to depend on the general outlook of the teller). Some authorities give *chisos* as the Apache word for ghost, but it is more likely a corruption of *hechicero* (sorceror) in Spanish.

31. Collected from Louis Darby, of Opelousas, Louisiana, in August of 1989.

32. Provided by John H. Snow, of Texas A. & M. University, College Station, Texas. Collected in 1989 from a freshman student of Mrs. Amma Davis of Sam Houston State University. There are many explanations for the Marfa Lights, but this is a variant of the most commonly accepted story. Other legends involving Indian chiefs and warriors are almost certainly romanticized fictions invented in this century.

The Marfa Lights came into new prominence when the NBC television series *Unsolved Mysteries* featured them in one episode. Videotapes of the Marfa Lights, like those taken of the Hornet Light by NBC affiliate KYTV in Springfield, Missouri, are faint and inconclusive.

Mr. Snow identifies two types of ghost lights: some, like the Marfa Lights, are thought of by local people as being simply lights; others, like the ghost lights at Stampede Mesa, are thought of as being ghosts.

33. Collected from Bill Frenchman, of Disney, Oklahoma, in August of 1989. Mr. Frenchman offers no explanation for the lights, but other tellers have alluded to the ghosts of miners in their hard hats with lanterns. The miners in such explanatory stories have always been victims of a cave-in or explosion, never having died from natural causes.

34. Provided by an anonymous informant in Albuquerque, New Mexico, in January, 1990. The story is also told of the Río Puerco area below El Cabezón. *See stories number 80 and 81.*

35. Collected from an anonymous informant in Albuquerque, New Mexico, in January, 1990. There are many stories about *braseros* (fireball, brazier, fire-pan) in the Río Puerco area. Numerous first-person narratives appear in *Recuerdos de los Viejitos: Tales of the Río Puerco,* collected and edited by Nasario García, published by the University of New Mexico Press, Albuquerque. These first-person narratives appear to be passing in and out of the oral tradition as they are retold by people who read them, as well as being told by people who heard them in their original oral form. It is impossible to tell which source any given narrative has. Many explanations are offered for the fireball phenomenon, ranging from the igniting of sulphurous gas near El Cabezón to the work of *brujos* (sorcerers). This type of narrative is a favorite in the Albuquerque area and is told with both great animation and complete belief.

36. Learned from numerous sources over the twenty years we have collected in the Ozarks, this is the most popular scary story in northern Arkansas and southern Missouri. It is known by names such as "Old Raw Head," "Raw Head and Bloody Bones," and "Bloody Bones and Rawhide." This variant contains the most prevalent motifs and represents the best tellings we have encountered. Technically, the Old Raw Head is a preternatural creature, not a ghost, but the implication that it is alive through conjuring (similar to witchcraft) places it into the Southwestern concept of ghost lore and witch lore being interchangeable.

37. Provided by a man in San Antonio who is a member of the Sons of Confederate Veterans. He declined to be identified and suggested that we seek out written sources. Sightings of the Confederate bridge guard were more common in the 1930s and '40s. The informant speculated that the bridge was either replaced by a new one or that the presence of Interstate 10 nearby had caused sightings to cease.

38. The White Wolf is a common theme in folk narratives; any animal albinism may be. There was a well-known white wolf in Montana in 1915, and there must have been many others in the West over the centuries. The white wolf story may be an offshoot of the Pecos Bill fantasy or of the Wolf Girl of Devil's River (*see story number 103*), or it may be nothing more than a romanticization of an albino wolf sighting. This narrative was collected in Abilene, Texas, in 1958, from Otis Johnson, who was a lad of eleven at the time. There is no historical connection between the name of Fort Phantom Hill and the events of this story.

39. Learned in 1988 from an unidentified white male California truck driver in his 60s who had seen the ghostly event. Later confirmed in a variant provided by Bill Frenchman of Disney, Oklahoma, who had also seen personally the "Ghostly Battle." Mr. Frenchman provided us with his variant in August, 1990.

40. Collected by New Mexico storyteller Teresa Pijoan de Van Etten from various informants in the Santa Fe area and provided to these editors on December 31, 1989. The story has many variants that reflect the ethnic origin of the informant. In another version, published in her book *Spanish-American Folktales* (August House, Little Rock, 1990), Sra. de Van Etten attributes sightings or hearings of the severed head to fiesta time in September, as would accord with Hispanic tradition; in the version provided to us, the head is seen or heard around Hallowe'en, as related by the Anglos living in Santa Fe. This story is the best known and most often repeated ghost story of Santa Fe.

41. Collected in the main library in Santa Fe from a patron who had heard the editors perform storytelling. Additional fragmentary information was provided by Kathy Costa of Oliver LaFarge

Library in Santa Fe, all in December, 1989. When the editors asked Sr. Luján if he knew such a story, he said that he did not.

42. Collected from one of the museum guards at the Museum of Fine Arts in Santa Fe, in December, 1987, during the *la LLorona* exhibit there. The same Hispanic man in his 50s provided story number 45.

43. The stories of the Ghost Girl of the Mimbres were reported in local newspapers in 1906 and thereafter; the legend itself seems much older. Learned from unidentified New Mexicans before 1988. The expression "on the Mimbres" refers to the Mimbres Mountains that sweep down from the Continental Divide.

44. Collected from Sra. de Kraul while at El Ropero, a fine artesania shop in Santa Fe in late December, 1987. The Kraul and Garcia families have worked to promote *la LLorona* as the true Hispanic folk character for the Santa Fe area. At The Word Process (P.O. Box 5699, Santa Fe, NM 87502), they have published a book of stories called *La LLorona: Encounters with the Weeping Woman.*

45. Collected from a museum guard at the Museum of Fine Arts in Santa Fe in December, 1987, during the *la LLorona* exhibit there. He also provided story number 42.

46. Collected from Teresa Pijoan de Van Etten on December 31, 1989. Sra. de Van Etten has heard the story and its attendant warnings to young girls not to drive alone in the area at night all her life.

47. Learned from Dr. H. H. Young in the 1960s; he heard it from students at Paul Quinn College in Waco, Texas. Although the black educators who shared this story did not believe it to be true, they readily passed it on as area folklore.

48. Learned from various Texas sources prior to January 1, 1989. The stories of "Bigfoot" Wallace are numerous and well-known. Some locals regard him as a half-legendary, half-real folk character to rival Davy Crockett.

49. Collected in passing from a young white male in his 20s in downtown Wichita, Kansas, November 25, 1990. He told the fragment as if he had heard it and did not believe it to be true. He did not remember there being any more to the narrative.

50. Retold by Texas folklorist George D. Hendricks, of Denton, from a story originally collected by Mary E. Hill, of Dallas, and appeared (in different form) in Mr. Hendricks's *Mirrors, Mice, & Moustaches* (S.M.U. Press, Dallas, 1966). This story has many variants but appears different from the "Vanishing Hitchhiker" story in that no one in this story recognized the ghost-girl. Other tellers have alluded to a spooklight associated with the White Rock Lady.

51a. The most famous ghost story from San Antonio, Texas. Originally collected from hearing-impaired students. *See note following.*

51b. Collected from Connie High on April 17, 1989, in San Antonio, Texas. At that time High was an intern at the Southwest Center for the Hearing Impaired. Sidney Brooks died Tuesday, November 13, 1917, on a training flight, and was one of the first cadet casualties in the new Army Air Corps. This story may appeal to the hearing-impaired because it deals with smell instead of sound. Using the descriptive technique of presenting the story in sign language was done to make it possible to recreate the story to deaf audiences exactly as it came to the collectors of this anthology.

52. Collected prior to January 1, 1989, anonymously from a teenager in Harrison, Arkansas (who is not the source of any other story in this anthology). It seems that most of the good ghost stories told in that part of north Arkansas are set in Newton County, a sparsely inhabited mountainous region where old oral traditions are kept.

53. Collected August 5, 1990, from storyteller Tom Phillips in Edmond, Oklahoma. Mr. Phillips works at Oklahoma Christian College and has gathered and told scary stories from college students since his own college days in the 70s. He does not claim that any of his stories are true; he doesn't deny that they are, either. He does state that he knew these brothers personally, and gave the family name, which the editors have declined to print.

54. Collected at Hallowe'en, 1971, from Henry A. Klussman, a free-lance writer from Houston, Texas, and the descendant of the girl in the story. In the Klussman family, the story is accepted as the truth.

55. Learned in the 1950s from the Rev. John Morgan Young, then of Dallas, Texas, and as retold by his sons Dr. H. H. Young and Dr. Morgan M. Young. The church was in Howe, Texas, but the Rev. Young's memory was unclear as to whether the house was in Howe or nearby Anna.

56. Collected from Teresa Pijoan de Van Etten in Placitas, New Mexico, December 31, 1989. The story of the Healing Lady of Los Luceros is the third in a trilogy of stories consisting of stories numbers 80, 81 and 56. Sra. de Van Etten personally knew occupants of the house in the last few decades. This story was told to Sra. de Van Etten by grandmother Monelle Holley, now of Plano, Texas, to whom the story is considered to belong.

57. Learned from California residents prior to January 1, 1989. Various visitors to Silver Dollar City have shared versions with the editors in recent years.

58. Collected from Patricia Smith, June 11, 1990. Mrs. Smith lived for a time in California and saw the ghost of Helen at the home of relatives. Various family names have been omitted from the story out of respect for living members of families involved. When the editors ask for ghost stories, expecting to get folktales, we often receive first-person narratives like this, which are fascinating.

59. Collected from Janet Shaw on June 11, 1990, in Harrison, Arkansas. Mrs. Shaw had only recently moved from the house in nearby Alpena, Arkansas, where "the ghost played pool."

60. Collected from Scott Denning, who had heard the story from Valerie Money, whose family had bought the house in the story. Mr. Denning provided the story to the editors at the Chile Hill Emporium in Bernalillo, New Mexico, in December, 1989.

61. Provided by Mary Grathwol, a librarian with the Library Storytellers of Santa Fe, New Mexico, in December, 1989.

62. Collected from Teri Murguía, from San Francisco, California, on July 26, 1989, when she was in Branson, Missouri. Certain family names were omitted at her request.

63. Collected from Terry Bloodworth of Kimberling City, Missouri, in August of 1990. The "House on Chalet Road" is in Hollister, Missouri, near Lake Taneycomo. Mr. Bloodworth's work as a glassblower does not interfere with his hobby as a fine storyteller.

64. Collected from George Wamser in July of 1989. Mr. Wamser lives in Oklahoma now, but his family lived in El Monte, California. The ghost in the house in the story is unusual in that it possesses or causes an aroma. *See also story number 51.*

65. Collected from Terryl Hébert of Kaplan, Louisiana, in June of 1989. M. Hebert is a hotelier and storyteller in the Cajun tradition.

66. Provided by the Albuquerque Public Library in response to a request for further information on a series of fragments related to the editors during their stay in New Mexico in 1987. The story was reported in a November, 1913, edition of the *Albuquerque Evening Herald* under the heading "Ghost of Old Spaniard Haunts Punta de Agua." The fragments are presented with lacunae filled in (comments in brackets) from our own research.

We offer two alternatives to details in the often-repeated story: In the newspaper account, the Spaniard is described as "wearing the uniform of a French soldier": we believe this to be the tabard-with-cross of *Three Musketeers* fame, a garment worn in Spain as well as France, with the cross of Calatrava, a purely Spanish emblem in spite of the presence of the *fleur-de-lys*. The newspaper story has the Spaniard say, *"Siste, viator,"* (stop, visitor) in Latin, apparently a language the tourist who saw the ghost had learned in grammar school; we suggest, based on fragments that have come to us, that the true message was in antique Spanish of the 1600s—which the ghost would more likely speak, and which the tourist would probably not have known. The original sighting was by a Wilbur S. Saener, of Winonk, Illinois, and some interested parties speculate that the "figure" has not been seen since, only reported by persons who wished the legend to grow and enhance the folklore of the region.

67. Provided by the Albuquerque Public Library in response to inquiries into a story that had appeared in 1952 in the *Tucumcari American-Leader*, and based on fragments provided to the editors at the Old Route 66 Café in Tucumcari in 1987. The story is still told in the area, primarily because of its punchline ending. Some versions of the story put the amount of payroll as high as $100,000 and refer to the money as being in "gold notes." Other versions apparently mention strongboxes full of gold bars or coins. The spiritualist explanation for the haunting is that the riders, so intent on their treasure, eternally reenact the opening of the boxes and the mysterious disposition of the gold (or banknotes).

68. The Riordan House is northern Arizona's most famous dwelling and seems to house Flagstaff's most famous ghost. Many interested parties speculate that the ghost is that of Anna, who died of polio, tradition says, within the house. Research by Paul Sweitzer, of the *Flagstaff Sun* newspaper staff, indicated that Anna died in a nearby hospital founded by the Riordan family. Our informant, who worked at the Riordan House under her maiden name Margaret Ybarra, refers to the ghost as that of Caroline, Anna's mother, still moving about the mansion, continuing to care for it after her death. The former Srta. Ybarra told the editors this personal experience, which we have extracted from a longer conversation while visiting at the Riordan House, now a small state park, on December 31, 1990. The Riordan brothers made their fortune in lumber, and the magnificent log mansion is still under restoration as of this writing.

69. Retold from versions common in the area of Guerra and Agua Nueva, Texas, heard in 1986. The severed hand gripping the reins is a well-known European folk motif. The phantom at El Blanco Rancho is also often described as being female, with a hideously decomposed face, perhaps as an alternative *LLorona*-figure. Each version bears different, usually conflicting, details.

70. Retold from the local legendry as provided by a waitress in a German-American restaurant, The Gasthaus, on November 17, 1990. Cripple Creek has many mining-related ghost stories, but they belong to a different collection.

71. Collected prior to January 1, 1989, from a family from Wichita, Kansas, who told the story solely for amusement and as "local Kansas lore," using the name "The Wraith of White Woman Creek."

72. Learned from Homer H. Young, Ph.D., in the summer of 1962. Dr. Young was a graduate of Austin College in Sherman, Texas, and played football in the 1920s when some players shaved their heads under their leather helmets. Rival Trinity University was founded in 1869 in Tehuacana, Texas, and moved in 1902 to Waxahachie and to San Antonio in 1942. Chief Tawakoni was a real person, but much information about him is legendary. The Wichita Indians were moved from the Canadian River area of Oklahoma to the Wichita Indian Reservation in 1859.

73. Provided by Arturo Jaramillo on December 30, 1989, at Rancho de Corrales Restaurant in Corrales, New Mexico. Sr. Jaramillo is one of the Torrez/Romero/Jaramillo family members who now own and manage the restaurant, formerly known as the Territorial House. The story of the Embertos' ghosts is one of the best-known ghost stories in Sandoval County, just as the restaurant is one of the best in the county.

74. The tale of the ghostly guardian on the Neches is retold by Texas folklorist J. Frank Dobie and a host of others. Versions vary, but interestingly enough, the quote of the man in the hole (sometimes called C——— and sometimes called Clawson) is always exact: "I have seen Hell and its horrors." Some have suggested it was a ruse, and the partner returned for the treasure; others prefer the ghostly—and ghastly—explanation and ending given here. Editor Richard Alan Young first heard this tale from his uncle Homer Harry Young, Ph.D., while spending the summer of 1962 in the Houston area. *See also the note for story number 10.*

75. There are several places in America known as Hell's Half-Acre. The more legendary one is in Wyoming, along the Oregon Trail. Another is in Arkansas, and various versions of the explanation have come to the editors over the years, usually from hunters. The narrative first entered print when a Miss Clara Eno submitted a story to Alsop's classic story collection *Romantic Arkansas* in the 1920s.

76. This widely-known tale is told throughout New Mexico. One New Mexican told us this variant and mentioned the version found in B. A. Botkin's *A Treasury of American Folklore*. Our version, collected in December, 1987, has details not in the Botkin variant and lacks some details therefrom.

77. This is a Hispanic story that some people say "ought not to be told." A grotesque variant on the "Golden Arm" theme, it is one of the oldest in the repertory of editor Richard Alan Young. It has been heard, among other places, at a gathering of college student members of Kappa Kappa Psi Fraternity in Tempe, Arizona, in August, 1968.

78. Collected from Tom Phillips, a former Harding College employee, on August 6, 1990. Mr. Phillips is a food service manager in his 30s who shares tales with the students at his college workstations.

79. Collected on June 25, 1990, from Sean Bishop of Altus, Oklahoma, telling about his true experiences in northern New Mexico in 1980. Mr. Bishop is a commercial pilot as of this printing. In the summers between years at the Air Force Academy, he worked as a ranger at Philmont Scout Camp in Cimarron, New Mexico, leading Scouts on camping and backpacking expeditions. While scary stories are stock-in-trade around Scout campfires, Mr. Bishop swears these are the truth. (*See also story number 16.*)

80. Collected from nationally-known storyteller and petroglyph expert Teresa Pijoan de Van Etten in Placitas, New Mexico, on December 31, 1989. Sra. Van Etten has published her own anthologies of Native-American and Spanish-American stories (*see the note for story number 40*). This and stories numbered 81 and 56 form a trilogy, which she told in sequence.

81. The second in the "El Cabezón Trilogy." See note 80 above.

82. Collected from George White, a member of the jury that convicted Odus Davidson, by Patricia Greeson, his granddaughter. Learned in childhood in the 1950s. Provided to the editors June 11, 1990.

83. Provided by Georgianna Greeson to the editors June 11, 1990. Mrs. Greeson was a resident of Arizona at the time of the events.

84. Provided by Fred and Vivian Hurlburt, storytellers from Golconda, Nevada, in January of 1991. Mrs. Hurlburt pointed out to these editors that Nevada has many ghost towns but few ghost stories. "Cousin Jack" refers to a Cornishman, and a *pastie* is a fried meat pie.

85. Collected in December, 1987, from one of the Acoma Indian women who serve as guides for tours of "Sky City," an Acoma pueblo in New Mexico. The 600-year-old pueblo sits atop a once impregnable mesa, and the ancestral home of the people is nearby Enchanted Mesa, called Katzimo (spelled here phonetically) in the Keres language of Acoma.

86. This event happened in 1964 to Pat Echeté. She offered an alternate explanation: there was at that time a gas-well flare near the site, but its flame and glow were yellow; she discounts this explanation. She relates that this was the most popular ghost story in that area (St. Charles Parish) in her youth. Collected June 11, 1990.

87. Collected from Kathryn Cavert on June 11, 1990, at a large ghost-story telling session. Mrs. Cavert was a California resident at the time of the events of the story.

88. Learned from Dolan Ellis, the official balladier of the State of Arizona, in Scottsdale, Arizona, in December, 1985. Mr. Ellis has also written and published a song by the title of "Lady of the Ledge," and saw the lady while at Old Oraibi years ago.

89. Learned prior to January 1, 1989, by the editors while touring the area of Victoria, Texas, in the winter of 1984.

90. Provided by Kathy Costa and the Library Storytellers of Santa Fe, New Mexico. Mrs. Costa is a librarian at Oliver LaFarge Branch Library. Mrs. Costa and her sister Mrs. Grathwol (*see note for story number 61*) told many stories for the editors seated around a warm fire in the *horno* fireplace at Mrs. Costa's home in Santa Fe, January 3, 1990.

91. Collected by Terry Bloodworth from Mike Jenkins and passed along to the editors in October, 1990. Both men have worked in entertainment in the Branson, Missouri, area for many years.

92. Provided by Fred and Vivian Hurlburt, storytellers from Golconda, Nevada, in January of 1991. Most Nevada ghost stories deal with mining, and most are centered around the Virginia City area.

93. Collected from Johnny Brewer from Grove, Oklahoma, in August, 1989.

94. Collected from Terryl Hébert in August, 1989. M. Hébert, a hotelier and Cajun storyteller, had learned it from his father, Frank Hébert during his childhood in Crowley, Louisiana.

95. Provided by two brothers living in Scottsdale, Arizona, who often camp in the Superstitions and are acquainted with the legends, lore, and humbug of the mountains. Working as muleskinners at Rawhide theme park in Scottsdale, they provided this story, which may be passing into and out of the print medium, to the editors in early January, 1985. They tell all lore of the Superstitions as the truth, even conflicting stories.

96. Collected from Tracy Gerlach, owner of Process One in Harrison, Arkansas, at a ghost storytelling session June 11, 1990. The print mentioned in the story is in the collection of the editors. Thousands of questions come to mind when one looks at the print. The photo shows no signs of fakery; the lab at Process One is not equipped for photographic fakery. Could it be a prank by one of the hunters . . . black cloth draped over a tree? The narrative has all the "stuff of urban legend," third-hand narrative, casual details, limited—but tempting—evidence, the terrible fate of those who saw the apparition, and so on. Mr. Gerlach offered one last comment: "The guy said apparitions are often that tall."

97. Collected in 1977 from Eddie Smith of Ogden, Arkansas, in Little River County. The town of Fouke sits in the marshy area at the confluence of the Red and Sulphur Rivers in southwest Arkansas, in Miller County. The monster was seen between 1955 and 1975, and the movie "The Legend of Boggy Creek" relates most of the reported sightings in semi-documentary form. Some suggest the creature is real—not a hallucination or myth—but is nothing more than a full-grown chimpanzee that escaped from a circus truck or exotic-pet owner. As an example of the species' longevity, readers of the tabloids were surprised to learn from the June 5, 1990, *National Enquirer* that Cheetah of the Tarzan movies was alive and well at age 55. Cheetah was at that time as large as his owner-trainer Tony Gentry, who brought the chimp from Africa in the 30s. Gentry was 86 and devoted to his simian star, who outlived most of the human stars of the Tarzan and other jungle movies in which he appeared. While there have been no recent sightings of the Fouke Monster, it remains an Arkansas-Texas phenomenon of immense folk popularity. There are Fouke Monster jokes, Fouke Monster folksongs, and so on.

98. This story was learned in fragmentary form from a merchant in the market in Nogales, Sonora, across the border from Nogales, Arizona, January 1, 1988. There are many versions of the story, ranging from European to Southwestern. One excellent version, perhaps more complete than this one, is entitled "Doña Sebastiana" and appears in *Cuentos* by José Griego Maestas and Rudolfo Anaya, based on the stories collected by Juan B. Rael.

99. This folktale about Death being tricked was reconstructed from two summary/fragments collected in Arizona and New Mexico in 1984–1988. Ethnically, the informants were more "cowboy" than Hispanic, and elements of the Appalachian folktale "Mean John and the Devil" seem to have been interpolated, either by poor memory or conscious adaptation. The central character, Pedro de Urdemalas, is a classic folkhero in Spain, where Miguel de Cervantes Saavedra wrote a play by that name in 1617. The name "Urdemalas" means "Wreaks Pranks" or "Trickster;" he is often compared to—and his name translated as—"Artful Dodger," after the character in Charles Dickens's *Oliver Twist*. A truer Hispanic version appears under the name "Pedro de Ordimalas" in *Cuentos* by José Griego y Maestas and Rudolfo Anaya, based on narratives originally collected by Juan B. Rael in New Mexico and Colorado in 1977. Our primary source was a conversation with native Arizonans while we were appearing at Rawhide, a theme park in Scottsdale.

100. Collected from Teresa Pijoan de Van Etten in Placitas, New Mexico, December 31, 1987. The story is Seneca in origin and is told now by many tribal groups. In the Tewa Indian language tradition, stories are usually told in the frost months when the snakes are in their dens. An exception is made for stories that involve only human characters and for stories about flight. Sra. de Van Etten, a reknowned storyteller and petroglyph expert, grew up in the San Juan Pueblo north of Santa Fe. She is the author of *Ways of Indian Wisdom* and *Ways of Indian Magic*, published by Sunstone Press in Albuquerque, and *Spanish-American Folktales*, published by August House, as well as other books. The editors have heard numerous versions of the Flying Head story, which is a favorite among children. The Van Etten family have been the gracious hosts of three storytelling sessions around the fire in their home in Placitas on the *fin del año* (New Year's Eve) of 1987, 1988 and 1989. The eve of a new year represents a crack in time, between the years, and it is a time when spirits could walk and graves open: the perfect time for ghost stories. The inspiration for this collection comes largely from these storytelling sessions, and the editors wish to express their appreciation to the Van Ettens for their contributions to the collection.

101a. Many historians in Texas and New Mexico repeat variations on the story of the Blue Lady. Her existence was reported by Fr. Alonso de Benavides in his *Memorial*, written in 1630. Fr. Damián Manzanet wrote in 1690 of her previous appearances to the Caddo Indians (or Tejas Indians.) The young mystical authoress María de Jesús de Agreda, who wrote *The Mystic and Divine History of the Virgin, Mother of God* in 1627, claimed that she had experienced "out-of-body" visitations to New Mexico, making her a "living ghost" by the definition of many psychic researchers. Historian Charles E. Chapman identifies de Agreda as the Blue Lady, but other writers leave her a supernatural mystery. The editors have heard versions and fragments of this story in New Mexico and Texas. This version was collected from Anglos and Hispanos; for a Pueblo Indian version, see next story.

101b. Provided anonymously from a source in the Santo Domingo Pueblo. The Blue Lady is revered by Indians, Anglos and Hispanos. *See also the Anglo and Hispano version in version above.*

102. Collected from students at the University of Texas at El Paso during an intercollegiate meeting with members of Kappa Kappa Psi Fraternity from the University of Arkansas in 1966.

103. The Wolf Girl legend has circulated among men and boys for more than a century in Texas. The mere fascination of seeing a naked girl running wild was enough to make this a prime campfire story in the 1950s, when this editor first heard it. L. D. Bertillion says, in *Straight Texas*, edited by J. Frank Dobie and Mody C. Boatright, in 1937, (Texas Folklore Society, Number XIII) that wolves "strongly marked with human characteristics" have been seen by him personally in that area. This grotesque postscript resembles a Greek myth more than a Texas legend.

104. Retold from the account of a teen-aged girl named Winona, who preferred not to be identified further, at a storytelling session in the early 1980s. She was a Texas resident at the time of the events of the story, which she related as the truth. The events so closely resemble the East Texas Hairy Man storyline (see the Introduction) that folklorists would assume it is merely a variant thereof. It was told, however, as the "Gospel truth."

105. This fragment was learned in Texas, near Abilene, from a Boy Scout storytelling session in the 1950s. The White Steed is told about from Texas to Arizona in story, poem, and song, always without a plotline.

106. The story about the "witch" Sally Baker was learned by Ken Teutsch of Walker's Creek, Arkansas, in his boyhood; he provided the "myth" and the postscript true story of his family's "debunking" of the myth on July 21, 1990. Mr. Teutsch believed the witch tale until he spoke with his father in the 1970s. As a writer in television and other media, Mr. Teutsch's poignant postscript gives remarkable insight into the process by which commonplace events may be expanded to legendary proportions through the medium of the oral scary story. Mr. Teutsch insisted that both the myth and his personal involvement be included consecutively to suggest that part of the folkloric process.

107. This Tewa story is told in Santa Clara and San Ildefonso Pueblos, and was provided by Teresa Pijoan de Van Etten in 1990, with changes being made in the story to remove its spiritual power without changing the events of the story. Mushboy was made at other times and had other adventures as well. Mushboy is a favorite with children, and this story was conveyed in English. We and the teller shared a laugh as the teller struggled to say Medicine-Meal Mush Boy, a tongue twister in English but not in Tewa.

108. Provided by Teresa Pijoan de Van Etten, of Placitas, New Mexico, this Hopi story came from the Arizona Hopi Homeland through a marriage. While it is not a sacred story, which the editors of this collection would not be entitled to hear and share, this story does have small changes made by the storyteller to remove its spiritual power and make it a touching moral lesson that may be read by anyone. If there is any error in our recording of this story, it is through ignorance, not disrespect. The story was told as an example of "teaching stories," which instruct children in proper behavior. Some of them are also scary stories that children love to hear over and over. Native American spirit stories resemble European ghost stories in this respect.

109. Provided by Judy Pruitt, storyteller for Rawhide theme park in Scottsdale, Arizona. This ghost train is often confused with, or its legend merged with, another ghost train seen in the distance across burning desert sand: a mirage caused by wavering hot air and a distant dust-devil that resembles a smoking stack. Mrs. Pruitt told this legend around a campfire in the Old Mission Patio at Rawhide on New Year's, 1991.

110. Collected from Teresa Pijoan de Van Etten in Placitas, New Mexico, December 31, 1989.

111. Provided by Barbara Pijoan and Teresa Pijoan de Van Etten of Corrales and Placitas, New Mexico, respectively, in December, 1989.

112. Collected by Teresa Pijoan de Van Etten and passed along to the editors on December 31, 1989. The story is well-known in the area around Española.

113. There are dozens of versions of the Stampede Mesa story, with some sources saying the names of participants have been forgotten, others offering pseudonyms (like Jones) and still others claiming to know the actual names of one or more historical characters. In some versions the rustler (or nester, in some versions) is killed before the stampede, in others he is killed for revenge and left to rot after he causes the stampede. The editors have heard this story from numerous informants in Texas since the 1950s. Storms often cause stampedes, but cattle could also be stampeded by something as small as a rabbit jumping in front of a lead steer; often the stampede's cause remained a mystery. Semi-literate cowboys relied largely on experience and verbal memory, so lore passed on by other cowboys had great significance and could cause superstition: a ghostly explanation for an unexplained stampede made as much sense as any. On another note, the physical phenomenon of an image projected on low clouds is rare but documented: it was first named The Spectre of the Brocken for its appearance on a specific peak in Switzerland. Light from a setting or rising sun is focused through a "lens" of warm air or cold air and a focused shadow of a man on the peak is cast on the clouds beyond him. This phenomenon could theoretically have occurred, even only once, at Stampede Mesa, and the lore that arose around it would endure indefinitely. The Stampede Mesa story has merged in this variant with the Riders in the Sky motif, made famous as the song "Ghost Riders in the Sky" by Gene Autry and, later, Johnny Cash, and epitomized, some say, by Frankie Lane's rendition.

114. Learned from Chinese-Americans from California prior to January 1, 1989. The corpse-walkers operated in the high mountains of China and Tibet, but legend has it that one or more also provided the grisly service to the families of Chinese who died mining high in the Sierra Nevada in California in the 1800s.

115. Collected by Teresa Pijoan de Van Etten from Charlotte Perry-Martínez, who was told the story by her neighbor; he had been the *hijo desobediente* and had gone to the dance in Placitas, New Mexico, decades before. Provided to the editors in December of 1989.

116. Collected from Father Regis at the Church of San Miguel, on the Old Santa Fe Trail in Santa Fe. The stories associated with the bell and told by the Christian Brothers to all visitors are considered ghostly in that they deal with the Holy Ghost and the intervention of supernatural powers into the natural world. This miracle story would not be considered a ghost story among Protestants or Northern Europeans, whose "ghost traditions" are so different from the Hispanic views on the subject. Collected January 4, 1990.

117. This story is retold from the collection work of Texas folklorist Peggy Shamburger Hendricks, as provided to the editors in November, 1989. This story used to be told to Mrs. Hendricks by her great-aunt Betty Shamburger Atwood of Tyler, Texas, who had in turn learned it in about 1900 from her family's nurse and cook, Aunt Hattie. Aunt Hattie was of mixed native American and Negro ancestry, and the story shows both heritages. While Aunt Hattie's words of almost a century ago have been filtered through retelling, the heart of the story is perfectly preserved in this excellent version. This story is known by many names and variants. In the Southeast, it is called "Barney McCabe" or "Wylie and His Sister." In the Southwest, it is called "Wham, Jam, Jenny-Mo-Wham" or other variants of the witch's chant.

118. Retold from a California hunter, who provided the narrative in response to a hunting "tall tale" from the Ozarks, prior to January 1, 1989. The white male in his 50s told the story as the truth although he did not actually say if he had seen the booger deer personally.

119. Collected from Terry Bloodworth, a Judsonia, Arkansas, native, on October 25th, 1990, in Stoneridge, Missouri. The name "Creature-in-the-Hole" was used to describe this river monster; that name has been applied to numerous other creatures and sites in Arkansas and Missouri.

120. Collected from "Pa" Paddy by Terry Bloodworth in the 1960s and passed along to the editors October 25, 1990. Mr. Paddy firmly believed the story, according to Mr. Bloodworth; the "changing man" or "shape changer" is a character in the folklore of Gypsies, American Indians, Ozark hillbillies, and others.

121. Provided by Debbie McGown Steinmetz of West Jordan, Utah, January 21, 1991. The Three Nephites have appeared singularly or as a trio since the inception of the Church of Jesus Christ of Latter Day Saints. The way in which the Nephite narratives seem to blend with the tradition of the urban legend of the "Vanishing Hitchhiker" is a phenomenon that fascinates folklorists. The act of vanishing immediately after doing a good deed or making a prediction has been a practice attributed to the Nephites since their first appearances.

122. The Dineh (Navajo) hero Killer-of-the-Alien-Gods had many, many adventures; his adventure with He-Who-Kicks-People-Down-Cliffs is fairly well-known in the Southwest due to its mention in a Tony Hillerman novel.

Several Indian and non-Indian Southwesterners have given us fragments of this story, but for a telling close to the Dineh original, we have retold the event from *Navaho Legends* by Washington Matthews, *Memoires of the American Folk-Lore Society*, Volume V (New York, G. E. Stechert & Co., 1897). We have included one fragment from an informant: we were told that the story comes from the area of Navajo Mountain, Utah, and that the *anayei* (demon) lived on Gray Mesa in northern Arizona. The mountain the Dineh call Mount San Mateo is Mt. Taylor, New Mexico, and another explanation for the origin of El Cabezón is found in the story "The Devil's Neck" in this collection.

123. The legend of the White Riders is common in the Southwest, and has passed out of the oral tradition into print, and back into the oral tradition again. The story is sometimes recited as a poem or song, and sometimes told as a narrative. This version purports to be from the Drag-Eight Ranch, and was provided to the editors by an Arizona retiree, complete with obligatory turquoise-set string tie, at a story-telling session at Rawhide theme park in Scottsdale, Arizona, on New Year's Day, 1991. The gentleman was an Anglo, in his seventies, who told the story as the gospel truth.

124. Collected from Bob Coody on December 31, 1990. Mr. Coody told this personal commentary with a nostalgic smile. The editors have extracted from a longer conversation this narrative about the spirits in the physical anthropology collection. It must be noted that the Museum of Northern Arizona treats the collection with the proper respect and works closely with the Hopi people, whose ancestors the collection represents. Mr. Coody is a librarian at the Northern Arizona University Special Collections Library in Flagstaff.

125. The Monster of the Mogollón Rim is a well-known Scout story used to frighten tenderfeet around the campfire. The editors first encountered a variant of this story with Scouts in New Mexico; an argument could be made that all the monster-in-the-night-that-gets-bad-Scouts stories are variants on a single theme. Most camps have a "patron spook" whose lore grows with each generation of Scouts and is perpetuated reverently in the most ancient of human rituals, story-telling around the campfire.

The monster may be an Anglo version of the Navajo "Skinwalker," who challenges young men to prove their bravery against him.

126. A certain number of the stories in this collection are composites, reconstructed from fragments or constructed from variants wherein the lacunae in one version are filled by details from another, and vice-versa. These stories were collected prior to January 1, 1990, some as long ago as thirty years, and are not substantiated by collection notes. They are now elements of the repertory of Richard and Judy Dockrey Young, collected from the oral tradition, as told to them by the hundreds of kind informants and contributors they have met through the years. This is one such story.

127. Collected from Homer H. Young, Ph.D., who as a teenager was the perpetrator of the knocking on the carwall. He told the story with great amusement in the 1950s and 1960s; the events took place in the 1920s. The story was told as the truth.

128. Collected in fragments from Yoichi Aoki in 1973, with contributions by Marilyn Aoki in 1984 and Suzette Raney in 1990. Called "Yotsuya Kaidan," ("The Ghost Story from Yotsuya", or "It Happened in Yotsuya") this story has so many variants that some bear no resemblance to others, beyond the name itself. This is the favorite ghost story of the Nisei people of California.

129. From the repertory of Judy Dockrey Young. *See the note for story number 126.*

130. Provided by Dennis and Judy Pruitt, of Phoenix, Arizona, in January of 1991. Mrs. Pruitt is the storyteller at Rawhide theme park in Scottsdale. The person to whom the story happened wrote it down and used the title "Hand of Time." Certain words have been omitted that might have identified the family involved.

131. Collected in Fort Hays, Kansas, on November 26, 1990, at McDonald's over breakfast, from an elderly white lady who told it as the truth. A lifelong resident of Fort Hays, she spoke reverently of Elizabeth, Fort Hays's fairly famous ghost.

132. "La Llorona" from "La Llorona in Yuma" published in *Southwest Folklore*, Volume V Number 1, Winter 1981. Collected by Belinda F. Lopez in Yuma, Arizona, in 1981 from "Informant

A.D., 37, male, half Mexican-American and half white [meaning Anglo]," and included in the above-named article written by Arizona folklorist Keith Cunningham. Reprinted by permission of the editor. This story is notable because of the motif of the Spanish man "legally" marrying a Spanish woman to promote his career and improve his social position. The collector, Srta. Lopez, pointed out that this version is not the most common one. Although collected in Yuma, Informant A.D. had first learned the story in neighboring Algodones, in Mexico, and the story would also be well-known in Imperial County, California.

133. Texas folklorist J. Frank Dobie gives a history of Jean Laffite in *Coronado's Children*. The pirate was born in France or Spain—stories vary—and perhaps at St. Malo or Orduña; either birthplace would give him an exotic lineage, Breton or Basque respectively. On existing historical documents, he spelled his name "Laffite," the spelling this collection employs. As a blacksmith shopowner on Bourbon Street in New Orleans, he took up with privateers on Barataria Island and became their entrepreneur/leader. Operating with letters of marque entitling them to raid the ships of one nation in behalf of a warring nation, the privateers raided indiscriminately and sold the goods and slaves in New Orleans.

When the War of 1812 broke out, the British offered Laffite a commission to attack New Orleans; instead he reported the plot to the Americans. At first Laffite was rebuffed, but when the battle of New Orleans came about, Andrew Jackson accepted Laffite's service in manning two artillery batteries. President Madison pardoned the "banditti" that fought for the U.S. in the battle. In 1816, Laffite moved his headquarters to Galveston Island, near present-day Houston. When his men began to prey on American ships, the Navy surrounded his enclave and ordered him out in 1820. Dobie suggests that Laffite died in Yucatán in 1826. Others claim he died in a battle with a British merchantman or was lost at sea in a storm. Like much of Laffite's life, his death was a mystery.

Laffite's headquarters, called the Maison Rouge, was real, and at least some of the treasure stories must be true also. This story came to the editors from many conflicting sources before 1989.

134. There are several theories about the origin of the name "Petit Jean." He may have been a short Frenchman killed by Indians, or "he" may have been the lady of the local legend. The people around Morrilton tell this version, with its lovely ghost. The editors have heard many versions of this legend before 1989.

135. Collected in New Orleans from an anonymous informant in November, 1984. The historic Marie Laveau died in 1881; her death was reported in the New Orleans newspapers. The second Marie must have been her daughter and a perfect filial image of her. The actual grave was originally unmarked, but its location is pinpointed by voodou tradition. Since voodou is a religion, practitioners are naturally skeptical of outsiders recording their traditions.

136. Collected from a young Hispana receptionist at the Kit Carson House Museum on January 4, 1990.

137. Retold from an account by a New Mexico listener at a storytelling event in December, 1989. When the editors asked the curator of the Bent House Museum if the story were true, he smiled and answered only, "You'll hear all kinds of stories about this place."

138. Provided by L. E. Gay of Santa Fe in June of 1990. Mr. Gay is a rare-book dealer and knowledgeable of Santa Fe and New Mexico lore.

139. Learned from Texas visitors to Silver Dollar City prior to January 1, 1989.

140. Collected in June of 1989 from Louis Darby of Opelousas, Louisiana. M. Darby is a Cajun fiddle-player and sometime storyteller.

141. Collected from Roger Knight from St. Louis, Missouri, in July of 1989. Mr. Knight in his 20s once worked at the Lunt Mansion as a server.

142. Provided by a librarian at Harwood Library in Taos, New Mexico, the night of January 4, 1990. She declined to be identified. Mabel Dodge Luján and Tony Luján were mavens of Taos artistic society for years; they were beloved and controversial. Other fragmentary tales of falling statues and moving furniture have also been heard by these editors, but this short tale is the most substantial we have received.

For Further Study . . .

For storytellers and story researchers who wish to pursue further study of ghost and supernatural narratives from the American Southwest, we recommend the following books and sources:

❖ *Researcher's Guide (to Archives and Regional History Sources)*, edited by John C. Larsen, Library Professional Publications, The Shoe String Press, Inc., Hamden, Connecticut, 1988. See especially the articles "Oral Histories" by Willa K. Baum and Bonnie Hardwick, and "The Ethics of Archival Research" by Floyd M. Shumway. (ISBN 0-208-02144-2)

❖ *Directory of Oral History Collections,* by Allen Smith, Oryx Press, Phoenix, Arizona, 1988. See especially the entries under the headings "Folk Medicine Archive," "Folklore/Folklife," and "Folklore Archive," page 108. (ISBN 0-89774-322-9)

❖ *Directory of Archives and Manuscript Repositories in the United States (Second Edition: National Historical Publications and Records Commission),* Oryx Press, Phoenix, Arizona, 1988. See especially the entries under the heading "Folklore," page 788.

The best source of folklore material is the "folks themselves." By going to the Southwest, or by corresponding with individuals living or reared in the Southwest, a storyteller or story researcher can best obtain folk narratives. If such an excursion or such communication is not feasible, here are suggested publishing houses and resource providers for story materials in print:

❖ August House Publishers, Post Office Box 3223, Little Rock, Arkansas 72203, telephone 1/800/284-8784. In addition to this anthology, August House publishes other folklore and stories collected or edited for reading, research, and telling. Write or call for a catalog.

❖ The National Association for the Preservation and Perpetuation of Storytelling (NAPPS), Post Office Box 309, Jonesborough, Tennessee 37659. Write for their current "Storytelling Catalog" or purchase their current *National Directory of Storytelling*. The *Directory* lists storytellers, storytelling organizations, newsletters, resources, festivals, conferences, and centers for storytelling.

Index of Stories by Chapter, Showing States of Origin

Stories from the Introduction

The Ghost of Fort Sill, Oklahoma
I Saw Her!, New Mexico
Spooklight at Hornet, Missouri
Bailey's Lantern, Texas
The Dolores Light, Texas
Feu Follé, Louisiana
El árbol de la horca, New Mexico
Spirit Writing, New Mexico
East Texas Hairy Man, Texas
To Keep His Ghost Away, Arkansas

Ghost Jokes

1 The Pawpaw Lie, Oklahoma
2 You Can't Get Out, Oklahoma
3 I Can't Get In, Arkansas
4 The Haunted Car, Texas
5 A Ghost Story for Folklorists, Arkansas
6 Scary Song, Arkansas

Urban Legends

7 Last Kiss, Texas
8 Laffite's Hook-Arm, Louisiana
9 The Baby's Milk Bottles, California
10 Pair of Pants, Texas
11 Freshman Initiation, Missouri, Texas
12 Call from the Grave, California
13 Eleven-Eleven, Oklahoma, Arkansas
14 *La LLorona* at Waldo, New Mexico

Ghostly Lights

15 Michael and the Ghost Light, Arkansas
16 Dawson Cemetery, New Mexico
17 Senath Light, Arkansas
18 Ghost Light in Red, Arkansas
19 Ball Lightning, Arkansas
20 Ball of Fire, Kansas
21 The Lights in the Nursing Home, Arkansas
22 Ball of Fire II, Texas
23 The Texarkana Light, Arkansas, Texas
24 The Big Thicket Light, Texas
25 The Miami Spooklight, Oklahoma
26 Spooklight at Hornet, Missouri
27 Hornet Burial Ground, Missouri
28 The Split Hornet Light, Missouri
29 The Still Hornet Light, Missouri
30 Ghost Light Along the Chisos, Texas
31 Bayou Bourleau, Louisiana
32 The Marfa Lights, Texas
33 Lights at Silverton, Colorado
34 Ball of Fire III, New Mexico
35 Ball of Fire IV, New Mexico

Ghosts of the Roadways

36 Raw Head and Bloody Bones, Missouri, Arkansas
37 The Guard at San Marcos Bridge, Texas
38 White Wolf, Texas
39 The Ghostly Battle, California
40 The Head on the High Road, New Mexico
41 The Headless *Caballero*, New Mexico
42 *La Malogra*, New Mexico
43 Ghost Girl of the Mimbres, New Mexico
44 *La LLorona*, New Mexico
45 *La LLorona* II, New Mexico
46 Hitchhiker at Tierra Amarilla, New Mexico
47 Booger Dog, Texas
48 The Headless Outlaw, Texas
49 Ghostly Express, Kansas
50 The Lady of White Rock Lake, Texas

Haunted Houses

51a The Ghost Smokes A Pipe, Texas
51b Ghost Who Smoke Pipe, Texas
52 The Ghost Door, Arkansas
53 The Ghost at Hughes, Arkansas
54 The Baker's Ghost, Texas
55 The Haunted House at Howe, Texas
56 The Healing Lady of Los Luceros, New Mexico
57 Winchester Mansion, California
58 Helen, California

Other Haunted Places

Supernatural and Preternatural

Possessed By Spirits

Lifestyles of the Dead and Famous

Index of Stories by States of Origin

GHOST STORIES FROM THE AMERICAN SOUTH

To the memory of Joe B. Rigdon, a Southern mountaineer, who never had the opportunity for contact with books or scholarship. Knowing that a book was dedicated to him would have surprised him more than anyone else.

ACKNOWLEDGMENTS

Compilers and authors of most books rely on the help of others for material necessary to make their proposed volume a reality. This tradition certainly holds for the present collection, for without outside help this manuscript would never have made it to the publisher's desk. A large number of people allowed me to intrude upon their busy lives and, in every case, responded graciously and kindly, willingly supplying me with the material found in this book. Such unselfishness deserves recognition, and I gladly give that here to Bill Clements, Bob Cochran, Frank de Caro, Nana Farris, Bill Ferris, George Foss, Bill Lightfoot, Brenda McCallum, Bob McCarl, Tom McGowan, Dan Patterson, Chuck Perdue, Sharon Sarthou, Ellen Shipley, Ethel C. Simpson, Marcia Wade, John O. West, and Charles K. Wolfe. They are, of course, not to be held responsible for any interpretations or errors found here; for those I claim sole responsibility.

W.K.M.

$\mathcal{C}$ONTENTS

# INTRODUCTION

THIS VOLUME OF SUPERNATURAL NARRATIVES IS, UNLIKE MOST SUCH VOL-
umes available today, taken from the folk tradition of the southern
United States. A majority of the texts were collected in the last twenty-
five years, although the tales are set in time periods ranging from the
Revolutionary War to the present. Most of the items given here have
never appeared in print before; in all cases, they have been maintained
by oral narration. Some very widely known stories are given here, while
others have not previously been known outside of a single family or
community. They are related only in that they are in some sense Southern, meaning not that they are unique to the region but merely that
they are told there.

These are examples of Southern folklore, primarily ghost legends,
with some space given to closely related supernatural beings such as
witches and banshees. I make no claim that all supernatural folk legends
found in the South are set forth here or even that the ones to be found
here are the most popular examples currently in existence. I have made
a concerted attempt, however, to provide material representative of the
entire Southern region.

Some items were taken from my own fieldwork, but most came from
other collections and archives. Call it fate, accident, luck or chance; the
point is that the informants whose texts fill these pages were not chosen
by any design on my part. They just happened to have appropriate
material which they could make readily available to me. Certainly,
many other volumes of supernatural narratives could, provided informants could be ferreted out, be compiled, for almost every community

and many families in the South have people who pass on these traditions.

A number of terms used in this volume may be unfamiliar or confusing to many readers. First is the word *folklore*, which in popular usage is generally reserved for anything that is quaint or odd. That is not the precise meaning of the word, however, and not the one used in this book. Here, *folklore*, refers to material that is passed on orally and, usually, informally; is traditional; undergoes change over space and time, creating variants and versions; is usually anonymous in the sense that most bearers of folklore are not concerned with the original creator; and finally, folklore is usually formulaic.[1]

Another term which calls for definition is *legend*. Legends are one of three types of folk narratives, the other two being folktales and myths. Folktales are regarded as fictional by both teller and audience and are told primarily for entertainment. Myths are set in prehistoric times, involve the activities of gods, demigods and animals and are believed by the teller to be true. Legends are set in historic times, are concerned with secular characters and call for a position of belief or disbelief.

Equally confusing is the common word *ghost*. Its ambiguity results because many terms—ghost, revenant, wraith, specter, apparition and spirit, to name a few—are used for essentially the same phenomenon. Often the actions of these agents are indistinguishable from those of witches. Ernest W. Baughman comments on the difficulty of distinguishing between these various figures:

> It is very difficult to tell whether the haunters under this category are ghosts, witches, or familiar spirits. The actions of these agents are very much alike. About the only distinction that can be made is that made by the informant: if the informant thinks of the agent as a ghost, then the agent is a ghost, regardless of the similarities of the actions to those of witches or spirits. The famous "Bell Witch" of Tennessee is usually a ghost by any criteria used; yet it is almost invariably referred to as a witch.[2]

Complicating the matter of definition is that the returning dead come back in several forms. First, they may come back in the same body they had while alive; second, they may appear in some sort of spectral form; third, they may be invisible and known only by the deeds, noises or mischief they commit.

In this book, for the sake of simplicity, a *ghost* is defined as a being returned from the dead in human or animal form or having some features of humans or animals. Those returning dead which lack human or animal features are labeled *supernatural creatures*. *Witches* differ from ghosts mainly in that they are living people with supernatural powers rather than dead people who have returned. The *banshee* mentioned earlier is regarded as a ghost although placed in a chapter dealing with non-ghosts. In a treatise on Irish or Scottish folklore, a banshee would likely be classified as a *fairy*, but these small, delicate supernatural creatures are extremely rare in American folklore.

One further definition is in order, namely "the South." That is easily answered, for it refers to the states of Alabama, Arkansas, Florida, Georgia, Kentucky, Louisiana, Mississippi, North Carolina, South Carolina, Tennessee, Texas and Virginia. In other words, the South means here most of the states represented in the Confederacy during the Civil War.

Having established some working definitions, it remains for me to discuss those who preserve and propagate these legends, that is, the informants. Remarks about individual narrators are included in the section of notes in the back of the book, but some general consideration should be given to the type of person who communicates legends about the supernatural.

The stereotype exists that the best bearers of any sort of folk tradition, ghost legends included, are rustic illiterates. As with most stereotypes, this has an element of truth but is also misleading. Certainly the rural unschooled know and tell such stories, but by no means do they have an exclusive hold on them. Ghost narratives flourish in cities just as well as they do in bucolic areas; indeed, they may even be more common there simply because there are more people to hear and tell them. Suffice it to say that most Southerners—in fact, most Americans—know or know of such tales, which they have heard related by friends and acquaintances, sometimes as firsthand experiences but more often as something that happened to a friend of a friend.

What type of person tells ghost stories? The foremost qualification for a bearer of this or any type of folklore is intelligence; a second requirement is a good memory. Without these, he will not be able to recall the lore and certainly will not be able to supply the details that remove a text from the status of a mundane incident to that of an item of interest that others want to hear.

Notice that I mentioned intelligence, not education, for the two are not synonymous. A person with no formal schooling may still be quite intelligent; furthermore, education has little if any bearing on whether or not a person will relate any type of folklore. As the texts in this volume illustrate, many ghost legends are perpetuated by college students, while others come from people with minimal schooling. To put it briefly, almost any intelligent person with a good memory who has the interest can, and will, tell stories concerning ghosts and other supernatural creatures.

Though there are many people who fit that description, certain narrators are better than others. To distinguish between these good narrators and those who can tell a tale but don't, Swedish folklorist Carl Wilhelm von Sydow offered the concept of active and passive bearers of tradition. He defined active bearers as those "who keep tradition alive and transmit it, whereas the passive bearers have indeed heard of what a certain tradition contains, and may perhaps, when questioned, recollect part of it, but do nothing themselves to spread it or keep it alive."[3]

One mark of the active bearer is that he tells a story as though it is his own, not necessarily as a personal experience (although it may be), but one that is related with authority as if it is his possession. The active narrator has thorough command of a text and presents it strongly. He will flesh out the basic narrative with dialogue and various dramatic devices so that it becomes a performance, not just a skeletal presentation of the merely essential details.

The passive bearer, on the other hand, presents his material almost apologetically and relates it as a secondhand possession, frequently resorting to phrases like "they say" or "it is said," not for clarification but because he is ill at ease with it.

Perhaps the difference between an active bearer and a passive bearer's treatments of a ghost legend is best illustrated by concrete examples. First, a text from Tavares, Florida:

Four or five years ago the exciting thing to do on a Friday or Saturday evening was go to Monkey Jungle. Monkey Jungle was a long winding road with many overhanging trees. The road eventually wound up where it began, thus creating a large circle.

It was believed that on a full moon after you crossed eight railroad tracks and stopped on the ninth, you would see a black body carrying her head. It was told her son had been hit by a train. So the next night she laid her head on the tracks for a train to run over.[4]

Second, a text from Harrisonburg, Virginia:

> There is a haunted house in Mt. Sidney. The first owner was a lady who went crazy. Since then there have been several owners who say the house is haunted because at night they hear footsteps, and the blinds are open in the morning that they drew the night before.[5]

Third, a narrative from Jonesboro, Arkansas:

> There was an old cemetery down the road from their farm. Uh, uh, of course, they called it a graveyard. Their, uh, grandparents had always told them that this old grave there was the grave of a drunkard. The legend was that once when he was drunk and eating cherries, he choked to death on a cherry pit. And then, of course, this tremendous cherry tree grew at the spot where his head would be in the grave. It was quite old and had low, spreading branches. All the children who lived around were just frightened to death of it because of the legend. And, uh, that's just about all I can think of except that, you know, one summer evening, late, at twilight time, Big Mother was riding a horse down the road when in some manner the horse wandered off into the graveyard. You know, when she found out where she was, she became frightened and that frightened her horse and he began to run. He crossed the grave and the low hanging branches dragged her off the horse. That's just all I know, I don't know how she got home or anything.[6]

These three narrators clearly have an uninvolved, almost disinterested, manner of presentation. They all recall the basic details of the legends they are relating, but they make no attempt to heighten the dramatic effect of the stories and, in the case of the third text, there is some hesitancy even in remembering the details recalled. Reading a transcript of their renditions is like scanning an outline rather than the complete play. Compare them with the following three texts. First, one from Forrest City, Arkansas:

> The bank was robbed by a man who held the bank up by himself with a shotgun. He was apprehended a short time later but didn't

have the money with him. A policeman panicked and shot the man on sight before the man had a chance to tell anyone where he hid the money. As the man was dying, they asked him where he hid the money, and he said he hid it in the old graveyard south of town behind the huge oak tree.

The police immediately go there to look for the money, but they never find it. They assumed that the man lied and that the town lost the ten thousand dollars. Then some teenage boys decide to investigate and they find a couple of dollars buried under the tree. The cops investigate again and find nothing. Time after time only a few dollars at a time was found under the tree; but when it's investigated by police nothing has been found by their digging. Everyone believes that the money is somewhere under the tree, but they believe the man put a curse on the money. Everyone believes that the curse will go away some day so they keep trying to find the money.[7]

Second, another narrative from Arkansas, this one from Batesville:

There was this woman who hated her husband. So one night she murdered him and cut him up into thirteen pieces. About a week later she was lying in bed when she heard a voice calling, "Where are my legs?" She just put her pillow over her head and soon the voice stopped. The next night she heard the same voice asking, "Where are my arms?" and the next night the voice asked, "Where are my hands?" She finally got a little afraid and went to stay at a neighbor's house for a night. Nothing happened there so she went home again the next night. That night she heard the voice again wailing, "Where is my left thumb?" over and over and over. Suddenly her left thumb began to twitch and it was twisted off.[8]

Finally, there is this text from Hot Springs, Arkansas:

Mrs. Florencie Williams lived in a large house on Grand Avenue. Her son, Bob Williams, had been sheriff and was shot to death. Thus, Mrs. Williams lived with Mrs. Woodcock only.

Mrs. Woodcock was a friend of my grandmother Henderson. She told Granny that many times when she came into the house, at night after 10:30, at the top of the stairs there were three figures. When she reached the top of the stairs the figures would disappear into the walls. There was one certain door upstairs which would not stay closed. No matter how many times Mrs. Woodcock would close it, it would *click* and open.

At a place in the upstairs hall was a big mirror. At certain times of the year there would appear on the mirror a ghostly looking thing as if someone had soaped the mirror for a Hallowe'en prank. Mrs. Woodcock would rub it off and it wouldn't appear until the next year.

Mrs. Woodcock told Granny that often she would walk up the stairs and she would hear a *click, click* noise following her up. When she stopped, it stopped. It sounded like a child playing in high heels or shoes with copper taps on the heels.

Mrs. Florencie never had any flowers in the house—at least she never went out to buy any and didn't have a garden. But sometimes in the dead of winter, when there weren't any fresh flowers for miles around, they would smell tube roses. The smell would start out faint and then increase to a terribly strong smell.

Every so often, every picture in the house would be found turned at an angle clockwise. Mrs. Woodcock and Mrs. Florencie would straighten them up and later would find them crooked again.[9]

In the last three texts an altogether different tale-telling ability is evident. The narrator is in total command of the narrative; there is nothing lackadaisical or hesitant about the presentations. None is offered as a personal experience, but all of the stories in a sense belong to the person telling it. That state of authority is almost totally lacking in the three earlier yarns.

A not uncommon situation is for passive and active bearers to change their relationship to folk tradition. Passive bearers might become active if they hear a tradition long enough that they become conversant with it and take it actively in hand. On the other hand, active bearers may become passive for various reasons. For example, a child may know actively several items of children's folklore but become passive concerning them once he has outgrown his childhood. An active bearer may also become passive when there is no longer an audience for the traditions he knows. But with legendary material such as is presented in this volume, most active and passive narrators remain so all of their lives.

Granted that there are both active and passive narrators, where do they narrate? What is the ambiance in which ghost legends are narrated? The answer is simple: they are told in most places where more than one person can be found. The performer/audience distance is usually not so great as that between a concert pianist and those attending his recital, but one thing is certain: without an audience, the narrator will cease to narrate.

In times past, the home was a place where ghost and supernatural legends were told, and it remains an important arena for the transmission of such material. Often ghost stories are told just between members of the immediate family, but on other occasions, a special social gathering, such as a party for friends, elicits such activity. In the South, country stores are an important forum for the exchange of tales, although usually in these situations the transmission is between members of the same generation rather than from an older generation to a younger one. The same holds for another popular place where ghost legends are told: the college dormitory. A typical dorm session is described by a female student:

On November 23, 1974 it was very rainy and dark. Around 9:00 I went to Room 627 to visit. The wind was hollering through the cracked window. One of the girls put a candle in the middle of the room, and turned out the lights.[10]

Campfires, offices and automobiles, during long trips, could also be cited as places where ghost stories are commonly related.

Why do people tell ghost stories? There is no single answer to this question, because most tales are told for more than one reason. The late William R. Bascom divided the various functions of folklore into four basic types: *compensation, validation, education* and *integration*. These terms sound good, but what do they mean? Again, perhaps the best way to demonstrate is by example. For the first function, that of *compensation,* consider the following story:

Children heard of a piano playing in a church outside of Osceola, about four miles out of town. They were curious and set out to satisfy their curiosity. They said they actually heard the piano playing but they were afraid to go inside of the church to verify the noise they heard. They left immediately in a hurry to get back to Osceola. The driver of the car was going very fast on loose rocks, a gravel road, and lost control of the car and hit an embankment. Two was dead on arrival at the Osceola hospital and three escaped with minor injuries.[11]

The collector of this narrative made the following assessment: "I believe that this legend served to compensate for the accident. There was an accident and two people were killed. So, to compensate for the man's inadequacies [losing control of the car], there is the implied belief that the supernatural connected with the playing piano caused the accident." Undoubtedly, this tale serves several other functions, but it is plain that its main purpose is that which the collector has underscored.

Validation, the second of the four functions in Bascom's scheme, involves justifying cultural rituals and institutions. For example, a woman related the following narrative, which she said contains a message warning everyone to "live a Christian life, because you never know when you will die."

About forty years ago when I was twenty, my boyfriend and I were double-dating with my best friend and her fiancé. We were going to a wedding party that Saturday night that was being given in honor of my girlfriend, who was going to be married the following Saturday. The party was similar to wedding showers today in the gift-giving custom only. The showers then were more of a party in nature and your fiancé, boyfriend or husband were invited also.

After the presents were opened, a party began in full bloom. There was a tremendous amount of food enjoyed, then music and dancing began. We had all been having a good time for about two hours when I developed a migraine headache. My headache continually worsened until I couldn't stand it for another minute. I had to go home. My boyfriend and I caught a ride with another couple that was leaving because we had rode in my girlfriend's fiancé's car, and of course, since they were the honored couple, they weren't ready to leave yet.

I got home around eleven o'clock and I went straight to bed. At one o'clock my mother awakened me with a horrible phone call. My girlfriend had been instantly killed in an automobile accident on the way home from the party. Her fiancé hadn't been seriously injured. The accident occurred when they were topping a hill and a car with a drunk man driving hit them head on. The girl was only nineteen, and everyone was shocked and grieved that someone so sweet, young and beautiful could have been killed so horribly. Those that were close to her were hurt the most, including me and her family, of course.

After she was buried in the Catholic cemetery, her parents bought her a beautiful tombstone in the shape of an angel. Legend has it that every time someone visits her grave, the angel tombstone points her finger at them and the pointed finger follows them around the graveyard until they leave. It's been said that the finger lights up at night with a golden glow. I have seen the finger point at me when I visited the grave. It's as if the statue has suddenly come to life as it points at you while you're walking. I believe you can see these things because my girlfriend was such a virtuous girl and the angel tombstone was an appropriate memorial of the innocent young girl who had lived a Christian life.[12]

What the legend really means is, of course, a matter of speculation. Some persons might say that it contains an anti-religious message. According to others familiar with the story, the girl's parents "were possessed with their religion, and they believed practically everything was a sin"[13]; these observers might argue that the legend contains a lesson for parents who are very strict. To the informant, however, the main function the narrative served was validation of the Christian outlook on life.

That folklore often functions as a form of *education* should be obvious to most readers. Many people are familiar with fables or folktales that point out some moral. In some societies, formal instructions are given in various forms of folklore. That is not often the case in the United States; more frequently, legends are used to make such points as that enunciated by this informant, who said a ghost appeared to remind people of the evil of unjust execution:

Forty years ago a man was hung on the bridge in Forrest City across from the courthouse. He was hung because he killed a man in self-defense, but the police said that he killed the man purposely. A friend of mine knew the man, and he said that they were at a bar drinking when the man and a stranger got into an argument. The stranger pulled out a gun. The man grabbed the gun, and after a struggle the gun went off and shot the stranger. My friend saw what happened, and he said he knew it was self-defense. After a short unjust trial, the man was pronounced guilty, and he was hung the following day.

I heard for many years that you could see the man hanging from the bridge on the anniversary of his death. I didn't believe it for years until a friend invited me to go with him and see the man hanging there, about fifteen years ago, on the anniversary of his death. A light flashed where he had been hung and you could actually see a vision of a man hanging for about three minutes, and then it was gone.[14]

Folklore also is used to maintain conformity to accepted patterns of behavior, or *integration*. While this is partially achieved through the previously mentioned functions of education and validation, Bascom's concept of integration differs in that it can refer to situations in which folklore is used to exert social pressure. It can also refer to situations in which oral traditions are used against individuals who attempt to deviate from patterns of convention. Most instances of folklore used to achieve integration are not so extreme; usually it does little more than bind those who know an item of lore into a group. This is precisely the integrative function that the following legend serves:

> About a mile from the rural town of Chapel Hill, Tennessee, a railroad track crosses a gravel road. In the 1890s an engineer for the Louisville & Nashville Railroad was killed here. This man got too close to the edge of the cab, and as they sped around a sharp curve he fell from the train. He was decapitated as the train rolled on.
>
> Every night at 9:30, the L&N freight train passes this area. Shortly afterwards, a light appears which sways back and forth. This is supposedly the headless engineer searching for his head.[15]

Because the present book is devoted to orally transmitted ghost legends, which differ from the literary stories most readers are familiar with, a few words about the two types of narratives are in order. Of course, oral and literary legends are alike in some respects, such as the tendency to concentrate on a leading character, but the differences are greater. One of the major distinctions is that folk legends usually have no title. Typically, the traditional ghost tale begins with some statement like, "You recall old Arnold Hill? Well, did you hear that story about him and the sailor's ghost?" And if these tales have a title at all, it is of only the most general, descriptive sort.

A second feature of folk legends is that they generally consist of only one scene. Compare, for example, the following tale with a more complex literary legend:

> John Green and Jim Cook were walking to church one night back in 1905 or 1906. They were going to Cook's Chapel down near Savoy. As they walked along they saw a group of men up in front.

The boys decided to catch them and walk together. The faster Jim and John walked, the faster the men walked and the taller they grew until they were as tall as the trees. The men came to a big rock by the side of the road; here a hollow led off into the woods. When the men came to this rock, they turned off behind it and disappeared. When the boys got to the spot, they could see no one. Later, Jim and John went back there and looked over the whole area during daylight but they could find nothing unusual. They always believed this vision had a meaning for them but they never knew what.[16]

Unlike literary legends, which are the work of the writer, folk legends are not composed by the presenter; he is merely the means by which the story is passed on and perpetuated. Even in the case of narratives based on personal experiences, the audience is, in certain respects, more important than the narrator, for without them the legends cease to be told. On the other hand, composers of literary legends write in hopes of capturing an audience and produce material that may, or may not, be successful. Thus, William Austin wrote "Peter Rugg, the Missing Man," which was so successful that it passed into local legendry.

Another notable difference between oral and literary legends is that the former lacks constant form; instead, it is in a continual state of flux. Even when repeated by the same narrator, two tellings of a story are never identical. Oral legends are generally related in vernacular language, because that is the way most people ordinarily speak. Regarding his narrative as something that actually happened, or is said to have happened (as is not the case in literary legends, especially literary ghost legends), the teller of folk legends relates his text in the language his audience will understand, that is, his daily speech. Certainly some literary texts are couched in vernacular language; mostly, however, the literary tradition attempts to avoid the colloquial.

There is also an added physical dimension to the orally transmitted ghost legend which often makes it difficult to capture in print: the narrator's use of his voice and body to dramatize the text. Facial expressions, manual gestures, and vocal intonation and inflection are utilized to bring a story to life. Factors of time and space also condition the performance, and, of course, the audience has a more direct impact upon the text than is the case with a written piece. Certainly, then, the oral ghost narrative differs markedly from the literary one.

Others have preceded the current volume with collections and analyses of Southern ghostlore, but there haven't been as many as one might think, especially when one discounts nonscholarly efforts. One of the most successful early efforts was made by Charles M. Skinner, a one-time newspaper correspondent who produced five volumes of American legendry between 1896 and 1903. The first of these, a two-volume *Myths and Legends of Our Own Land* (1896), was followed by *Myths and Legends of Our New Possessions and Protectorate* (1899), which was followed in turn by the two-volume *American Myths and Legends* (1903).

As these titles indicate, Skinner's focus was on legends of all sorts found in the United States and her possessions rather than on supernatural legends from the South. Most of the space is given to items from the Middle Atlantic and New England States, but even so, a goodly portion of the 1896 and 1903 volumes deal with the South and some of those texts deal with the supernatural. All of the selections were "improved" by Skinner, who related the tales in what Richard Dorson calls a "limpid Hawthornesque prose."[17] Although frankly a popularizer, Skinner did collect material from oral tradition and made some attempt to provide his books with some scholarly trappings, such as prefaces demonstrating how the legends fitted into regional clusters. Nevertheless, he also took items from various printed sources that often remain unidentified. Most of his texts deal with Colonial and Revolutionary times; he deliberately stayed with eras beyond the memory of the living mean, because "the past is more picturesque than the present."[18] Rewritten texts, the failure to identify sources, and the lack of comparative material place Skinner's volume outside the realm of ideal folklore scholarship.

Newbell Niles Puckett's *Folk Beliefs of the Southern Negro* (1926) was originally written as a Ph.D. dissertation at Yale University. It does include one chapter dealing with ghosts and witches, although it consists mainly of descriptions of beliefs about these beings rather than complete texts. Puckett's book is a study of acculturation and, despite a title that implies otherwise, consists of materials gathered from elderly people and rural illiterates. He also associated folklore with the past, a misleading concept to which many other scholars have subscribed. Thus, he spoke about "the necessity of haste in collecting this fast-disappearing lore."[19]

Although Frank Clyde Brown began collecting his folklore prior to Puckett, his work was not published until long afterwards. Indeed, it did not find its way into print until after Brown's death when it appeared as the seven-volume *Frank C. Brown Collection of North Carolina Folklore* (1952–1964). Brown had come to Trinity College (now Duke

University) in 1909 as a Professor of English, and three years later started gathering various types of folklore found in the Tarheel State.

Brown's interest lay mainly in folksongs and ballads, but he did collect several folktales and legends, a large number of which deal with ghosts and the supernatural. Brown did record his informants' names and usually their place of residence and the site of the collection. In recording these, he did not consider such factors as degree of belief or nonbelief; contextual data; or what role the narrative had in the community in which it was kept alive. There is also ample evidence that much of what he recorded was "memory culture," that is, material recalled from the past but no longer actively told. Brown's total work is useful, if for no other reason, because it is one of the most extensive collections from a single state ever published. In regard to ghost legends, however, it is a relatively small body of work.

One of the most prolific American collectors of the genres of folklores sometimes collectively called the verbal arts (meaning those items like songs or stories that are regarded by their perpetuators as requiring artistic performance) was Vance Randolph. A native of Pittsburg, Kansas, he spent most of his adult life in the Ozarks of Arkansas, Missouri and Oklahoma. Among his numerous publications were articles on witchcraft; a booklet titled *Ozark Ghost Stories* (1944); and a book originally issued as *Ozark Superstitions* (1947).[20]

This last volume is especially valuable because of its bibliography listing everything written on traditional Ozark beliefs as of the publication date. Two lengthy chapters deal with Ozark ghost stories and witchcraft. The stories are generally rewritten summaries, but a few are offered in the actual words of his informants, who are identified by name and place of residence.

J. Mason Brewer was one of the leading black folklorists of his day. Throughout his long career, he taught in colleges in North and South Carolina and Texas. Like the other scholars mentioned here, he was interested in many types of folk narrative found in the South, and several of his books do include some ghost tales. His *Dog Ghosts and Other Texas Negro Folk Tales* (1958) is seemingly devoted to the subject; the title, however, is misleading. Only the last of the book's five sections deals with ghost stories. Brewer includes informant names, ages at the time of collection and places of residence. He also tries to reproduce his texts exactly as they were related to him; for the convenience of his readers, however, he regularizes the dialect, which lessens the value of including dialect spelling. Another shortcoming in the collection is that Brewer, like too many other collectors, offers no comparative material.[21]

(On the positive side, Brewer avoids one trap that many collectors often fall into, namely, the geriatric syndrome. Rather than recording only from elderly informants, he garners legends from many age groups. His informants range in age from twenty-one to ninety-seven.)

Two collectors of Kentucky mountain lore did include comparative data, but their work had other problems. Marie Campbell's *Tales from the Cloud Walking Country* (1958) was devoted to tales "from across the ocean waters" that were grouped around individual raconteurs.[22] The texts were mostly märchen, or fairy tales, with only a few ghost narratives included. Recent evidence suggests that some of these tales were fabricated out of whole cloth. Whether or not this is so, it is clear that the material Campbell reported was representative of a "memory culture" rather than a living one.

To a certain extent, this is also true of the work of Leonard Roberts, who definitely sought out the oldest elements of folklore but did manage to report some more recent items. His focus was on märchen, but in *South from Hell-fer-Sartin* (1955) and *Sang Branch Settlers: Folksongs and Tales of a Kentucky Mountain Family* (1974), a few selections deal with ghost and supernatural legends.

Ray B. Browne's *"A Night With the Hants" and Other Alabama Folk Experiences* (1977) not only includes comparative data and notes on informants but a transcript of a folk storytelling session. By this means, Browne provides as close a flavor of the natural context as one is likely to find. Despite the title, there is much in Browne's book that does not have anything to do with ghosts or the supernatural. Still, the majority does. Although Browne has no apparent age bias in his collecting, most of his texts come from persons of advanced age. Despite his claim that the volume "represents a good cross section of the folktales of the state," the truth is that only a very small section of Alabama is represented.[23] Even so, it is the only collection of printed ghost legends from the state and gives more information about the setting in which such narratives are often related than any other book yet published.

One of the most prolific authors among American folklorists was the late Richard M. Dorson. Of his more than two dozen books and hundreds of articles, only two deal with Southern ghost lore, and even in these the subject receives scant attention. A few brief items, such as John Lawson's report of a spectral ship that appeared to colonists of present-day North Carolina, are included in *America Begins: Early*

American Writing (1950).[24] Several supernatural texts are contained in *American Negro Folktales* (1967), itself a compilation of two earlier books, *Negro Folktales in Michigan* (1956) and *Negro Tales from Pine Bluff, Arkansas, and Calvin, Michigan* (1958).[25] Dorson includes informant and collection data, as well as comparative notes, but the volume's major value lies in the extended introductory essay containing, among other features, a discussion of the "Art of Negro Storytelling."[26]

Two other works which deal tangentially with ghost narratives are John A. Burrison's *The Golden Arm: The Folk Tale and Its Literary Use by Mark Twain and Joel C. Harris* (1968) and Harry Middleton Hyatt's *Hoodoo, Conjuration, Witchcraft, Rootwork* (1970–1977). Burrison's monograph concerns a tale that is always told as fiction but is based on an ancient folk belief that a dead man or animal cannot rest until its physical remains are intact. Hyatt's several volumes contain data gathered during many years of collecting, primarily among blacks, which focus on the four aspects of belief listed in the title. The first volume contains several texts concerning ghosts as well as informants' statements about the stories.[27]

William Lynwood Montell's *Ghosts Along the Cumberland: Deathlore in the Kentucky Foothills* (1975) is the most recent scholarly treatment of Southern ghostlore. As the subtitle suggests, Montell deals with more than ghosts, namely, death beliefs, death omens and folk beliefs. The major importance of this volume is that it deals with material from a very small region, an area of southcentral Kentucky known as the Eastern Pennyroyal. Surprisingly, there are very few other studies of ghostlore, or any other type of folklore, from such essentially homogenous sections of the South. Filled with comparative data, information on collectors and informants and discussions of various aspects of deathlore, *Ghosts Along the Cumberland* reveals just how strong a hold tradition exerts on daily life in the South.[28]

That, to my knowledge, constitutes the entire body of published books on Southern ghost legendry. Such popularizing efforts as Hans Holzer's *Best True Ghost Stories* (1983) were not mentioned because of both their nonscholarly design and their nonfolkloristic approach. Holzer and similar pop-parapsychologists are primarily concerned with demonstrating that ghosts exist and are "indicative of man's continued existence beyond death."[29]

This is not the aim of folklorists, who are interested in ghost narratives as an element of traditional culture. Whether or not ghosts exist, they are psychologically real. People do believe in them and tell stories about them, which makes them deserving of consideration and study. Questions that concern folklorists are, Who sees and talks about ghosts? Under what conditions? What do they mean as cultural artifacts? Hopefully, some answers to these queries are given in this book in the prefatory comments to each section and the notes for each entry.

Now it only remains to discuss one of the eight categories this book contains. Why does a volume of ghost stories have a section on witches? There are at least two reasons. One is the desire on my part to provide some examples of other types of closely related supernatural lore, especially since these traditions are often perpetuated by the same people who tell ghost stories. More important is the already mentioned fact that in societies such as the South where both witches and ghosts exist, there is no sharp distinction between them.

So much for the preliminaries. Now on to some stories of the eerie and supernatural that are told in the South.

W.K. McNeil

Ozark Folk Center
Mountain View, Arkansas

NOTES

[1] For a more detailed discussion of these points, see my book *The Charm Is Broken: Readings in Arkansas and Missouri Folklore* (Little Rock: August House, Inc., 1984), pp. 11–13.

[2] Ernest W. Baughman, *Type and Motif Index of the Folktales of England and North America* (The Hague: Mouton & Co., 1966), p. 143.

[3] Carl Wilhelm von Sydow, *Selected Papers on Folklore* (New York: Arno Press, 1977; reissue of a work originally published in 1948), pp. 12–13.

[4] Reported in 1978 by Terry Fox from Tavares, Florida. Fox was apparently recalling a legend that was popular during his teenage years. This is Baughman's motif E422.I.I.(b) "Headless woman—appearance only."

[5] Collected September, 1965 by Elmer L. Smith from an unidentified informant in Harrisonburg, Virginia. Baughman's motifs E281 "Ghosts haunt house" and E402.1.2 "Footsteps of invisible ghost heard" apply here.

[6] Collected June 15, 1974 by Katherine McCracken from an unnamed white female in Jonesboro, Arkansas. There is no motif number cited by either Baughman or Thompson that directly corresponds to the element of the cherry tree in this text.

[7] Collected by Brenda Hedrick from an unnamed retired contractor in Forrest City, Arkansas. The man had lived in Forrest City for the past fifty-five years; the bank was robbed about thirty-five years before. He claimed he saw some of the money that was found and strongly believed that the money was cursed by the robber. Baughman's motif E291 "Ghosts protect hidden treasure" is relevant.

[8] Collected in 1975 by Lynn Runyan from an unidentified informant in Batesville, Arkansas. This is very reminiscent of Type 366 *The Man from the Gallows* and Baughman's motifs E235.4

"Return from the dead to punish theft of part of corpse" and E419.7 "Ghost returns when part of body is removed from grave." Runyan's text differs from most in that the corpse is mutilated without being buried and the ending lacks the sudden scare tactic of hollering at a listener "You've got it!" or some similar phrase, and it does not have the unrealistic silver or gold arm, which is of course the reason this tale is often called "The Golden Arm."

⁹Collected by Ruthann Luedicke in 1961 from her aunt, Ruth Henderson Martin. The informant was a native of Marshall, Texas, but at the time of this collection lived in Hot Springs, Arkansas. Martin also contributed the text about the dead soldier at Pleasant Hill, Louisiana, who returned for his missing teeth (21 in text), and more information about her is given in the notes for that narrative. Relevant motifs here include E281 "Ghosts haunt house" and E402.1.2 "Footsteps of invisible ghost heard." There is no assigned motif number for the ghostly flowers; the closest is F815 "Extraordinary plants."

¹⁰These comments appear in a paper turned in to Dr. William Clements, Arkansas State University, Jonesboro, Arkansas, by Katherine Lemay.

¹¹Collected June 16, 1974, in Jonesboro, Arkansas, by Artie Faye Taylor from Mrs. Annie Jackson, a twenty-five year old black woman. The informant was a language arts teacher in elementary schools in Osceola, Arkansas. The relevant motif is E402.1.3 "Invisible ghost plays musical instrument."

¹²Collected in 1974 by Brenda Hedrick from an unnamed sixty-year-old woman. The woman is a devout Catholic, and according to Hedrick, "her religion is so intense that she has never missed going to church unless she was extremely sick." The relevant motif is F990 "Inanimate object acts as if living."

¹³Collected in 1974 by Brenda Hedrick from an unnamed retired electrician in Forrest City, Arkansas. The man was sixty years old and a lifelong resident of Forrest City.

¹⁴Collected in 1974 by Brenda Hedrick in Forrest City, Arkansas, from an unnamed retired farmer who lived near the town. The relevant motif is E274(a) "Ghost haunts scene of unjust execution."

¹⁵Collected in 1978 by Carl May from an unidentified informant. The relevant motifs are E422.1.1 "Headless revenant" and E530.1 "Ghost-like lights."

¹⁶Collected July 1, 1981, by Beulah Faye Tucker Davis from Belle Davis Green in Fayetteville, Arkansas. There is no motif number listed that exactly fits the incident described in Green's story; the closest is the general motif D600 "Miscellaneous transformation incidents."

¹⁷Richard M. Dorson, "How Shall We Rewrite Charles M. Skinner Today?," in Wayland D. Hand, ed., *American Folk Legend: A Symposium* (Berkeley: University of California Press, 1971), p. 69.

¹⁸Charles M. Skinner, *Myths and Legends of Our Own Land,* 2 vols. (Philadelphia: J.B. Lippincott, 1896), vol. I, p. 257.

¹⁹Newbell Niles Puckett, *Folk Beliefs of the Southern Negro* (Chapel Hill, North Carolina: University of North Carolina Press, 1926), p. viii.

²⁰The book was reissued in 1964 by Dover Publications, Inc., as *Ozark Magic and Folklore.* Despite the title change, there were no alterations in the book's contents.

²¹J. Mason Brewer, *Dog Ghosts and Other Texas Negro Folk Tales* (Austin, Texas: University of Texas Press, 1958).

²²Marie Campbell, *Tales from the Cloud Walking Country* (Bloomington, Indiana: Indiana University Press, 1958), p. 9.

²³Ray B. Browne, *"A Night with the Hants" and Other Alabama Folk Experiences* (Bowling Green, Ohio: Bowling Green University Popular Press, 1977), p. xx.

²⁴Richard M. Dorson, *America Begins: Early American Writing* (Bloomington, Indiana: Indiana University Press, 1971; reissue of a work originally published in 1950). Lawson's account appears on p. 159, and other supernatural incidents involving a Southern setting are on pp. 151 and 156.

²⁵Richard M. Dorson, *Negro Folktales in Michigan* (Cambridge, Massachusetts: Harvard University Press, 1956) and Richard M. Dorson, *Negro Tales from Pine Bluff, Arkansas and Calvin, Michigan* (Bloomington, Indiana: Indiana University Press, 1958).

[26]Richard M. Dorson, *American Negro Folktales* (Greenwich, Connecticut: Fawsett Publications, Inc., 1967). "The Art of Negro Storytelling" appears on pp. 47–59.

[27]Harry Middleton Hyatt, *Hoodoo, Conjuration, Witchcraft, Rootwork* (New York: Alma Egan Hyatt Foundation, 1970), vol. I, pp. 19–56.

[28]William Lynwood Montell, *Ghosts Along the Cumberland: Deathlore in the Kentucky Foothills* (Knoxville: University of Tennessee Press, 1975).

[29]Hans Holzer, *Best True Ghost Stories* (Englewood Cliffs, New Jersey: Prentice-Hall, Inc., 1983), p. 5.

1 𝓗AUNTED HOUSES

One very popular image that is conjured up by the word **ghost** is an old abandoned house with loose, banging shutters and doors that seem to be closed by some unseen hand. To a certain extent, this stereotype is justified, for houses are the favorite hangouts of ghosts. Generally, the houses are not abandoned, and in most narratives, no mention is made of the size of the residence. Usually the haunting is done by male ghosts, but neither are female ghosts rare. The haunting usually takes place in communities that have a long history of settlement and a relatively stable population. As the following selections illustrate, ghosts haunt houses for various reasons and, in most cases, are not harmful to human beings although they may often prove to be a nuisance. A few Southern ghosts have no specific motivation, but these purposeless wraiths are rare.

The first story given here appears in this section rather than in that on witches only because the informant called it a ghost story. Nevertheless, many of the incidents that occur in this narrative are commonly encountered not only in Southern ghostlore but in that of the United States. The narrative featuring the supernatural antics of Sally Carter is a good example of a tale in which the ghost returns not for just a single reason but for several. The story about Sam Graves is one of many Southern legends involving the ghostly reenactment of a murder. Another text reveals the story of a young suicide who refuses to leave the house where she died; presumably, she is unable to rest in her grave because she ended her life prematurely. Other stories in this section include one about a haunted bed in which no one can sleep, another concerning an ineradicable bloodstain, several concerning strange ghostly noises, and one about a ghost that pulled cover from the bed where people were sleeping.

Here, then, are some typical Southern ghosts. They usually return for some specific reason that is often revealed in the course of the narrative, although in some cases it never comes clear. In every case, their story is of more than passing interest.

143

UNCLE I.H. DECIDED TO BUILD A HOUSE FOR HIS NEPHEW. THE PLANS were drawn and soon some itinerant carpenters and painters came along to help in the construction and painting of the house. The nephew, Mr. S., lived in a log cabin just back of the construction site. An agreement was reached whereby the itinerant workers could sleep in the new building and board with the S. family. Mr. S., his wife and small daughter lived in the cabin. One day, as the house neared completion, one of the carpenters walked in and told Mr. S. that he was leaving the job because someone had put a hex on the place and he could not sleep at night for all the noise going on in the new house. The doors opened and closed all night, there was a tapping sound in the walls, strange things were happening in the hallway. Mr. S. assured him that in all probability some of the neighborhood boys were ticktacking the house; he would therefore clean up the debris that very day and would in all probability solve the mystery. True to his promise, he cleaned the house and surrounding premises that day, but he failed to find the ticktacking evidence. Mr. S. decided that he and his wife and child could move in the new structure and all this foolishness would stop.

Unfortunately, this did not give the carpenter peace of mind, nor did it help the S. family. At night they would see a casket roll up to the side of their bed. They would light a lamp and there would be nothing there. As they would try to settle down again, their bed would rise from the floor. The house moaned and creaked all night long. The wagon belonging to the little girl raced up and down the center hallway. The doors opened and closed all night.

Mr. S. watched the workmen closely and came to the conclusion that the painter was the offending person with devilish powers. He confronted him with this information, and the painter acknowledged that he was possessed with powers from the devil and every night before he went to sleep he released these evil spirits to do their work.

One day Mr. S. had to go to town, and Mrs. S. prepared dinner as was her custom and called the workmen in to eat. The painter in question asked her how she would like to see her kitchen table start walking. She was frightened but rather sternly replied that if he wanted to keep eating there, he had better leave his tricks away from the kitchen.

The house was eventually completed, and as the painter took his departure, he was warned that he had better take his evil spirits away with him. He departed, but it was noted that doors in the house, closed and latched they might be, without warning would come open and be standing ajar.

This house was eventually partially burned, and in its place a new house was constructed. The only part of the old building put in the new was the front door. The new front door could be latched, firmly closed, but with no warning could come open. Mrs. B. and her family all believe this is the ghost of the devil-possessed painter still doing his work.

WELL ANYWAY, THAT FIRST SUMMER WE WERE THERE WE WOULD ALL BE out in the field working, and Momma would be there at the house, and her first grandchild, Leontine, would be there with her, and Momma said the first time she noticed anything she thought she heard a bunch of people coming up out front talking and she wondered who could that be, because she knew it wasn't time for us to come from the field for dinner, and she went out, looked everywhere and didn't see a soul. Well, that's the first thing she told us when we came to the house for dinner, that she heard noises, and she thought it was somebody coming up out front. Well, she didn't see anything. So it went like that and . . . one Saturday night Louie and Beulah came to stay all night with us, and that left Mildred and me to sleep upstairs, and after the lights were out, well, we were lying there in bed and all of a sudden my cover began to move off of me and I told her, "Stop pulling all the cover!" And she said, "Sister, I'm not pulling the cover," and I knew she wasn't because she was perfectly still. Well, next thing we knew we were rolling downstairs. It scared us.

Well anyway, Louie was there from the time we moved in until the next October he married. And he slept up there one night and he was the first one that told us the cover slid off him, and we knew very well there wasn't anybody up there. Well, we didn't go back up there to sleep anymore. So that went on, oh, I don't know, a long time. We didn't go back up there to sleep anymore. Papa tried to get us to, but we told him he could if he wanted to but we wouldn't.

So then that fall, we started to school, and the school building was close, where we walked, and in the evenings there was a little pond— We had to pass this pond coming from the school to the house, and I happened to look up at the upstairs window, and until today I can see that; it looked like a big, a huge Newfoundland—what do you call these dogs, not a Newfoundland but a St. Bernard. It looked just like a huge St. Bernard dog reared up to that window and just as plain as if I'd been standing there. Well, Sook saw it too. We both did. I said, "Look," and she looked and there was that dog. It looked just like a big St. Bernard dog reared up to that window. Well, it was after that in the evenings when we'd come home and get along by this pond, I don't know why we didn't hear anything or see anything until we'd get near this pond. Then we'd hear an organ start playing "Nearer My God To Thee." Nana, that's absolutely the truth, and if Mildred were here she'd tell you the same thing. Well, it just excited us so that we didn't know whether something had happened to Momma or what. We were just almost afraid to go to the house.

We were all excited and telling Momma about it, and she kind of laughed it off. Then she got to telling us about hearing those voices more than once. She said she'd gone out of the house to look and see who was coming up out front. Well, it went on like that, and then in the wintertime one Sunday night my boyfriend was there, and he and Mildred and I were sitting in front of the fire, and we knew this spinning wheel was upstairs but we knew there wasn't anybody up there because Momma and Papa and Jake were in the other room, and it was in the winter and that spinning wheel started a'spinning. Oh, it sounded like you'd gone and taken your finger, you know, like you spin a wheel to and it would stop on a certain number. It just spun and just roared, it ran so fast. Well, this boyfriend of mine, he said, "What's that?" We told him, "It, well, they always said it was Mr. Yancey upstairs." That's what Emma, everybody around said. We weren't the only ones that ever heard it either.

Then Momma had a wire clothesline up there where she hung her clothes in the winter, and that thing . . . One night this same fellow was there, and it sounded like you had taken your finger and pulled that wire down tight and turned it loose and it made a funny noise again, and I was telling Jim about it this morning, and he said, "Do you actually believe in all of that?"

I said, "Well, if he was here, he could tell you the same thing, but he can't be here to tell you because he's dead."

Oh, and again it was in the wintertime, and Mildred and I had gone to bed, and then, well, she and I all the time slept across the hall from where Momma and Papa slept. We'd gone to bed and was just lying there talking and whenever we closed the door that went into the hall, and we heard this noise, and you know how a dog—when he has run quite a distance and when he gets hot—how he will lap his tongue, you know, and make the noise, and that was the same kind of sound we heard. It came out of the hall and you could hear it. It sounded like you could hear his claws hooking in the carpet as it went across. It went to the big fireplace and just disappeared. And we jerked the covers over our heads, and I don't know how long we kept the cover over our heads, we were so scared. But finally when I got nerve enough, I eased the cover back and I called for Papa and told him what we'd heard, and I said, "Light the lamp and bring it in here." Well, he or Momma, one lighted the lamp, but they didn't come across that hall. We rolled out of that bed and went across that hall and we didn't go back in there that night either.

And that's the only time we ever heard that. But we kidded Momma and Papa about being afraid. They were scared too, and I don't know whether they had heard noises in the house either, but . . . We lived there three years, and we heard things once in a great while. But he always said it was the rats running across the floor upstairs.

145

WHEN MY GRANDDADDY BOUGHT THAT PLACE DOWN HERE, WHY, THEY moved over from the other side of the mountain. And so they had a lot of stuff to move. They brought over a load or two of stuff, two wagonfuls, and brought some of the women over and they stayed all night. Well, the menfolks went back 'cross the mountain fer to get some more furniture and stuff. Well, there was three women, I think. They was kinda brave. So they brought lard and all kinda groceries and stuff, you know, fer to have, and that's what they brought with the first load. So they had a great big dog they brought along with 'em for these women to keep with 'em if anything bothered 'em.

They said they had a big jar, a big stone jar, and they had lard in that and they put it in that big press back in that room. They put this lard and some meat and stuff in thar. Well, the women stayed thar that night, and the menfolks went on back over the mountain to get another load. So they said way in the night then they heerd sump'n fall in the dining room 'bout that old closet, 'bout that press whar they put the lard and stuff. One of these women said to the other one, says, "Lawd have mercy," says, "let's get up and go in thar." Says, "That dog I bet done knocked that big jar of lard over." And they got up and lit the lamp and went in thar, and the door was fastened to the press and everything, wasn't no lard out nor dog wasn't in thar nor nothing. And when they come thar they had back in that hall a part where they used to keep the saddle under the stairsteps.

And I heerd my granddaddy, after he lived down thar, said they could hear 'em go out thar every night and draggin', you know, taking the saddle out, you know, and hearing the belly cinch and the buckle part, you know, dragging across the floor when they went on out the door, went on down the steps. Had the saddle on their arm and the buckle on the belly banging over, dragging on the floor. Said they heerd that and they went in thar to see if somebody got the saddle or was going out. Some of the boys, they's always going out a'riding, trying to catch a horse after night. Thar's the saddle and all back in thar just like they'd left it.

IN 1826, MARY CARTER WAS MARRIED AND MOVED THERE (TO THE HOUSE in Huntsville, Alabama). In 1836, Sally, who was Mary's sister, came to visit. There she caught the whooping cough and died. She is buried in the family cemetery. Before my grandmother moved there, two other families owned it and in between the house was unoccupied for long periods of time. They moved there in 1919, and the woman who was moving out told them to not let Sally's tombstone get toppled over.

So one time, my grandparents were having a party and they invited a whole bunch of people and they had to stay overnight. So my cousin Charles Martin had to sleep in the upstairs hall. During the night a storm came up, and he looked out over the balcony and saw a ghost standing there. She had long blonde hair, and she had on a long white robe, and she walked very softly through the screen door and sat down on the inside. She put her hand on his forehead and said, "Will you please help me? A tree has knocked my tombstone over." So the next day, Charles got up and told everybody what happened, and he finally got my grandfather and some more men to go over to the cemetery, and the tombstone was toppled over. So they put it back up. They thought Charles had dreamed it all up; they didn't think it was any big deal.

After that—my daddy and my aunt grew up in that room—and after they left, this man moved in, he rented the house from my grandmother. He was a very heavy chainsmoker, and Sally didn't like it. You know she didn't like smoke, because every time somebody was smoking she would slam doors and things like that.

I've heard that on her grave the headstone fell over, and every time they put it up it falls back over. It won't stand up for anything. If you stand on her grave at night she will haunt you that night, she will follow you home. This friend of mine heard that she was in love with this guy and he didn't love her back, so she jumped off that balcony into a rosebush. You hear all kinds of stories—and they just get bigger and bigger—that really didn't happen.

THERE IS THIS HOUSE IN SAN ELIZARIO THAT'S HAUNTED. BUT HE'S A funny ghost that haunts it—he only likes women. If a girl goes into the house, he pinches her. The house belongs to some people named Lujan. I think they were related to me. Anyway, they all died.

Some people moved into the house. The ghost kept bothering the wife—pinching her. They didn't like it, so they moved out. Some more people moved in. The ghost pinched this wife too. When they went to bed she could feel the ghost feeling her and rubbing his hands on her legs. But they got used to the ghost.

Why don't you go see for yourself?

ONE EVENING ON A LITTLE FARM OUT WEST OF WARREN, SAM GRAVES SAT down at his kitchen table to have supper. For reasons unknown, he and his wife had been having trouble. Before Sam had a chance to help his plate, his wife, who had prepared the nice supper, walked up behind him with a rifle and shot him point-blank in the upper part of his back. Stunned, Sam slumped over the table, filling the plate before him with

HAUNTED HOUSES • 237

blood. Then he rose to his feet, staggered across the room out the front door and sat down on the front porch steps. His wife dropped the single-shot rifle and grabbed up the butcher knife from the table. She ran out to where her bleeding and stunned husband sat and started stabbing him repeatedly with the knife. Once again, Sam got up and half stumbled, half crawled out to the orchard and died.

This happened in 1922. Mrs. Graves had been apprehended and executed. The little farmhouse stood untouched for many years. Everything was left just as it was the evening of the murder. Even the dried-up blood stains were still in the plate on the table. But years later, a member of a logging crew swore he heard a shot come from the house as he was walking by the vicinity. He was alone, but he went in the house to investigate. He was horrified when he saw the plate on the kitchen table filled with fresh blood. At first, people back in Warren thought he was crazy. The logger took some men back out to the haunted farm, but all they found was a plate of dried blood looking like it had for years.

But people changed their minds when they realized it had been exactly ten years to the day since Sam Graves had been murdered. Still today, many people who remember the incident believe that Sam Graves gets murdered again and again on that horrible anniversary.

THIS IS A PERSONAL ACCOUNT OF A GHOST STORY THAT OCCURRED A LITTLE more than forty years ago, and at that time the house which I visited had been empty some three or four years. I was staying at the Edgewater Beach Hotel on the Gulf Coast with my Aunt Harriet, who was a professional journalist. She was editor of a paper at that time; until 1959 she held that position. She was a woman of truth, integrity . . . and she didn't hold much with ghosts, but we made this excursion at the specific request of a friend of hers whose house this was.

The friends had been long-time friends of hers, and they owned a large plantation-type home on the Gulf, but they had not been able to live in it for several years because their daughter, who had been a teenager, had committed suicide in the house and her ghost was reported to haunt the house. At any rate, late one evening after dinner and moving well past my bedtime, we got into the car and drove down toward the beach with Aunt Harriet's instructions that we were going to examine something that she considered to be a phenomenon, and that although she didn't believe in ghosts, there were some unusual occurrences taking place in this house, and we were just going to see what *was* there. And then, she was going to report back to the parents and tell them that obviously there was no such thing as a ghost there, and that it was all right, but we were supposed to be able to explain what was occurring at the house.

So we drove up to the house and entered it with the key Aunt Harriet had gotten from her friends, and we arranged chairs in the front hallway, and we sat there quietly for some time. It must have been more than an hour, and I suppose the appropriate witching hour, which should have been midnight, had gotten close. But I really don't have much concept of time because I was a child and because one doesn't have much concept of time when one is just sitting in an empty house waiting on something to happen. But along about what I suppose to be midnight, we heard a noise in the upstairs hall and it sounded distinctly like footsteps, and the footsteps came out of a bedroom and closed a door and then proceeded to come down the hall, and my eyes went to the top of the stairs, and although the light inside the house was very dim, I expected to be able to see a figure standing at the top of the stairs. Of course, I did not. The steps hesitated for a moment and then continued to come down the stairs slowly but steadily, and as the steps got toward the foot of the steps, which were directly in front of me, I could see, even in the dim light, a depression in the carpet, and then the steps touched the marble hallway and clicked across the foyer and then went back down the hall just a little way toward the double music-room doors, and those doors opened.

Naturally, I was terrified, but I looked to Aunt Harriet to see what she was doing, and she was sitting perfectly still, and I knew that I should sit perfectly still too. So, we watched the doors open and heard the steps continue across the floor until they came to the piano, which was within our vision with those double doors open. We watched as the piano stool came back. The top to the piano was raised—the keyboard—and then, after a few moments, assuming that this person, whoever it was, was arranging themselves at the stool and in front of the keyboard, began to play and continued to play through about three pieces of Chopin, and then the music stopped, the keyboard was lowered. The piano bench went back, and we heard the steps come back out of the room. The double doors were closed and then . . . *tap* . . . the steps tapped again across the marble foyer and touched the bottom of the steps, where they hesitated as though whoever it was that was performing for us was watching *us* or looking at us, because they turned. Poised for a moment and then went up the steps . . . back up the hallway upstairs, went back into the bedroom, and the door was closed.

That was the end of what was, for me at least, a singular event. And Aunt Harriet said, "It's now time to go." So we closed the house up and left, got back into the car, and on the way back into town, I asked her if this was indeed the ghost and if this was the girl who was supposed to have killed herself and was now haunting the house and if this was why the parents couldn't stay there anymore. And she told me with one line, and that was the last one on the subject, "There is no such thing as a ghost."

WELL, ONE NIGHT I WENT DOWN TO MY COUSIN'S TO STAY ALL NIGHT. WE set around and talked for a while after supper, telling tales and jokes. 'Long toward bedtime they ast me where I wanted to sleep. I said that if hit made no difference, I was gonna sleep in that danged hainted bed back in t'other room. They tried awful hard to argy me out of it, but I uz long, long headed and finally had my way. We went in and I looked all around to see that there wasn't anybody who uz gonna pull a trick on me. Then they went on back in the other room, and I shucked off my clothes and crawled in bed. I hadn't more'n got fixed when sumpin down at the footboard began to pull the kivver; it would pull it down and I'd pull it back. Well, I got tired of that and give a big jerk. That hadn't more'n happened when every quilt on the bed sailed right over the foot of that bed. "Bring in a lamp," sez I, "some danged fool's trying to play a trick on me." In they came with a lamp, but there was the room jist as empty as a ol' bee gum. Nobody could've gotten in or out either. They begged me agin to come on and sleep in the "big house" where they was, 'cause nobody ever could sleep on that bed. "Lemme try it agin," sez I. They agreed. So I rolled up in the kivver and hugged up to the feather bed and straw bed, and then, *wham,* the whole kerpoodle landed right over on the floor, straw bed, feather bed and all. When they come runnin' in with the lamp, there set that bed a'trembling like a leaf. No sir, I didn't sleep on it and ain't nobody else ever slept on it either. That bed was hainted shore's you're born.

YOU MEAN THAT PLACE DOWN IN THE HOLLER? LORD, YES, HIT'S HAUNTED, allers has been as fur back as I kin recollect. I don't know whur ye'd call hit a hant er not. Hit's a sort of evil sperit that hangs over hit all the time. Wuzn't ye never inside of hit? Well, ef ye'll go and look, ye'll find a powerful red stain on the floor, right behind the front door. I ain't never knowed nobody that lived thar sence Jim and Allie Honeycutt moved out. She said that as long as she lived thar that no matter how hard she'd scrub that place with soap and water hit wuld jest git brighter, ever time, and hit never would come off. I never knowed how that red stain got thar, but Pap, he allers 'lowed that some pore feller wuz kilt thar in time of the war. Ye know they say that at one time they wuz a gang of robbers had their den thar, and they'd go out and git people, lettin' on like they wuz friendly to 'em and nobody would ever know what went with 'em.

Nobody ever lives thar now because as shore as they do, they's some member of their family certain to die. Ye know Little Joe Dugger, he moved his family in thar and 'lowed he'd live thar. But they warn't thar no time till their gal tuck sick with the fever, and the raincrows and screech owls, hit was a sight to hear 'em. They jist kept on a'hollerin' till she died, and then they jist kep up their lonesome croakin' till Milly, she jist told Joe that they wuz all a'goin' to die ef they didn't git away from thar, and they moved out.

Then Jim Honeycutt, ye know he lived thar fur awhile and his little boy died. Allie said hit wuz a fever, and I don't know what hit wuz. 'Peared to me like hit wuz some kind o' curious trouble that jist come up outer the ground.

Everybody that I've ever heard tell of that lived thar allers had trouble. Some of their folks wuz shore to die. Don't I remember the night that Abe Canter's wife died? They wuz a'livin' right thar in that house. Bob and me set up till twelve, and that night I had a dream. I dreamt that this here yard all around here wuz all lit up, jist as ef hit wuz a fire, and I looked agin and I seed a white angel a'comin' and hit jist floated down right easy, jist like a soap bubble when hit's in the air before hit gits busted. Then hit looked at me with hits face jist a'shinin' and hit pinted hits finger at me, and hit says, "Ye've been a'sinnin'." Yes hit did! Hit says, "Ye've been a'sinnin'," jist as plain as me a'speakin' to you, and I says, "Yes," says I, "I've been a'sinnin'."

Then hit looked at me agin, hit did, and hit says, "Go and sin no more!" Yes hit did. Then I waked up, I did, and I still seed that angel plain as day. So I jist punched Bob and I says, "Bob," says I, "Hit's sin, jist sin, that's caused hit all."

THE NEXT STORY IS ABOUT A HAINTED HOUSE THAT WAS NEAR A CAVE, IN this vicinity. The old house had been there ever since before the Civil War. And people lived in it all of this time. And there was a place way back in the mountains, still of course—the place is still there. There is no house or anything. It was called the old Russian place. They're supposed to have a lot of money buried up there. And the man that buried the money had killed a man and took his wife. All the men nearby were gone to war. This was during the Civil War. So he did all of this and he kept the money. And everybody wondered where it was. And everybody tried to find it and nobody could. But they moved to this house, down closer to other people, this old Linebarger house I call it. And they just kinda took over where they lived, nobody bothered them much because he was kind of a bad man.

And the man that got killed had a son, and he had been off in the war. He came back, and all of this had happened. Of course, he didn't like that, and he decided he'd just get even with the guy. So he just sent him word that he was going to kill him. Well, the old man didn't believe him.

But early one morning someone knocked on the door. The woman went to see who it was. And it was before the man got up. They had a big old room, they had this bed in the room, and there was a big fireplace, big rock hearth—the fireplace was rock—and a big mantle. This man, this young man came in. She screamed, and he came on in. And the old man was in the bed, just lying there. And he saw who it was. And he said, "Get out of bed, I am going to kill you." He had his gun in his hand. The man that was in the bed had his gun under his pillow. He went for his gun. The man shot at him, missed, and the bullet went into the mantle, under the rock, and it went into this piece of wood. And the man that was in the bed raised up, grabbed his gun. But before he could do all of that, the guy shot again, shot him right in the forehead. He fell back dead.

Well, of course, there was never anything done about that either that I ever heard of. And I don't think there was anyone who ever said there was. But they took him and buried him. And they never did bother to take the bullet out of this mantle. Now I seen that place, many times. And this bullet stayed there just for people to show off, until the house burned several years later.

But after that the house got hainted. Now strange things happened there, so they said. Sometimes someone would knock on the door, and it would open; you'd go see who it was, there wasn't a soul there. But it would sound like they would step right in the room. People thought it was the ghost of this man who came to kill this man who was in the bed. Then, sometimes, the back door would open. And they'd have to go close the door. They told all kinds of things, you could hear a man walking sometimes across the room just like the man that opened the door. Maybe he'd come from the back and he'd walk across the room and out the front door. But you wouldn't see a thing.

This went on for many years. But finally the house burned; after that, nobody ever saw the ghost. This house was located right close to a cave. Whether that had anything to do with it I do not know.

I WAS NEVER AFRAID OF HAUNTS IN MY LIFE. AND WHEN WE MOVED UP there to a house near Prestonburg, Kentucky, why the house had been empty a long time. I didn't know what was wrong. I just thought he couldn't rent it, you know. And I went out to my neighbor's house, and she said, "Do you know that that house is haunted?"

I said, "No, I didn't know it."

"Well, it is, and you'll soon know it."

Well, it wasn't very long until, sure enough, it come. They was in the hall—one of my little girls was in the hall. We had a hall in the house. She was in there, and this other one was between the dining room, and she went out to the backyard. And so it knocked on the door, just as hard as it could knock. She said to the other girl, "You couldn't scare me." She thought it was her, trying to scare her. Then she looked out there and seen her shrieking and she went out there to tell her about it, and while she was telling her about it, why the table turned over and broke all the things it seemed like we had in the world. Broke all the dishes and everything else. When I come back they was settin' over at the barn. I said, "Children, what in the world's the matter?"

"Oh, Mama," they said, "everything we got's broke. Everything on earth we got."

And I went over there, and they was just like they was when I left. They wasn't turned over, nor nothin' bothered at all. And that's the way it was. I knowed the house was haunted, but I never could see nothin' myself. It scared the children to death, but it never bothered me. I'd go out in the night and get coal. 'Way in the night, to the coal house. And I'd go down in the cellar. And I never could see nothin'. I'd think about it . . . and I never could see a thing. It never come when I was there, either—only when I was gone. And you know we stayed there two year and I wasn't afraid.

THE MODE OF TRAVEL BACK THEN WAS BY HORSEBACK OR ON FOOT. THIS particular man was walking with a pack on his back, and around dusk became tired so he stopped at an old two-room shack to spend the night. But before he entered the old shack he happened to notice that there were nine unmarked graves at the back of the shack.

He hesitated about staying all night, but he was so tired he lay down in one of the rooms to get a night's rest. But all of a sudden he heard voices in the next room who said, "Sharpen the knife, this one will make ten." The voices were eerie but came clearly from the next room. He was carrying a gun, so he burst into the other room, but to his amazement only a flickering candle was on the floor and nothing else. He ran out of the house until he came to a house down the road and told his story to the people living there. They said, "Oh! that old shack has been empty for years, we call it the haunted house of the nine graves."

155

JOSÉ WAS VERY SAD. HIS WIFE HAD JUST BEEN BURIED, AND NOW HE WAS alone.

"Poor José, you are very silent. Can I help you?" said Donaciana.

José looked up and saw his neighbor. She had brought him some food and flowers.

Soon after this, José fell in love with the kind Donaciana and married her.

One hot night, José slept outside in the moonlight. Donaciana had gone to visit her sister in a neighboring village, leaving José alone. All at once he began to shiver. Something cold was pressing his feet. He was almost paralyzed with fright. Maria's ghost stood at the foot of his cot. It was her hands that were pressing his feet.

With a yell, he ran into the house and barred the door.

After a sleepless night, José went to the village with his story.

"My son, do not be afraid. Maria was a good woman. She means you no harm. When she comes again, ask her what it is that she wants from you," said the kindly priest.

José thanked him and returned to his home.

That night José slept outside again. When he felt cold hands grip his feet he said, "Maria, what do you wish of me?"

"José, I am glad that you are happy, but I cannot rest in peace. I owe the grocer, Xavier, *seis pesetas,* and I cannot rest in peace until you pay the debt. Give him the money, José, and let me rest peacefully."

In the morning, Xavier's first visitor was José. He paid the *pesetas* and was never again troubled by Maria's ghost.

156

WELL, I'LL TELL YOU ONE EXPERIENCE. WE WERE RIGHT DOWN HERE TO Headquarters. My daughter-in-law what was with me tonight, well, that was her homeplace. We were settin' up there with her mother one night just before she died. Her sister were there and had a cot there, and I was sittin' 'side the bed where the lady was layin' and I was wipin' the sweat off her and givin' her cold water. There was a big door right there, and the wind were just as still and calm as it could be. All at once that door flew wide open, and the lady and her sister layin' over there, and another lady was settin' over in a chair kindly dozin'. And I reckon it was around twelve o'clock in the night. We was settin' there. That door flew wide open. So her sister got up and she shet that door, and when she turned her back that door flew wide open agin. Wasn't a piece of wind anywhere a'blowin'. Well, I said to the neighbor settin' there, I said, "Well, what do you think of that?"

She said, "I don't know." Said, "There's not a piece of wind."

We sit there. So I got up then and went in the kitchen and got a cup of coffee and came back. Dinin' room right over there. The little hall right in that way where you go in the livin' room. Dinin' room right there. 'Twas prompt twelve o'clock. We were settin' there. Just had the light turned down low because the lady was ill. We 'as lookin' for her to pass on any minute. All at once we heered the pot tops just a'rattlin' in the dinin' room, and I knew they had cleaned up already. Had a long table, oh, the table were long because they had so many, you know, to eat when they were younger people and they never did smallen the table down. The pot tops and the lids just rattled. And I thought to myself, "Well, I just wonder who that is in there in the pots."

So the lady was settin' over there, and Mrs. Foster then were layin' over on the bed. I just kindly eased over to the door and I peeked around the door to see if I seen anybody, see if there were pots on the table. Wasn't no pots. Table settin' just like they'd left it. We could hear the pot lids. Hear 'em when they take 'em off and hear 'em when they put 'em back. I set myself down, and all at once it looked like they brought in 'bout a dishpan full of knives and forks and spoons and dumped 'em over in the middle of the table. You never heerd such a fuss in your life. And it was even twelve o'clock, but you could see that house there used to keep slaves there, you see, and I told the lady there, I said, "I reckon the pore old slaves is gettin' the tables all ready for 'em to eat." I said, "The pots is rattlin', the lids is rattlin', even poured out the knives and forks on top of the table."

That's 'fore the lady died. She died next morning, nine o'clock. I said, "Well sir," I said. "I don't believe daylight'll ever come tonight." I waited till four o'clock in the mornin' before I left down the road by myself. Yes, sir, when daylight did come, I moved it on home. And the girl here, one of 'em, sent word over there for me to come back over there, that their mother had passed on. Well, her mother, when she died, I was settin' up there with her, and so when they laid her out over in the parlor room, her brother was there, and the whole house was settin' full of people. So they was a man and his wife was from up there, and I used to work with 'em in the orchard, and I were tellin' him about hearin' things. He looked at me and he said, "I wish I could hear sump'n. It wouldn't scare me a bit."

I said, "I wish you could hear sump'n too and see what I see."

So 'long about 'leven o'clock, here us just the neighbors settin' up in this room, and my daughter-in-law's mother layin' 'cross the hall in the parlor room, and her brother and her sister-in-law was settin' there in the floor. All at once we heard the awfullest noise fall. We thought the casket had fell off the stand in the floor. And her brother jumped up with his flashlight and said, "Law," said, "sister's casket has fell off."

Well, he run with the flashlight—we didn't have 'lectric lights then like we have now—he run with his flashlight, and we all follered him, and when we got into the parlor room there set the casket just like the undertakers had set it. But we couldn't give no 'count. We could even feel the floor jar across that hall and into the settin' room that we was settin'. Look like you could feel the floor kindly shake. Right there at Headquarters.

Lord, man, I could just set and talk all night about them ghost tales. We just heerd those things down there and I told Lucille, I said, "I wouldn't stay there by myself." Oh, there was ghosts always seen down there.

I WAS AT MY GIRLFRIEND'S HOUSE ONE DAY AND DECIDED TO SPEND THE night. Her grandmother, who was dead, had been crippled and walked with a limp. That night, when everybody was asleep, we all heard footsteps in the house. (My friend's mother told us what happened to her in the morning.) The footsteps went through the kitchen, into the bathroom and into my friend's mother's bedroom. As the footsteps walked, we heard a limp—*da dum da dum*.

In the morning, her mother told us that in the night she had heard the footsteps also. Then she suddenly had sensed that somebody was behind her. Suddenly, she felt a hand on her shoulder! She began to pray very hard. She was so frightened and was praying so hard that she finally fell asleep.

Later in the day, we were all in the kitchen talking. It was in the winter, and there was snow outside. I smelled the scent of perfume in the kitchen and asked who had put it on. Everybody said that it wasn't them. Then it seemed to fade away as if it were going another way. Then it came back.

My friend then reminded me that she had told me that her grandmother often came to visit them. They could tell she was there because of the perfume she was wearing. No one else in the house used that scent of perfume. When they smelled this scent, they would know that she had come for a visit. The second time I smelled the scent, it was so strong, like it was standing right next to me. It was weird! I got scared and left.

I USED TO PLAY TENNIS IN A PARK IN AN OLDER SECTION OF EL DORADO. There was a house across the street, owned by H.L. Hunt. The house and grounds took up an entire city block. By the time I was playing tennis in the park in the '60s, no one lived in the house. There were signs around the house saying "KEEP OUT," but it was always fun to go sneaking around somewhere you weren't supposed to be.

I think any old house left empty for a number of years assumes a story or legend. Someone will go in and hear noises and some kind of a legend will grow out of it. This is the way legends are made. I don't think the legend things you hear are true. There might be some small thing of truth in it, but it is blown way out of proportion.

Anyway, the story about this house was something like a party going on at the house. Hunt's girlfriend was there, and she fell down the stairs and broke her neck. When you go in the house and hear these noises, people think it is Hunt's girlfriend coming back looking for him.

The house was torn down several years ago.

159

MY MOM AND DAD USED TO LIVE IN PARAGOULD. MOTHER SAYS IT WAS real weird. The house had a creepy upstairs that they never used. The stairway came down in the dining room. Mom had a dark green curtain hanging at the end. Every night when they would go to bed, they heard someone walking up and down the stairs for about twenty minutes. Daddy looked a couple of times and didn't find anything.

Later they heard the lady that lived there before them used to walk those stairs for exercise every night before bed. People said that she had left a lot of cats behind, and the cats were looking for the woman. My mom got so scared after that that she used to follow Daddy to the field.

It went on for about forty-five minutes one night. Daddy was determined to do something. He got a flashlight and a gun and went to the stairs. When he pulled back the curtain, something jumped out on him. They looked all through the house and didn't find a thing.

Later, cats started showing up all over town. No one knew where they were coming from. Then Mom saw a cat on the eating table. She swears it was a strange cat. Some time later they found out the lady had died in Little Rock. The cats were searching for her spirit. My mother really believes that.

My parents lived in a haunted house right after they were married. A man froze to death in the house about four or five months before they moved there. They said when it started turning cold that people began to talk.

Well, the first night it snowed they got in a disagreement about hogging the cover. Every morning at breakfast they would accuse each other of taking all the cover during the night. One night before they went to sleep, the cover began to move. Mom said something to Dad. He said, "Me?" The cover was being pulled off at the foot of the bed.

The next day they started looking for a house. It took them awhile to find another place. That was the only thing they noticed. They talked to the thin air at night. They said they would talk, and the cover would move different ways.

I'm getting married during Christmas. We have rented an older type here in Jonesboro. I'm sort of wary.

2 OTHER HAUNTED PLACES

Although old houses are the favorite hangout for ghosts, the otherworldly creatures can be found haunting just about any place. In American tradition, they frequently haunt battlefields, mines, highways, boats, graveyards, gallows and wells.

In the stories that follow, ghosts haunt a tree where a youth was executed by guerrillas, battlefields, hollows, a mill, a lake, a courthouse, a rock, cemeteries, a college and a casketmaker's shop. They haunt these places for various reasons including unjust execution, suicide, restless souls, a desire to eternally torture their victims, as a sign of divine retribution, to complete business left unfinished at the time of their death, or because they have forgotten something and are returning to find it.

These varied reasons are the ones most commonly found in Southern tradition. The ghost tales recounted here range in age from the Revolutionary War up to the present time. As with most ghosts, these are generally more of a nuisance than they are harmful.

161

GOLD HILL LIFTS ITS PEAKS FAR ABOVE THE FERTILE VALLEYS OF EASTERN Forsyth County. On the tiptop is a large opening, now crowded with debris and undergrowth, its rocky, perpendicular sides glazed by wind and rain. This is the deserted gold mine that still holds the spirit of Elizabeth Reed. Every time the wind whips around the crags and crevices, there issues from the depths of the pit an agonizing wail. Sometimes it is the faint wail of a child. Then again, it is the shriek of a woman.

It was during the Revolutionary War that Richard Reed was killed in a battle with the British, and his wife, Elizabeth, went mad.

One day Elizabeth sat crouched in her chair watching her grandmother prepare the noonday meal. As the old woman busied herself between the table and fireplace, Elizabeth's eyes took on a deep cunning. She hated the old woman who watched her every move and hated the squalling baby that lay in the cradle. She hated everyone except Richard, her husband the British had killed.

But that wasn't true. Richard wasn't dead. The old woman was keen. She had hidden Richard in the deserted mine on the top of Gold Hill and was leaving him there to starve. The night before, an owl had sat in the tree beside her window and told her all about it. It told her that the old woman had tied Richard's hands and feet, then flung him into the pit, but that he wasn't dead and that she could get him out if she did as the owl told her.

Elizabeth's hands began to move. She plucked at her sleeves and gnawed her nails, all the time watching Old Granny through slitted lids. How ugly she was with her gray hair straggling down the back of her neck and her skin the color of a tanned rawhide! And the baby was no better. Elizabeth turned her gaze to the child in the cradle. It was a squirming piece of flesh that only ate and cried. She would far rather have a rabbit that was woolly and soft. She despised the baby, she wanted nothing but Richard, and she was going to have him. The owl had told her if she threw her baby into the Gold Hill mine that Old Granny would give her Richard, so as soon as she could slip the baby away, she was going to fling him into the mine; then Richard would be hers again.

Elizabeth turned her gaze back to Old Granny. She stood facing the table, kneading dough. There was flour on her blue-checked gingham apron and a fine dust showed on her yellow arms. Elizabeth rose quietly from her chair. Noiseless and swift as a cat, she darted across the room to the baby's cradle, reaching out her hands for him. Just as she touched him, she saw the old woman turn and rush toward her.

"There, there," she heard Granny say, "don't you worry, Lizzie. You just sit quiet and rest. Granny will take care of little Richard."

Elizabeth sank back in her chair, her eyes gleaming balefully. That was always the way. They wouldn't let her get her hands on the child. She knew what they were thinking, Granny and the neighbors too. They thought she was crazy, but she wasn't; it was Granny who was crazy. The owl told her so, and the bird told her that Granny was keeping the baby from her, just as she was keeping Richard from her. Elizabeth held up her hands and began awkwardly to count her fingers. She lowered her lids to keep from seeing Old Granny, who had moved to the other side of the table and stood facing her, alert and watchful. Suddenly Granny gave a cry and rushed to the door, looking out into the garden.

"The calf!" she cried. "It's in the garden eating the peas!" She ran out across the yard, calling to the calf.

For a moment Elizabeth sat motionless, and her eyes began to glitter. She leaped from the chair and ran to the cradle. Snatching up the child, she dashed out the back door and into the woods, fleet as a deer. As she passed the spring beneath the sycamores, her laughter broke, shattering into a shrill, vibrating echo that floated out behind her, reaching the ears of Old Granny, who was tying the calf.

Elizabeth climbed the steep incline nimbly. She was free at last, free with the baby they wouldn't allow her to touch. She was going to do as the owl said, take the baby to the mine on top of Gold Hill and fling it down into the dark depths. Then Old Granny would free Richard and give him back to her. Higher and higher she went. The trees pressed close about her; the thorns of the bayberry vines tore her face and arms, leaving bright crimson streaks, and the sharp stones in the narrow path bruised and cut her bare feet, but she staggered on. She stopped, panting for breath, when a sound held her motionless.

Behind her was the sound of voices. Even as she stood quiet, a shout broke the stillness. It was Granny and Uncle Bill, the Negro who fed the horses, coming after her, but they mustn't catch her. Hugging the baby tighter, she turned and sped up the last steep incline. It wasn't far now.

Her breath came in short, broken gasps. Behind her she could hear the thudding sound of running feet and Old Granny calling her name, but she only ran faster. A minute now and she would be there. Already she could see the dark opening of the mine just a few feet ahead. With a last desperate effort she reached the hilltop.

At her feet the pit gaped wide open. Somewhere in that dark hole Richard was waiting, and in a few moments he would be with her. Leaning forward, she held the baby over the pit. As she did so, she heard the hoarse, panting cry of Old Granny, begging, pleading. The girl began to laugh, wild shrill laughter that stabbed the stillness of the forest with bloodcurdling mockery. She raised the child high above her head and flung it far out into space, watching it fall down, down, into the blackness of the mine. Then she whirled and faced Old Granny, who reached her, grasping her arm a moment too late.

Elizabeth continued to laugh as Old Granny fell on her knees, gazing frantically down into the mine. She watched with burning eyes as Uncle Bill fastened a rope to a tree, dropped it into the opening and clambered down. She even began to sing, a chanting tune of exultation. He was going after Richard. Soon she would see him again and they would be happy. The owl was right; Richard hadn't been shot in the war. He was alive and down in the mine where Granny had left him to starve. She moved nearer the opening and peered in, watching the Negro as he came slowly upward.

What was that he had in his arms? It was too small for Richard. As he drew nearer her face whitened; her lips drew back against her teeth and her eyes flamed beneath her frowsy hair. The man was bringing the baby back, a broken and bruised baby. She didn't want it; she wanted Richard. As the man reached the edge of the mine and climbed out and laid the lifeless child in Old Granny's arms, Elizabeth cowered back, watchful and sullen. So the old woman wasn't going to bring Richard out of the mine. She was going to keep him down there. Elizabeth chewed her lips, her hands plucked at each other. Then she slit a leaf to small fragments with her sharp nails, and a queer choking sound rattled in her throat. She would show Old Granny that she couldn't keep Richard imprisoned in the mine. She would go down into the pit herself and bring him out.

She moved forward, creeping craftily toward the rim of the pit, her eyes on the sobbing old woman who had forgotten her. Slipping past Old Granny, Elizabeth reached the crumbling edge of the mine. For a moment she tottered there, leaning slightly forward, both hands clasped to her breast. Suddenly a wild, piercing cry tore from her throat.

"Richard!" she screamed. "I see you. I'm coming!" Flinging her arms high, she leaped forward. For an instant her body hung suspended against the bright blue walls of the sky, then disappeared into the dark depths of the mine.

Today, when the wind beats against the crags of Gold Hill, wails still issue from the dark recesses of the old pit. Sometimes it is the agonizing wail of a child in pain, but more often it is the bloodcurdling scream of a mad woman that echoes and re-echoes from the rocky, storm-glazed crevices of the mine—the mine that is still haunted by the spirit of Elizabeth Reed.

THIS WAS DURING THE CIVIL WAR. AND THIS WAS A BIG OAK TREE, STOOD on the side of a little country road that went through the country. And it had big limbs reaching out on all sides, kindly straight out. Not the kind of tree that the limbs point toward Heaven, the other kind, the kind you hang a man on. And in this community there lived a family and all of the people were gone to war except one boy, and he liked to speak his mind. But if you would keep your mouth shut you'd live longer; if people came by and they were for the North, then if you were for the South that caused trouble, and vicey versy. If you believed that other way around and they believed the other way around, you were just in for trouble.

This boy didn't mind to speak his piece. The jayhawkers came by, and, uh, he started to tell them off so they just took him out to this tree and hung him. People was afraid to go get him down, and he hung there all night long till the next day, and somebody had nerve enough to go and cut the rope, take him down and bury him.

Now for years and years this tree stood there. But it was hainted. They could see, on certain nights, an image of this boy hanging there on the tree. But it had a funny light around it. They all said they knew the boy went to Heaven because of this beautiful light they would see—they thought they could see—and that he had lived right and all of those things. But it got so people were afraid to go through the community where this was, where this tree was. Nobody had ever bothered to cut the tree down. It stayed there until, I suppose, it just died a natural death. But they always saw this boy, the image of this boy hanging from the tree.

163

ONE OF THE LAST BATTLES WAS FOUGHT AT PLEASANT HILL, LOUISIANA. Great-Grandmother Mommom had moved to Pleasant Hill just after the Civil War was over. One day, Mommom and her sisters were crossing a field on which men had fought and she found a beautiful set of teeth, not false but real teeth. She took them home and put them in a box with some cotton. That night, Mommom, Great-Aunt Lottie and Jo Jo were sitting around the fire talking. Mommom looked up, and in the window she saw a face of a man. He had red-blond hair, awful eyes and blood all over him. She screamed and then fainted. After Lottie and Jo Jo revived Mommom she told them what she had seen. Finally, they all went to bed and forgot about the incident. The windows rattled and the doors squeaked all night, but they thought it was the wind making the noise.

The next morning they looked around the house but did not find any footprints. That night Mommom, Aunt Lottie and Jo Jo saw the face at the window again. They grabbed a light and ran outside to see who or what it was but could not find anything or anyone. The next day they took rakes and brooms and raked and swept the ground (there wasn't any grass) so that if anyone should come there would be tracks or prints. The face appeared again. The next morning they looked outside but there weren't any tracks at all. The face kept on appearing for a while. Then the family decided that Mommom should take the teeth back. Mommom took them back and buried them in the field.

After that the face didn't appear. Summer came and Mommom, Lottie and Jo Jo and the family would sit on the porch quite a bit. (The porch stretched across the front of the house.) One evening they saw a ball of fire dancing up the dogtrot, and the peculiar noises started again. Finally, one morning they went out and found that something or someone had moved the whole front porch away from the house. And there weren't any footprints. They moved out of the house immediately!

MARK'S MILL, NEAR WARREN, WAS THE SCENE OF A BATTLE DURING THE Civil War. There is a story about a Confederate officer who got wounded in the face by an exploded artillery shell. A Confederate supply train had been attacked by the Yankees, and that was the cause of the battle. Now the officer knew which wagon was carrying the gold shipment, and somehow he managed to crawl back through the bushes to the wagon, although he was blinded. He set fire to the wagon so it would burn down around the gold to prevent the Yankees getting hold of it. The blind and wounded soldier was taken to a field hospital where he died, not knowing what became of the gold. It has been said that ever once in a while you can see the soldier's ghost walking blindly about the battlefield with his arms outstretched, looking for his gold.

Another story connected with Mark's Mill has to do with some dead Yankees. After the small battle was over, the Yankees had to get out fast. They didn't have time to bury their dead, and they knew the Confederates wouldn't bury them. So they dropped as many as they could down a well. People say that if you hear some moans and groans echoing around the vicinity it is the dead Yankees wanting out of the well.

165

IN THE EASTERN PART OF JOHNSON COUNTY, NOT FAR FROM THE HISTORIC little stream of Roan's Creek, there is a large gap which extends some distance back into Doe Mountain known as Songo Hollow. This section is very heavily forested and thick with underbrush. People seldom pass through it, especially near nightfall for it is a haunted region and has been so since the Civil War.

On a little knoll in the wilderness there is a heap of stone, once a chimney, which marks the site of Samuel Songo's cabin. Little is known among the settlers, except for the fact that he was noted as a man of great physical strength. He immigrated to Johnson County from Kentucky and brought along with him a beautiful wife. But it was rumored throughout the settlement that Songo belonged to the hostile party of a feud that was brewing, and early one morning as he was leaving his cabin, he was shot by an enemy in ambush. No one knew who killed him, and they had not known him long enough to care.

Two hunters passing the road that was then the stagecoach route to North Carolina heard a woman scream, and when they made their way to the cabin, they found that Mrs. Songo had stabbed herself with her husband's hunting knife and was lying in the doorway. The neighbors came and buried them near their home. But no one cared to live in the cabin where the strange couple had spent so short a time, for their rest was sure to be disturbed by the weird screams of the pretty wife of Samuel Songo as she grieved over the death of her husband and killed herself in despair.

166

DURING THE WAR BETWEEN THE STATES, WHEN THE POTTER–STANFIELD feud was raging in the upper part of Johnson County, the Bloody Third rang with rifle shots from the skirmishes of the guns in battle, and the members of the victorious parties brought their prisoners across the hills. These victims were tortured, imprisoned or killed outright.

In the torturing process, the cave, called the Jingling Hole, played a most unique part. Since this cave has a straight descent of ninety feet, the victorious party—whether Potter or Stanfield—often placed an iron rod across the entrance. To this rod the culprit was forced to swing by his hands while his gloating captor tapped on his knuckles with the breech of his rifle, first on one hand and then on the other in rapid succession, causing an active display of gymnastics as the prisoner swung from hand to hand. Usually these victims were able to stand this torture and were released with bruised and blistered hands, to be preserved for future adventures; again, there was a casualty, as the victim rolled into the lake at the bottom of the cave.

The neighbors say that at night when they go 'possum hunting in the fall, they hear strange noises around the Jingling Hole. If they listen carefully they hear moans and groans, especially if the wind is blowing, and there is also the hollow sound of a gun breech cracking on knuckles, for the spirits of the Potters and Stanfields are not at rest but must still be torturing their victims.

167

THE BIGGEST STORY I EVER HEARD WAS THAT DURING THE CIVIL WAR AN old fellow named Jack Walker lived up the river there on *this* side. And you know they had livestock back then at open range here, and the old feller was over there huntin' hogs when he had a nigger slave run away from him. A fellow, Bone, over there was runnin' the mill and the nigger slave run away from him and went over there and Bone was a' coverin' him up. And this old feller Jack Walker went over there and found him or somethin', got in contact with Bone some way, and Bone killed him. Buried him in the mud but didn't kill him dead, and he left old man Walker's one hand out of the mud, they found him that way.

And there wasn't any courts then, during the war. They impounded a jury and tried him, public trial, and they found him guilty. And hung him over there at the lake. And one of my great-aunts—I think it was a great-aunt—spun the rope that they hung him with . . .

But he and old man Walker had a run-in some way about the nigger, and he killed old man Walker. He was a—Bone was—a Yankee sympathizer.

And they was an old mill house there, but that mill sinking into that lake, I've never knowed that to be a fact. I've never heard what went with that old mill house, but they *said* that it was standing there when Bone was hung. And I've been told that that water rises and falls, you know. And there's a deep end of that lake where there ain't no bottom to it. They've never been able to find the bottom to it. And that lake, sometime it'll fill up full, and sometime it'll go down to a lower level. And they said right after Bone was hung that water rose up in that pond, up to the eave of that mill house.

168

It was day, and the river ran as it had always run, and then it was night, and with the next day there was a lake where the river had been. It was a large lake, and the river ran beside it. In between there was an island of farm about fifteen hundred acres in size, and it was to become very good farmland. A lake was born, and that is how the Indians told the white men it happened.   The lake was known as "the lake" for many years, for it was a lake without a name. The white man came, and they cleared the land and planted it in cotton. It was a plantation, and there were slave huts along the side of the lake. The people would fish in the lake, and they would go back and forth in boats to see their neighbors.

There was one old Negro who crossed the lake to see some people who lived on the other side, but he was never to return. The people sitting on their porch watched his small boat make its way back across the lake. They could see the light of the old man's lantern, but as he reached the middle it went away. They drug the lake all the next day, but they could never find him.

Some have said they have seen the old Negro with his lamp walking on the waters of the lake in the night. Many are scared of the lake, and they will not go near it in the darkness; many say that it is foolish, and the man does not walk on its waters. But today the lake is known by everyone at Spirit Lake.

169

ONE NIGHT AT A PARTY WHEN THINGS BECAME DULL, THE CONVERSATION shifted aimlessly from one subject to another. In the course of this rambling conversation, a young man of the group teasingly belittled the bravery of women. The young ladies were immediately offended. They would prove that they were as brave as any man or group of men in the country. In fact, in order to prove their contention, a delegation of them would voluntarily go into the graveyard at the side of the hill without male escort.

But how would one know that they had really visited the graveyard and not merely hidden away until sufficient time had elapsed to make the young men think they had been there? They would solve that, too. They would carry forks and stick them upright in newly made graves, and these the young men could see the next morning. It was agreed, so the girls went.

The night was dark. A low-lying fog lay around the hills, and the trees dripped with moisture. The ghostly meetinghouse shining dimly nearby did not tend to add confidence to the hearts of the girls. The graveyard lay a good distance around the meetinghouse and up a hill.

When they reached the graveyard, there was hardly enough courage left to take them in, but they took each other by the hand and thereby gained needed confidence. Finally, they were at the newly made graves. They stopped simultaneously and each embedded her fork to the hilt in the wet clay. Then they each arose—all except one! The awed girls who had risen had heard a slight shriek, and when they looked at their feet, there lay the white form of one of their companions. They fled. They thought a ghost had her.

The next morning the sun dispelled the fog enough to light up the stark face of the dead girl on the new-made grave. Some men pulled her up from the yellow mound. It was not a ghost that had her at all. It was the fork. In sticking it in the ground, she had caught her low-hanging skirt in the tines, and it had become fastened to the grave. She had died of heart failure.

ONE NIGHT PAPA WAS COMING FROM CHURCH. IT WAS DARK AS PITCH. Well, he walked along this old gravel road, and just before he got to the creek, near this old creek bed—and he had to cross the creek to get to the house—well, he heard something, like rock or gravel, you know, rolling, and he looked around and there was a man. He was just laying there on the ground and said he just lit up. He said the man got up and started walking up the creek bank and tried to get him to follow him. Why, it nearly scared him to death! He said he was never so afraid in all his life. He said he heard something like someone stepping on a dead stick and looked away, and when he looked back, it was gone.

THE COURTHOUSE IS CARROLLTON, ALABAMA, IS LISTED AS, UH, ONE OF the things in Alabama that's listed in *Ripley's Believe It or Not.* The reason it's listed is that a long time ago, there was supposed to be a hanging, a black man had murdered a white man for some unknown reason to me, and when the man claimed to be innocent—And they housed him in the jail in Carrollton. Carrollton is the county seat of Pickens County, the county I grew up in. And when they took the man up to the gallery in the courthouse, the weather was real bad and they were going to hang him inside, and he told the sheriff and the others present that—that he was innocent and if they hung him that they would find out a white man had killed the man and that they would have hung an innocent man. So when they got ready to hang him an electrical storm came up and just as they hung the man this bolt of lightning struck the courthouse and the man's picture was transposed on the north gallery window.

And legend has it that this window has been removed a number of times and each time this face reappears on it. Now whether this is true or not I don't know, and of course, we that lived in Pickens County believed that they wouldn't take it out for anything, 'cause it's a little-bitty place and this is really its only claim to fame.

EIGHTY YEARS AGO, IN ALICEVILLE, ALABAMA, A MAN WAS ARRESTED AND tried for murder. All through the long trial the man pleaded innocence, but a verdict of guilty was handed down, and the judge sentenced him to be hung. After he was hung, it was discovered that the man had been innocent, and the real murderer was caught. Since that awful discovery, the image of a man's face has been outlined in the windowpane of the cell he stayed in throughout the trial. They have tried to wash it off but couldn't. A few years back, a rampant hailstorm knocked out or broke every window in the building except that one. Then they removed the pane and replaced it, but the image returned in the new one, and there it can still be seen.

NEAR THE TOP OF STONE MOUNTAIN IN JOHNSON COUNTY, THERE IS A large rock that juts out over a precipice known as Fiddler's Rock. It was here that Martin Stone charmed the rattlesnakes with his fiddle and met his untimely fate.

It seems that Martin Stone was noted as a fiddler. At dances, parties and all social gatherings, Martin and his fiddle were the center of attraction. Often on quiet Sundays in the summer, Martin sat on the big rock and played his fiddle. From their den underneath came the rattlesnakes, attracted by the music. They wriggled, danced and rattled, keeping time in a most uncanny manner. When Martin grew tired of playing, he often stopped and amused himself further by reaching for his shotgun and priding himself on the number that he could kill before they glided back into shelter.

But one day, as Martin played, he became fascinated with the wriggling, writhing mass below him. In and out twined the smooth golden bodies, reflecting the ever-changing lights and shadows. He forgot to reach for his gun, the bow dropped from his nerveless fingers, and slowly he felt himself sliding downward toward the snakes.

The next day, a neighbor found his lifeless body, in which had been buried the fangs of many rattlesnakes. Nearby lay the fragments of his broken fiddle. The neighbors buried him and mourned his loss. But ever since they have avoided Fiddler's Rock as a haunted place, for on summer evenings, when the wind is in the trees, the whine of Martin's fiddle may still be heard as he charms the rattlesnakes and, in his own fascination, forgets to reach for his gun.

WELL, IT SEEMS IT HAPPENED MANY A YEAR AGO; MAMA KNOWED THE woman that was married to that man. I don't know of his real name; they called him Lightnin' as a nickname, 'cause he moved about so slow. Well, I don't know for sure but that he took to drinkin' and then to beatin' on his wife. She was a real good person and says she loved her husband, so she never did nothin' to make him stop.

His drinkin', it got worse and worse, till one day he up and left. Well, nobody knowed where he got off to, but some say he drowned in the river 'cause he couldn't swim. Shortly after that, his wife, she took real sick. She said she had the high fever, but everybody knowed she was sick in the heart 'cause that man of hers, he was gone. I don't understand why she could worry herself sick over a man that drunk most of the time—even on Sundays—and beat her up till she was black and blue and could hardly walk. But black womans—they's that way about their mans. Well, Lightnin', he never come back to her, and by and by she died. Some folks say it was out-and-out murder 'cause he was what drove her to that grave. But nobody done nothin' about that 'cause couldn't nobody prove it.

Then that man, he come home one day lookin' to see where his wife was gone. Nobody done told him she was dead most 'cause of him. He didn't believe it when he found out she was dead. He said somebody killed her or took her off and hid her out from him. Everybody was real scared of him 'cause he was filled with all them evil demons from drinkin'. One day he went out to the graveyard—that one on the hill— and he found her grave. Nobody knows for sure, but some folks say he dug her up to see for hisself that nobody was lying to him. He found her body and bones and all and then killed himself. Some folks say he died from grief, but I think he drunk hisself to death.

And to this very day, you can hear him a'beatin' on her some nights and you can hear her screamin' and moanin' 'cause their souls they ain't rested. Don't nobody go by there at night if you can help it, for that man, he's liable to chop you up or something else real bad. And if you do has to walk by there, don't never dare look at the graves, but look straight ahead and walk on by real fast.

I remember one night when we was kids, we got real brave and decided to walk by there, and sure enough you could hear that poor old woman screamin' but you had to listen real close. We was scared half to death. I had the shakes for a week and plenty of nightmares too. I ain't never once gone by there again walkin' at night—and I don't let my kids neither.

Some people now say it ain't true, but it is, 'cause I heard it myself. It's just like some folks not believin' in the good Lord, but it's true too, 'cause I seen him once. But that's another story, and you know about that already anyhow. Well, that's the story.

WELL, ON A NIGHT IT WOULD BE STORMING, EVERYBODY AROUND IN THE community would gather at my Grandpa's house because he had a cellar and nobody else did. And some of the older people would tell us kids about, uh, that building that was across the road from my Grandpa's house. They would tell us kids that caskets were still stored in the loft of the old casketmaker's shop. It was a long time ago, before any of us were born, and the guy that made the caskets had been dead for a long time.

Well, like I said, we'd all be sitting up there on the porch and watching the storms, and sooner or later one of the older people start talking about—about the building and how it had once been a cas-ketmaker's shop and the man-who-owned-it's name was Ashberry Sago. And his son Morris would be sitting up there, and he would come up on the porch and he would tell about what a good business he had because he was the only casketmaker around there at that time. These caskets were good—they look a lot like they do today—even though completely handmade down there in that shop. Well, the people around there didn't like him too much because he always looked at you as though he was mentally measuring you up for a casket and wondering how long you would make him wait before you died and give him your business.

No one knows exactly how he died or when, but the older people say that caskets are still stored in the loft of the old shop and that one is an unfinished casket for a child, and on stormy nights you can hear him hammering away on an unfinished casket for a child who has long been cold in her grave. It is commonly known that until recently his casket lay unoccupied because of his mysterious disappearance. However, only a short while ago the old shop was torn down.

WELL, ASHBERRY—WE CALLED HIM RIP—MADE CASKETS FOR ALL THE local townsfolk. He did this for over fifty years—actually more than that if you count his father. A doctor moved in one day, where Rayburn lives now, but was so scared—this was in 1924 or thereabouts—he moved out. Well, this old casketmaker seemed always his happiest when death was in the air. He would look you up and down when he saw you —made you feel kind of crazy. The oddest thing about this old man was that he made his own casket and prided himself on this fact and would even show people when they had a death in the family. Well, he had a call for a child's casket and set to work on it, but before it was ever finished he disappeared. The people believed he would always return. During the stormiest part of a storm you can hear him at work trying to finish out his work. I tell kids if they ain't good, he will build them a casket.

ONE NIGHT ME AND A FRIEND OF MINE WERE WALKING BY A GRAVEYARD AT night. While we were passing the graveyard, we heard a noise coming from it. We then walked over into the graveyard to see what was making the noise. When we got into the graveyard, we saw a baby crying on one of the tombstones. My friend picked the baby up, and then we started down the road toward his home.

As we walked down the road, he noticed that the baby got heavier and heavier. He then looked at it and saw that it had turned into an old man with a gray beard. He tried to put him down, but he couldn't. The old man told him that he would never be able to do it until he took him back to the place where he found him. He took him back and left him there. The baby was a ghost!

I REMEMBER WHEN I WAS ABOUT EIGHT YEARS OLD, ONE NIGHT I WAS walking home from the theater. I only lived a few blocks away. It was about eleven. I saw a horse in the far end of the city graveyard. The horse was bending down over a grave and pawing. When he saw me, he ran away. It struck me as sort of strange to see a horse in the graveyard.

The next morning I told my granny about the horse. She told me this legend about a man who'd been a soldier in World War I. He was in the cavalry, and he was a bugler. He died a long time before the night I saw that horse, and he is buried in the cemetery. Granny told me that a lot of people had seen that horse and heard the bugler in the cemetery. The people said during a full moon is when you can hear the bugle and see the horse at the grave. I saw the horse, but I didn't hear the bugle.

177

I LIVE JUST OVER THAT LITTLE RIDGE, I'VE LIVED THERE TEN YEARS. WE built a little house there. There was the most impossible, impossible, unbelievable things that could have ever happened at that place. It was when you least expected anything that it happened. The first thing we ever noticed was one night, there was a light over our house, a big light like the sun was shining right there, and it was real dark. My husband first noticed it and he called me out there. It came over the spring—we had a spring out there and a tree by it—and you could have counted ever limb on that tree. Well, we stood there and watched that until we got too tired and went to bed.

Then, the next thing, one night—the moon shined that night—we walked out in the yard and was standing there looking around. Over in the field where we had cows and horses out, we heard this horse coming. It sounded just like a man coming up the road, and then all of a sudden it stopped—the sound. And there was not nothing. My husband said that beat any damn thing he'd seen.

Then one night he was gone and the children had done gone to bed. Now my oldest stepdaughter wasn't asleep. I was just settin' there a'readin' and I heard the kitchen door latch rattle, and I thought it was the dog a'bumpin' the door with its nose. Well, then the front door latch started rattlin'. It was just an old house we built ourselves, it had these big old hinge doors, and when you'd open them the hinges would squeak. Well, these doors started *scree-ak-ing,* like somebody was opening them easy, you know. Well, I raised up my head and my stepdaughter raised up her head on her elbow. It went back to *scree-ak-ing* back about halfway, and then it stopped. And that door didn't no more move than that door's moving now. Both of us just sat there and looked at it, there wasn't nothing we could do. You talk about a creepy feeling.

Then one evening the children went to the spring to get some water; it was the fall of the year and the leaves were dead. They said, "Mama, something fell out of this tree out here and we can't find it and it's making the awfullest racket you ever heard." And I went, and the leaves was laying there, they wasn't stirring, but it went like a dog having a fit or dying or something out there in them leaves. Well, I thought that maybe there was something in under the leaves, and I took me a stick, and I raked and I raked. There wasn't nothing under there, there wasn't even a board under there. And then when I quit, it started again.

It was just everything. Sometimes I'd take my kids and go to the store, and I'd look back and I'd wish that everybody was out of them mountains and wouldn't have to go back no more.

I WENT TO SCHOOL, COLLEGE, IN ARKADELPHIA AT HENDERSON STATE Teachers College, Henderson State College. Now, OBU (Ouachita Baptist University) is in the same town, right across the street from Henderson, and so they are great rivals. When I was going to college there, this was a tradition as well as a legend.

Back when Henderson first became a college it was called Henderson Brown College, and it was a Methodist school. One year a boy from Henderson fell in love with a girl from OBU. Their friends tried to break them up because they were from different schools and different religions. Finally they succeeded in getting them apart, and while they were dating other people the boy fell in love with someone else. The girl from OBU was upset about this, and she tried to get her lover back, but there was nothing she could do, so she committed suicide during homecoming week.

Every year during homecoming week the ghost of the girl from OBU

—she is called the Black Lady—comes back through the girls' dorms at Henderson looking for the girl who stole her lover. Every year during homecoming week the junior and senior girls at Henderson get together and go through the freshmen dorms and scare the girls. The freshmen have heard the story of the Black Lady, so they know what is happening.

ONE TIME, IT WAS LATE AT NIGHT, I WAS WORKING AT NIGHT SCHOOL with Mr. Carlisle. It was registration night, and we had collected a lot of money, and he said he was going to leave me in Room 521, which is way down the hall, to go to the guidance office to turn on the alarm. I said, "You are not going to leave me here alone with all of this money." At the time, I did not know anything about the ghost.

He said, "Well, come on and walk down there with me." While we were walking, just before we got to the cutoff down here, he says, "When we get to the 300 hall I want you to look and tell me what you see."

When we got down there, I looked and I said, "What in the hell is that?"

He said, "That's the ghost," and I took off. He was outlined in white; he was a real tall man. He was standing in the middle of the hall. We have breezeways, and it looked like that was where he was standing, and that was why I saw him, because of the light reflection. I never believed in ghosts. I did see him; he was standing there with his hands on his hips. He was not doing anything; he was just standing there with his hands on his hips. I could tell he had on a skinny tie. It was a real thin tie; he had on a suit and a white shirt; that was why the tie showed up. That is all I saw. I left, and Mr. Carlisle had to find me. I was scared to death. Mr. Carlisle explained to me that it was Mr. Pair. He said that Mr. Pair is seen a lot, especially at night.

From that time on, I started hearing a lot of stories. It seems like they used to have a problem with the alarm going off for no apparent reason. You often heard it said that Mr. Pair had scared away anything that might happen to Airport (High School). It's strange because nothing has ever happened to the old part of the school. He has never been seen in the new parts, and they have been broken into. Nobody has ever broken into the old part. Mr. Rivers says that he will not hurt you; he may make you hurt yourself, but he will not hurt you.

3 HEADLESS AND SCREAMING GHOSTS AND REVENANTS

*Perhaps because of the popularity of Washington Irving's **Legend of Sleepy Hollow,** ghosts are frequently thought of as headless figures on horseback. Certainly, a strong folk tradition—derived primarily from England —of headless ghosts on horseback does exist. Headless ghosts, however, are more often found walking, sometimes carrying their head under their arms. On other occasions the headless figure is standing at a certain spot and jumps up behind the rider as the horse passes by.*

*In the following tales, the actions of various headless Southern ghosts are related, some of them having only a small portion of body visible. Also recounted here are the activities of some invisible "returners" from the dead, or **revenants.** As these texts demonstrate, the headless ghosts and revenants often appear for a specific reason, perhaps as an omen of impending death or to avenge an injury.*

180

MY GRANDFATHER USED TO TELL ME WHEN I WAS A LITTLE GIRL ABOUT ONE of his sons which he used to live with. He said his son had a good wife and two children, but his wife wasn't strong and had to lie in bed most all the time. My uncle wasn't good to her because she couldn't work. She loved him, but he would only curse her when she tried to tell him.

Years passed on, but matters grew worse instead of better. My uncle fell in love with a Negro woman, and he began going to see her. Every night he would leave his sick wife at home and go to see the Negro woman. One night his wife prayed and asked him to stay with her, but he would not listen to her. He went on to see the Negro woman.

Then, about nine o'clock, he started back home. As he went up the hill a small man stepped in front of him. He spoke, but the little man didn't answer. My uncle began to shoot at him but couldn't hit him. Then he started to run. Just then, the little man jumped on his back and put two woolly paws around his neck. This thing stayed on his back, and every step he took, it seemed to get heavier. He carried it for about three miles up the mountain before he came to the house. Just as he got to the steps, the little man jumped off and ran.

The little man came again the next night to the big farmhouse and kept him awake all night. He would come every night and walk through the hall and up the stairs. The doors would not stay shut, and the windows would rattle. The little man could not be seen, but he could be heard. One night, grandfather sprinkled flour on the stairs to see if any tracks could be seen next morning. But next morning they couldn't see any tracks. They would even bar the stair door, but it would come open. This never left until this sinful man fell on his knees and began to pray. After that he was never bothered any more, for he became a religious man.

THE WAY THIS HAPPENED, I WAS COMIN' ALONG THE ROAD UP THERE ON the Markland Hill and thought I was overtakin' Oscar Tipton. I did walk up a little fast. Wanted to see him. And I was gainin' on him. Then when he got about to the bars there on top of the hill, he turned in. Well, I kep' a'goin' it and when I got up there an' looked in at him I see that he had no head. And then I shore straightened out them roads. A little while atter that, eight or ten days I reckon, they brought Butler home dead. Butler was Aunt Frances' boy. Died of measles and double menthole, in the Army. I don't know what that double menthole is, but that's what they called it. Now it looked to me like that was a warnin' or somethin'.

WELL, I'LL TELL YOU SOMETHING: ME AND MY DAD, BACK WHEN I WAS A boy, we'd wagon from—you know that was the only source of getting groceries—Ramsey, Virginia, out there through Norton, and we'd drove our wagons down. We had covered wagons loaded down with meal, flour, lard, coffee—you know, we'd get all the groceries and bring 'em back. And so we couldn't make it with the horses and all in one day's time, you know, leaving out of the Kentucky River there and going over to Norton. We'd have to, you know, camp out at night.
So we's up there, and we got out and it was a'blowin' snow; it was in

November, and we got out and we got our firewood, you know. We kept our bedrolls with us all the time, and a lot of times if it was real bad, why, we'd manage some way to crawl in the wagon, but if it was real good weather we'd just build a fire—we always kept plenty of firewood, and we had our bedroll to keep us warm. We'd do our own cookin'—cookin' on a campfire.

We had a boy with us . . . about seventeen, eighteen years old, and he was tellin' an awful big lie. He kept on saying, "Who's that man goin' yonder with no head on? Who's that man goin' yonder with no head on?" Finally I looked up. I wasn't payin' no mind to him 'cause you couldn't believe anything he said. My dad, he didn't believe in anything like that at all, and I looked up and seen it myself. Yeah, I really looked up and seen it. And so, uh, I woke my dad up. And he said, "Has he learnt you to start lying, too?" And I said, "No." We called him Pap, you know, that's the old way, the mountain way, Pa or Pap or Pappy or something like that.

And I said, "No, Pap, sure as we're here I seen it." I said, "Watch now for yourself, and don't say you didn't see it, 'cause I seen it four or five times crossin' that road."

And he looked, and that was the worst surprised man, when he seen that, that I ever seen in my life. And he said, "I'd have never believed anything like that in my life. But that's really happened." And the old man, he never went to sleep anymore that night. He set there and kept a good fire—good and warm—said, "Now I believe you."

It looked like a man, and he was a well-dressed man. Looked like he had on a real fresh-pressed serge suit, and, uh, it looked like you could have seen his head stickin' up, but he had no head on *whatsoever*. You could see his neck stickin' up—he had a long neck. He went across there—you'd never see him come back across, he was always going that same way every time.

183

THE MOST FAMOUS OF THE SEWANEE GHOSTS IS THE HEADLESS GOWNSMAN. The legend goes that in years gone by, some time in the past, there was a group of theologues, or seminary students, cramming for mid-semester exams. It was late into the night, and one of the students, being particularly diligent or particularly guilty, whichever the case may be, wanted to study considerably later than his roommates. An argument and a scuffle ensued, and the candle the student was studying by went out. When the fellow reached over to find the candle his head fell off, the theory being that the poor theologue had crammed his head so full of information that it just spun right off.

Now the headless gownsman was supposed to have been seen by a lady named Mrs. Tucker or Rucker or somesuch. It seems Mrs. Tucker was returning late one night from Forensic Hall. She was returning home and met a figure whom she assumed to be a student, since he had a gown, and Sewanee students do wear gowns, those who have been inducted into the Order of Gownsmen. Anyway, they wear their gowns to class, indeed, anytime they leave their rooms except to go to sporting events or to work or such things.

At any rate, Mrs. Tucker met this gowned figure and assumed it to be a student and expected it to greet her as she met it. But it didn't happen; the gowned figure kept getting closer and closer to her. It made no effort to get out of her way; it didn't speak to her. As it brushed by, she turned around and it was gone. She also said that she thought she saw a face on it but couldn't recognize it as anyone she had ever seen.

Now this wouldn't be too unusual on most university campuses, that is to say, someone not recognizing a given student. But this is exceptionally rare at a place such as Sewanee. The student body of the university itself being limited to something like six hundred students and Sewanee being a relatively isolated community, everyone pretty well gets to recognize the faces of everybody else.

At any rate, ever since Mrs. Tucker's experience people have reportedly seen the headless gownsman. Now usually, the reports come from someone who saw someone who talked to someone who knew someone who saw the headless gownsman. It's still alleged that the head of this gownsman that fell off from having too much knowledge crammed into it remained in Wyndcliff Hall. Now, Wyndcliff Hall don't no longer exist. When the theologues moved out it was torn down, and the theologues moved into what is now known as St. Luke's Hall.

In those days, the days when the legend of the headless gownsman originated, all the seminary students were single, or the large majority of them were single, and in St. Luke's Hall the single seminarians live on the fourth floor, which is up above the classrooms and the library. Now the head of this gownsman, as I say, is to have remained in Wyndcliff Hall. But when they tore Wyndcliff Hall down and the theologues moved into St. Luke's Hall, the head of this gownsman moved in there.

It is said to be ominously present during times of exams, especially mid-terms and finals. Each year someone claims to have some sort of scuffle with the ghost or sees the ghost in his room. It is said to come down the stairs and then count the stairs as it comes down, always the right number of bumps per the number of steps it comes down. Normally, it only shows up during the exam period. Now this is the head of the headless gownsman.

There is at least one sighting per year of the headless gownsman. Again, most reports come from someone who saw someone who talked to somebody who heard somebody say they had seen him.

THIS IS THE TRUTH. I WAS A LITTLE BOY AROUND ABOUT SIX OR SEVEN years old. We were down the street picking berries at night. We had two flashlights and we seen something come out the bushes, and it was real black and had white hands and it was beckoning for me and my sister

ONE NIGHT WE COME UP HERE TO OLD MAN SIPES, LIVED OVER THERE IN
the Brown house. I'd been over there to see him about some hay, and I
went on 'cross that bridge and on down the road. Earl had the cows—
he was just a little feller—and I went up to the house to see about the
hay while Earl was drivin' the cows.

Went on down the road, and I looked down beside of me and there
'as a dog walkin', just trottin' along. He just trotted on alongside of me.
And he was a big black-lookin' dog—big dark dog. That dog stood up
that tall, but he just trotted along like he was one of those big police
dogs. You've seen those big dark police dogs. He was big as one of those
big police dogs, and he just trotted right alongside of me.

I was smaller than I am now. I didn't weigh but 'bout a hundred and
twenty-five. Looked like to me my breath was comin' and goin', and
that dog just trottin' on alongside of me. He never barked. He never
made no noise. He just trotted right alongside of me just like he'd
a'been my pet dog.

And when we got there to Mr. Blake's gate, he just walked right
around in front of me, and I just slowed down when he walked round
in front of me; he went right through that gate crack, and that dog
disappeared. And I ain't never seen that dog from that day to this, and
I'm tellin' you, man, I never did look fer him. Naw sir, that 'as the
biggest dog I'd seen in this country, and I ain't never seen that dog no
more, but that dog disappeared; when he went through that gate that
dog just disappeared right in the air. Never did see him. Never did see
whichaway he went nor nothing, but I heerd the chain and heerd the
gate rattle and I saw him when he went through and when he got on
the other side, but soon as you turn your eyes it's gone.

Talk 'bout steppin', I didn't come back up this road no more after
dark. When I got home I told Earl, I said, "I seen a ghost tonight."

He said, "Where'd you see him, Mama?"

I said, "Right up there. Right down below the old Brown bridge." And I said, "He walked right side of me till I got to Mr. Blake's gate, and he just went right through that crack. When he went through that crack I could hear that gate shakin' and the chain, and when I looked that dog were gone."

Didn't see no more dog. I quit comin' up this road after dark by myself.

I WAS COMIN' DOWN THESE BRIDGES AT COAL RUN ONE TIME, AND IF THE river was up or anything you had to walk the railroad. So I went to the show uptown and it was about twelve o'clock (midnight), and there come a big storm. You know where Cedar Creek is, don't you, that cut in Cedar Creek? Well, I saw two eyes a'comin', looked like they was about that far (a few inches) apart. Every time it would lightning I couldn't see those eyes, but when it was dark I could see those eyes a'comin'. I didn't know what to do, so I got off on the ground, up on the tracks, and I got me two big rocks and I throwed them at it and I didn't dent it nor nothin'. Just went on through it. I didn't have no light atall, that's all there was. No, it wasn't no train. It was something in the middle of the tracks. You couldn't hear it. All I could see was just them eyes. After it got past me, I didn't see it. It went on by me; I got off the tracks onto the ground. That's the worst scared I've ever been in my life. I was about eighteen years old.

4 $\mathcal{G}$HOSTS AND HIDDEN TREASURE

One of the most popular reasons for American ghosts to return is to reveal the whereabouts of hidden treasure. The theme is ancient, being first reported in a Buddhist myth but coming to this country primarily by way of the British Isles, where it is still a very strong tradition. Frequently reported from England, Wales and Ireland—although rarely from Scotland—the idea of a ghost returning to aid humans in finding hidden treasure has remained popular in the United States since Colonial times. Usually, it is a male ghost that returns, but there are many reports of female specters. Sometimes the ghost returns as a dismembered corpse, but frequently it takes no human form. The ghost may return as a dog or some other animal or as an object or a phantom ship. Sometimes it is a ghost light that points out the treasure, at other times merely a noise. In most instances, the ghost disappears, never to return again once the treasure is found.

Accounts of ghosts and hidden treasure are contained in the several texts that follow. In most respects the Southern apparitions discussed here are typical of those generally found in American tradition.

188

Not far from Mountain City, in a section called "The Bloody Third," stand the ruins of an old stone house around which hangs a peculiar legend of "the haint that couldn't be fathomed." The house remained vacant for some years after the Civil War, until Dr. Houston, a promising young physician with a brilliant mind and an unfortunate taste for drink, bought it, settled there and took up the surrounding mountain practice.

A short time after moving into this house, the members of the Houston family were often disturbed by queer noises. Early in the evening came a decided patter of feet on the floor. With three distinct knocks on the door, this invisible guest would enter. Then came the patter of feet on the broad oak stair as it made its round of the room above returning by the same route, back to the large fireplace in the broad living room, after which it took its departure, giving three farewell knocks.

Mrs. Houston, being a woman of strong character, was not afraid of the ghost, but she was curious to know its origin, so she sprinkled flour thickly over the stairsteps, hoping to get an imprint of the airy foot. She then listened to the pat on the stairs, but no track was ever made. All was smooth whiteness. She grew to know when to expect it and accepted it calmly. But if the doctor happened to be at home when the tapping occurred, he was much disgruntled and would often follow it upstairs and back, mumbling as he came.

As the neighbors became more wrought up and curious in regard to this strange apparition, several reliable men of the vicinity gathered and decided they would investigate the situation. They made pallets on the floor in the hall and arranged to sleep in front of the door so as to intercept the footsteps, but their sleep was not satisfactory. A sudden gust of warm air settled heavily on their chests, and they were nearly suffocated, being held down in meek submission while the footsteps passed over them. The men rose quietly the next morning and left. They were never known to mention the subject to their friends, and when questioned in regard to it they briefly told their experience, making no pretense of understanding it.

One evening Dr. Houston came in drunk. He sat with the pistol cocked, waiting for the ghost. As the three knocks sounded on the door he bounded forward to meet it and followed it up the stairs shooting and cursing volubly. The footsteps were not disturbed by the doctor's violence. They made their rounds with regular tread. As three farewell knocks sounded, Dr. Houston emptied his pistol into the outside darkness several times and closed the door.

Strange to say, this visitor never returned, but years afterwards, when the huge fireplace was torn away, a skeleton was found underneath the hearthstone, and fastened to the ledge of rock was a huge roll of Confederate bills. It was thought that the unfortunate victim had been killed for his money, which was fastened to the ledge for safekeeping, but the murderer was killed before he could return for his booty.

THERE WAS AN OLD HOUSE DOWN AROUND SNOW HILL THAT PEOPLE SAID was haunted. Things had been seen there and things heard, and the man that owned the place said that anybody who could stay there all night could have it. There was a Mr. Jones who decided to give it a try, and he took his family with him to spend the night. Late that night, after the children had been put to bed, Mr. Jones and his wife were sitting by the fire reading the Bible, when a black cat came down the stairs and passed through the room and went out the door. Mr. Jones went on reading the Bible, and a while later, a man in a black overcoat came down the stairs and disappeared. Mr. Jones kept on reading the Bible. Later on, the same man in the same black overcoat came back down the stairs, and Mr. Jones asked him, "What in the name of the Father, the Son and the Holy Ghost do you want?" The man in the black overcoat then told him to go upstairs. He told him where there was a part of a room that had been sealed off and that inside it he would find a black overcoat with some money in the pocket. Mr. Jones went upstairs and found the money. The overcoat was the same as the one the ghost had been wearing.

Now I don't know if it's true or not, but she told it to be true. She was out chopping cotton. This was after she got married and moved down around Hugo. Her baby was sick, and every now and then she'd go back to the house to see about him. Once, when she was walking back to the house, she saw a woman coming towards her down the path. And then the woman disappeared. Well, Mrs. Tillman had to keep going back and forth from the field to the house, and the same thing happened twice more. The third time she asked the woman, "What in the name of the Father, the Son and the Holy Ghost do you want?" Nearby there stood an old walnut tree beside a graveyard, and the woman told Mrs. Tillman to step off ever so many steps from that tree toward the graveyard and dig and she'd find some money. She did, and she said she found some. Like I said, I don't know if it's true or not, but she told it to be true.

My daddy told me this when I was a little boy. It happened when they were living on this man's farm in one of the old houses. And, you see, most of the land around there had been owned by the McCormicks —they were the rich people back in them days. And they say the last two sisters died. But they buried some enchanted money before they died. And they said what made them think that it was some money at the house—say because they be all the time hearing things and get them feeling like people get when they meet a ghost or something.

Well, they—Daddy and some more fellows around in there—they decided to try and dig that money. So they all got together with their bits of knowledge and everything. So they all decided to make a ring using cups and saucers that were filled with salt and surround the place where the money was. You see, the evil spirit couldn't cross over that ring. They did this. Then they had a man to get on each corner of the house to watch, because the money was right under the edge of the house. After the men got to every corner of the house, they started digging.

After a while, he said they heard something coming through the cotton field. And they looked up. He say there was something that looked like a great big hog coming down through there! It was coming right at them, so they ran into the house. He said that after they got into the house, that thing ran under it and just shook that whole house like a tornado had hit it! So that scared them off, and they didn't try to dig that money no more.

Somehow the word got out to those professional guys out of McColl, South Carolina. So when they came up there, they brought a man that could talk to spirits. This man brought a Bible and some whiskey with him. He said that if the spirits that were guarding the treasure were drunkards, he could get them to come to him with the whiskey; if they were religious, he could get them to come with the Bible.

So this man walked down to the edge of the woods to contact and ask the spirits for the money. After the man got down to the woods, Daddy said that they saw the two old women that had died. When the man offered them the whiskey, they would not come. Then he offered them the Bible. One then came close enough to him so that he could talk to her. He asked her for the money, and she finally agreed to let them dig the money. And they got the money!

192

I REMEMBER ONE NIGHT BEFORE THE FIREPLACE, THERE WAS MY UNCLE—MY father's brother—tellin' not only me as a child, but my father, about this occurrence across the mountain. As I say, many folks from this side of the mountain went over in season to work for the big farmers in the valley. These mountain people used to go over into the valley in the fall of the year at harvest time in late summer to harvest the wheat. They'd go back in autumn to harvest the corn crops. Everything was done by hand in those days, that is, as far as cuttin' corn. And then after the corn was in, they would cut wood for the winter for these big farmers over there.

And so as my uncle related, he had started out—in those days you didn't work by the clock, you worked by the sun—he started out just before daylight so he could get to his work. He had started that mornin' up the hollow, up to the woods, a hollow called Lewis's Run. Most hollows had a stream in 'em; a stream was a run. And he said it was a dreary lookin', spooky lookin' place. And he said the farther he got, the worse he felt. He felt cold chills. And he said he looked up the hollow and he saw a woman in old-time attire like his mother used to wear. And he said he didn't think anyone lived up there, so he asked himself, "Well, why would a woman be way up in this mountain this early in the mornin', a wild-lookin' place like this."

He said he kept walkin' and she kept comin'. And said when she got near him the clothes in particular didn't look natural, and he noticed she never batted an eye, she never blinked an eye just like she was lookin' through him and walked right by him and said he felt a chill and turned around. There was nobody there. And he said he went on up until he got to a good place to cut the wood and said the more he worked, the more apprehension he felt about being up there, and he started out. And said when he got back to the self-same spot that he had met this woman comin' down, he saw her comin' back again. And he said his heart stood still then. And he had always heard, if you were confronted with anything supernatural or anyone from the grave, to ask them in the name of the Lord what they wanted.

And he said when she got up in front of him that time, she didn't attempt to pass. She stopped right in front of him. And said it just paralyzed him, ev'rything but his tongue, and he said he did manage to get out, "What in the name of the Lord do you want?" And he said she pointed to a cliff on another mountain and said, "You see those rocks over there?" She said, "For one hundred years my bones been layin' in a cave under those rocks." Said, "I was murdered one hundred years ago, and my body was hid there, and if you will go git my bones and give 'em a Christian burial," said, "you'll be greatly rewarded for it." And said she just disappeared.

He come out and he told these people in the community what he thought he saw, and he tried to get someone to go with him, and they laughed him to scorn. Naturally, the experience he'd had the first time had unnerved him enough he wasn't goin' to take a chance of meetin' her again in a remote place, so he didn't go. But I heard him swear in my father's house that that was absolutely true. That's how I heard it; he was tellin' my father.

THERE WAS ONCE A HOUSE THAT HAD A ROOM WHERE NO BED COULD BE kept in a certain corner. This was called Old Sutton's corner. A family lived there, and the husband's mother lived with them. Now this corner where no bed could be kept was a very desirable place since it was in the corner by the fireplace. Every time a bed was placed in this corner it would jump out in the middle of the floor.

Well, one night, just as the family was fixing to go over to a neighbor's to stay till bedtime, Granny, as she was called, said that she was going to have her bed in that corner. The son told her that Old Sutton would get her, too. She said that her bed was going in that corner, Sutton or no Sutton.

The family went on, and it was late bedtime when they started back home. After they crossed a little ridge and got to where they could see the house, it was full of fire, the blazes of light shooting out at the windows. All the family started running toward the house, very scared as to what might have happened to Granny. When they got through the yard gate, all the fire and light went out of the house. They went in the house, and there set Granny's bed out in the middle of the floor with her looking scared. She was not hurt at all, but she never did try to put a bed in that corner again.

Years later, when the house was torn down, a roll of money was found hidden in the walls of the house near the corner where nobody could get a bed to stay. And that was the last of Old Sutton and his troubles.

MY WIFE'S BROTHER AND HIS FAMILY BOUGHT A PLACE AND MOVED INTO the house that was on it. There had been some talk that nobody had been able to live at this place, but they never thought much about that, just thought it was some scary tale people had got in their head and started telling. They moved on in anyway.

There was a big rock fireplace in the big house, but they didn't sleep in this room; they slept in the back room. Well, it hadn't been long after they moved till they began hearing noises at night—just like the big rocks might be jumping out of the chimney and bouncing around over the floor. When they'd go in the room, everything would stop and there'd be no more noise, but as soon as they'd go back to bed it would start all over again. Finally, Henry's wife said she couldn't stand it any longer, and so they just sold out and left.

Well, the feller they sold to had the same trouble, so he just tore down the house to build another. When the old chimney and fireplace was torn down, they found a jar of gold pieces hidden right above the jambs. When the new house was put up, there was no more noises or trouble of any kind. It was all because of the hidden money.

195

MY GRANDPA LIVED ON THIS HILL PLACE, AND GREAT-GRANDPA LIVED down there at the well. One night Papa wanted to go to church. Grandma and her sister, Bertha, didn't want him to go. They said, "Don't go off and leave us."

Grandpa said, "There ain't nothing going to hurt you, and they ain't nothing for you to be afraid of." Grandpa said, "I'll have my gun."

Well, he went on down there to church and started back. Well, there's a white oak tree down the road that stood on the right. Well, he got up there even with the tree, and there were those two graves on the upper side of the road. Well, this woman came out from behind the tree and started running toward Papa. Well, Papa just stopped. He said she had big brown eyes and long brown hair and was just standing there looking right at Papa. And he said he could see her bat her eyes and the moon was shining as bright as day.

He said he just stood there looking at her and never said a word. And he heard a noise and turned his head, and when he looked back she had disappeared. Well, Papa told some of the older people what he had saw and all, and they said, "If you had said, 'Lord have mercy, what do you want?' she would have told you." What folks told Papa was that her husband was buried there, and there was money buried with him.

5 TRAVELING GHOSTS

Most ghosts are bound to a single place, but there are those who carry their haunting farther afield. Usually the wraiths move about by horseback or automobile, rather than by supernatural means. This activity has a lengthy and somewhat elderly tradition, being found throughout Russia and much of Europe. It is documented that as early as the 1660s, people were telling stories about these traveling ghosts, and they were undoubtedly being discussed prior to that time.

Some such tales involve a dead lover who returns and carries his sweetheart behind him on horseback. His goal is to carry her with him into the grave; in most versions he succeeds, but in a few, the girl is rescued at the last moment. Perhaps the best known European legend concerning a wandering ghost is that of the Flying Dutchman. In this story, a sea captain, because of his wickedness, is doomed to eternally sail his phantom ship without coming into harbor. "The Flying Dutchman" is the exception to the rule that the traveling ghosts do not cover distances of more than a few miles.

In the texts that follow, we will encounter some ghosts traveling in the South. Included among them is "The Vanishing Hitchhiker," a ghost tale that differs from most of the others in this section in that the ghost is a woman.

196

MY GRANDFATHER, W.T. DOLLAR, HE WAS A DRUMMER, A HORSEBACK drummer for R.J. Reynolds Tobacco Company of Winston-Salem, and he drummed tobacco, you know, sold snuff and chewing tobacco. And the first thing, he always rode up by White Top through Konnarock when he was heading home, and he would always have to ride by the Devil's Stairs at sundown, and something got on the horse behind him, you know, and his horse started fretting, and he couldn't control it. His horse got kind of out of control with him.

And there's a church still standing, known as the Oak Grove Baptist Church now. When he come by there—when he got to the church— the horse just came to a complete stop without his controlling it, and when it did, why, it was just something getting off his horse, and he rode on in, which he lived about, oh, three quarters of a mile up the road at the homeplace. It's burned down now, you know. It was behind Paul Elliott's garage where an old junkpile is now.

He said when he got home, there was something, something on his horse. It looked like white marks of some kind, something you might say looked like chalk marks or something in the shape of somebody's legs or something—like somebody's legs on his horse's flanks, you know. He wiped to see if it was sweat from where the horse was a'frettin', but it wasn't, he said; it wasn't sweat. It was white marks like somebody had gotten on there with something on behind the saddle there. Whatever it was, wasn't on the saddle there; it was on behind the saddle. Ever what it was, sitting there behind him, had hung down and touched the horse's flanks, and my grandfather at that time, as anyone could witness, kept the best horse, 'cause he depended on his horse for his livelihood.

Now from that day on, it was always told to me, you could never get my grandfather to pass the Devil's Stairs at night. If he was caught below there, he'd always spend the night with Dr. Minnie Blevins, who lived in a house which is still standing there just below the road there in that real stiff curve.

A LONG TIME AGO, AN INDIAN COUPLE WAS TO BE MARRIED, ANOTHER ordinary marriage, as it may appear. But as time went on, the economic status of the family went from fair to very poor. When the couple had its first baby, a boy, the father knew he couldn't feed him, so after thinking about what was best for the child, he went to the river, and after asking God for forgiveness he dropped the child in the river. The husband believed he was doing the right thing and repeated his feat as each child was born. Each time, the townspeople heard the wife screaming, *"Ay, mi hijo (Oh, my son)"* in an eerie tone.

When her last son was born, she was determined to let him live. She went down to the river, and after her husband dropped the boy, she went after him. Since she wasn't skilled in the art of swimming, she drowned along with her son.

Nobody thought much of it after her death, but one foggy night, one of the farm workers saw the ghostly figure of a woman and child in the river. The woman screamed in her high-pitched voice, "Oh, my son!" After that night, the ghost appeared on the water and the nearby land. The husband couldn't sleep because he heard these eerie sounds. Finally the husband, knife in hand, jumped into the river and tried to kill the woman. After his unsuccessful try, his body was never found.

After the story was spread around, people reported seeing her in different places. But the local people said that she appeared only on rainy, foggy nights.

As a young lady, I often met José in the grove of trees near the river. Much kissing and loving took place, but I was always careful to leave the area well before midnight. One night shortly before my engagement, time got away from me and I failed to leave before twelve. A cold chilling wind came up suddenly from the north with a furious intensity. A cat screamed, and a plaintive wailing sound came to my ears. It grew louder and louder until a blast of wind caused a white-robed figure to whisk past me. As the figure darted by, I saw that it had no face. I fell to my knees and sought God's help. Before long the wind stopped, and I could no longer hear the mournful cries. To this day, I have not returned to that cursed spot.

Late one night, my uncle and one of his friends were coming home late from the cantina. They always took too much tequila, you know, and so it was pretty late. All at once, they saw this lady, about a block away, walking toward the canal. She really had a good figure.

Well, you know how guys are when they've had too much tequila— they get interested in the ladies. So they hurried to catch up, and they even called to her, but she didn't wait. She walked on down by the canal. Finally they were just a few yards away, and they called to her to wait. Slowly, she turned around—and she didn't have a face! She lifted up her hands toward them, and she had shiny claws, like tin. And she was coming toward them, like she was going to get them, you know.

Well, they turned and ran, with the woman right behind them, till they got to a bright streetlight, where she disappeared. My uncle never went to the cantina after that—He didn't want to meet La Llorona again.

198

WELL, ONE TIME THERE WAS AN OLD COLORED MAN LIVED OVER HERE—you talkin' about ghost stories—and he lived right close to my grandfather, and he worked for the Browns. The Browns owned a farm, and he was a hand on the farm, and my granddaddy lived right close to him, and he used to go down to talk with him some nights. They was great cronies.

So he goes down one night, and he had a big chat with my grandfather at headquarters. So as he was comin' on back home—They was always sayin' that there was ghosts, and he said, well, he was never scared of no ghost. So as he was comin' on back home, just between his home and my grandfather's—They had a big old tobacco house stood right on the side of the road. So as he's comin' on in the night by that, just as he got about the opp'site side of that old tobacco house, why there was a woman walked right out through the drawbars, right to the road, and he looked around and he looked at her, and he spoke to her and he says, "Is that you, Miss Dolly?" That's my mother. And he walked on, and she walked right along beside him, and he 'gin to walk a little faster and she did too.

So they went on about twenty yard, and he had a creek he had to go across before he got to his house. And as he walked a little faster, she did too, and so he struck a trot and she did too. So when he got to the creek he just lit out a'runnin' and he took right through the creek, and when he got through the creek she stopped. And he was out of wind.

He had just about twenty yards to go when he went to his house.

And 'fore he got to the house he hollered for his wife, said, "Open the door, Ida!" And when he got to the door, 'fore she could open it, he fell agin' it and knocked the door open. And he fainted when he fell inside. And she run, "Lord, what's the matter?"

"Oh," he said, "there's sump'n got after me." Said, "There's some woman followed me up the road, but she never would speak and she disappeared and I don't know whar she went."

That was all I know. That happened down here—well, I'm fifty—I think that happened about sixty years ago.

THIS IS A STORY ABOUT THE OLD TIMES. A LONG TIME AGO, MY DADDY used to tell me about these old men that walk around on the road. 'Fore you know it, they had turned their head around backwards. One night my daddy and my brother, they were going down the road in Clarksdale. They were walking down the street on Hallowe'en night, and they see this man had turned his head around backwards. He was hollering like a cow. Daddy tried to catch him, and this man said, "You can't catch me. I'm a bad man. You can't catch me."

When he said, "You can't catch me," my daddy jumped on his back and tied him down and said, "Turn your head around back like it was."

And the monster turned his head. When he turned his head, my daddy knowed it was a old friend of his. He let the old man go, and he came back home.

One rainy and wintery night, a man was driving down this road and slowed up to come into this curve. As the headlights flashed around the curve, they showed that a young girl was standing in the road waving. The man stopped immediately and offered the girl a ride home, and she accepted by simply nodding her head.

The man was overwhelmed by the young girl's beauty and fell in love with her before she ever spoke a word. The young girl directed the man by pointing her finger and never saying a word. The man thought that she was just shy and didn't press a conversation. They finally reached her house, which was about five miles off the main highway, and the man got out to go around and open the door.

When he reached the other side of the car, he discovered that the young girl was no longer in the car. Thinking that she had already gone in the house, he went up and knocked on the door. An old, tired-looking lady came to the door and asked him in. When he asked to see her daughter, she looked surprised and began to explain that her daughter was killed on that very night just five years ago. She was on her way home from a party when it happened. She explained that this same thing had happened on the four previous years before now: she had been picked up, brought home, and disappeared for another year.

THE STORY TOOK PLACE IN REDFIELD, ARKANSAS, A LITTLE COMMUNITY about halfway between Pine Bluff and Little Rock, Arkansas. Supposedly, a man was driving along the road on a rainy, stormy night, and on the side of the road a young girl flagged him down. He stopped, and she told him that they had car trouble and would he give her a lift to her home. He agreed. So off they drove.

On reaching Redfield and pulling up in front of the house that she had pointed out, the man got out of the car, walked around the car to let the girl out. On reaching the other side and looking through the window, he discovered the girl had disappeared. The man was bewildered and confused. Not knowing what next to do, he walked up to the house and knocked.

A middle-aged couple came to the door, and he related the story to them of what had happened. They didn't seem to be too shocked. As a matter of fact, they told him that this had happened a number of times before on this particular date. And they went on to tell him that about four years before, their young daughter was out celebrating her birthday —that date—with her boyfriend. She was killed south of Redfield in a car wreck, along with her boyfriend. And they went on to tell him that this same thing had happened two or three times before, on this particular date. Evidently, every year on their daughter's birthday she would try to come home.

200c

ONE NIGHT A MAN WAS DRIVING ALONG THE HIGHWAY BETWEEN LITTLE Rock and Woodson and noticed a girl standing on a bridge. He stopped and asked her if she wanted a ride. She explained that she was on her way home for the Christmas holidays and her home was just a few miles away in the small town of Woodson. Upon arriving at her home, she asked him to go to the door to see if anyone was there, because it looked very dark. Therefore, he went to the door and knocked, and when a woman came to the door, he explained to her that he had brought her daughter home for the Christmas holidays. The woman looked at him, astonished, and told him she was sorry but her daughter had been killed in a car accident one year ago from that very night. Puzzled, he went to the car and opened the door. There was nothing in the car but a coat. After carefully examining the coat, the woman stated that the coat was one of her daughter's.

200d

THERE WAS A TAXI DRIVER, WHO, ONE DAY, AFTER WORK WAS DONE, WENT on a spree. He drove all around the town, up one street and down another, and finally he came upon a dance. He stood for a long time in the doorway, seeing what he could see, and finally noticed a very pretty and charming girl. He went up to her and asked her to dance with him. She accepted, and they danced until very late. Then she decided to leave, and the taxi driver offered to take her home in his car. She accepted, and on the way home, she felt very cold. He took off the coat and gave it to her to put around her shoulders.

When they reached her home, she asked him to let her out at the garden gate. The girl got out, opened the gate, and went inside. The taxi driver went on home and went to sleep.

Next morning when he awakened, he recalled that he did not have his coat and decided to go to the girl's house to ask for it. He rapped on the door, and a woman answered. He said to her, "I'd like to speak to the young lady who lives here. We were dancing together last night."

The woman was a bit surprised and told him that her only daughter had been dead for many years. The driver protested that such was not possible, because they were dancing just last night and she had brought his coat home with her. The woman replied that she was sorry but that her daughter had died a long time ago. "Come with me," she said, "and I will show you her tombstone." So the mother and the taxi driver went to the cemetery. How surprised they were to find that upon the tombstone was hanging his coat!

The man fell ill, and a few days later he was dead.

IN 1973, I WAS COMING HOME LATE ONE SATURDAY NIGHT. AS I AP-proached the end of the bridge which leads out of Batesville, Arkansas, going towards Little Rock, a girl appeared. It looked like she came out of nowhere, and she was dressed in white. To avoid hitting her I had to slam on my brakes, real hard. I stopped the car and noticed the girl still standing there by the road. I noticed the girl's dress was long, white and torn. She had a cut above her eye. I asked her, "What happened?" She explained that she had been in a car accident and needed a ride home to get her father to pull her car out of the ditch it was in.

"OK, I'll take you home," I commented. "Are you OK?" She told me that she was fine and gave me directions to her house. She did not talk any more. I took the directions she had given me to her house, but when I got there and turned around to say something to her, she was gone.

I knocked on the door. Her father came to the door. While I was trying to tell him what happened, her mother came to the door with a white dress and told me she had been killed two months before—in a car accident, the same place I had picked her up. I also learned that other people had seen her.

Now, on the night (anniversary) of her accident, don't be surprised if you see her yourself. She will appear just out of nowhere and ask for a lift. Oh, yes, she will be wearing white—a white dress—and it will be after twelve o'clock.

ONE TIME THIS MAN HAD BEEN WORKING LATE AT NIGHT IN HIS OFFICE AND had to walk home because he had missed the bus. He was walking right by a graveyard and about to turn the corner when a lady stepped out and lit his cigarette that was hanging from his mouth. They began talking, and he asked her if he could walk her home. She said she would like that very much. The man walked her to her home, which was just a short distance away, and had a very enjoyable time.

The man enjoyed it so much that he decided to call on her the next night. He went to the house where he had taken her the night before and knocked on the door. A man came to the door and asked to help him. The man said he wanted to see his daughter, Anne. The owner of the house said, "You must be joking, my daughter has been dead for twelve years." The father took the man inside the house and showed him a picture of his daughter, Anne. It was the same girl he had walked home the night before.

The father said he would show the man her grave. They went to the grave, and there was her name on the tombstone. On top of the tombstone was a cigarette lighter that someone had left. The name on the lighter? Anne.

6 ᴍALEVOLENT GHOSTS

Most ghosts are harmless to anyone with a clear conscience, but there are some that are vengeful and malevolent. Often the ghosts of dead lovers and husbands and wives return to haunt their faithless sweetheart or spouse. Second marriages of husbands or wives especially occasion spectral visitation. Sometimes it is a parent who comes back to make life unpleasant for his or her children; on other occasions the ghost returns to slay a wicked person or to take revenge on its murderer or on someone who injured or cheated it while it was alive. Frequently, the dead returns to punish a person who has stolen part of the corpse or who has in some way disturbed the grave; at other times it is to punish someone who is mistreating a relative. These are the major reasons for the return of vengeful Southern ghosts, some of whom are discussed in the following section.

201

IT HAPPENED SOMETIME IN THE LATE 1800S, IN THE SUMMERTIME. A young man by the name of George Scott had been going with this girl, a lovely Southern girl, and she loved him dearly. They were planning to get married in the early fall. He decided for some reason that he . . . well, wasn't ready to get married and broke the engagement. She was just grief-stricken. Before long she became ill, caught typhoid fever, I think. She got worse and worse and finally died. He was upset about it, but not too much, because he went on with the other boys to see other girls.

Around Christmas, he and a bunch of young men were going to a party. They had to walk back home in those days. It was two or three miles on a narrow, winding road, so narrow only one buggy could pass and grown up on both sides. They had to go past the very graveyard where his girlfriend was. As they got right opposite the graveyard, they saw this funny-looking fog, a white form coming toward them. The other boys took off and flew, scared to death, and left him, but George Scott stood stock-still, petrified, because he knew who it was and it couldn't be anybody else. He didn't speak, and she didn't either. The white shape touched him. Its hand was icy cold. Then it vanished.

The others had gotten to the house, where they told what had happened and excited everybody. Some went back to see if they could find him, and they did. He was still in a daze. A few months later his health went bad, and he died young.

And that's not all. He was buried in the same cemetery not far from where the girl was. His parents put up a white tombstone about four feet high. After he'd been dead about forty years, the news got out that there was the likeness of that girl's face on his tombstone. It was some kind of discoloration, very visible, life-size. She'd been dead, of course, a long time, but people who'd seen her picture declared for sure it was she and nobody else. People came from miles around to see it.

202

No sir, I don't reckon ghosts come out nowadays like they did two generations ago. Why, when I was a boy, folks in Rockford wouldn't go within hollerin' distance of the old graveyard after dark. In those days people really believed in ghosts, and from what I've seen I ain't exactly sayin' I don't.

Speakin' of ghosts reminds me of a story that's been told for years around Rockford. It's about an old fellow the kids called Still Face because he never smiled. He didn't have anything to do with anybody and lived with his old maid sister Hettie in a ramblin' house above the river. He had an old hound dog and spent a lot of time up the river huntin'. He was pretty fond of his sister, and they stayed at home most of the time. Folks didn't pay much attention to them.

Then one day Hettie took sick and in a week was dead. It almost killed old Still Face. He didn't have any other kin, so the folks got together and went to his house to make arrangements for the funeral and to sympathize with him. After the funeral the old man went home alone and didn't show his face for a week or so.

Then one night, about ten o'clock, old Charlie Wilson, who carried the mail from Yadkinville to Rockford in a two-horse wagon, was comin' up the road near the graveyard. He was late because a thunderstorm washed out the road pretty bad. It was lightnin' and thunderin' something awful, and old Charlie cussed and whipped the horses, tryin' to get in before the road got worse.

Well, just as the wagon got to the graveyard, there came a low, moanin' sound from among the tombstones. Charlie's hair stuck up. Suddenly the thunder crashed, and a flash of lightnin' lit up the cemetery. What he saw made him lose his false teeth and crack his whip on the horses' rumps. A human figure—ghost or livin'—was sittin' on top of a tombstone, right at the edge of the graveyard, with a rain-drenched dog beside him. Charlie didn't wait to see any more.

When Charlie got to town, everything was dark except a dim lamp-light in old man Gink's store window. He went in breathlessly. When he told what he had seen, old man Gink swore it was only a tree swayin' or a stump or else some durn fool cuttin' through the cemetery on his way home. But didn't neither one of 'em figure that old Still Face might have gone out in the graveyard to his sister's grave and got caught in the storm.

Well, about three days later, along about midnight, a hound dog started howlin' over toward the old man's house. It kept howlin' all night, and folks thought it must be Still Face's dog. They could tell by its long, mournful howl that something was wrong. It didn't usually go on that way. The next mornin' some of the neighbors went over to the house, and sure enough, there was the old man lying in bed, deader'n a doornail.

Some of the pious citizens didn't want the old man buried with their kind in the graveyard because they figured he might contaminate their souls. So they decided to send his body to Yadkinville. They put him in a coffin and put it in the back of Charlie's mail wagon, which was leavin' for Yadkinville about four o'clock. There were no passengers for Yadkinville that day, so Charlie had to make the trip alone. He begged some of the boys down at the store to go with him, because he knew it would be dark before he reached Yadkinville. But none of them cared to ride with a corpse. As he was leavin', one of the boys hollered jokingly after the disappearing wagon: "The mail must go through, Charlie, so don't slack yer duty!"

Old Charlie whipped his horses into the river at Shallow Ford about sundown and was soon up on the other side, heading his wagon down the road toward Crutchfield and Yadkinville. He sat up in the front seat looking straight ahead, cluckin' his horses on and wishin' he could see somebody comin' down the lonesome road.

By the time Charlie had gone four miles from town, a cloud had come up and everything else black as pitch, except for a dim, flickerin' kerosene lantern swingin' on the side of the wagon. The woods on both sides were dark and still.

Then, suddenly, from the back of the wagon there came a low tap-pin' sound that got louder and louder, till it was an awful racket. It sounded like somebody strugglin' and kickin' to get out of a box. Charlie stiffened in his seat. That noise was comin' out of the coffin! Then came a ghastly shriek, and, with a crashin' of splinters, the coffin lid flew off.

Old Charlie jumped to the ground, and when he took his first breath he was half a mile down the road, runnin' like a streak of lightnin' toward Rockford. Me and some of the fellers was in the store when he staggered in, drippin' wet with sweat and muddy water. He fell into a chair, white as a sheet, and after catching his breath, told us what happened. Some of the boys said they didn't believe it, but I saw some doubtful looks in them fellers' eyes!

Next day, old John Borden, who lived on the island down the river, saw the horses, still hitched to the mail wagon, grazing on the other side of the river. The boys went over and found the coffin just like Charlie said. The lid was split, and the hinges had been broken off.

Nobody ever figured what happened to old Still Face. Some thought the old man wasn't really dead but had some sort of sleepin' sickness and, when he came to in his coffin, ran off into the swamp and died. Others thought the fellows had played a joke on Charlie. They figured some of 'em had carried the old man's body off and put one of the boys in the coffin.

Charlie quit the mail job and a few years later took sick and died. Nobody went near the graveyard on a dark night for a long time after that. Even now, when a storm comes up at night, and it's lightnin' and thunderin', a lonesome howl floats in from over the hills toward the graveyard, and the folks around town swear it's the ghost of the old man's hound huntin' for his master.

A LONG TIME AGO THERE WAS AN OLD NEGRO WHO HAD WORKED IN A sawmill near Crossett all his life. He was very good at his job, and some of the newer Negroes thought he was a know-it-all, so they gave him a rough time. One day, the old man had taken all he could stand, so he hit the man who was fooling around with him, even though they were on the job. The young Negro struck back at the old one, knocking him into the buzz saw. The old man tried to break his fall with his hands, resulting in both of his arms being ripped off just below the elbow. The old Negro's life was saved, but he couldn't work in the mill anymore. The sawmill was his life, so he just wandered off and nobody ever heard of him again. Some time later, the young Negro who had started the fight was still working at the mill. He was found cut half in two by the saw. The Negro who was working with him at the time swore he saw two arms reach out of the shadows and push the screaming man into the buzz saw. Many other Negroes believed this also, but the judge at the murder trial didn't. The Negro was accused of murder and executed.

BACK IN 1925, AFTER THE EL DORADO BOOM HAD SETTLED DOWN, THERE was a drilling company that pressured people into letting them drill for oil on their land. Now, many people were farmers, and they wanted to stay that way. Besides, most people knew how crooked this company was, so they didn't want any part of their business.

In one case, an old man had a farm out in the middle of the east field. The drilling company was reasonably sure there was oil on this land, but the old man didn't want his little farm turned into a mass of oil slick and salt flats. The men at the drilling company tried to reason with the old man, but he was stubborn. So they sent a bunch of roughnecks out to rough him up a little bit and try to convince him to sign with them so they could drill and collect their outrageous profits. But when they got out there, the old man grabbed a gun to protect himself, so the men had to kill him. He was found out in front of his house, lying in a large pool of blood.

The drilling company never did get to drill on the old man's property because the land was left to his son who lived in Chicago. The men never got convicted for the old man's murder, but later the drilling company got run out of town on other charges. So many years passed, and finally the son allowed the land to be drilled. The drilling crew had been working for days on the rig, trying to go down deep enough to hit the precious oil that no one could be sure was down there.

There was one older roughneck on the crew who, the men noticed, had been acting very strange ever since he started on this particular job. Every time he came out to the lease he started getting jumpy and afraid of every little thing. Then one night, the night shift was going about their normal tasks when a faint rumbling started deep in the ground. It got louder and louder. The well was coming in! The older roughneck stood there horrified while the other men tried to cap the well off before it gushered out over the top. But they weren't fast enough. The gusher rumbled and sprayed out the top of the derrick. The hard-working men were distracted by the older roughneck screaming, "It's blood! It's blood!" He fell screaming into the oily dirt and squirmed around as if he was being burned to death as the oil from the gusher rained over him.

Before the other men got the oil stopped it quit flowing of its own accord. This only meant one thing. There was not enough oil left in the hole to fool with. When they got back to the man lying in the dirt, he was dead. Later, everyone decided that the dead roughneck had had a hand in killing the old man some years back. Many people just figured that his conscience drove him crazy and he had a heart attack. But many people thought the old man's ghost came back to bewitch him and get revenge on him. Which do you think?

205

THERE IS A TERRIBLE SWAMP OUT SOUTHWEST OF MAGNOLIA CALLED BEAR Creek Bottom. It is full of quicksand, snakes and gators. Many years ago it was a lot wilder. One story about the swamp is that of a three-man search party.

Ever so often, someone would turn up missing after going hunting down in the swamp, either getting lost or getting killed by the animals and reptiles there. An old Negro who lived a little way down in the swamp knew his way around the swamp but wouldn't ever go down in it anymore because he thought the woods were alive. Everyone thought he was crazy, but they would get directions from him to go in.

Then one day, a man turned up missing who had three very close friends who went down into the swamp to search for him. They stayed in so long that people feared they were dead. Finally, one of the men staggered out of the swamp and fell alongside a road, where he was found. He had completely lost his mind; his whole body was cut up, and he had splinters stuck all in him, and his hair had turned white. He was mumbling that the woods were alive, over and over. Some people thought that he had seen his two friends die some terrible swamp death which had scared him out of his mind and caused him to run many miles through the underbrush. But many people remembered the old swamp nigger's warning, and they wondered if the very woods in the swamp were alive.

7 WITCHES, BANSHEES, BLOODSTOPPERS, GHOSTLY LIGHTS AND SUPERNATURAL CREATURES

To most Americans, witches are something out of the past, people who were charged with having, or claimed to have, certain supernatural abilities. Contrary to this notion, the tradition of witchcraft did not die in Colonial times but has persisted down to the present—and not just in out-of-the-way places but even in some of the largest cities in North America. Recently, in Miami, a man killed his wife reportedly because he thought she was a witch. Similar incidents have been reported from Indianapolis and Detroit, and in Georgia, a convicted murderess claimed to be a witch. One of Phil Donahue's recent shows was devoted to a discussion with four witches from a Wisconsin association of witches. Such cases are proof that there are people who strongly believe that witches and witchcraft are a real force in today's world. In folk tradition, the witch is generally a woman, often hideously ugly, usually using her supernatural powers for evil reasons. There are, however, also "white witches," who use their abilities for good.

While witches are common in Southern, and American, folklore, other supernatural figures are relatively rare. Certainly none of the European supernatural beings is less frequently found in this country than the banshee, a type of bearer of bad tidings (usually a portent of death) who often appears in legends from Wales and Ireland. They are not entirely unheard of in this country, for Wirt Sikes reported in his book, **British Goblins** (1880), an incident which happened in the 1870s in Evansville, Indiana: a banshee appeared prior to the deaths of five members of the same family. According to Sikes, "the circumstances attending the banshee's visits were gravely described in a local journal as a matter of news." (p. 247) Still, it is *generally correct to say that banshees belong to old-world folk tradition rather than that of the new.*

While the banshee is not often reported in the South, ghostly lights, supernatural creatures merely called "the thing," and bloodstoppers are. Often the ghostly lights serve as omens, and "the thing" is usually sent to try and make a bad person do better. Bloodstoppers—people possessing the power to staunch the flow of blood from wounds or cuts, generally by means of verbal charms that are effective against disease, evil and witchcraft—are a different order of the supernatural. They use their powers on people for reasons that most often have little to do with good or evil or how the person receiving the charm has lived his life. Most of the charms date from pre-Christian times but are revamped to fit Christian tradition. A majority of the charms involve belief in the power of sacred or magic words, such as "Jesus," and usually only specially gifted persons can use the words effectively. A person born with a caul, and a seventh son of a seventh son are both supposed to be exceptionally skillful at bloodstopping. But even though the belief in bloodstopping is common in America, relatively few examples have been collected, due solely to lack of inquiry.

The few examples in the following section offer some representative stories from the South about bloodstoppers, witches, banshees, ghostly lights and other supernatural creatures.

206

THE MUDDY WATER OF THE TAR RIVER IN EDGECOMBE COUNTY NEAR Tarboro moves sluggishly between the reedy, oak-shadowed banks as slowly and sullenly as it did centuries ago. The grist mill that once stood on the curve below the dam is gone, and no sign of the dam remains. But on misty August nights, when the yellow moon tilts on end and the rain crow calls for rain, the cry of the banshee that haunts the river splits the mist in a shrill, wild scream that echoes from bank to bank and dies away above the treetops in a throbbing, dismal moan.

During the Revolutionary War, David Warner, an Englishman, ran the Tar River mill. He was a staunch Whig and hated the English. He used his mill for the grinding of wheat and corn for the rebel army, furnishing them freely of his own food and allowing them to use the mill for grinding their grain. From dawn to sunset the mill clattered, the water turning the mill wheel often far into the night.

From the open door, the lantern light sent a golden path out into the darkness. Warner moved from hopper to bin and from bin to hopper, his shadow falling across the lantern glow, sometimes dwarfed and sometimes tall. He was a big man with a shock of black hair and black beard whitened with flour dust. His eyes were keen as an eagle's, and there was a fierce strength in his arms and wrists. He could lift a sack of grain with one hand and fling it over his shoulder, and with one turn of his wrist he could snap a tenpenny nail in two.

It was noonday in the heat of August. David Warner stood in the doorway of the mill listening to the lazy hum of jarflies and the raucous call of the katydids, when far down the road he heard the thudding sound of galloping horses. He knew before the runner came to warn him that the British were coming.

"Close your mill and hide. The British know you for a rebel, and they will kill you."

Warner looked at his big wrists and shook his head. "I'd rather stay and wring a British neck or two," he said grimly.

"But you can't stay and fight a whole army single-handed." The runner's teeth were chattering.

"Then," declared the miller, "I'll stay and be killed. What is my life?" He went back into the mill, and the runner followed.

The mill wheel was turning swiftly and Warner was sacking meal when six British soldiers crept to the door. Pretending not to see them, the miller said to the runner who was helping him, "Try to save every precious ounce of it, my lad, and we'll deliver it to General Greene. I hate to think of those British hogs eating a single mouthful of gruel made from America's corn."

When the soldiers heard this, they rushed in and seized the miller, cursing him for a rebel and beating him. Warner fought bravely, but five men held him fast. When they told him they were going to drown him in the river, he laughed in their faces and jeered, "Go ahead, go ahead, but if you throw me in the river, ye British buzzards, the banshee will haunt ye the rest of your life, for the banshee lives here. When the moon is dark and the river's like black ink and the mist is so thick ye can cut it with a knife, ye can see her, with her yellow hair falling about her shoulders, flitting from shore to shore, crying like a loon. And sure as the stars are in the sky, if ye drown me she'll get ye." Then he cursed them all 'round and dared them to carry out their threat.

For a moment the five men hesitated, whispering together. "Let's wait," said the tallest, "until the commander arrives. He will decide for us."

"Yes," agreed the second soldier, "let's wait."

But a big soldier with evil eyes and cruel mouth cursed and said, "Why wait? We are sent on ahead to make the way safe. We'll get rid of this rebel before he makes trouble."

The soldiers carried the miller down to the river bank. They bound his hands behind him. They tied a great stone around his neck and another to his feet. Then they threw him into the river. As his body sank from sight beneath the sullen water, a piercing cry ripped from the red clay ledges—the cry of a woman in the agony of death.

The soldiers stood frozen with fear. At first, there was nothing save a thick mist above the water. Then the mist took on the form of a woman with flowing hair and a veil for her face. The men turned white with horror.

"The banshee," whispered one. "The banshee," whispered another. But the soldier with evil eyes who had been so ready to drown the miller was too frightened to speak. He turned and fled to the mill.

At nightfall, the commander and his men arrived. The officers made their sleeping quarters in the mill house, and the soldiers pitched their tents beneath the trees. Soon campfires glowed against the night and made the shadows seem blacker. The new moon arose, tilted on end, thin and yellow. Far off a rain crow called for rain. From down the river came the banshee's cry—the cry of a woman in the agony of death.

The commander with his officers rushed from the mill house, and the soldiers ran from their tents—all except the soldier with evil eyes and his two mates who had helped him drown the miller. These three sat as if frozen, motionless, with their hands over their eyes, trying to stifle the agonizing wail.

The officers on the river bank saw a thick cloud of mist over the water; they saw it take the form of a woman with flowing hair and a veil for her face. When the soldiers climbed to the claybank ledge, no woman was there. The weird cry echoed far down the stream.

The three soldiers were so frightened that they confessed their crime. The angry commander, for their punishment, decreed that for the rest of their lives they should stay at the mill, grinding grain and listening to the haunting wail.

During the day they ground grain for the British, and at night the cry tormented them. Then one night the banshee came closer. She appeared in the doorway of the mill, a tall, mist-shrouded figure with flowing hair. She flung back her veil and faced the frightened men. The soldier with evil eyes cowered far into the corner, but the other two leaped to their feet, lured by the misty apparition before them. The banshee floated away just beyond their reach. Blindly they followed, heedless of where she led them. They came to the river. There they stumbled, fell into the water and were never seen again.

After that, the evil-eyed soldier who was left alone went raving mad. All through the night he wandered the woods, calling the miller's name. The cry of the banshee answered him. One day, his body was found floating face upward in the very place in the river where he had drowned the miller.

Years have passed, but to this day, in August, when the rain crow calls for rain and the moon is yellow and tilted on end, the mist will rise in a thick, white shroud. Slowly it will take the form of a woman with flowing hair and a veil for her face. Then sharp and shrill will come the banshee's cry—an agonizing wail that rises higher and higher, beating against the distance where it fades away in a dull, throbbing moan.

207

WHEN THE AMERICAN COLONIES WERE BEING SETTLED, GERMANS CROSSED the Atlantic, landed at Charleston. Then, as more and more arrived, they spread out over the state, living mostly along the rivers. Finally the area along the Saluda River was settled by German Lutherans. The Germans were Lutherans, you know. They were very law-abiding, good Christians; they read their Bibles regularly, they built churches and schools, practiced strict moral laws, attended church every Sabbath, prayer meetings every Wednesday night. They did every good deed possible; oh, they were a pious group, all right.

The old devil believed he could change them. So one night he really tried. Oh, he really tried to get in with these good people, so he dressed himself up; he looked like a—well, he was a good-looking man when he really dressed up and tried to date the girls; well, he did date the girls, but when they'd go out with him, they soon found out that he was the devil and they'd give him the kick. And then he tried the young men. He told them he knew where he could get something for them that would make them feel good and make them happy, and here he comes with a bottle of gin or liquor or whatever you call it and offered it to them, to see if he could make them drunk.

Oh, he did his best, but these were good pious people, and he couldn't make out, couldn't make them do anything he wanted them to do. Oh yes, he pretended to be a pious, Christian man too, and he went to church with them, especially on Wednesday nights, and oh, how he could pray! But he was a rascal, all right. They soon found out that he had the devil in him anyway. One time he asked a young lady to go horseback riding with him. That's the only way they had to go about in those days, you know. Anyway, even the horse knew that he was the devil; he threw him off.

So when he had tried every trick he could think of and failed, he really had to admit that he would have to give up. He was so angry that he was almost on fire. In the hurry to get out of the community, his burning feet set the woods on fire, and to this day one can see his track where he stepped on the large flat rock that lies on the hill between the Old Chapin Road and Wise Ferry Road, near the backwaters of Lake Murray and Old Tan Yard Creek.

YEARS AGO THE OLD LOG CABINS, THEY DIDN'T HAVE LOCKS ON THEIR doors like they have today. They had a hole honed through the door and through the door facing, and they run a chain through there and put a padlock on it, and they also had a hole in the door there where the cat could go in and out of at night.

And this one woman kept having this dream. She would dream of a night that she would hear the chains a'rattling on the door there, and every time it rattled, there would be a big black cat jump up on her head and get on her chest and it would just almost smother her to death. She said she just couldn't hardly breathe with the cat on there— was just like a dead weight. And this happened just night after night.

She finally told someone about it, some of the neighbors, and the neighbors that she told said, "You know this old lady that lives down the road here by herself, she is a witch, says she got mad at you about something, and this is her. She turned herself into a cat." And said, "The next time she does that, you get her by the foot and bite her, and that will stop her."

So the next night this woman went to bed and said just before she went to sleep, she heard the chains rattle and the door, and here come that cat and jumped right up on the bed and on her. It was so heavy she felt like it was going to mash her plumb through the bed, and said she couldn't hardly breathe. Said she grabbed the cat by its front paw and stuck its foot in her mouth and bit it real hard, and said the cat screamed out and squalled and jerked its foot back and took off out through the door. And she heard the chain rattle as it went out the door.

And the next day some of the folks walked by the house where the old lady lived down there and she had her hand all bandaged up, and she died just a short time after that. But she wore that bandage on her hand as long as she lived. After she died some of them took the bandage off, and there was teethmarks on her arm.

I'VE HEARD MY FATHER, JESSE BOLLING, TELL A TALE ABOUT JIM BAKER OF Baker Flats. This Jim Baker was my great-grandfather. Now I don't know. I don't believe my father or mother would lie, an' I've heard them tell some awful tales about people being bewitched. They believed it. This one I'm goin' to tell was about Jim Baker.

He left my great-grandmother in North Carolina when my grandmother was a baby an' got him seven women and came back here an' lived in the Baker Rocks back yonder on top of Black Mountain. My folks thought he was a witch. After he'd finally left the flats an' settled on head of Cumberland, he married again an' settled down, but they still thought he was a witch. Father said that he was just a small boy, but Uncle Jerry and Uncle Jim were grown men.

One mornin' they heard a gun fire way back on Carmel Mountain, an' Granddaddy said, "That sounded to me like a witch's gun." Now they believed if a witch could fire a gun, as fer as it was heard the woods would be rung. That is, the ring within the sound of the gun would be bewitched, and nobody could kill a deer with his gun.

Well, Uncle Jerry went out a'huntin'. He saw some deer an' fired at 'em but didn't hit any. Hit was just that way on an' on. Uncle Jim went out, an' his gun wouldn't even fire. He had the lock an' powder pan worked on. He got new flints, but hit didn't do any good. So at last Granddaddy said he'd test it out. So he went out an' run tight up in a herd of deer. He was so close he could almost touch 'em, an' he was a dead shot. So he fired an' never hit a thing. He tried again. Same luck. Some pigeons lit in a tree, an' he fired at them an' killed one. He come back home an' went up on the point an' skinned the bark off a tree an' drawed the picture of Jim Baker an' stepped back fifty steps an' shot at it in the three highest names, Father, Son and the Holy Ghost, an' hit it.

He hadn't been back in the house when Jim Baker's wife come over to borrow some meal. They told her they were out. She went back, but hit wasn't long till she was back to borrow Grandma's winding blades. They were using them. The next morning, before they got out of bed, they heard her holler at the door, an' when they opened the door she was standin' there an' said, "Jerry"—that was Granddaddy's name—"if you don't come over an' do somethin' for Jim he won't be alive an hour."

He took a thumb lance an' went over there an' bled him a little, an' he got well right then. An' the spell was off their guns.

JIM ROYAL WAS AN OLD SLAVE THAT THEY CLAIMED KNEW A LOT ABOUT black magic. His people had learned it in Africa, brought it here with them. Now there's a legend about Jim Royal. I have heard old-timers, and I can remember back fifty years ago when these tales were current.

Jim Royal, they said, could take his violin and smash it over the back of a chair. It would fall to pieces. He would toss the pieces down, and it'd go back together again. 'Course that's a little hard to swallow and always has been. And they said his master would send him out to hoe corn. He'd go out to the fields to see how he's gettin' along. Jim would be up on the stump playin' the fiddle and the hoe just workin' the corn right along. 'Course that made him sort of a valuable slave, I guess. Hoe wouldn't get tired by itself.

So there were tales told about him that were remarkable. And now this incident I'm going to relate, it's not unknown today, and I guess the other things could be just as true—just as possible, rather. It seems he was always welcome as an entertainer at ev'ry gatherin'. There was some sort of mountain shindig, apple butter boilin' maybe or sump'n goin' on in a place over in Greene County, and Jim Royal was there. And they had heard that he could walk through fire, and he said he could. It seems that the information he give out was his own undoin'.

There was a big still on the fire and ev'rybody drinkin'. Mountain people always drink. So there's room enough under that still for a big log fire, great big still, you know. They had bonded stills in those days. So some of these people that claimed they knew Jim Royal could do it asked him to get back in this fire and play his fiddle. And they told the crowd, "He can play his violin back in that fire and won't singe a hair on his head nor one on the fiddle bow." And they all wanted to see it. Well, it was sorta cramped quarters under that still.

According to the legend, he made one condition which if he hadn't'a made he probably wouldn't've lost his life—that they throw no spirits on the fire; no whiskey to be throwed. And 'course whiskey was runnin' out the other end of the still by the bucketsful, runnin' off in wooden buckets and pour'd in barrels. And they claimed he got back under there and was playin' his violin when some of these big, rough mountaineers, probably drunk, picked this bucket of whiskey up from under what they called the worm of the still, walked around and threw it under there and burned him up.

That's the legend of the death of Jim Royal.

How Linkus Shiflett learned to play the fiddle from Jim Royal, that's what I'm comin' to now. Linkus never claimed to have any of the pow'r or the ability to do those kinds of things that Jim Royal had, but he did tell how he learned to play the violin. Now Linkus Shiflett was classed as a good man by all people that knew him. He had that reputation: a kind man and certainly not a liar as far as I could ever learn. And they asked him how he acquired such a talent. They say he was wonderful, just a mountain boy, you know, grew up a mountain boy. First violin he ever had he had to make out of a gourd.

So he told me, after Jim Royal was gone, that he had asked Jim Royal if he could teach him to play the violin like he did. He said, "If you wanta go through the ordeal that it would require," said, "yes, you can be as good a violinist as I am." And he asked him how. He designated an old outhouse somewhere. They built outhouses in those days for smokehouses or to put root crops and vegetables in and things like that.

Jim Royal told him to bore nine holes through an ironwood tree, that was the first process, to bore nine holes through this ironwood tree. And ev'ry mornin' for nine mornin's he was to go and run his fiddle bow through all those nine holes nine times each. And there was various other things that he was required to do that have slipped my memory now, but the one that stands out the most is the last one he was told.

He said, "Now you have one more test." And he designated this old outhouse that Linkus must go to on a certain day and he must never speak. When he got out he wasn't to speak until he got back home. And he said he must stand his ground no matter what he saw or what happened, he mustn't speak or he mustn't move. So, accordin' to the legend, Linkus said that ev'ry horrible thing imagined would come in that outhouse and said he stood shakin'. But he said part of the time he was paralyzed and couldn't move. But said he stood it all until at last a big black snake crawled through the logs and come in and began to wrap himself around his neck and he started to put his head in his mouth—he was standin' there with his mouth open—and said he broke down and shook the snake off and broke and run.

And so when he saw Jim Royal again, he told him about it. Said, "I stood my ground for ev'rything else, but I couldn't stand the snake puttin' his head in my mouth."

"Well," he said, "you got to go through with it all or you'll never learn to play."

And he wanted to play the violin so bad he set another day to go. He said that time he stood his ground and said it was worse, ev'ry hideous thing that he could imagine come into that building to torment him. And last thing, the snake come in again and he crawled up, and when he crawled up that time the snake put his head clear back to his throat three times and dropped to the ground, crawled away, was nothin' there. Linkus said he went on back home.

From then on, he said, he could play the violin as good as Jim Royal.

And he was a famous violinist for these mountains. So that was his version of how he acquired his ability to play the violin so well. My grandfathers have heard him play. Some of the oldtimers that I knew have heard him play.

WELL, I NEVER KNEW GEORGE HERRING MYSELF. HE WAS A SUPPOSED wizard. I knew his sons, Jake Herring and Noah Herring. I knew their children and their grandchildren. I went to school with their children— with George Herring's grandchildren. But George Herring didn't live too far from where we lived in Greene County. We lived at the base of the mountain in Shiflett Hollow on the Simmons Gap Road after you cross the mountain.

The legend I heard of George Herring begins with another man—an old Negro that used to live close to George Herring after the Civil War, Old Solomon. Whatever other name he had I never learned. So it was claimed that Old Solomon was—well, the folks called him a witch. He was supposed to be a warlock or a wizard. He's a black man, and he and George Herring had some difficulty somewhere along the line.

Herring's cattle began to come up, and he noticed a chalk mark or sump'n across a path in his field that these cattle come in on from pasture, and he said as fast as his cattle come up, accordin' to the tale, they dropped dead right in the barnyard. Had four or five all died right there. And he said he searched the field and he found different symbols and things across these cowpaths, and he said he knew that Old Solomon had killed 'em.

So George Herring, accordin' to the legend, knew he couldn't do anything with Old Man Solomon, not havin' enough power to counter- act it, and he decided to leave. He was gone for a long, long time, and none of his family ever knew, but he went to learn more about black magic. Where he went he knew of a man that was supposed to possess magic powers, that dealt in black magic. But anyway, he came back a lot smarter man in magic than he left home.

The children was there when he came back. That night he made all the family go to bed. He dared anyone to even speak. In those days the family usually slept in one big room or some up in the attic, you know. The houses built different—old-timey houses. And they built up a log fire in the fireplace. Fireplaces and chimneys were huge in those days. And he sat down in a chair in front of the fire and he drew symbols all around on the floor. Said he sat there till midnight watchin' the clock and said at midnight a black cat come down the chimney through that fire and landed out in the floor toward these symbols. He kicked it back into the fire and stomped it into the fire, but it got away and went back up the chimney.

And next mornin' some of Solomon's relatives or his family came to borrow, and they kept comin' to borrow, and Herring dared his family to loan 'em anything. The last thing they come after was a needleful of thread and they were refused. And the next mornin', they said, accordin' to legend, Old Solomon was burnt to death. So that's taken with a grain of salt, but most people in those days believed it and they said Old Man Solomon was suddenly burned up. They had a doctor and he died from it next mornin'. People that knew George Herring, I've heard 'em tell it.

I USED TO HEAR 'EM SAY THERE WAS A FELLOW LIVED IN HERE, THEY CALLED him, let's see, Jim Royal. He was colored. Said he was a little-bitty nigger and said he looked just like a man like everybody else. Said he used to have a little white horse, just as white as snow and the purtiest thing. He used to ride on that horse, and he'd sail—said he'd just actually sail in the air on that horse. Anybody'd get after him or the law would get after him for anything he'd do, he'd take a little switch and touch that little white horse on the flanks and he'd holler, "Up we jump, and here we go." And said that little horse would get up and just sail through the air. 'Course that was 'fore my time, but I heard the ancestors say he could fly on his horse and he was a great fiddle player and he could do more kinda magic tricks.

Jim Royal's daddy was gonna whip him one time. Said his daddy went to beat on him, and he looked and he was beating a stump and Jim Royal was up on the hill laughin' at him. He must have been the devil.

Jim Royal played a fiddle quite a bit, and they said he could set up in a brush pile; they'd set the brush pile afire, and he'd be playing his fiddle and he could vanish. He'd set on a stump and play with the fire burning all around him; he wouldn't burn playing his fiddle while the fire was burnin' all 'round him, and first thing you know Jim Royal'd be vanished.

'Course you know that was fairy tales they was tellin', but the old people say it was so. All that was handed down, and they believed all that stuff about Jim Royal.

IT'S JUST LIKE OLD LADY. I WAS A GIRL THEN. AND SO ERNEST NOLE AND his wife come to visit Ernest's people. And the old lady was named Old Lady Lizzie. And there was a man by the name of Frank Roberts, and she was riding him every night. She would ride him. And so he asked one of the boys to come and spend the night with him.

Said, "I just don't feel like spending the night."

Said, "Well, please come stay. It's a witch riding me every night." And said, "I want you to get a big stick."

See, people didn't have brooms with handles in 'em like now. They swupt with fennel leaves or weeds and broom straws; they didn't have brooms with handles in 'em like they got now. They go out in the fields and things and get this old dog fennel; they called 'em old yellowtops.

Said he gone get them and that's what they used for brooms. So he say, "I want you to get a good seasoned stick."

So he did. So they laid down. You know, they tell me you be makin' a fuss tryin' to get up but you can't. See, it be like—something like to smother you to death. And said, "Now, but you hear me make that fuss," he said, "then you hit her." And when he started making that funny fuss, he struck her. And she was an old lady, and she went home. And she sicklied and died; she never did get over that hit. It kilt her. That's right; it kilt her.

It was a long time ago, when people first came from eastern Virginia and western North Carolina and settled here in the Cumberlands. A settler, whose name has been forgotten, had a large flock of sheep. Suddenly his sheep began to die, one a day, seemingly from no particular cause. He watched his flock and would see a ram or ewe suddenly fall dead while it was feeding along in the best of health.

He believed his sheep were bewitched so he hied himself to an old woman who was reputed to be a witch doctor. She told him to go home and skin out the ham or shoulder of a sheep that had just died and put it in an oven and bake it and by no means allow anyone to come in the house and borrow, steal or in any way get anything out of the house, above all a drink of water. So he skinned a sheep that had died that same day and put a shoulder on in the oven to bake. The witch doctor had said to let it warm up slowly and start baking gradually for best results. He followed the directions, and it was two hours before the shoulder was warmed up to the baking stage.

About that time he looked down the road and saw a neighbor woman coming, walking as if she was in a hurry. She came on, entered and asked to borrow some meal. They had no meal. She then asked for a drink of water; and there was no water up. She took her departure, but in a short time she was again seen approaching, walking faster than before. This time she seemed unstrung and could not stand still and wanted to borrow some salt—no salt in the house; and again she asked for water, which was politely but firmly refused her. All the time she was eyeing the oven on the hearth, and this time before she left she asked what they were baking and tried to accidentally overturn the oven.

She had not been gone long until she was seen coming again. This time she was running. The shoulder was getting a nice brown now. She rushed into the house and screamed, "For God's sake, get that off there! You are killing me. Look here!" And she ripped off her clothes and exposed her own shoulder baked to the same crisp brown as the mutton shoulder. The woman recovered, but if she ever practiced her witchery again it was not found out.

THERE WAS THIS GIRL WHO LIVED NEXT DOOR OR BEHIND MY GRAND-mother's house in Juarez. She wasn't too old and was very pretty. She didn't like to do what she was told. If her mother said to do something, she wouldn't, even if it was something that she really wanted to do. She wasn't old enough to go on dates, but she was pretty enough.

One night she told her mother she was going to El Gato—that's a bar where they go to dance and it's not very clean and you've probably never heard of it—and dance with her boyfriend. Her mother was so mad that she shut the girl in her room and went to a bar herself. The girl sneaked out a window and went to El Gato with her boyfriend, and while they were dancing, she saw this good-looking man dressed in green come in. He smiled at her, and she went right over to him and danced with him for a long time. He was real good-looking, but he had a limp and he could still dance.

When it was late, she decided to go home because her feet were tired, and he was going to take her. When they got outside, people heard a loud scream and ran out. The girl was all scratched and bloody on the sidewalk, and a rooster was flying down the street. As she died, she said, *"Eres pata de gallo."* This means that it was the devil, because he is always a cripple in the left foot. The people got out their rosaries and started saying them and ran home.

The next day the sad mother came and took her body to bury. She told the girl, "I told you not to go out, or the devil would get you." The priest would not bury her in the cemetery, and so they just dumped her in the desert for the coyotes.

My grandmother told me this story as the truth, but I don't really think that they just dumped the dead body on the desert. That's against some law.

THERE WAS A GIRL LIVING IN THE HOUSE NEXT DOOR TO MY AUNT. SHE was very pretty but too young to go on dates. One night she went to the Acapulco Bar on Pershing Drive to dance and have a good time. Her mother had told her not to go because it was Friday and she had to go to church. She went anyway. There she met a dark, handsome man who danced every dance with her.

After the bar closed, he was going to walk her home. All of a sudden, he was sort of like a goat and danced all over her with his hoof. *Pata de chivo,* it is called. She saved herself by taking out her rosary and showing it to him. He ran away, but she was almost dead and had to have a lot of sewing done on her where he tramped. She still has a hoof-shaped scar on her face, but now she goes to church every Friday and is very obedient.

This story tells what will happen if you don't mind the teacher and your mother.

ONCE THERE WAS A GIRL WHO LIVED NEAR MY GRANDMOTHER. I DIDN'T know her, but my aunt did. She was very pretty, and all the men liked her and tried to date her. She didn't help at home. Her mother worked very hard in El Paso so that the girl could have nice things and go to school. The girl wanted to go to a cantina and dance one night. The mother was very tired and asked the girl to stay home and take care of her little brother. The girl wouldn't. She went to the cantina and danced with all the men.

Finally a stranger came in. He was very good-looking and walked with a slight limp. He passed all the other girls by and danced only with this girl. He seemed very rich, and the girl was very interested in him. While they were dancing, someone tore his trouser leg, and everyone could see the *pata de gallo*. Someone screamed, and the lights went out.

When the lights came on, the girl was half in and half out of the door, and she had been scratched to death. As the people picked her up to carry her away, they heard a loud laugh and a cock crow. It had been the devil.

THERE WAS A GIRL AT JEFF WHO WANTED TO GO TO A DANCE REAL BADLY. Her mother said she couldn't go because she was sick and wanted her to stay home with her. So she locked herself in her room, got dressed, turned out the lights as if she had gone to bed, and slipped out of the window.

She was walking down the street when a good-looking guy passed in a convertible. He passed her a couple of times and then stopped and asked her if she would like a ride. She said no. Then he asked her where she was going, and she told him to the dance. He said wasn't that funny, that was exactly where he was going, too. So he gave her a ride to the dance.

They got to the dance and were dancing one of those fast rock-and-roll dances, and he was turning her around and around. Somehow he had danced her outside into the alley. All of a sudden, the people heard loud, terrible screams from outside! They went out and found the girl had been all scratched and torn, and her face was all torn and bloody. Next to where she was, there was a bush that was all on fire and glowing. They knew then it was the devil! The girl died.

THERE WAS A GIRL WHO WAS MARRIED BUT WAS LIVING WITH HER MOTHER because her husband was overseas. She wanted to go to a dance one night, but her mother forbade her to go. She fought with her mother and hit her. As the mother was dying, she moaned and moaned.

The girl went to the dance anyway. She danced with a handsome man who was dressed in a tuxedo. Suddenly the lights went out, and when the girl looked down, she saw that he had feet like a rooster, and she knew he was the devil. Before she could get away from him, he scratched her face real bad and made moaning noises like her mother had.

I know this is true because I saw her the next day, and her face was all covered with little tiny scratches.

WELL, MY DAD HAD A GE PLACE THAT BURNED ABOUT SIX YEARS AGO. MY dad had a picture of his dead brother on his desk, and it did not burn. The picture was taken a few days before my uncle died in a car wreck. The picture was made for Janet. Dad asked for a copy, but he got the real one and Janet got the copy.

After that Mom got a real nice frame for it. When it was dark, the frame sort of shined. People have even tried to burn the picture with a match or lighter. The thing just won't burn. Mom started getting scared; she told Dad that the picture watched her all the time. So to please Mom, Dad put it away in a box of pictures. Now it can't be found. That is strange.

218

I WAS COMING DOWN THE HIGHWAY, AND A LITTLE BOY GOT HIT BY A truck. He would have bled to death. I was the third car. The truck hit him just as he got across from the school, right across the road. He saw the truck coming, and he thought he could make it.

And I walked up to the kid. He was bleeding out his ears, out his mouth—It looked like everywhere he was bleeding. And I walked up there, and I gave these words. And then this white fellow that hit him pushed me, and he says, "We're going to put him in this truck."

I said, "No, you're not." I said, "You're not going to put him in the truck. I'll put him in my car. He's not too bloody. You gonna put him back there where those animals been?" He'd been haulin' animals.

I put a sack or something down there, you know. I decided to put him in my car. By that time another car came up, and they took him here to a doctor before he, uh, bled to death . . . I stopped the bleeding before they picked him up. You see, he had lost so much blood, they couldn't give him blood fast enough. They rushed him to Albany. And he died in the Albany Hospital.

But had he been in my car he wouldn't have never bled that much.

THIS GIRL UP ON THE HILL HERE, SHE CAME OUT HERE ONE AFTERNOON and she said, "You know what?" She said, "Precious, I've been worried all day. You know Minnie Mae Wooders? Did you know I saw her last night in a pool of blood?" Said, "I don't know how she got hurt or what happened to her. I've been tryin' to call her, and I haven't gotten her yet."

I said, "Well, just keep tryin', 'cause she might be sick."

You know where she was? Went to a funeral down there at Valdosta, and somebody ran into their car and she was drivin' the car. And they took 'em all to the hospital there.

Now she foresaw that.

I HAD A SISTER ONE TIME THAT KNOCKED A WINDOW STICK OUT—WAS propped up like that window there—knocked out, and some way or other she bit a big artery in her tongue. Bit it plumb in two. 'Bout nine o'clock one morning. And she bled until nearly sundown, and just about bled to death.

And there was a fellow on up above us named Charlie Williams. And my uncle, I remember, he rode a horse up there, and just about the time he got there, had time to ride the horse up there, the blood stopped. The doctors had tried all day to stop it, and they hadn't stopped it. And that blood clotted on her tongue. And the next morning it come loose, and she swallowed it and it like to choked her to death. And that thing never did bleed no more. Now I know them things.

I WAS BATCHIN' THEN, UP THERE IN VIRGINIA. BEEN OUT ON MY HORSE, and my little old dog had followed me. When I got to the lane—guess I was about two hundred yards from the end of it—I spied two men. They was walkin' together purty fast, keepin' step. I watched 'em. They had four times as far to go as I did. I kept on watchin' them an' never took my eye off of 'em till they got to the lane. Then the little old dog jumped a rabbit, and I turned to look.

That quick they disappeared or turned into somethin', one. They was a black thing about the size of a sheep thrashed around an' took up through the field, tearin' up brush heaps where there wasn't no brush heaps an' makin' a lot of noise. It didn't look like nothin' I'd ever seen. Don't know what it was, but they had turned into it.

I went on an' got to the Anneson bottom. Crossed it, an' it was gettin' dusk. Somethin' began to make a noise under my mare's nose. Couldn't see a thing, but I watched for the black thing to show up again. I went on through, an' a light flashed. It scared the mare, an' she started runnin', run till I got hold of the bridle and quieted her down. Never could tell what it was.

When I was fourteen, a young fellow came up to the house courtin' me. I stayed in the kitchen because I didn't like him, but after a while he came around to the back door and told me to see the light out there in the field.

I stepped outside. There was a big ball of fire comin' up the lane at our landlord's house next door. Our landlord was Barry Nelson. That light danced up to the gate and went out until it got right over the house. It came back on then and came down and touched in the field by the house. Then it went back the same way it had come. Yep, back over the house and up the lane.

The next day a woman that lived in that house was chopping cotton in that same field. When she got to the spot where that light touched down, she fell over dead. That's right—at the exact spot where that light touched down, she fell over dead. I saw it.

8 GRAVE HUMOR

Although many ghost stories and tales of the supernatural are related to provoke fear or prove the existence of ghosts, a large number are also told for humorous effect. Ray B. Browne, in *"A Night With the Hants" and Other Alabama Folk Experiences* (1977), says that approximately half the stories told in Alabama on death and the hereafter are humorous. He attributes this high percentage to an attraction/repulsion with death and the dead. There is a morbid, almost pathological, interest in corpses, ghosts and hants, but at the same time there is a realization that there is something unhealthy about such interest. Thus, the comical treatment arises as a means of balance. Browne's statistics don't seem to hold up in other Southern states (although no one has really bothered to make a count), but his reasons for the existence of humorous narratives about ghosts and the like may have great validity. Whatever the case, the following section includes some examples of Southern grave humor.

223

ONCE THERE WAS AN OLD MAN WHO GREW QUEER IN HIS OLD DAYS, AND when he died he asked that a peck of hickory nuts be buried under his head so he could crack them and eat his favorite delicacy when he became hungry.

Two thieves lived in the community, and one night they decided to steal a sheep. One of them was to wait in the graveyard while the other went up on the hillside and picked out a choice sheep and brought it down.

While the rogue waited in the graveyard, he happened to think of the hickory nuts underneath the dead man's head, and being hungry and having some little time to wait, he dug them up and began to crack them leisurely. Two farm boys happened to pass near the graveyard just then and they heard the cracking. They went home swiftly.

"Grandpap," they said, "old Jim Higgins is risin' out'n his grave and cracking the hickory nuts under his head."

"Nonsense," said the old man, "I don't believe it."

The boys swore that it was so.

"Don't believe it," said the old man, "and if I didn't have this rheumatism that's had me down for the last ten years I'd go and see for myself."

The boys considered for a moment and finally answered. "Grandpap, we'll carry you on our shoulders if you want to see it," they said.

"I'll go on your shoulders to show you there's nothing there," said he. And he got ready to be carried on their backs to the graveyard.

When they came near enough to hear the cracking, they walked stealthily and crept very close to the fence and might have seen the grave of Jim Higgins if the bushes hadn't been hiding it. There was silence for a time, and then there was rustling down the hillside, and the thief with the sheep appeared from behind the clump of bushes. The white sheep, from that distance, loomed up as a ghost and seemed to rise and swell to magnanimous proportions before the startled eyes of the two boys and their grandfather. The rogue who was cracking hickory nuts was unaware that the visitors were near. He ceased cracking when he saw the sheep.

"Is he fat or lean?" he asked.

The spoken word was all the boys needed. They then threw the old man to the ground and addressed the ghost.

"Fat or lean, take him!" they said and ran for home.

As they reached the porch, one of them said, "Boy! I bet that ghost has done got Grandpap."

"He ain't either," said the old man from inside the house. "I beat you in."

224

WELL, THIS IS A SMALL STORY ABOUT A FELLOW CALLED GRAVEYARD JOHN. Ole Miss died, and John worked around the house. At that time, it wadn't no funeral home, and they had Ole Miss there in the house. Ole Miss had on some diamond rings and things, and John was spotting that stuff. He supposed to been sweeping up, but the people that was in the waiting room say, "John, keep a'sweeping now."

"Yes ma'am, Ole Miss, I'm sweeping."

He'd sweep and peep through the crack.

Say, "John, why don't you go on and sweep. I want you to git everything cleant up 'fore all the visitors git here."

"Yes ma'am, Ole Miss, I'm sweeping." So John peeped through the crack. He shake his head and say, "I'm gonner git that tonight"— talking 'bout them watches and rings.

Finally, John got everything cleaned up and that night he went to the cemetery to dig Ole Miss up. Ole Miss wadn't dead. She had went off in a trance. John, he got the top off the box, and he got his head down in there, and he thought he heard something, and he jumped up out the grave. He say, "Aw, naw. That wadn't nothing. I'm going back there. I'm gonner git them rings. I ain't gonner let nothing scare me off of them rings."

John went back there, and he got one of the rings, but one ring was on there so tight he couldn't git it. When he tried to git that one off,

Ole Miss clamped him, and out the grave he come with her on his back. John wadn't hollering nothing but "Dey! Dey! Dey!"

She fell off at they house, and when she went in that upset the family. Say, "Oh, what you doing here?"

Say, "John saved my life. Wherever he is, don't y'all bother him, because he saved my life."

Say, "Well, we'll try to find him. I hope he don't run clean off." "Well, I do too."

So the next day they set out to look for him. They say, "Y'all talk to him easy. You might git up to him."

They got out there and found him in a sage field. Say, "Here we lay right here." They went there and they talked to him and say, "John." "Dey. Dey. Dey. Dey. Dey. Dey. Dey."

"John, we ain't gonner bother you."

He jumped up and said, "Dey! Dey! Dey! Dey got me!"

I HEARD MY FATHER TELL A STORY ONE TIME. HE WAS BORN AND RAISED IN Logan, West Virginia, and he never did go back to his hometown after he married my mother. He said that they had a big house one time, and these people thought it was haunted. And they hired him and another guy to watch it. Fifteen or twenty dollars back in those days was worth a hundred now. And they watched this house that night, and he said they was laying there that night and there was a noise like a man walking through the house, and my dad said he was so scared he didn't know what to do. Sounded just like this man walkin' over the floor. And they watched and watched and they couldn't find out where it was coming from or where it was going, and finally they found what it was making all the noise. Somebody had caught a muskrat in the house and this steel trap had growed in its leg and it learned to walk with that steep trap. And every time it walked, it would make this noise. My dad showed it to this man and they stayed a couple of nights afterwards and found that they had really caught whatever it was that they had caught.

226

Now an old man was going through the country, and he come to a house and he asked if he could stay overnight. The man told him he didn't have room in his house, but that there was a house on down the road he could stay in but that the house was haunted.

The old man said he wasn't afraid of hants, and so he went on down the road until he came to this house. It was about dark when he looked in. But there was a lamp sitting by a table, and so he went inside, lit the lamp and sat down in the chair.

Well sir, we sat there and nothing happened until nearly midnight, and then a big black cat poked his head in at the door and said, "Me-ow!" And the man, he didn't say anything. The big black cat walked all around in the room and then hopped up on the table, wrapped his tail around the lamp and just lay there a'lookin' at this man with them big green eyes he had.

About then the man heard a *thump, thump, thump*, upstairs in the loft, and then a *thump, thump, thump*, on the stairsteps, and a man's head rolled down the stairsteps right into the room. Yes sir, it did, a man's head, and it stopped rolling, and the eyes in that head looked right at the man in the chair.

But this man didn't say anything, he didn't, and then he heard *thump, thump, thump*, again on the stairsteps, and a man with no head came down the steps. A man with no head, yes, and this man with no head walked over to the man in the chair and he said:

"Two of us here, I see."

"Yes," said the old man, "but there ain't goin' to be very long."

With that, he jumped as far as he could out the door, and he started running, and he ran and ran until he was plumb give out, and he sat down on a log to rest, and in a little while the man with no head sat down beside him and said:

"Had a pretty good race, didn't we?"

"Yes," said the man, "an' we're goin' to have another one."

So he jumped up from the log and he ran out of the woods into a corn field, and a rabbit was running there, and the man said to the rabbit, "Get out of my way, rabbit, and let somebody run that can run."

THIS MAN WAS WALKING THROUGH A GRAVEYARD ONE NIGHT, AND HE accidentally fell in an open grave. The grave was so deep that he was unable to get out by himself in spite of his many attempts. The caretaker was off duty that night, and no one was there to hear his cries for help. It was real cold that night, and by morning he was nearly frozen. He heard someone coming through the graveyard and cried out to him:

"Help! It's cold down here!"

The man passing through came up to the grave and, looking down, said, "I guess so, someone took all the dirt off you."

Notes

In the following notes as much detail is given on the informants as is available to me. This includes name, age, place of collection and residence, attitude towards the narratives, manner which the text is generally used, and other biographical material. Where any of these features are absent it is because they were not supplied by the collectors. Some fieldworkers provide copious accompanying information with their texts while others give nothing more than the informant's name. Early collectors, such as those working for the WPA in the 1930s, were particularly guilty of paying little attention to such matters. Happily, most of the collectors whose work is utilized here were cognizant of the necessity for such accompanying details. Earlier folklorists were mainly concerned with texts rather than context while more recent scholars realize that both are important.

At the end of the comments about the texts are motif numbers. These refer to the systems employed in Ernest W. Baughman, **Type and Motif-Index of the Folktales of England and North America** (The Hague: Mouton & Co., 1966) and Stith Thompson, **Motif-Index of Folk Literature,** 6 volumes, revised edition (Bloomington, Indiana: Indiana University Press, 1955), the standard indices of narrative elements found in American folk tradition. Baughman's numbers are cited first because he is more directly concerned with American folk narratives, but in some cases, he does not list parallel material. In these instances Thompson's numbers are given. References to type numbers refer to Stith Thompson's **The Types of the Folktale** (Helsinki: Suomalainen Tiedeakatemia Academia Scientiarum Fennica, 1961).

143. Collected in 1974 by Wanda Lee Johnson from a sixty-one year old businesswoman identified only as Mrs. D. B. of Paragould, Arkansas. The informant is the daughter of the family who lived in the house, and her older sister, the child of the story, also believes that the story is factual. Johnson titled this "The Legend of the Door That Refused to Stay Closed" but that seems to be her own contribution, for there is no evidence that the informant had any specific name for it or that she even referred to it as a legend. The narrative serves as incontrovertible proof of the existence of ghosts and witchcraft for both the informant and her sister.

For those unfamiliar with the term "ticktacking," it is a word referring to a type of practical joke played by many young pranksters. By means of a controlling cord and weight, a device is rigged up whereby a person can tap on windows and house walls from a distance. The name probably comes from the sound made by the device when it is in operation.

Although the informant referred to this as a ghost story, it is really a story of witchcraft, the ghost only being mentioned at the very end of the narrative and then only as a suspicion, not something that had been sighted. The tale is reminiscent of the Faust story (motif M22 "man sells soul to devil") in that the painter claimed to have acquired his powers directly from the devil and, in order to do so, presumably had to sell his soul. Also pertinent are motifs D1273 "Magic formula 'charm' "; D1710 "Possession of magic powers"; E281 "Ghosts haunt house"; G224.4 "Person sells soul to devil in exchange for witch powers"; G265.8 "Witch bewitches objects"; G265.8.5(b) "Witch bewitches house"; G265.8.3.2 "Witch bewitches wagon"; G249.8 "Witches open doors and windows"; G269.5 "Witch causes haunted houses"; and Thompson's D1641.13 "Coffin moves itself" and F1083.0.1 "Object floats in air."

It is interesting that the son of the house's builder believes none of this story.

144. Collected March 1, 1978 in Henderson, Kentucky, by Nana Farris from Mrs. Frank Reed, Sr. The informant was discussing a series of personal experiences that occurred while she and her family lived in an old two-story log house during the years 1914–1916. Mrs. Reed frequently laughed during the course of telling her experiences, the laughter evidently a nervous reaction rather than an indication that the tale was humorous and not to be taken seriously. Reed evidently tells of her experiences as a testimony in favor of belief in the supernatural. Apparently she is a skillful narrator because she made use of vocal dynamics to point out significant points in her narrative and she imitated the voices of characters, such as her boyfriend, who figure in the tale. She also made use of hand gestures to indicate such activities as spinning and drawing bed covers back.

Motifs include E279.3 "Ghost pulls bedclothing from sleeper"; E402 "Mysterious ghostlike noises heard"; E402.1.3(b) "Ghost plays organ"; E423.1.1 "Revenant as dog"; and E561 "Dead person spins"; E545 "The dead speak." An incident similar to the talking sounds heard by Mrs. Reed appears in Ray B. Browne, *"A Night With the Hants" and Other Alabama Folk Experiences* (Bowling Green, Ohio: Bowling Green University Popular Press, 1977), p. 27. Thompson's E545.1 "Conversation between the dead" is also relevant.

145. Collected September 3, 1965, by George Foss from Lloyd Powell, Browns Cove, Virginia. Powell was born in Browns Cove in 1905 in a house that had been in his family since the 1860s and continued to live in the same community until his death in 1977. In his later years he lived with his sister Hilma Powell Yates in a building that originally served as the overseer's home for a large plantation/farm once owned by their family. The main house of the property was called "Headquarters" because for a brief period during the Civil War it had been used by Stonewall Jackson as headquarters for his troops who were on their way to help Robert E. Lee defend Richmond. Apparently, Powell related this tale primarily as an example of the sort of narratives about the supernatural once commonly told in his community. In other words, it was both entertainment and an important bit of local history for him.

The only relevant motif is E402 "Mysterious ghostlike noises heard."

146. Collected March 27, 1977, by Debbie McWilliams from Kathy Thornton in Tuscaloosa, Alabama. Thornton, from Huntsville, apparently is a relative of the family that currently owns Cedarhurst, the house in which the supernatural incidents concerning Sally Carter took place. As the last line indicates, Thornton thinks many of the stories about Sally are absurd. Still, she firmly believes her cousin's experience and that of other family members, even though she probably recounts them mainly for entertainment.

Motifs include E235.6 "Return from dead to punish disturber of grave"; E281 "Ghosts haunt house"; E281.0.3* "Ghosts haunt house, damaging property or annoying inhabitants"; E402.1.7 "Ghost slams door"; E419 "Other restless dead"; and E422.4(a) "Female revenant in white clothing." The idea of a ghost returning to see that its tombstone is erect seems not to have been previously reported from folk tradition; neither has the idea of the tombstone that constantly falls over. A similar story is found in Hans Holzer, *Best True Ghost Stories* (Englewood Cliffs, New Jersey: Prentice-Hall, Inc., 1983), pp. 44–46, concerning a Connecticut woman named Betty Tylaska. Her great-great-grandfather haunted her house until she discovered his tombstone in the basement and set it properly in a cemetery. There is also a tradition concerning the victims of the West Plains, Missouri, explosion of 1928 that says their tombstone constantly shifts (there were many unidentified victims who were buried in a common grave).

147. Collected December, 1964, by Mary Scott from Pedro Lujan in El Paso, Texas. The informant was a twenty-two year old student at Texas Western College (now the University of Texas at El Paso) who, apparently, told the story for entertainment. He did not recall where he heard the tale or from whom. The legend, however, is well known in Texas and has been around for some time. Its first published report came in 1937 in Charles L. Sonnichsen's article, "Mexican Spooks from El Paso," pp. 120–129 in volume 13, *Publications of the Texas Folklore Society* (Austin: Texas Folklore Society, 1937). According to Sonnichsen the ghost is of one Don Mauro Lujan and the house has been around since the 1870s. Sonnichsen's version contains several elements not mentioned by Pedro Lujan, including a buried treasure whose location is revealed to the family by the ghost. There are also more details about the relationship between the husband and the ghost. It is said that when the husband comes home late he must ask the ghost's permission to get in bed with his wife.

Motifs include E281.0.3* "Ghost haunts house, damaging property or annoying inhabitants" and E281.3(b) "Ghost lays hand on girl awake in bed." There seems to be no motif number listed for the amorous ghost who pinches women, an act that seems mischievous rather than malicious. Witches and, in European tradition, fairies often resort to pinching but in those cases the deed is done as punishment of their victims; this doesn't seem to be true in Lujan's narrative.

148. Collected in 1962 by Jan Calhoon from Dale Pope of Warren, Arkansas. Pope was the son of a farmer who lived near Warren all of his life. Apparently he didn't believe the tradition because it is related as a tradition held by others. For him, seemingly, it was just a good story. Motifs are D1003 "Magic blood—human" and E337.1.1 "Murder sounds heard just as they must have happened at time of death."

149. Collected October 31, 1982, by Jane Watson from Fran Franklin, Monticello, Arkansas. Mrs. Franklin is Assistant Professor of Speech at the University of Arkansas at Monticello where she is very popular with students. She firmly believes in ghosts and frequently relates this narrative, even using it in her classes, not only for entertainment but for other reasons as well. Watson, a former student, reflecting on the matter recalled, "It showed us, the students, a personal belief held by the instructor. It also worked to bind us together as a group, initiating free-flowing discussions between members of the class. These conversations almost always showed us another facet of one another." That a well-educated and respected person like Mrs. Franklin told a ghost story as truth also produced some perhaps-to-be-expected side effects. Watson notes, "One lovely lady from Star City, Arkansas, who is near seventy years old, was quite surprised that someone like Mrs. Franklin believed in ghosts. This discovery led her to blushingly tell the legend of her own about a ghost that inhabited their old home."

Motifs include E281 "Ghosts haunt house"; E334.4 "Ghost of suicide seen at death spot or near by"; E338(e) "Female ghost ascends, descends stairs"; E402.1.2 "Footsteps of invisible ghost heard"; and E402.1.3 "Invisible ghost plays musical instrument." Most of these motifs were first reported from oral tradition in the early 1800s but are much older.

150. Collected by Lewis David Bandy in 1940 from an unnamed white informant who also contributed the other haunted bed story in this volume, Text 193. Evidently, the narrator believed in the veracity of his story, but it also served an entertainment function. There is a sense conveyed that he was somewhat proud of having such an interesting and unusual experience to tell listeners. He was also a person who fancied himself somewhat daring and adventurous as attested to by his attempts to outdo whatever unseen force controlled the bed in the "back room." The use of words like "wham" and "kerpoodle" sound somewhat literary but not unlike the sort of language that might be used by a person who is histrionic.

Motifs here are E279.2 "Ghost disturbs sleeping person"; E279.3 "Ghost pulls bedclothing from sleeper," a motif that is well-known in the folk tradition of both the British Isles and the United States; E281.3 "Ghost haunts particular room in house"; E421.1 "Invisible ghosts"; F1411 "Fear test: staying in haunted house"; and Thompson's H1376.2 "Quest: learning what fear is." In its general tenor this text bears some similarity to Type 376 "The Youth Who Wanted to Learn What Fear Is" in which a youth sets out to find fear, something of which he is ignorant. He tries several frightful experiences such as playing cards with the devil in church, stealing clothes from a ghost, staying at night in a cemetery or a haunted house, playing ninepins with a reassembled dead man, or being shaved by a ghostly barber.

151. Collected by Caroline McQueen Rhea in 1932 from a Mrs. Liddy (probably Lydia) Potter near Mountain City, Tennessee. She was apparently responding to a question, for her opening sentence is definitely not studied, but responsorial. Her very active participation in the story indicates that it is one she deeply believes. Her concluding remark "Hit's sin, jist sin, that's caused hit all" reveals that the legend also conveys a religious meaning to her. It seems likely, though, that it also functions in a sense as entertainment since it is a vividly recalled unusual series of incidents.

Motifs E422.1.11.5.1 "Ineradicable bloodstain after bloody tragedy" and E422.1.11.5.1(a) "Ineradicable bloodstain in stone or wood floor after bloody tragedy at spot" are applicable here although, as Mrs. Potter indicates, it is unclear just what happened to cause the stain. The motif is quite old in folk tradition and common in Denmark, the British Isles, and the United States. Other motifs found here include E574 "Appearance of ghost serves as death omen"; and the following two listed only in Thompson: D1812.5.1.12.2 "Bird calls as evil omen" and E714.1 "Soul (life) in the blood." Bird calls as an evil omen crops up in Korean folk narratives but is relatively uncommon in American tales. There are, however, a variety of folk beliefs common in the United States concerning owls and raincrows. One holds that a dog's howling portends death, especially when preceded by an owl hooting. Another says that merely seeing an owl, particularly at night, is a sign of impending death. Sometimes it is the color of the owl that is important, white and red owls being particularly bad omens. According to some accounts death results only if you are the only one to hear the owl's hoot. The raincrow, or cuckoo, is widely regarded as a sign of rain but rarely as an indicator of imminent death. Perhaps the key to understanding this aspect of folklore about the raincrow is contained in a Slovenian folksong which speaks of a treasonous act committed by a cuckoo, as a result of which Jesus was captured by his enemies. As a result the bird was punished by being made a harbinger of doom.

152. Collected November 19, 1976, by Anna Farrier from Elizabeth E. Apple, Huff, Arkansas. Mrs. Apple is well-known in her community not only as a narrator of interesting tales but also as a singer of old-time songs. She had most of her tales from her father who is probably the source of the narrative given here although that is not so indicated by Farrier. Apple has also made a concerted effort to gather interesting stories about local happenings and, as postmistress at Huff for several years, she acquired without much effort many such narratives from people picking up their mail. As the beginning of this text indicates, this tale was recorded during a session at which Mrs. Apple contributed several narratives, most of which dealt with the supernatural.

Motifs are E281 "Ghosts haunt house"; E402 "Mysterious ghostlike noises heard"; E402.1.5. "Invisible ghost makes rapping or knocking noise"; E402.1.2. "Footsteps of invisible ghost heard"; E421.1 "invisible ghosts"; and E451.8(c) "Ghost laid when house it haunts is burned."

153. Collected by William E. Lightfoot from Daisy Branham Banks, June 30, 1974, at her home on Jane Brown Branch near Prestonsburg, Kentucky. Mrs. Banks was born in Floyd County, Kentucky, in 1881 and lived in the area all of her life. She knew a good deal of supernatural lore and gave Lightfoot stories about witchcraft and of markings caused by fright in addition to this personal experience regarding a haunted house. Yet, despite this fund of material, she was no believer in all of these things. Speaking of witches she remarked, "Yeah, the people believed in them. I never did, but people did believe in them." She was less skeptical about marking, recalling that she had "been awful bad scared once that one of mine would be marked, but they wasn't, they wasn't marked. I made sure they wasn't marked." She did this by making up her mind not to be scared by any frightening thing that happened to her while she was pregnant. The opening line of the story given here indicates her attitude towards ghosts and revenants. This sentence also suggests that Banks regarded herself as an open-minded, somewhat fearless person; this feeling is perhaps the main reason she tells the tale.

The major motif here is E281.0.3* "Ghosts haunt house, damaging property or annoying inhabitants," which is usually a puzzling narrative element because it is very difficult to tell whether the haunters are ghosts, witches, or familiar spirits, precisely the problem here. Other motifs are E338.1(aa) "Ghosts knock on door"; E421.1 "Invisible ghosts"; and E599.6 "Ghosts move furniture and household articles."

154. Collected November 7, 1975, by Lloyd Thornton from an unnamed fifty-eight year old white housewife in Jonesboro, Arkansas. The story was one that had been told to her by her father nearly fifty years earlier in her hometown of Lorado, Arkansas. The "back then" referred to in the first line of the story is a reference to some indeterminate time twenty-five to fifty years prior to the time she was told the story—that is, approximately one hundred years before Thornton recorded this text. This was one of many ghost stories told by her father and, apparently, the informant saw this solely as entertainment. She noted that her father's stories took the place of radios and television which, in the mid 1920s, were nonexistent in Lorado. She also frequently referred to the narrative as a legend, an almost certain indication that she did not believe the story to be true.

This sounds remarkably like a märchen but a search through Stith Thompson's *The Types of the Folktale* fails to turn up any exact parallel. Motifs include E281 "Ghosts haunt house"; E281.0.1 "Ghost kills man who stays in haunted house"; E402.1.1. "Vocal sounds of ghost of human being"; E545 "The dead speak"; and Thompson's E545.1 "Conversation between the dead."

155. Collected in 1964 by Jacqueline Miller from Mrs. William Ramsey, a housewife in El Paso, Texas. No other information is offered about Mrs. Ramsey so it is hard to determine her attitude toward the story or how she used it. Clearly the woman was a skillful narrator, indicated by the extensive dialogue and the general manner of presentation, and had probably related this legend several times.

Motifs include E322 "Dead wife's friendly return" and E415.4 "Dead cannot rest until money debts are paid."

156. Collected September 3, 1965, by George Foss from Mary Woods Shiflett, Browns Cove, Virginia. Mrs. Shiflett was born in 1902 and, at the time of collection, had been widowed for several years. A very energetic person, she supported herself, until illness confined her to a Baltimore nursing home, by cutting timber, running moonshine stills, making quilts, making apple butter, and housing up to a dozen welfare children at a time as foster parent. Since the story is related as a personal experience it may be told partly as proof of the existence of ghosts, but it also has a significant entertainment function. Shiflett's statement, "I could just set and talk all night about them ghost tales" indicates a considerable pride in having unusual experiences to relate.

Motifs include E402 "Mysterious ghostlike noises heard"; and E723.7.3 "Wraith opens and closes door." A very similar story from Alabama is given in Browne, *"A Night With the Hants,"* pp. 220–223.

157. Collected in 1967 by Pat Simons from Connie Herrera in El Paso, Texas. Miss Herrera also told the legend about the devil who appeared at the dance at Thomas Jefferson High School in El Paso (Text 216d), and more information about her is contained in the notes for that text. Since the story is related as a personal experience it is obvious that Herrera considers it more than just an entertaining story although it probably is related by her for that reason as well.

Motifs include E281.3(b) "Ghost lays hand on girl awake in bed" and E402.1.2 "Footsteps of invisible ghost heard."

158. Collected by Morris Emison, December 8, 1974, from her twenty-seven year old sister in Blytheville, Arkansas. The informant is a high school speech and drama teacher who taught for two years in Kansas but, at the time of the interview, worked in Blytheville. She digresses briefly to offer a theory about how legends originate, an action that makes it clear she does not believe the legend is factual. This view is already evident from her use of the term *legend,* a word rarely used to describe anything one believes. Actually, she only summarizes the legend, suggesting that she is a passive narrator for whom the story serves no function beyond entertainment. This latter view is enunciated by the informant who said, "This story, like the others I will tell you, would probably be told when a bunch of people get together and tell ghost stories and the like." The other stories she told were mostly ghost legends although she did tell a local character anecdote and a humorous story.

Motifs are E281 "Ghosts haunt house"; E310 "Dead lover's friendly return"; and J1782.3 "House noises thought to be ghosts."

159. Collected in Jonesboro, Arkansas, November 20, 1974, by Katherine Lemay from a twenty-year-old female college student from Ida, Arkansas, who is identified only as Carrie Ann. The informant is skeptical but not ready to call the story false. When asked if she believed the story she answered. "I'm not sure. I can't say no because my Mom would not lie, but I've never seen anything of the sort." Clearly, then, she sees it mainly as an entertaining, albeit unusual, story and, to some extent, so do her parents although they also believe they are providing a factual narrative. The informant told Lemay that her parents were recently talking about the house when "they were entertaining some friends. One of the women is super superstitious." The last sentence suggests the possibility that the informant might believe more deeply if she were not afraid of being called "super superstitious."

B546 "Animal searches for dead man" and E402.1.2 "Footsteps of invisible ghost heard," a motif frequently reported since the early 1800s, apply here.

160. Collected in Jonesboro, Arkansas, November 23, 1974, by Katherine Lemay from a nineteen-year-old female college student from Hope, Arkansas, who is not identified by name. Apparently, the story is mainly utilized by the girl for entertainment as the occasion for telling it was a rainy night in a college dormitory where several girls were telling ghost stories in a darkened room. She is, however, not entirely sure that the incident couldn't have happened and is therefore a bit leery about her marriage starting off with a supernatural experience like that encountered by her parents as newlyweds.

The motif here is E279.3 "Ghost pulls bed clothing from sleeper," one with a long history and many published examples. For another story about a ghost who tampers with bed clothing that ends differently see Holzer, *Best True Ghost Stories,* pp. 77–79.

161. Collected by Ethel M. Cottingham and Travis Jordan from John L. Masten. No date or place of collection are given but it was recorded for the WPA in the mid-1930s and, based on the setting of the story, probably was collected in Forsyth County, North Carolina. The text has a very literary quality, noticeable even in the opening paragraph which contains descriptive words that would rarely be used in oral passages. There are, of course, some people who speak in such stilted language but there is good reason to believe that this text is the result of improvement," either by Cottingham or Jordan or by some other unnamed party. The best evidence for this suspicion is the nature of much WPA folklore collecting, which was done for the purpose of gathering material that could be used for literary transmission. In many states the tests gathered were rewritten rather than presented in the exact words of informants. Since only Masten's name is given it is impossible to determine exactly what function this narrative served for the informant. Because the collectors were, in most instances, concerned with getting tales that were interesting and entertaining it is probably reasonable to assume that Masten found the story entertaining. It also undoubtedly offered an interesting explanation for some unusual and mysterious noises.

Motifs include E402.1.1.3 "Ghost cries and screams"; and Thompson's P214.1 "Wife commits suicide (dies) on death of husband"; and T86.3 "Mistress springs into dead lover's grave."

162. Collected October 14, 1976, by Anna Farrier from Elizabeth E. Apple, Huff, Arkansas. For more information about Apple see the notes for Text 152, collected by Farrier from her. Mrs. Apple had this tale from her father, and several others in her repertoire are from the same source. Evidently this, and other narratives she related, were both entertaining to her and regarded as part of local history.

The word *jayhawker* originally applied to a group of anti-slavery guerrilla fighters on the Kansas-Missouri border that was later incorporated into the Union army. This group was notorious for their burnings and killings. Eventually Confederate propagandists branded all Union sentiment in Arkansas as the work of jayhawkers. History books today generally refer to Union raiders as jayhawkers and Confederate raiders as bushwackers. Ozarkers make no such careful distinctions; to them all guerrillas who specialized in terrorizing those left at home during the war are usually labeled jayhawkers. Most informants still regard these persons as thugs or deserters or worse who were taking advantage of the Civil War to line their own pockets. Narratives about jayhawkers are still commonly encountered throughout the Ozarks. For a discussion of some of these see James J. Johnston's, "Jayhawker Stories: Historical Lore in the Arkansas Ozarks," *Mid-South Folklore* IV:1 (Spring, 1976), pp. 3–9.

In some folk traditions there is a taboo against taking down the body of a hanged man, but of course, that is not why the people in this narrative were afraid to take the boy's corpse down. Their only worry was the jayhawkers who might return and kill them. Motifs are E274 "Gallows ghost"; E274(a) "Ghost haunts scene of unjust execution"; and E530.1 "Ghost-like lights."

163. Collected 1961 by Ruthann Luedicke from Ruth Henderson Martin of Hot Springs, Arkansas, who had the story from her grandparents. Evidently, Martin viewed the narrative as a bit of family history as well as just an interesting, unusual story. The battle at Pleasant Hill, Louisiana, took place April 9, 1864 and, contrary to Martin's text, was far from being one of the last Civil War battles in Louisiana.

Motifs include E235.4.6(a) "Theft of teeth punished by scare from ghost who returns, takes teeth," a motif primarily found in Afro-American legendry; E328* "Dead returns for something forgotten"; E338(a) "Male ghost seen"; E338.1(b) "Ghost looks in at window"; E421.2.1 "Ghost leaves no footprints"; and E422.1.11.2 "Revenant as face or head." The second ghost here, like those in several American narratives, seems to have returned for no specific purpose. For more on this aspect of ghostly behavior see Louis M. Jones, *Three Eyes on the Past: Exploring New York Folk Life* (Syracuse: Syracuse University Press, 1982), pp. 35–59, especially see pp. 46–49. the "dogtrot" mentioned here refers to a specific type of architecture that developed in the United States about 1825. Dogtrot houses are one-story buildings composed of two equal units separated by a broad open central hall and joined by a common roof. The term probably arose as a colorful description of the open central hall as a place where dogs could trot through at their own leisure.

164. Collected in 1962 by Jan Calhoon from Dale Pope of Warren, Arkansas. More information about Pope is given in the notes to Text 148. There were two reported Civil War engagements at Mark's Mills, one a skirmish on April 5, 1864, and the second the battle on April 25 of that year. According to Col. John M. Harrell in *Confederate Military History,* X (New York: Thomas Yoseloff, 1962; reprint of a work originally issued in 1899), p. 260, "this engagement took place in a forest of pines not far from the west bank of the Saline River, in a spot usually lonely and undisturbed by any sound ruder than the winds in the treetops." The battle lasted approximately four hours, and losses were quite heavy for such a relatively short battle, casualties numbering close to a thousand. So the engagement at Mark's Mills was a "small battle" only in the amount of time it lasted, not in the loss of lives involved.

Motifs include E334.5 "Ghost of soldier haunts battlefield"; E402 "Mysterious ghostlike noises heard"; E402.1.1.2 "Ghost moans"; and E410 "The unquiet grave."

165. Collected in 1932 by Caroline McQueen Rhea from Dave Greer near Mountain City, Tennessee. Greer was a member of a pioneer Tennessee family and apparently knew several ghost legends, of which he told Rhea at least two (see notes to Text 172). Even so, he was not a particularly skillful narrator, for his texts are basically summaries. Probably they were told primarily for entertainment which, if so, makes the lack of dialogue a major deficiency. Moreover, there is a literary sound to this text since some of the language is not typical of that usually given in oral narratives. Nevertheless, his descriptive passages do provide a dramatic backdrop for the story, placing the setting in a heavily forested, secluded region that has been haunted since the Civil War. The sense of drama continues through the yarn for the murderer was never identified. Neither was the reason for Mrs. Songo's suicide ever discovered. But, while these features provide interest in the story they also leave an essentially incomplete tale, one with no denouement.

Motifs are E275 "Ghost haunts place of great accident or misfortune"; E337.1.1 "Murder sounds heard just as they must have happened at time of death"; E402.1.1.3 "Ghost cries and screams"; K910 "Murder by strategy"; and several given only by Thompson. These are the general motif K950 "Various kinds of treacherous murder"; and the more specialized K959.4 "Murder from behind"; P201.1 "Feud between two branches of family"; and P214.1 "Wife commits suicide on death of husband."

166. Collected by Caroline McQueen Rhea in 1932 from Mrs. W.C. Wright of Silver Lake, Tennessee. Actually, Mrs. Wright did not relate the story but wrote it out, presumably because she was somewhat shy about telling the narrative to Rhea. This suggests that she was not a person who ordinarily related legends, at least not to strangers. In short, she was a passive narrator of this type of lore. The text she provides is etiological; that is, it explains the origin of a somewhat unusual place name. While such explication is Wright's main purpose she also seems to view the yarn as entertaining.

Motifs here are E402 "Mysterious ghostlike noises heard"; E402.1.1.2 "Ghost moans"; E411 "Dead cannot rest because of a sin," a motif that is rarely encountered in America although it is well-known in the British Isles; and three cited only by Thompson. These are S100 "Revolting murders or mutilations"; S110.5 "Murderer kills all who come to certain spot"; and S180 "Wounding or torturing." Surprisingly, neither Thompson nor Baughman gives a motif number for a feud between two families which is one of the most distinctive features of this narrative. For more about the Bloody Third and the Jingling Hole see the first text in Section 4 of this book.

167. Collected August 4, 1977, by William E. Lightfoot from Joe T. Fletcher, a farmer near Waterloo, Georgia. Fletcher was born in 1905 and has earned his living as a farmer since 1935. Mr. Fletcher knew a number of legends and anecdotes that he related to Lightfoot. The words he uses in this text make it evident that he is not really a believer in the supernatural disappearance of the mill. He calls it "the biggest story I ever heard" and emphasizes that "I've never knowed that to be a fact," further noting that "they" said it happened. All of these things suggest that the story functions for him partly as entertainment and partly as a bit of local history. Lightfoot collected another version of the Crystal/Bone Lake legend from a Carlos Ross of Sycamore, Georgia, who claimed that the supernatural disappearance was just fiction. According to him, what really happened was that "the water riz up on the old gristmill. And they finally moved it, I guess, sold it for junk, the people did. After he was hung."

Relevant motifs here include F713.2 "Bottomless lakes (pools)"; F940 "Extraordinary underground (underwater) disappearance"; and Thompson's D910 "Magic body of water." The term "open range" refers to a time when grazing grounds were not fenced off and, thus, open to anyone's cattle. This condition no longer exists in Georgia or in most other states.

168. Reported 1959 by Drew Velvin from Lewisville, Arkansas, but his source is not named; Velvin himself is possibly the informant. There is a reportorial quality about the text ("Many are scared," "Many say," etc.) suggesting that the story is mainly entertainment for the narrator. The opening in mythological times is a nice touch, especially when contrasted with the immediately following passage bringing the story down to contemporary times. This indicates that the person has some experience in relating stories designed to hold audience attention.

Motifs are E530.1 "Ghost-like lights" and E599.7 "Ghost carries lantern." Spirit Lake is located about four miles from Lewisville.

169. Collected by Robert Mason in 1939 from his grandmother in Cannon County, Tennessee. The tale was a favorite entertainment in Mason's family, particularly on windy and rainy nights which created an appropriate atmosphere. Repeated retellings, and the entertainment function, perhaps account for the somewhat literary descriptive passages used in this text. Sections like "a delegation of them would voluntarily go into the graveyard at the side of the hill without male escort" are certainly more typical of a carefully rehearsed written account than of a spontaneous oral text.

This tale is a widely known type classified in Stith Thompson's, *The Types of the Folktale* (Helsinki: Folklore Fellows Communications, 1964), p. 475, as 1676B "Clothing caught in graveyard." Known in Finland, Sweden, Holland, Iraq, Italy, Hungary, England, and the United States, it has been collected by various folklorists for almost a century and was most likely around for a long time before any collections were made. The Tennessee text differs from most versions in that the girls visit the graveyard in a group rather than singly. In addition, they stick forks into the graves rather than stakes. Although quite old, the story is still very popular; I have collected versions in Arkansas in the past three years and know from other folklorists that it is well-known in other parts of the United States. Baughman lists this both as a tale type and as motif N384.2(a) "Person goes to cemetery on a dare: he is to plant a stake in a grave or stick a knife or fork or sword or nail into a grave (or coffin). The knife is driven through the person's loose cuff, or the nail is driven through part of the sleeve, or the stake is driven through the person's long coat tail."

Other motifs here are Thompson's F1041.1.11 "Death from fear" and H1416 "Fear test: spending night by grave."

170. Collected by W. K. McNeil from Ella Fletcher of Onia, Arkansas, April 14, 1981. Mrs. Fletcher was born in 1907 and is a firm believer in ghosts and tells this, and some other ghost stories involving various members of her family, as evidence that ghosts do indeed exist. She was being interviewed about local history and, when asked about any unusual events that had happened in the community, brought up the subject of ghosts and proceeded to tell this story about her father. The incident described here happened near a famous house in the community of Onia that is now called the Uncle Bud Moore House. Built in the 1890s and burned down in the 1960s, the Bud Moore House is well-known in Onia as the scene of a number of unusual happenings. At one time Mrs. Fletcher lived in the house and told me about some of the supernatural things that occurred while she was a resident. One such incident that especially impressed her involved her daughter. In Mrs. Fletcher's words: "People told us before we moved there, they said, 'You won't stay there, you'll see things and get scared.' Well, my daughter, well, she went out on a date one night, and when any of the kids were out I couldn't go to sleep until they came home. Well, she come home and didn't make no racket and shut the doors, and I didn't hear her come home. Well, her bedroom was there in the back corner and she had come in and got undressed and went to bed. Well, her door to her bedroom kinda drug on the floor when it was shut and it was hard to shut. Well, along in the night, I'd say about ten, I heard this door drag like someone was shutting it. Well, next morning I got up and went down and was making breakfast and my daughter came down in her gown in the kitchen and said, 'Mama, I heard something last night.'

"I asked her what time she got in last night and she said, 'About nine.' Well, I heard that door drag and she said she heard it too. It was something, it was! Now, I was across the hall and I heard it."

Motifs involved here are E281 "Ghosts haunt house" and E402.1 "Noises presumably caused by ghost of person." The relevant motifs in her story about her father are E332.1 "Ghost appears at road and stream"; E332.2 "Person meets ghost on road"; and E332.2(h) "Ghost seen on road at night." When Mrs. Fletcher says that the man "just lit up" she does not mean that there was a luminescence about him but merely that he got up.

171a and b. The first text was collected November 10, 1974, by Janet Thomasson in Jonesboro, Arkansas, from an unnamed white female informant who, at the time of the collection, was forty-four years old. The informant grew up fifteen miles from the scene of the story and first heard about the face in the window from her grandmother. As her concluding words indicate, she is not quite ready to refute the legend but is well aware of its publicity value. She told Thomasson that "when we had visitors from out of state, we always drove down to Carrollton to show them the face on the window." She added that "it looks almost like a negative rather than a picture, its eyes, nose and mouth, but it's like an oil slick on water." For the informant, then, the main function the legend serves is entertainment, but it does have some broader implications. For the citizens of Carrollton it provides a graphic reminder of the pitfalls of hasty judgment, as a result of which an innocent man was executed. The legend also gives the town a "claim to fame" and an illustration of the idea of divine retribution, that is, those who punish will be punished.

The second text was collected in 1975 by Jim Harkins from his father, Jim Harkins, Sr., now living in Oklahoma City but a native of Aliceville. Although similar to the Carrollton legend this one about Aliceville is not exactly the same. Since the two towns are located only about fifteen miles apart it would be interesting to know if two traditions have been blended together here. An interesting difference is that the race of the innocently executed man is not mentioned in the second tale. Probably the Aliceville legend serves essentially the same functions as the Carrollton one.

Motifs here are E532 "Ghost-like picture" and E532(a) "Ghost-like portrait etched in glass."

172. Collected by Caroline McQueen Rhea in 1932 from Dave Greer near Mountain City, Tennessee. Greer also related the legend about Songo Hollow (Text 23), and more information about him is given there. This tale explaining the origin of a place name doesn't sound so literary as the one dealing with Songo Hollow. While explanation is certainly the main point of the narrative, the structure and method of presentation suggest that entertainment is also one of its most important functions. There is little intrusion of the narrator in the story, much character delineation, and an ordering of events with a specific time slot for each.

Motifs are E402.1.3 "Invisible ghost plays musical instrument"; E402.1.3(a) "Ghost plays violin"; and four given only in Thompson. These are A1617 "Origin of place-name"; D1233 "Magic violin (fiddle)"; D1441.1.3 "Magic fiddle calls animals together"; and Z355 "All snakes but one placated by music."

173. Collected November 2, 1982 by Stacy VanAusdall from Faye Newsome in Harrisburg, Arkansas. At the time of the interview Newsome was sixty years old, meaning that she was born in

1921 or 1922. Mrs. Newsome, who worked in the home of the collector's family, is said to have "extensive knowledge of everyone in the small town of Harrisburg (1984 population, 1,910)" and particularly of the Negro community there. Apparently, she is also a skillful narrator for the collector notes, "Faye's style and method of telling it very deliberate and precise. She sat very relaxed with her hands folded in her lap while she told the story she has undoubtedly told many times before. She speaks very quietly and pauses a great deal for dramatic effect." Her skill, however, is mainly in the manner of telling, not in the text, which is essentially a summary of the legend. The last paragraph makes it clear that Newsome believes the story but, within the Negro community of Harrisburg, it probably serves many functions. First, it is a moralistic temperance narrative in which a drunkard drives his wife and, ultimately, himself to the grave, but even in death their souls can't rest. Presumably others inclined to partake of alcohol should beware lest they find the same fate. Second, it provides an explanation for some unusual noises that have apparently been heard by many people. It, then, is entertainment, a story proving the existence of ghosts, a temperance yarn, and an explanatory tale.

Motifs include E273 "Churchyard ghosts"; E401 "Voices of dead heard from graveyard"; E402 "Mysterious ghostlike noises heard"; E402.1.1.2 "Ghost moans"; E402.1.1.3 "Ghost cries and screams"; and E410 "The unquiet grave."

174a and b. Both versions collected by Johnny Lloyd Redd, the first in June, 1976, from Linda Sue Redd Harris and the second, also in June, 1976, from Jess Seawell. The first text was recorded in Jonesboro, Arkansas, while the second was recorded in Maynard, Arkansas. Harris was a twenty-six year old secretary who, at the time of the collection, lived in Jonesboro but until she graduated from high school lived in Stokes, Arkansas, where she heard much conversation concerning Ashberry "Rip" Sago. Seawell, a seventy-three year old retiree at the time of collection, knew Sago as a young man. Although one informant knew the old coffinmaker personally, both tell the legend essentially for entertainment. Seawell's last line indicates, however, that he also uses it as a kind of exemplum predicting a terrible end for kids who are not good.

Motifs include D1856 "Death evaded"; E354* "Dead returns to complete task"; E363.3(c) "Ghost warns of approaching storm"; E378* "Ghost continues to remain in usual surroundings after death"; E402 "Mysterious ghostlike noises heard"; E402.3 "Sound made by ghostly object"; E419.8 "Ghost returns to enforce its burial wishes or to protest disregard of such wishes."

175. Collected by Gilbert Cooley in 1974 from an unnamed black male from Dillon, South Carolina. Cooley also collected an almost identical story from another informant from Rowland, North Carolina. Since it is related as a personal experience the informant clearly believes the story and, possibly, tells the tale as proof of the existence of ghosts. This is a version of a well-known legend called by folklorists "The Baby with the Fangs" and is primarily associated with Mexicans and Mexican-Americans. It is also known in Cuba and Bolivia and possibly other Latin American countries. Unlike Cooley's text, most versions indicate that the baby is a witch or the devil. Typically the legend has a man traveling at night, either on horseback, driving a car, or walking. He finds the baby beside the road, lying on a grave behind a tombstone, in a barn, or under a bridge. He picks the child up and carries it off. The baby soon starts to grow, rapidly becoming too heavy to carry, turns into a witch, develops unusually long, sharp teeth or fangs, grows long sharp nails, horns and tail. The man drops the child or simply disappears.

Few versions of this legend are related as personal experiences. Possibly Cooley's informant merely told the story as a personal experience to heighten the dramatic effect. Motifs are Thompson's D55.2.5 "Transformation: adult to child"; D56 "Magic change in person's age"; and D56.1 "Transformation to older person."

176. Collected Summer, 1974, by Pat Blake from an unnamed twenty-six year old male computer operator in Jonesboro, Arkansas. Clearly the informant believes the story since it describes a personal experience but he also sees it as entertainment and is somewhat proud of having such an unusual experience. He told Blake, "I can remember telling it to friends when we were telling ghost stories, and when we traded stories about weird things that had happened to us." To the many others who told about the bugler and his horse the legend probably served some other purposes. By emphasizing this supernatural event that occurs in a cemetery after dark, youths were hopefully discouraged from loitering in graveyards after nightfall. The story can also be seen as a comment on the loyalty of animals. Like many other supernatural occurrences this one is said to happen usually when there is a full moon.

Motifs are E520 "Animal ghosts" and 521.1 "Ghost of horse."

177. Collected March 12, 1977, by Eric Batchelder from Oma Little in Paint Rock, Alabama. Mrs. Little told Batchelder a number of supernatural stories but considered this the most unique, perhaps because it was a personal experience. Actually, this account of the haunted hollow is not a story so much as it is a series of related incidents. Motifs are E338.1(c) "Ghost opens doors and windows repeatedly"; E402 "Mysterious ghostlike noises heard"; E402.2 "Sounds made by invisible ghosts of animals"; E421.1 "Invisible ghosts"; and E530.1 "Ghost-like lights."

178. Collected December 8, 1974, by Morris Emison from her sister in Blytheville, Arkansas. For more information about this informant see the notes to Text 158 in Section 1 of this book, which concerns H. L. Hunt's house in El Dorado, Arkansas. This legend functions as entertainment for the informant but probably it also serves to create a feeling of unity and tradition among the student body of Henderson State University. In short, the Black Lady represents the school spirit (pun intended). OBU is Ouachita Baptist University.

Motifs include E230 "Return from dead to inflict punishment"; E411.1.1 "Suicide cannot rest in grave"; and Thompson's T81.2.2 "Scorned lover kills self."

179. Collected in 1983 by Jill Pimentall and Craig O'Dell from Kathy Jones, Gaston, South Carolina. Since the story is told as a personal experience, the informant obviously believes the story is a factual account. Even so, she still finds it hard to believe in ghosts but, clearly, she enjoys telling this tale. She told the collectors that she had related this story two hundred times. The ghost is supposed to be of George I. Pair (1924–1962), the first principal of Airport High which, at the time of its construction in 1958, was the second high school in the Cayce-West Columbia, South Carolina area. The Mr. Rivers mentioned by Jones was Ed Rivers, custodian at the school and a close friend of Pair's, who has reported seeing the ghost several times. The incident described constitutes Jone's only encounter with the apparition.

Although Jones sees the narrative mainly as an eerie personal experience validating the existence of ghosts, the numerous reports of sightings by others possibly serve a broader, more useful function. Would-be vandals may be scared away by stories of the school's supernatural "guardian." There is also a sense of pride in stories about the ghost for he gives Airport High a distinction that no other schools in the area have, their very own resident wraith. This feeling is particularly conveyed in an article titled "School Spirit Haunts Halls of Airport" that appeared in the Monday, October 31, 1983, issue of a local paper, *The Eyrie*. In an almost bragging manner the author of the article asks, "But did you know that Airport has its own resident ghost?" and proceeds to describe some encounters that faculty members have had with the spirit of the former principal. For whatever the reasons the legend is perpetuated, it is certain that those who pass it on believe in the reality of Pair's ghost. From evidence presented by the collectors it seems to be taken very seriously by both students and faculty members. Most persons who have sighted the apparition are convinced he is there to protect the school which, reportedly, he loved above everything except his family. One informant voiced this opinion succinctly when he said, "I always wind up by telling people that he is not going to hurt you unless you are trying to do something to hurt the school."

Motifs are E300 "Friendly return from the dead"; E330 "Locations haunted by the non-malevolent dead"; E422.4.5 "Revenant in male dress"; and E425 "Revenant in human form."

180. Collected in 1938 by Henry Wacaster Perry from Orpha Harrison, a white woman living in Carter County, Tennessee. She heard it from her sister-in-law, who had learned it from her grandfather. That it is a story the grandfather "used to tell" and, that it is about one of her uncles suggest that it was used in the family as an object lesson. This is also indicated by the missionary-like ending that emphasizes, "This never left until this sinful man fell on his knees and began to pray. After that he was never bothered any more, for he became a religious man." It seems likely, though, that the narrative functions as entertainment also.

Motifs utilized here include E421.2.1 "Ghost leaves no footprints," a motif common in English, Canadian, and American folk tradition but first reported from England in 1850; G303.3.1 "The devil in human form"; G303.3.1.21 "The devil as a great hairy man"; and three cited only by Thompson, S60 "Cruel spouse"; S62 "Cruel husband"; and V254.4 "Devil exorcised by 'Ave.'" The Tennessee text bears some similarity to Thompson's type 760 "The Unquiet Grave" in which a man burns his three wives but can find no rest in the grave. A girl takes the dead man to a priest and secures his pardon for the murder of his wives. That type, of course, is a fictional tale whereas Harrison's narrative is told as an actual happening.

181. Collected in 1938 by Henry Wacaster Perry from John Harrison, an elderly white resident of Carter County, Tennessee. Like several other stories in this book, Harrison's is a reminiscence of a personal experience. In other words it is what folklorists call a *memorate* (pronounced "mem-o-rat"), a narrative of a personal happening usually involving the supernatural. Perry had heard the story numerous times prior to its recording one winter evening in 1938. Thus, the tale clearly serves an entertainment function but the narrator also believes this is actually what happened. His concluding line "Now, it looked to me like that was a warnin' or somethin'" shows just how seriously Harrison takes his story and why he frequently tells it. Just what the disease, double menthole, that claimed Butler's life is remains as much of a puzzle to me as it was to Harrison. Possibly the illness was something like pneumonia.

Motifs include D1812.5 "Future learned through omens," which is also a frequently encountered folk belief as well as a traditional narrative element; E574 "Appearance of ghost serves as death omen"; and two listed only by Thompson, E783.6 "Headless body vital" and M341.1.2 "Prophecy: early death." For both of these motifs Thompson cites an Irish myth as his only reference.

182. Collected by William E. Lightfoot from George Tucker on March 13, 1974 at Big Mud Creek near Beaver, Kentucky. Born November 6, 1917, Tucker is well known not only locally but nationally as a banjo player and he has appeared at numerous folk festivals and on several records. Evidently he believes in the events related in the tale for it is presented as a personal experience. It is unclear whether or not the opening is an indication that Tucker is proud of the story which is "something" or he is merely responding to a request from the collector to give him something of a supernatural nature. Tucker provides some dialogue and is a skillful taleteller, but, from a purely narrative standpoint, this text leaves something to be desired. We never learn what the host was after or why he is haunting this particular spot. In other words, like some other ghosts described in this book, he appears for no apparent reason.

The motifs here are E422.1.1(a) "Headless man—mention of appearance only" and Thompson's F511.0.1 "Headless person."

183. Collected by Andy Fulkerson in 1974 from Reese Hutcheson, a twenty-nine year old Episcopal priest in Paragould, Arkansas. Hutcheson received his theology degree in 1971 from the University of the South at Sewanee, Tennessee, and, at the time of collection, was parish priest for All Saints' Episcopal Church in Paragould. During the course of the interview, Hutcheson made it clear the legend was for him nothing more than entertainment, and it probably serves the same function for most students from the University of the South who discuss the topic. The typically rather uneventful college life can be made somewhat more exciting by a ghost. But even if Hutcheson had not expressed a certain skepticism toward the existence of the ghost, it would be evident from his text. The entire legend is told as if it is someone else's story that he is merely reporting. Such lines as "the legend goes," "supposed to have been seen by," "said to be," "said to," "reports come from someone who saw somebody, etc." are not words used by a narrator who deeply believes the story he is relating. Yet despite Hutcheson's skepticism, he commented that "still, some very weird noises come down those hallowed halls very early in the morning after having studied hours on end."

Probably the legend mainly serves a function of entertainment, and there is indeed something humorous about a person getting so much knowledge that his head falls off. The narrative can also be seen as an admonition not to put off studying until the last minute. Those who do not heed the warning run the risk of sharing the fate of the student who did so much cramming that his head fell off. Motifs are E422.1.1.5* "Miscellaneous actions of headless ghosts" and Thompson's D1641.7 "Severed head moves from place to place."

184. Collected in 1968 by Bill Ferris from Gene Autrey, a ten year old black boy in Leland, Mississippi. He also contributed the text about the ghost who turned his head backwards (Text 199). His attitude towards this text is indicated by the first sentence. The only relevant motif here is E422.1.1(a) "Headless man—mention of appearance only."

185. Collected by William E. Lightfoot and Tom Alder from Martin "Marty" Weathers of Glenville, Georgia, August 15, 1977. Weathers was a sophomore at Abraham Baldwin Agricultural College in Tifton where this text was recorded. He, and a friend from Barnesville, Georgia, named Bill Henry, contributed several legend and custom texts to Lightfoot even though they "were perpetually bewildered that 'college professors' were seriously interested in their customs and stories." Weathers was apparently an excellent informant, but the text given here is not especially distinguished as a narrative. Essentially it is just a summary of the legend; Weathers even seems uncertain about some of the essential details, such as why the girl had to stay late. Some of his wording indicates that for him the legend serves only an entertainment function. For example, he refers to it as a kind of "garbage," hardly the categorization that would be given by a believer.

The relevant motifs here are E275 "Ghost haunts place of great accident or misfortune"; D334 "Non-malevolent ghost haunts scene of former misfortune, crime, or tragedy"; E402 "Mysterious ghostlike noises heard"; and E402.1.1.3 "Ghost cries and screams." On August 10, 1977, five days before Lightfoot and Adler recorded this text, Lightfoot and Dave Stanley collected another version of the Omega Bridge legend from Teresa Lindsey, an employee of Abraham Baldwin Agricultural College. According to Mrs. Lindsey, "When I-75 was first built a woman, and I think two children, were riding down there and they were killed on that curve. And the noise that I guess your tires make from the curve is supposed to be the screams from her children as they died."

186. Collected August 30, 1965, by George Foss from Mary Woods Shiflett, Browns Cove, Virginia. For more information about Mrs. Shiflett see the notes to Text 156. Since the story here is told as a personal experience it is clearly related not just as entertainment. Probably Mrs. Shiflett told the story primarily as a testimony to the existence of ghosts.

The main motif here is E423.1.1 "Revenant as dog," but Thompson's F401.3.3 "Spirit as black dog" is also suggested. Browns Cove is just a few miles from the Skyline Drive of the Blue Ridge Parkway, a region that has a lengthy tradition of spectral black dogs. In the *Journal of American Folklore*, 20 (1907), pp. 151–152, a Mrs. R. F. Herrick, who mostly wrote articles on ballads, submitted the following information on "The Black Dog of the Blue Ridge":

> In Botetourt County, Virginia, there is a pass that was much travelled by people going to Bedford County and by visitors to mineral springs in the vicinity. In the year 1683 the report was spread that at the wildest part of the trail in this pass there appeared at sunset a great black dog, who, with majestic tread, walked in a listening attitude about two hundred feet and then turned and walked back. Thus he passed back and forth like a sentinel on guard, always appearing at sunset to keep his nightly vigil and disappearing again at dawn. And so the whispering went with bated breath from one to another, until it had travelled from one end of the state to the other. Parties of young cavaliers were made up to watch for

the black dog. Many saw him. Some believed him to be a veritable dog sent by some master to watch, others believed him to be a witch dog.

A party decided to go through the pass at night, well armed, to see if the dog would molest them. Choosing a night when the moon was full they mounted good horses and sallied forth. Each saw a great dog larger than any dog they had ever seen, and, clapping spurs to their horses, they rode forward. But they had not calculated on the fear of their steeds. When they approached the dog, the horses snorted with fear, and in spite of whip, spur, and rein gave him a wide berth, while he marched on as serenely as if no one were near. The party were unable to force their horses to take the pass again until after daylight. Then they were laughed at by their comrades to whom they told their experiences. Thereupon they decided to lie in ambush, kill the dog, and bring in his hide. The next night found the young men well hidden behind rocks and bushes with guns in hand. As the last ray of sunlight kissed the highest peak of the Blue Ridge, the black dog appeared at the lower end of his walk and came majestically toward them. When he came opposite, every gun cracked. When the smoke cleared away, the great dog was turning at the end of his walk, seemingly unconscious of the presence of the hunters. Again and again they fired and still the dog walked his beat. And fear caught the hearts of the hunters, and they fled wildly away to their companions, and the black dog held the pass at night unmolested.

Time passed, and year after year went by, until seven years had come and gone, when a beautiful woman came over from the old country, trying to find her husband who eight years before had come to make a home for her in the new land. She traced him to Bedford County and from there all trace of him was lost. Many remembered the tall, handsome man and his dog. Then there came to her ear the tale of the vigil of the great dog of the mountain pass, and she pleaded with the people to take her to see him, saying that if he was her husband's dog he would know her. A party was made up and before night they arrived at the gap. The lady dismounted, and walked to the place where the nightly watch was kept. As the shadows grew long, the party fell back on the trail, leaving the lady alone, and as the sun sank into his purple bed of splendor the great dog appeared. Walking to the lady, he laid his great head in her lap for a moment, then turning he walked a short way from the trail, looking back to see that she was following. He led her until he paused by a large rock, where he gently scratched the ground, gave a long, low wail, and disappeared. The lady called the party to her and asked them to dig. As they had no implements, and she refused to leave, one of them rode back for help. When they dug below the surface they found the skeleton of a man and the hair and bones of a great dog. They found a seal ring on the hand of the man and a heraldic embroidery in silk that the wife recognized. She removed the bones for proper burial and returned to her old home. It was never known who had killed the man. But from that time to this the great dog, having finished his faithful work, has never appeared again.

Unlike the canine in Herrick's narrative the ghostly dog that appeared to Mrs. Shiflett was apparently motiveless.

187. Collected by William E. Lightfoot from Reuben Lowe, November 20, 1973, in Pikeville, Kentucky. Mr. Lowe, who was born in Pike County in 1909, is a retired coal miner who now earns his living as a farmer. He and his wife, Ruth, told Lightfoot a large number of supernatural tales concerning witches, burnstoppers, thrash (thrush) healers, measurers, magic healing, ghosts, and markings caused by fright and seemingly strongly believed in the validity of such traditions. In some cases, though, he had some difficulty recalling how the tradition worked. For example, in discussing a measurer (someone who cures a child's illness by measuring techniques) he commented: "What *we* always done was to measure a baby's length and to, to a . . . I believe it was a sourwood tree . . . and cut a notch on it that high. And by the time it gets above that . . . something or other. I don't know. My wife knows. I just can't think of what happens here." Considering his degree of belief in the supernatural and his several personal experiences pertaining to ghostly things, it seems certain that he tells such stories as evidence of his belief and as testimony on behalf of such things as ghosts. Possibly, they also serve a secondary function such as entertainment. The town mentioned in the text is Pikeville, Kentucky, and the incident occurred circa 1927.

The only relevant motif here is E422.1.11.1 "Revenant as an eye" which has rarely been collected in folk tradition. The only previous reporting is in Charles M. Skinner's popular volume of 1903, *American Myths and Legends*, which consists of rewritten folk narratives. Unfortunately, Skinner does not identify his source but his text was set in Pennsylvania.

188. Collected by Caroline McQueen Rhea in 1932 from Mrs. Harrison Donnelly of Shouns, Tennessee. Apparently the tale was told primarily for entertainment; at least that's what its very structured arrangement suggests. If anything, it is a little too well ordered and reads more like a literary piece than an oral narrative. The impersonal sequential arrangement is typical of literary efforts as is some of the language utilized here. A reference to the ghost as an "invisible guest," to the doctor who "bounded forward" to meet the ghost, to his being "much disgruntled" and having "an unfortunate taste for drink," as well as several other phrases given here suggest a literary style rather than an oral one. There are, of course, some people who speak in such stilted language and Mrs. Donnelly may have been one. The net effect is that her use of euphemistic language suggests that she is both appalled and intrigued by the events she relates.

Motifs include E371.4 "Ghost of man returns to point out hidden treasure"; E402 "Mysterious ghost-like noises heard"; E421.1 "Invisible ghosts"; E421.2.1 "Ghost leaves no footprints," a motif first reported from England in 1850; and E451.8 "Ghost laid when house it haunts is destroyed or changed."

189. Collected June, 1973, by Michael O. Thomas from his aunt, Lee Thomas, in Kinston, North Carolina. The informant spent most of her childhood on farms in Lenoir and Greene counties, the latter being the county in which Snow Hill is located. Miss Thomas first heard this story as a young girl from a Mrs. Tillman, one of the daughters of the Mr. Jones in the narrative. The incident reportedly took place between 1910 and 1912, and at that time the house was old. Part of the room was sealed off because "the owner of the house had died of smallpox, and nobody wanted to handle his things." Miss Thomas said that Mr. Jones found "several thousand dollars" in the overcoat.

Motifs include E371 "Return from dead to reveal hidden treasure"; E402 "Mysterious ghost-like noises heard"; H1411 "Fear test: staying in haunted house"; and Thompson's E373.1 "Money received from ghosts as reward for bravery"; E436.2 "Cats crossing one's path sign of ghosts"; and E545.12 "Ghost directs man to hidden treasure."

190. Collected June, 1973, by Michael O. Thomas from his aunt, Lee Thomas, in Kinston, North Carolina. She heard this story when she was a young girl from a Mrs. Tillman who claimed to have had this encounter with a ghost. Reportedly, the incident took place on a farm near Hugo, North Carolina, in 1916 or 1917. This story, like the preceding text which was also told by Miss Thomas, was probably related by the informant mainly for entertainment but she was also aware that it was part of local history.

Motifs include E545.19.2 "Proper means of addressing ghost"; and Thompson's E373 "Ghosts bestow gifts on living" and E545.12 "Ghosts direct man to hidden treasure."

191. Collected in 1974 by Gilbert Cooley from an unnamed black male from Rowland, North Carolina. The informant had this story from his father who told him that "enchanted money" was money that was being guarded by a spirit. He told Cooley that during the Civil War the master would take a slave along with him when he was ready to bury some money. Once the money was in the ground the master would tell the slave to stay there and guard the treasure. Then, while the slave was obeying orders, he would be shot by the master so that the slave's spirit was left to guard the money. In this story, however, the slave's spirit is aided by that of the two old women in the task of guarding the money.

Motifs include E291 "Ghosts protect hidden treasure"; N576 "Ghosts prevent men from raising treasure"; and Thompson's D1815.1 "Knowledge of ghost language." Salt is frequently used in folk tradition as a means of protection against witches but its use as protection against ghosts is rare.

192. Collected July 15, 1961, by George Foss from Robert Shiflett in Browns Cove, Virginia. Shiflett was born in 1905 in "Shiflett Hollow" in Greene County, Virginia. His father, Erasmus, was a storekeeper in the area and the family moved to the mouth of Browns Cove in Albermarle County when Robert was a young child. Shiflett was known locally as "Raz's Robert" since he was the son of Erasmus. He was the brother-in-law of Mary Woods Shiflett, the widow of his oldest brother, who also contributed several narratives dealing with the supernatural to Foss. Robert died in 1979. The story may have been considered mainly as entertainment by Shiflett but it was also a bit of family history.

Motifs include E231 "Return from dead to reveal murder"; E235.2 "Ghost returns to demand proper burial"; E371.5* "Ghost of woman returns to reveal hidden treasure"; and E422.4.4 "Revenant in female dress."

193. Collected in 1940 by Lewis David Bandy from an unidentified white informant of Macon County, Tennessee. Although Bandy tells nothing more about the informant, there is no evidence in the text suggesting that it serves any function other than entertainment. Indeed, the structure of the text, with its almost formulaic opening and closing lines, is reminiscent of the *märchen* or fairy tale. Like many of the other texts in this volume this one has at least one narrative element more common to fairy tales than to legends. This feature is the "magic" fire which leaves Granny scared but unhurt.

Motifs included here are E291.2 "Form of treasure-guarding ghost"; E451.5 "Ghost laid when treasure is unearthed"; F473.1(ga) "Bed is thrown down and away from certain corner if it is set up there," which is very rare in folk tradition; N532 "Light indicates hidden treasure"; and Thompson's D1271 "Magic fire."

194. Collected by Lewis David Bandy from an unidentified white informant in Macon County, Tennessee, in 1940. Evidently the narrator believed the story was factual because he offers the concluding line, "It was all because of the hidden money." Motifs used are E371.4 "Ghost of man returns to point out hidden treasure," a narrative element widely known in England, Wales, Scotland, Ireland, Canada, and the United States and first reported by Scottish collector Robert Chambers in 1826; E402 "Mysterious ghostlike noises heard"; and E451.8 "Ghost laid when house it haunts is destroyed or changed." Although motif E402 is very common and widely known, the ghost who makes its presence known by the sound of falling rocks is relatively rare.

195. Collected by W.K. McNeil from Ella Fletcher of Onia, Arkansas, April 14, 1981. For more information about Mrs. Fletcher see the notes for her Text 170. Several widely traveled motifs appear in this text. They include E334.2 "Ghost haunts burial spot," and probably E371 "Return from dead to reveal hidden treasure" and E371.5* "Ghost of woman returns to reveal hidden treasure." The word "probably" is used because it is not altogether clear from the text whether the ghost is returning to reveal the treasure or to guard it. If the latter intent is involved then the motifs E291 "Ghosts protect hidden treasure" and E291.2.1 "Ghost in human form guards treasure" are relevant. The latter motif is well known in England, Wales, Canada, and the United States. Probably the best known instance of this motif is associated with a legend that the Scottish privateer and reputed pirate William Kidd (1645?–1701) buried a treasure on the Isles of Shoals sometime before his execution in 1701. According to the tradition that still-missing loot is guarded by a ghost. Comments made by Mrs. Fletcher throughout the interview suggest, though, that the ghostly woman was not guarding the money but rather, would have willingly told anyone who asked about it in the proper way that it was in her husband's grave. Also relevant here is E545.19.2 "Proper means of addressing ghost."

The idea of invoking the Lord's name in order to find out what a ghost wants is common in folk tradition, but the specific manner of address suggested here is uncommon. Generally, it is stated that the person must address the ghost in the name of the Holy Spirit and then ask its business three times. Some narratives say that the person must ask, "In the name of the Lord, why visitest thou me?" or "In the name of the Lord, why troublest thou me?" Yet others maintain that one must use the names in the Trinity in order to learn what the ghost wants. According to Mrs. Fletcher, merely having the Lord's name in the question asked of the ghost is the most important point.

Mrs. Fletcher found her father's reaction to the incident especially noteworthy: "He said he wasn't very scared. He said he sat down beside the road and thought he would rest awhile and he thought to himself, 'What was that woman doing behind that tree and how did she disappear?' I'll tell you, something like that would have scared me."

196. Collected in 1978 by Robert E. McNeill from Henry Dollar in Ashe County, North Carolina. Dollar was a thirty-nine year old white male with a high school education. Prior to being disabled by a gunshot wound he had been employed by a local chair company. The story related here was a personal experience of his grandfather that happened about the time of the First World War, i.e. 1916–1918. Thus, it was part of Dollar's family history, but it undoubtedly also functioned as entertainment. The Devil's Stairs is a local name for a spot in Ashe County, North Carolina that over the years has acquired a reputation as a place where macabre and mysterious things happen. Legends of supernatural happenings in the area postdate two deaths that occurred near there about 1910. The first, the accidental death of a black laborer by dynamite, happened about a year before the second, which was the murder of an unwanted baby by its mother. Many different types of ghostly sightings and encounters have taken place at the Devil's Stairs, including a number of reported versions of "The Vanishing Hitchiker" (see Texts 200 a, b, c, d, e and f). For more about these see McNeill's article, "Legends From the Devil's Stairs" in *North Carolina Folklore* 26:3 (November, 1978, pp. 149–156).

The main motif here is E332.3.1 "Ghost rides on horseback with rider" but E421.1 "Invisible ghosts" and E421.1.2(a) "Ghost scares horse" are also relevant.

197a, b and c. These three texts are versions of one of the most popular legends found among Mexican-Americans, that of "La Llorona"—"The Weeping Woman." The first text was collected in 1965 in El Paso, Texas, by Cathy Skender from a boy raised in Ciudad Juarez, Chihuahua, Mexico. Skender gave no other data on the informant so it is hard to surmise how he used the legend or what meaning it had for him. Possibly he viewed it simply as entertainment and his text gives some indication of this attitude. Such phrases as "people reported" and "local people said" are the words of a reporter rather than a true believer but hardly conclusive proof of disbelief. Parents frequently employ the tale as a means of keeping children in check and away from certain places, and because this informant had known it from early childhood, possibly he first heard it used in such a way.

The second text was collected by William Campion from an unnamed seventy-two year old woman in El Paso, Texas. Since it is presented as a personal experience it obviously is viewed by the informant as something more than just an entertaining story. The third text was collected in 1963 in El Paso, Texas, by an unidentified collector from an unnamed informant. Related as an incident that happened to a close relative, this text also was regarded seriously by the informant. Possibly the narrative served as a localized temperance yarn since the implication is that the men only saw the ghost after a night of drinking.

Although "The Weeping Woman" is primarily associated with Mexican and Mexican-American folk legendry, there is disagreement about its origin. In his article, " 'La Llorona' and Related Themes," *Western Folklore* 19:3 (July, 1960), pp. 155–168, Bacil F. Kirtley maintains that "La Llorona" is largely of European origin and merely adopted in the New World. Most authorities, however, argue that it is a Mexican tale that has been around since Aztec times and is probably adapted from Aztec mythology. The Aztec goddess known either as Civacoatl, Chihuacohuatl or Tonantzin appeared dressed in white and carrying a cradle on her shoulders as if she were carrying a child. The goddess walked among the Aztec women and left the cradle alone; the women discovered that the cradle contained an arrowhead shaped like the Aztec sacrificial knife. During the night the goddess roamed through the cities screaming and crying until she disappeared in the waters of lakes or rivers. According to this thesis the myth later became merged with the story of a real tragedy, a case of infanticide that occurred during the sixteenth century. A peasant girl murdered her three children who were fathered out of wedlock by a nobleman. After dispatching the babies the mother went through the streets crying.

Whatever its source, "La Llorona" is known throughout the Southwest and as far away as the Phillipines. Wherever her adventures are recounted, the Weeping Woman is said to appear in many shapes and forms. She has a seductive figure and a horse face; she is dressed in black and has long shiny black hair, tin-like fingernails, and a skeleton's face; she is dressed in white, has long black hair, long fingernails, and a bat's face; often she has no face; sometimes she is a vampire. Meeting La Llorona is always a frightening experience and sometimes leads to tragic results. More often encounters produce such results as causing drunkards to reform their ways.

Of the three texts given here, the first one is somewhat unusual in that it contains no description of the ghost's dress and physical features. This legend also has the husband killing the children, thereby avoiding the usual motif of the woman returning as a ghost as punishment for the murder she committed. The second text is typical in that the ghost appears at midnight, the most popular time for the appearance of La Llorona. Although wailing is mentioned, nothing is said about the reason for the crying and, in fact, no association of the ghost with her dead children is made; these features are relatively uncommon but not rare. The third text is unusual only in that the ghost makes no sounds.

Motifs are E402.1.1.3 "Ghost cries and screams"; E422.4.3 "Ghost in white"; E547 "The dead wail"; and E587.5 "Ghosts walk at midnight."

198. Collected September 18, 1963, by George Foss from Lloyd Powell, Browns Cove, Virginia. For more information about Powell see the notes for Powell's Text 145. Apparently, the story given here was related primarily for entertainment. Despite his statement in the narrative, Powell was not fifty, but fifty-eight, at the time he related this tale to Foss. The only relevant motif is E425.1 "Female revenant."

199. Collected in 1968 by Bill Ferris from Gene Autrey, Leland, Mississippi. Autrey was ten years old at the time he contributed this text. Even though the narrative has a beginning similar to the "once upon a time" opening of *märchen* there is no evident reason to believe that Autrey didn't accept this as a factual story. There seems to be no motif number that parallels this tale.

200a, b, c, d, e and f. These six texts are examples of what may well be the best known ghost legend in modern America, one that folklorists usually call "The Vanishing Hitchhiker." The first text was reported by Billy Kyser, Fayetteville, Arkansas, in 1959 as recalled from a telling by his junior high coach, Pat Jackson, while on the way to a 1953 football game in Little Rock. Apparently, Jackson had a wealth of ghost stories to relate, for Kyser remembered that he generally told them to team members while they were traveling to games. This information makes it rather evident that this and similar tales were used as an entertaining way to pass the time while on the way to a game.

The second text was collected June 16, 1974, by Susan Jennings from her husband, Horace Jennings, in Trumann, Arkansas. The informant was a twenty-nine year old football coach who first heard the story in high school and recalled that it was mostly told on overnight hunting and fishing trips. In other words, the legend's main function to him was entertainment.

The third text was collected in 1962 by Judy Armstrong from Nancy Riley of Little Rock, Arkansas. Mrs. Riley had heard the story numerous times in and around Little Rock, primarily from older residents. It is unclear from information provided by the collector what Mrs. Riley's attitude toward the story is. Does she believe it is an account of an actual incident or is it just an entertaining story that happens to be well-known? Woodson is a community of five hundred located about twenty miles southeast of Little Rock.

The fourth text was collected in 1963 by Eugene Bourland from Elizabeth Kelly, a long-time librarian for the city of El Paso, Texas. Miss Kelly knew several other ghost stories, most of which she heard from a woman that she met while working at the library, that she told mainly for entertainment.

The fifth text was collected November 19, 1976 by Anna Farrier from Patty Faye Baker in Batesville, Arkansas. Unfortunately, the collector provided no additional information about the informant, but, because the narrative is offered as an account of a personal experience, one can assume that it serves a function other than just entertainment.

The sixth text was collected by Billy Kyser in 1959 from Freddy Akers in Fayettevile, Arkansas. Akers heard the story from Charles Abbott, a friend from his hometown of Blytheville, Arkansas, and previously heard an almost identical tale from his grandfather. Although the story was heard in Blytheville, the story is supposedly set just across the state line in Missouri. Apparently the story was seen by Akers primarily as entertainment.

Although the legend is well, and widely, known in the United States it probably did not originate here. It was, however, known in this country at least as early as the latter quarter of the nineteenth century but most likely was imported from Europe—or the story that may have been its prototype probably was. There is, however, also reason to propose an Asian origin for the narrative because a legend collected from Chinese immigrants in California contains many of the same motifs found in most early American versions. There is also a Korean version that was popular in the days before World War II. But, it seems most likely that "The Vanishing Hitchhiker" is an example of a narrative constantly readapted to changing times (to take newer technology into consideration, among other things) but ultimately derived from earlier European legends about eternally wandering ghosts such as "The Flying Dutchman."

Earlier texts of "The Vanishing Hitchhiker," of course, lacked the automobile, referring instead to travel by horseback or in horse-drawn vehicles. The automobile did not become a common feature until the early 1930s. Much older is the element of the hitchhiker's actual presence in the vehicle and her status as the ghost of a particular individual. Frequently, she leaves some object behind—a book, purse, suitcase, blanket, sweater, scarf, footprints, or water spots in the car. The driver often learns her identity at the hitchhiker's home by showing the object to her relatives, or describing her, giving the girl's name, or from a prominently displayed photograph of her that often shows her wearing the same clothing her ghost is dressed in. Sometimes she has borrowed clothing from the driver and it is found draped over her tombstone. Frequently she is picked up on a rainy night on a secluded road, but occasionally the pickup is made at a club or dance. Frequently the girl has been killed two, three, four, seven, or ten years ago, but rarely thirteen, the number most popularly associated with bad luck and which is used in a popular song based on the legend.

Over the years elements of various alien traditions have been blended into the story of "The Vanishing Hitchhiker." Besides "The Flying Dutchman," which has already been mentioned, characters and elements from Hawaiian traditions about the volcano goddess Pele, Mexican traditions about the spirit La Llorona (or "The Weeping Woman"), and from Mormon traditions about the Three Nephites, disciples of Christ who are said to appear to Mormons in times of need, have all become attached to some versions of "The Vanishing Hitchhiker."

The legend has also served as an inspiration for several movie shorts and television plots, the most notable of which is a thirty-minute drama used on the television series "The Twilight Zone." It also provided the story for "Bringing Mary Home," a song popularized by Billy Edd Wheeler and featured on his album *Goin' Town and Country* (Kapp KL-1479) and for "Laurie (Strange Things Happen)", written by Milton C. Addington and recorded by Memphis singer Dick Lipscomb, who records under the name Dickey Lee. The latter was one of 1965's biggest pop hits, reaching number fourteen on *Billboard's* Top 100 and remaining on the charts for thirteen weeks. Lee's recording was released on TCF Hall 102.

Of the six versions here, the first one, Pat Jackson's, is typical of modern Southern texts in that the pickup occurs on a night when the weather is dismal but is unusual in that the ghost remains silent. The feature of love at first sight is borrowed from romantic fiction although most texts reported to date the driver is very taken with the passenger's looks and personality. The latter feature, of course, can be dismissed here because the ghost is mute throughout, a fact that makes the idea of overwhelming love at first sight even more implausible. The other elements of Jackson's text are standard fare in modern versions of the legend.

Text 200b, by Horace Jennings, shows few deviations from other modern versions. It takes place on a dismal night on a road near a small community (Redfield is on the main route between Pine Bluff and Little Rock but is so small its population is not listed on most road atlases). That the driver learns of her identity from both parents rather than just the mother is a slightly different element in an otherwise conventional text.

The third text, by Nancy Riley, differs from most modern Southern versions in that no mention is made of the weather and the ghost talks to the driver after he arrives at her home. That she is on her way home for a holiday is also somewhat unusual, providing additional reason for the annual return. The unique feature of the fourth text is that the man who picks up the girl dies as a result of the encounter. A common motif in American folk tradition is death caused by meeting a ghost but it is rare in the modern tradition of "The Vanishing Hitchhiker."

The fifth version is distinctive, for it is one of the few reports of the legend that is related as a personal experience. Is it possible that the person merely presented a widely told tale in this format for dramatic effect? Or did she really have a supernatural experience? Since the collector supplied nothing more than the name, date, and place of collection it is impossible to do more than speculate on this matter. Another unique feature of this text is that the girl's death occurred only two months prior to the pickup, rather than the usual year or several years. Yet she apparently appears on "the night of her accident" which must mean that she is seen on the same night of the week her accident occurred.

In several respects the sixth text is the most unique of those presented here and may, in fact, represent an older form of the tradition since there is no actual hitchhiking; the meeting takes place as the man is walking by a graveyard. That the informant heard essentially the same narrative from his grandfather suggests that it is older. It shows some resemblance to a Chinese story collected from immigrants in California in which the ghost of a young girl walks with a young man along the road to her parents' home and then disappears. A significant difference is that the Chinese girl walks behind the man, thus he does not know of her disappearance until he turns around. This is, of course, exactly the way the driver learns of her disappearance in most automobile versions of "The Vanishing Hitchhiker." In the Chinese text the young man learns her identity from the girl's father. Also similar is Dickey Lee's song, "Laurie," in which the narrator meets the girl at a dance and walks her home, during the course of which she borrows his sweater. He later discovers she "died a year ago today" and finds his sweater "lyin' there upon her grave." In "Bringin' Mary Home" it is his coat that is draped over her tombstone but she had been picked up in a car on a "lonely road on a dark and stormy night."

Probably, besides sheer entertainment, "The Vanishing Hitchhiker" is offered by most narrators as a kind of exemplum concerning the perils involved in picking up hitchhikers. There may, of course, be many other possible explanations for the vast popularity of this particular legend. A book could be written on the subject and, in fact, one has, sort of. A portion of Jan Harold Brunvand's *The Vanishing Hitchhiker: American Urban Legends and Their Meanings* (New York: W. W. Norton & Company, Inc., 1981) deals with the legend. A discussion with numerous texts is found on pp. 24–26. Brunvand, and others, have labeled "The Vanishing Hitchhiker" an urban legend but it is no more urban than it is rural although, in most modern versions, an automobile, a symbol of urban technology, is prominently featured.

The motif is E332.3.3.1 "The Vanishing Hitchhiker."

201. Collected in 1973 by William E. Holloman from a Mrs. Holloman of Goldsboro, North Carolina, who is the collector's grandmother. Evidently this was not a story she had told often in recent years for it was recalled only with difficulty after the collector asked her for some local legends or ghost stories. She had the story from her grandmother and apparently used the narrative primarily for entertainment, telling it at social gatherings where ghost stories were frequently told. These stories generally followed games, corn-popping, taffy-pulling, or similar activities after which "guests would gather around the roaring open fire. They'd sit on the floor and tell ghost stories. After each one, someone would try to cap it and make it a little worse." After these sessions, Mrs. Holloman recalled that some people would act like they were afraid to go home.

The story Mrs. Holloman gave her grandson seems to have as its two main characters a George Deans (1831–1889) and a Rachel Vinson (1839–1857). At least there were two such actual people although only this narrative indicates there was any relationship between them. Actually, the connection is even more nebulous for it is a George Scott, not Deans, mentioned by Mrs. Holloman, but there is no George Scott that seems to fit the details of the story. The parting of the lovers is reminiscent of that in "Barbara Allen" and other Child ballads. They break up for some unknown reason—the informant suggests cold feet on the boy's part—and the girl soon dies from typhoid fever which, the narrator hints, may have been brought on by grief. For more on this legend see William E. Holloman, "The Ice-Cold Hand," *North Carolina Folklore* 22:1 (February, 1974), pp. 3–8.

Motifs include E214 "Dead lover haunts faithless sweetheart"; E265.3 "Meeting ghost causes death"; and Thompson's F855 "Extraordinary image."

202. Collected in the 1930s by Claude Dunnagan from his grandfather who resided at Rockford in Surry County, North Carolina. Although the story about "Still Face" was told as an actual happening it seems likely its main function was entertainment. The narrator specifically emphsizes that it is "a story that's been told for years around Rockford" which, of course, is not irrefutable proof that the informant thought of it mainly as entertainment. Nevertheless, most Southern folk narrators do not use the word *story* for a narrative describing an incident they consider true and of serious import. Generally such a yarn is prefaced by some statement like, "Now this is no story, it really happened." The informant's attempts to explain "what really happened" to Still Face also indicate that he was at least skeptical about the supernatural aspects of the tale, as apparently were several other people in the community.

Motifs are E402 "Mysterious ghostlike noises heard"; J1769.2 "Dead man is thought to be alive" which is particularly popular in the South. Generally, this latter motif involves a story in which mourners are sitting up with a corpse that, due to some type of muscle contraction, sits up in the casket, causing the onlookers to think the dead man has come back to life. Also relevant here is Thompson's E261.2.1 "Coffin bursts; dead arises and pursues attendant."

203. Collected in 1961 by Jan Calhoon from Frank Allen of Crossett, Arkansas. Frank heard the story from a Negro he worked with who remembered the incident. There seems to be an air of superiority evident here, as though this is a story that "superstitious" people—meaning anyone that the narrator considers an inferior—believe, but one that he finds to be nothing more than an entertaining story. He emphasizes that "many other Negroes" believed the convicted man's tale about the two arms, possibly a deliberate choice of words suggesting that only Negroes believed the strange manner of revenge. Perhaps this is an erroneous interpretation of the narrator's views; his text may reflect nothing more than that the tale primarily circulated among Afro-Americans. All such speculation must remain guesswork because the collector provided no data with which one could draw any sound conclusions in this regard.

Motifs include E232.2 "Ghost returns to slay man who has injured it while living"; E234 "Ghost punishes injury received in life"; E422.1.11.3 "Ghost as hand or hands"; and Q285 "Cruelty punished."

204. Collected in 1960 by Jan Calhoon from Homer Davis of Urbana, Arkansas. Davis, who had lived in the area all his life, heard the story when he was a boy, which was approximately ten years before telling Calhoon the tale. The dilemma posed in the last line suggests that Davis thought of the story mainly as entertainment although he certainly believed events happened as described. Calhoon supplied the title "The Gusher of Blood" but there is no evidence that the narrator gave it any title. The motif here is E232.1 "Return from dead to slay murderer."

205. Collected in 1960 by Jan Calhoon from Maurice Lewis of Magnolia, Arkansas. Lewis had the story from Dick Dickson, also of Magnolia. Apparently, the story was just an entertaining piece of fiction to the narrator, who refers to it as "one story about the swamp." A related tale with a less violent ending is found in William Lynwood Montell, *Ghosts Along the Cumberland: Deathlore in the Kentucky Foothills* (Knoxville: The University of Tennessee Press, 1975), p. 123.

Motifs that apply here are D940 "Magic forests" and F990 "Inanimate object acts as is living." Calhoon gave this narrative the title "The Woods Are Alive," but evidently, the narrator supplied no title.

206. According to the WPA records this very literary sounding text is given exactly as told to J.C. Stutts of Cary, North Carolina by C.D. Creech of Moore County, North Carolina. If this text really contains Creech's exact words then it is certain that he had told this tale many times and had it all carefully rehearsed. His descriptions of "reedy, oak-shadowed banks" and "the raucous call of the katydids" have all the earmarks of a literary, rather than an oral tale—in any event, a narrative that has often been told. Although only the informant's name and place of residence are given it is obvious that he mainly thinks of the story as entertainment. A very dramatic manner with lots of dialogue and considerable lyrical description are used, exactly the sort of thing one might resort to when trying to present a suspenseful and interesting yarn of the supernatural. The General Greene referred to here is probably Nathanael Greene, the youngest of the generals elected by the Continental Congress. This is one of the very few reports of banshees, not only in Southern folk tradition but in that of the entire United States.

Motifs include Thompson's F491.5 "Will-o'-the-Wisp's revenge"; M301.6.1 "Banshees are portents of misfortune"; and Q467 "Punishment by drowning." The rain crow mentioned here is more commonly known as the cuckoo and, in folk tradition, is generally regarded as an omen of rain.

207. Collected April 19, 1981, by Aida Rogers from Julia Harmon Rogers, Cayce, South Carolina; Mrs. Rogers is the grandmother of the collector. Although she tells legendary narratives about the Devil's Track she has never seen the place. According to the collector the Devil's Track "is like a large footprint with a distinct toemark. It is remarkably symmetrical, and it is about ten inches long and five inches wide. The track itself is carved in the side of the rock, not the top, which makes it hard to spot. Also a rotten log has fallen down over the rock, covering it with leaves, dirt, and other debris. But the print is clearly visible." Possibly the narrative is told for entertainment but the collector feels that it also serves other purposes. She says, "I think it was told to inspire moral rectitude and to establish respect for the community. And after dwelling on the matter, I believe my grandmother once told me the legend in hopes that I would not lose my temper, and storm, rage, and fume like the little devil I used to be." Thus, like most folk narratives this legend is not always told for the same reasons; its purpose may change with each telling.

This etiological narrative has a suggestion of the elements of "The Devil at the Dance" but that portion of the present text has an entirely different result because the devil is not successful in his disguise. Motifs are A980 "Origin of particular places" and Thompson's A1617 "Origin of place-name." Although the concluding sentence of this text is incomplete, it is given here just as reported by the collector.

208. Reported by James Taylor Adams circa 1940 from his own memory. He had heard the story as a child from his mother and said he had heard it several times since in "slightly different versions." Adams (1892–1954) was a native of Letcher County, Kentucky, who spent twenty-five years as a coal miner in Wise County, Virginia. Leaving the mines in 1930 he spent the rest of his life as a printer and witch in Big Laurel, Virginia. He edited a quarterly magazine, *The Cumberland Empire,* that included sketches, short stories, poems, and songs descriptive of southern Appalachia. He also published a book, *Death in the Dark: A Collection of Factual Ballads of American Mine Disasters with Historical Notes (1941).* For more information about Adams see Archie Green, *Only a Miner: Studies in Recorded Coal-Mining Songs* (Urbana, Illinois: University of Illinois Press, 1972), pp. 399–400. Thus, Adams was a person with a special interest in preserving various types of southern Appalachian folklore; for him it was much more than entertainment. His mother possibly believed in witchcraft although that is uncertain in this text.

Motifs include G265.4.1 "Witch causes death of animals" and G271.4 "Exorcism by use of sympathetic magic."

209. Collected February 4, 1941 by James Taylor Adams from Boyd J. Bolling, Flat Gap, Virginia. Boyd heard this story from his father and, as the text indicates, was inclined to believe the events described in the narrative were factual, primarily because of who told it, even though, apparently, he did not generally believe in witchcraft. Basically it seems that this narrative was told as local history and for entertainment.

Motifs include G265.8.3.1 "Witch bewitches gun" and G271.4.2(b) "Shooting picture or symbol of witch breaks spell (usually injuring or killing the witch)." The folk belief that if a witch or a member of the witch's family can borrow something from the family of the person who injured him then he will be cured is expressed here.

210. Collected July 15, 1961 by George Foss from Robert Shiflett, Browns Cove, Virginia. For further information about Shiflett see the notes to his Text 192. Shiflett regarded this story as part of local history, but mainly he found it an entertaining yarn. As some of his remarks indicate, Shiflett was not totally convinced that the marvelous events recounted in this legend didn't actually happen as described.

Motifs include D1700 "Magic powers"; D1721.1 "Magic power from devil" is implied; D1812.0.2.4 "Magic knowledge of witch (wizard)"; G200 "Witch"; G220.0.2 "Sex of witches"; G229 "Characteristics of witches: miscellaneous"; G249 "Habits of witches: miscellaneous"; G275.3 "Witch burned," which, despite popular opinion to the contrary, was a relatively rare way for a witch's life to end; G295 "Witch (usually male) does impossible deeds (usually with active aid of the devil)"; and Thompson's D1601.16.1 "Self-digging hoe," a motif that is primarily found in African and Asian societies.

211. Collected May 30, 1962, by George Foss from Robert Shiflett, Browns Cove, Virginia. For more information about Shiflett see the notes for his Text 192. Apparently, Shiflett told this story primarily for entertainment but also as evidence of the belief that local people once had in the power of witches. In Anglo-American folk tradition the violin or fiddle is often considered the devil's instrument, or box, and the legend given here corroborates the idea that musical ability really comes from the devil.

Motifs include D1751 "Magic passes from body to body"; G200 "Witch"; G224.10 "Witch power is transferred from one person to another"; and H1400 "Fear test." Although there are numerous texts and ordeals contained in various folktales and legends, the one reported here seems not to have previously been collected, which is why only the general motif is cited.

212. Collected July 15, 1961 by George Foss from Robert Shiflett, Browns Cove, Virginia. For more about Shiflett see the notes for his Text 192. Apparently, Shiflett regarded the narrative about George Herring and the others he related to Foss as local history but they were primarily valuable to him as entertainment. The degree of belief he had in the incidents described is evident from his statement, "That's taken with a grain of salt but most people in those days believed it."

Motifs include G200 "Witch"; G265.4 "Witch causes death or illness of animals"; and

G275.12(b) "Witch as cat injured or killed by injury to cat." The borrowing mentioned in this text refers to the belief that if a witch is injured it will get well if it can borrow something from the person responsible for the injury.

213. Collected April 18, 1963 by George Foss from Hilma Powell Yates, Browns Cove, Virginia. Yates was the sister of Lloyd Powell, another of Foss's informants, and, like him, was severely handicapped with a congenital degeneration of the eyes (their parents were first cousins). Born in 1903, Yates died in 1982. Evidently, she had little belief in the validity of the traditions about Jim Royal for she referred to them as "fairy tales" and "stuff." Still, she found them an entertaining aspect of local history.

Motifs include D600 "Miscellaneous transformation incidents"; G241.3 "Witch rides on horse"; and Thompson's D2188.2 "Person vanishes."

214. Collected in 1972 by Lovelace Cook from Carrie Patterson Shaver, an eighty-two year old black woman residing in Montgomery, Alabama. She definitely believed the incident described in her narrative really happened but there is also a possibility that this is a tale she sometimes told for entertainment. "Fennel leaves" refers to the perennial plant with yellow flowers that at one time was occasionally used for nature-made brooms.

Motifs include G241.2 "Witch rides on person" and G271.5(b) "Breaking spell by flogging witch."

215. Collected in 1981 by Gail Ogle from Burkett Casteel, a fifty-five year old white man living in Bristol, Virginia. Although Ogle provided no further information on the informant there is no reason to doubt that he believes this to be a factual report. True, the opening words "years ago" convey a similarity to the "once upon a time" opening of *märchen*, but that hardly constitutes evidence of lack of belief. Of course, Mr. Casteel may have been like some informants I have encountered who felt that witchcraft was practiced in times past but not in the past fifty years.

Motifs include G211.1.7 "Witch in form of cat"; G271.5(f) "Shooting or injuring in other fashion the form which the witch is using at the moment"; and G275.12(b) "Witch as cat injured or killed by injury to cat."

216a, b, c, d and e. These five texts are versions of a very popular legend known as "La Hija Disobediente" (The Disobedient Daughter) or "The Devil at the Dance." The first text was collected April, 1965, in El Paso, Texas, by Janyth S. Tolson from Ernesto Chasco. The informant was twelve years old and a native of Mexico but an American citizen who received all of his formal education in Texas public schools. Although his family spoke Spanish they could neither read nor write the language; Chasco was comfortable with Spanish and had some difficulty with spoken English. Ernesto heard the story from his grandmother who believed it was a true story, and he apparently accepted it as an account of an actual incident, mainly because of his respect for his grandmother. As the last two sentences indicate, Chasco didn't accept every element of the story as factual. *"El Gato,"* the place where the disobedient daughter went, is Spanish for "The Cat." The phrase *"Eres pata de gallo"* means, "You are [have] a rooster foot."

Both the second and third texts were also collected in El Paso in April, 1965, by Janyth S. Tolson. The second one came from Alice Duran, a twelve year old native of El Paso, who heard the story from a babysitter who specialized in frightening the children with scary stories. The last sentence of this text reveals Duran's view of the story and its purpose. *"Pata de chivo"* means "foot of a goat." The third text was contributed by Roberto Guillen, a fourteen year old schoolboy, who said the story was about a true incident. *"Pata de gallo"* means "rooster foot."

The fourth text was collected in El Paso in 1967 by Pat Simons from Connie Herrera, an eighteen year old clerk for a local dry goods store. Herrera had the legend from her mother who said the incident happened about twenty years earlier, i.e. circa 1947, at Thomas Jefferson High School in El Paso. At the time Mrs. Herrera was a high school student at another school in El Paso. She heard the tale from her classmates who told it as fact. Mrs. Herrera said that people at the dance claimed the burning bush next to the girl was the devil, who had disguised himself as the "good-looking guy."

The fifth text was collected in 1968 by Mary V. Mellen from Mrs. Delia Zavala of El Paso. The informant was a married woman in her thirties and the mother of three small girls. She believed the incident described in her text really happened and, in fact, claimed to have seen the girl's face all covered with tiny scratches. She said the girl this happened to was the sister of a girlfriend.

Typically, "The Devil at the Dance" consists of a taboo or prohibition against dancing but a girl desires to attend anyway. The devil is at the dance, his presence is detected, he departs, and serious consequences result from his departure. That is the skeleton of the story, but there is considerable variation within each of these elements. The taboo exists for several reasons such as Good Friday, Holy Saturday, Lent; or simply a prohibition against dancing is imposed by the parents or grandparents. Sometimes the devil appears at the girl's house, is discovered and forced to leave. Sometimes she goes to the dance with the devil. In several texts it is a young man rather than a woman who goes to the dance. Sometimes the devil is already at the dance when the girl or boy arrives, and in other texts he arrives from out of nowhere amid noise or, in darkness, after the lights go out. In several texts he doesn't show up until after the dance is over. He appears most often either as a handsome, well-dressed young man, a musician, a young woman, a pig, a cat or a goat. His presence is usually detected by a physical feature, such as a tail, horns, unusual feet, claws, long fingernails, a protruding back that grows larger or by his manner of dancing. Generally a child, the devil's dancing partner, grandparents of the disobedient youth or some other older person, or a cowboy calls attention to the devil's presence. The devil departs in various ways, sometimes after the use of a religious charm. He often leaves in a cloud of smoke, amid a sulphurous smell, in an explosion, by flying out the window or up through the ceiling, by running out into the dark, turning into fire or simply disappearing into thin air.

The devil's departure often brings about some tragic or supernatural result. Sometimes the dancers find themselves at a remote spot or back at home; in some cases the dance hall itself moves from its place. Often the girl disappears with the devil, goes insane, is burned to death, or has her face scratched by the devil. On some occasions the devil scratches a girl's father or his image appears on the door and windows. In a few texts a musician receives a gift of food from the devil but, upon returning home, discovers that the food has turned into lizards.

The first text here is typical of most texts of the legend except that the priest's refusal to bury the girl in hallowed ground is unusual, especially since there is no indication that she did not die in a state of grace. The second text possibly was told to explain a unique scar or birthmark on the face of someone known by the person who related the legend to the informant. It is unusual from most versions of "The Devil at the Dance" because the victim ends up basically being a heroine, but one who has learned the proper lesson from her experience. There is nothing unusual about the third text, but the devil picking up the girl in a convertible, mentioned in the fourth text, is relatively uncommon. Generally such modern means of transportation are not used by the devil of this legend. The fifth text is somewhat unusual in having the girl married, a feature found in very few texts, presumably because married women are thought to be old enough that they are no longer under parental authority.

Motifs include G271.2 "Witch exorcised by use of religious ceremony, object or charm"; G303.3.1 "The devil in human form"; G303.3.1.2 "The devil as a well dressed gentleman"; G303.4.5.4 "Devil has cloven goat hoof"; G303.10.4.4 "Devils appears to girl who wants an escort for a dance"; and Thompson's C836 "Tabu: disobedience"; G303.3.3.3.5 "Devil in form of cock"; G303.3.3.1.6 "Devil in form of goat"; G303.4.5.9 "Devil has cock's feet"; G303.5.2 "Devil is dressed in green"; and G303.10.4.0.1 "Devil haunts dance halls."

217. Collected in Jonesboro, November 16, 1974, by Katherine Lemay from a nineteen year old college student from Forrest City, Arkansas, named Martha. Although Martha believes the story, it is also apparently used for entertainment, because she told it without prompting to several acquaintances at ghost-telling sessions. Possibly the supernatural incident serves as a means of acquiring status in her peer group. This is not a story so much as it is a description of some "strange" happenings involving a picture. Thompson's D1266.2 "Magic picture" is the closest relevant motif.

218. Collected by William E. Lightfoot, July 28, 1977, from Precious Jackson in Sylvester, Georgia. Mrs. Jackson and her husband, Henry, are both physical and spiritual leaders in the black community of Sylvester. She is a retired schoolteacher, born about 1912, who believes she possesses God-given supernatural powers—such as bloodstopping and the ability to "talk" the fire out of a burn—that she tries to use wisely. Most of her stories concerning her power have happy endings, but in this text a tragedy results because she is not allowed to fully exercise her abilities. Thus, this and other stories about her abilities are told mainly as testimony to the validity of such supernatural powers as bloodstopping.

The relevant motifs here are D1504.1 "Charm stanches blood" and D2161.2.2 "Flow of blood magically stopped." "These words" referred to by Mrs. Jackson are a Bible verse used as a charm by many bloodstoppers.

219. Collected by William E. Lightfoot from Precious Jackson, July 28, 1977, in Sylvester, Georgia. For more information about Mrs. Jackson see the notes for the preceding text. A discussion of dream-signs among Afro-Americans in the South is found in Newbell Niles Puckett, *Folk Beliefs of the Southern Negro* (Chapel Hill, North Carolina: The University of North Carolina Press, 1926), pp. 496–505, a book that has been reprinted by Dover Publications, Inc.

The relevant motif here is D1812.3.3 "Future revealed in dream," a frequent feature of fairy tales and legends.

220. Collected by William E. Lightfoot and Carl Fleischauer, August 4, 1977, from Joe T. Fletcher, near Waterloo, Georgia. For more information about Fletcher see the notes for his Text 167. Both Mr. Fletcher and his father were bloodstoppers who practiced mainly on animals, especially calves that were newly castrated. The Fletchers would stop excessive bleeding merely by sticking a knife blade into the ground. As the concluding sentence in this text indicates, this memorate mainly serves as a testimonial to the validity of bloodstopping.

The relevant motif here is D2161.2.2 "Flow of blood magically stopped."

221. Collected by Henry Wacaster Perry in 1938 from Mart Rankins, a white resident of Carter County, Tennessee. Rankins, apparently, was a highly regarded local raconteur since he was called Uncle Mart, "Uncle" being a term common in Southern communities that has nothing to do with kinship but is instead is reserved for respected older gentlemen. He also had a wealth of supernatural narratives, mostly about witches, and interrupted a series of witch tales to present this narrative about "a black thing." The speed with which the "thing" changed from two men into its black form hints that witchcraft is possibly involved. At the very least the tale is offered as a testimonial to the existence of things that can't be explained in usual ways.

Motifs are E530.1 "Ghost-like lights" and the following found only in Thompson: E422.2.4 "Revenant black"; K1821 "Disguise by changing bodily appearance"; and Z143 "Symbolic color; black." The slang term *batchin'* is commonly used by men, regardless of marital status, who are living alone and taking care of the housework. The term, of course, comes from the word *bachelor* and has been widely used since the late nineteenth century.

222. Collected in 1973 by Ralph C. Worthington, Jr. from a Mrs. Jim Barnhill of Pactolus, North Carolina. The informant was not eager to share this story with the collector and did so only after a great deal of persuasion by Worthington and coercion by her husband. Her reluctance was occasioned by her fear of being associated with "wild, outlandish" beliefs. She also saw herself as an old-fashioned person whose beliefs could become the butt of jokes by non-believers. She prefaced her story with the words, "Now this is not folklore because I saw this with my own eyes. This is true."

Motifs include Thompson's D1812.5.0.3 "Behavior of fire as omen" and F964 "Extraordinary behavior of fire."

223. Collected in 1939 by Robert Mason from his grandmother in Cannon County, Tennessee. She apparently had a large stock of legend material—another of her stories, a version of Type 1676B "Clothing caught in graveyard," appears in Text 169. Although the action takes place in and near a cemetery it is unlikely that any narrator presents this tale as anything other than a humorous story. Indeed, a Cave City, Arkansas informant frankly calls it a tall tale and most people who know this yarn would probably categorize it similarly.

This is a very widely known narrative that Thompson gives as Type 1791 "The Sexton Carries the Parson." Known throughout Scandinavia, the British Isles, Europe, India, the West Indies and, of course, the United States, this story is at least as old as the medieval *Thousand and One Nights* and appears in most medieval and Renaissance tale collections. The Mason text differs from most American versions in that instead of two boys dividing nuts or other articles in the cemetery, two sheep thieves perform this central action. This is exactly what generally happens in European versions of the tale and suggests that the Mason version was learned some years ago and has been little influenced by outside sources. A unique touch is provided by the addition of a man buried with hickory nuts placed under his head. Almost equally rare is the feature of the misunderstanding resulting from overhearing the thieves occurring twice. This expansion is typical of the entire text which is far more extensive than most reported versions. Such expansion and the considerable dialogue here are the marks of a skillful narrator.

There are, of course, many possible explanations for the widespread popularity of this tale but one is certainly its versatility. A teller can insert whatever he wants to be counted and various versions have the hickory nuts used here, or walnuts, fish, pawpaws, and sweet potatoes, but almost anything that is countable could be used. Undoubtedly the punch line in which one thief asks the other "Is he fat or lean?" or, in some versions, "One for you and one for me" or "I'll take the one over by the gate" is also partially responsible for its popularity. The absurd misunderstanding, no matter in what form, is a perennially popular feature of folk tales and it, and the surprise ending in which a severely handicapped person is not only able to run fast but actually outrun the able-bodied boys, also help the story's popularity.

Motifs here are X424 "The devil in the cemetery" and X143.1 "Lame man is taken on hunt on stretcher or in wheel chair. He beats the dogs home when they tree a 'hant' or when a bear gets after them."

224. Collected in 1968 by Bill Ferris from Wyndell Thomas, Leland, Mississippi. The informant was ten years old at the time and, as the son of James "Sonny Ford" Thomas, a noted blues singer, occupied a position of some prominence in the local Negro community. It is unclear whether Thomas believed this a factual account or not, but his calling it "a small story" suggests that he regarded it merely as entertainment. This is part of the cycle of Afro-American folk narratives involving John and his Old Marster. Richard Dorson said that this series of tales "provides the most engaging theme in American Negro lore." John is a trickster in the form of a plantation Negro in the antebellum South, a generic figure who enjoys a degree of favoritism and familiarity with the owner. For more examples of John and Old Marster see Richard M. Dorson, *American Negro Folktales* (Greenwich, Connecticut; Fawcett Publications, Inc., 1967), pp. 124–171 and Alan Dundes, *Mother Wit from the Laughing Barrel: Readings in the Interpretation of Afro-American Folklore* (Englewood Cliffs, New Jersey: Prentice-Hall, Inc., 1973), pp. 541–560.

There are no motif numbers in either Baughman or Thompson that parallel this tale but Type 990 "The Seemingly Dead Revives" does cover most of the details. It has previously been reported from the British Isles and the United States as well as most of Europe. Five versions titled "The Jewelry Thieves" appear in Montell's *Ghosts Along the Cumberland*, pp. 207–209. Montell thinks the legend originated in Europe and came to America with German immigrants. Almost every known text of this narrative identifies the item of jewelry as a ring. In most versions the thief cuts the ring off of the fingers of the presumed corpse, an act that causes her to awaken.

225. Collected by William E. Lightfoot from Lou Thacker, July 25, 1973, at her home in Yorktown, Kentucky. Mrs. Thacker was born in 1927 and has always lived in the Big Sandy region of eastern Kentucky. She knows a large amount of supernatural lore, and her father was renowned locally as a blood-stopper. Mrs. Thacker told Lightfoot several accounts of bloodstopping, measuring, haunted houses, omens, and markings. Still, she is not a particularly skillful narrator as this text demonstrates. Her story has no dialogue and is presented in a rather uninterested manner, not unlike that which might be published by a newspaper reporter. There is a minimum of description with little more than the absolutely essential details being given. In short, this has all the earmarks of an oral narrative told by someone who is a passive legend teller. It seems that the only reason Mrs. Thacker remembers the story is because it was told by her father. Its function, then, is essentially the same as that served by a family history; it is, in fact, merely a piece of family history.

As Lightfoot comments, "This story is not a 'ghost story' as such, it does indicate an awareness of ghosts, and shows how belief in ghosts affects actual behavior." It seems likely, too, that the story is sometimes told as a humorous example of how belief in ghosts affects behavior. Two relevant motifs here are J1782.3 "House noises thought to be ghosts" and J1785 "Animals thought to be devils or ghosts." A similar story from Alabama appears in Browne, *"A Night With the Hants,"* pp. 161–162.

226. From Bert Vincent, *The Best Stories of Bert Vincent,* ed. Willard Yarbrough, (Knoxville, Tennessee, 1968), pp. 179–180. Vincent does not indicate the source of his story but, like most of the other stories in the book, it was taken from material sent in by readers of the Knoxville *News Sentinel,* most of whom come from Tennessee, Kentucky, Virginia, and North Carolina.

Perhaps the most popular motif here is one that is well known among both Afro-Americans and whites in the United States but is rare in other parts of the world. Baughman assigns this the number J1495.1 "Man runs from actual or from supposed ghost." It has been collected from Negro informants in New Jersey, South Carolina, and Florida, and from whites in New Jersey, Florida, Indiana, Wisconsin, Iowa, and Arkansas. That it is not even more widely reported is probably due to the fact that most American folklore collections have been focused on a relatively small portion of the country.

Other motifs here include E422.1.11.2 "Revenant as face or head"; J1495.4* "Man racing with ghost outruns rabbit" and three classified only in Thompson. These are D1610.5 "Speaking head" which is used in *Sir Gawain and the Green Knight,* in an Irish myth, and in Icelandic, Indian, and German narratives; D1641.7 "Severed head moves from place to place"; and E783 "Vital head" which refers to a head that retains life after being cut off. This latter motif is found, among other places, in stories from India, the West Indies, Spain, Ireland, and Iceland, although it usually occurs in *märchen* or fairy tales rather than in legends.

In most versions of this tale the cat is a revenent who talks to the man and later chases him, but here he merely provides a prelude to the real action. Since nothing is said about the informant it is difficult to determine what function this story serves for him. Judging solely on its submission to a newspaper column specializing in "interesting and unusual" stories it seems likely that the narrative is mainly used for entertainment.

227. Collected January 7, 1960, by Billy Kyser from Freddy Akers of Blytheville, Arkansas. Akers also contributed a version of "The Vanishing Hitchhiker" which appears in Text 200f. Akers heard the story given here in his hometown. A similar tale has a man falling in an open grave and, after several unsuccessful attempts to get out, decides to go ahead and sleep there. Then another man falls in the grave and while he is trying to get out the first man tells him there is no point, he can't get out. After hearing this the second man does succeed in getting out of the grave. Akers's text has an identical beginning but, of course, a different punch line from the other tale. There is no motif listed in either Baughman or Thompson that is relevant to the narrative given here.

APPENDIX 1
A Partial List of Folklore Archives Found in the South

Materials housed in these archives are generally available for use by qualified researchers, although there may be special conditions imposed on the use made of them. Anyone wishing to do research in these archives should make arrangements in advance of a visit.

ALABAMA

Archives of American Minority Cultures
P.O. Box S
University of Alabama
University, AL 35486

ARKANSAS

Regional Culture Center
Nana Farris, Director
Arkansas College
Batesville, AR 72501

Special Collections
University Library
University of Arkansas
Fayetteville, AR 72701

ASU Folklore Archive
Attn: Professor William Clements
Arkansas State University
State University, AR 72467

Folklore Archive
Attn: Professor Wayne Viitanen
University of Arkansas
Monticello, AR 71655

Ozark Folk Center
W.K. McNeil, Folklorist
Mountain View, AR 72560

FLORIDA

Florida Folklife Program
P.O. Box 265
White Springs, FL 32096

GEORGIA

Georgia Folklore Society Archives
Art Rosenbaum, Director
Electromedia Department
University of Georgia Library
Athens, GA 30602

Georgia Folklore Archives
Professor John A. Burrison, Director
Folklore Program
Georgia State University
University Plaza
Atlanta, GA 30303

Foxfire Fund Archive
Rabun Gap, GA 30568

KENTUCKY

Weatherford-Hammond Mountain
    Collection
Berea College Library
Berea, KY 40403

Western Kentucky Folklore, Folklife, and
    Oral History Archives
Helms-Cravens Library
Western Kentucky University
Bowling Green, KY 42101

Appalachian Collection
Ann G. Campbell, Curator
Department of Special Collections and
  Archives
Margaret I. King Library
University of Kentucky Libraries
Lexington, KY 40506

Appalachian Collection
Camden-Carroll Library
Morehead State University
Morehead, KY 40351

Appalachian Oral History Project
Appalachian Learning Laboratories
Alice Lloyd College
Pippa Passes, KY 41844

Robert Rennick Folklore Collection
Prestonburg Community College
University of Kentucky
Prestonburg, KY 41652

LOUISIANA

Archive of Acadian and Creole Folklore/
  Oral History
Dupre Library
University of Southwestern Louisiana
Lafayette, LA 70504

MISSISSIPPI

Mississippi Folklore Society Archives
  Committee
State of Mississippi
Department of Archives and History
P.O. Box 571
Jackson, MS 39205

Archives and Special Collections
University of Mississippi Library
University, MS 38677

NORTH CAROLINA

William L. Eury Appalachian Collection
Belk Library
Appalachian State University
Boone, NC 28607

North Carolina Folklore Archives
Curriculum in Folklore
University of North Carolina
Chapel Hill, NC 27514

Southern Historical Collection and
  Manuscripts Department
Wilson Library 024-A
University of North Carolina
Chapel Hill, NC 27514

Frank C. Brown Collection of North
  Carolina Folklore
Manuscript Division
Duke University Library
Durham, NC 27706

East Carolina University Folklore Archive
Department of English
122 Austin Building
East Carolina University
Greenville, NC 27834

Bascom Lamar Lunsford Collection
Mars Hill College
Mars Hill, NC 28754

SOUTH CAROLINA

Department of Anthropology
Attn: Professor Robert McCarl
University of South Carolina
Columbia, SC 29208

TENNESSEE

Archives of Appalachia
The Sherrod Library
East Tennessee State University Library
Johnson City, TN 37614

Center for Southern Folklore Archives
1216 Peabody Avenue
P.O. Box 40105
Memphis, TN 38104

Archive of the Southern Folk Cultural
  Revival Project
3390 Valeria Street
Nashville, TN 37210

Archives and Manuscripts Section
Tennessee State Library and Archives
403 Seventh Avenue North
Nashville, TN 37219

TEXAS

Sul Ross State University Archives
Wildenthal Library
Sul Ross State University
Alpine, TX 79830

University of Texas Folk Archive
Center for Intercultural Studies in Folklore
and Oral History
Social Work Building 306
University of Texas
Austin, TX 78712

North Texas State University Archives
A.M. Willis, Jr. Library
North Texas State University
Denton, TX 76203

Rio Grande Folklore Archive
Attn: Mark Glazer
Behavioral Sciences
Pan American University
Edinburgh, TX 78539

University of Texas at El Paso Folklore
Archive
Attn: Professor John O. West
Department of English
University of Texas at El Paso
El Paso, TX 79968

Institute of Texan Cultures Library
P.O. Box 1226
San Antonio, TX 78294

VIRGINIA

Kevin Barry Perdue Archive of Traditional
Music *and*
The University of Virginia Folklore Archive
Attn: Professor Charles L. Perdue, Jr.
Room 303
Brooks Hall
University of Virginia
Charlottesville, VA 22903

Virginia Folklore Society Archive *and*
The WPA Folklore and Folksong
Collections
Manuscripts Division
Alderman Library
University of Virginia
Charlottesville, VA 22903

Northern Virginia Folklife Center
Margaret R. Yocum, Director of Archive
George Mason University
4400 University Drive
Fairfax, VA 22030

Blue Ridge Heritage Library
Blue Ridge Institute
Ferrum College
Ferrum, VA 24088

APPENDIX 2
Directories

The following directories are also helpful in locating archival resources of Southern folklore.

Association for Recorded Sound Collections. *A Preliminary Directory of Sound Recordings Collections in the United States and Canada.* New York: New York Public Library, 1967.

Craig, Tracey Linton. *Directory of Historical Societies and Agencies in the United States and Canada.* Nashville: American Association for State and Local History, 1982.

Library of Congress. *National Union Catalog of Manuscript Collections.* Washington: Library of Congress, Catalog Distribution Services, Vols. 1–19, 1959–1981.

Shumway, Gary L. *Oral History in the United States: A Directory.* New York: Oral History Association, 1971.

Wasserman, Paul and Jean Morgan. *Ethnic Information Sources of the United States.* Detroit: Gale Research Co., 1983.

Wynar, Lubomyr R. and Lois Buttlar. *Guide to Ethnic Museums, Libraries, and Archives in the United States.* Kent, Ohio: Program for the Study of Ethnic Publications, School of Library Science, Kent State University, 1978.

Index of Southern Localities

The following entries refer to the text numbers utilized throughout the book. The locations referenced are mentioned either in the text itself or in its corresponding endnote. Additionally, some locations are referenced to stories contained in the general introduction; these are indicated by the number of the endnote which corresponds to that particular text. As with the main texts, the location may be mentioned in the text, the endnote, or both.

About the Authors

RICHARD AND JUDY DOCKREY YOUNG are professional storytellers who travel the United States collecting and telling stories of all kinds. Their other books include *Favorite Scary Stories of American Children* and *Ozark Tall Tales*.

W. K. McNEIL holds a Ph.D. in folklore from Indiana University, and is the folklorist at the Ozark Folk Center in Mountain View, Arkansas.